V1 ___ FK

VIRTUAL JFK

Vietnam If Kennedy Had Lived

James G. Blight, janet M. Lang,
and David A. Welch

ROWMAN & LITTLEFIELD PUBLISHERS, INC.
Lanham • Boulder • New York • Toronto • Plymouth, UK

ROWMAN & LITTLEFIELD PUBLISHERS, INC.

Published in the United States of America
by Rowman & Littlefield Publishers, Inc.
A wholly owned subsidiary of The Rowman & Littlefield Publishing Group, Inc.
4501 Forbes Boulevard, Suite 200, Lanham, Maryland 20706
www.rowmanlittlefield.com

Estover Road, Plymouth PL6 7PY, United Kingdom

British Library Cataloguing in Publication Information Available

**The hardback edition of this book was previously cataloged by the Library of Congress
as follows:**

Blight, James G.
    Vietnam if Kennedy had lived : virtual JFK / James G. Blight,
Janet M. Lang, and David A. Welch.
        p.   cm.
    Includes bibliographical references and index.
    ISBN-13: 978-0-7425-5699-7 (cloth : alk. paper)
    ISBN-10: 0-7425-5699-9 (cloth : alk. paper)
    ISBN-13: 978-0-7425-5765-9 (electronic)
    ISBN-10: 0-7425-5765-0 (electronic)
    1. Vietnam War, 1961–1975—United States.   2. Kennedy, John F. (John Fitzgerald),
1917–1963. 3. Johnson, Lyndon B. (Lyndon Baines), 1908–1973. 4. Presidents—United
States—Decision making. 5. Imaginary histories. I. Lang, Janet M., 1948– II. Welch,
David A. III. Title.
DS558.B554   2009
959.704'3—dc22

                                                                2008048413

ISBN 978-0-7425-5700-0 (pbk. : alk. paper)

Printed in the United States of America

♾ ™ The paper used in this publication meets the minimum requirements of American
National Standard for Information Sciences—Permanence of Paper for Printed Library
Materials, ANSI/NISO Z39.48-1992.

In memory of our friend and colleague,
Chester L. Cooper, who knew why,
and
To C., at her royal ease, in the garden

It's not possible for me to make a joke about the death of John F. Kennedy.

—KURT VONNEGUT[1]

CONTENTS

Virtual JFK to President Barack Obama: Is the Game in Afghanistan Worth the Candle?

> Deliberation is very troublesome to me, and I find my mind more troubled by the tumbling and tossing of doubt and consultation than by acquiescing in whatever shall happen after the dice are thrown. Few passions break my sleep, but the least deliberation will do it. The fear of the fall more fevers me than the fall itself. What if the game is not worth the candle? For a man often loses more by defending his vineyard than by giving it up.
>
> Michel de Montaigne, *Essays* (1580)

Nearly every page in this book contains evidence of our rejection of a fundamental maxim held dear by many historians: that it is impossible to do good by doing history. Many in the historical profession regard as positively toxic efforts such as ours to bring history to bear on contemporary policy issues. They are right to be cautious. History cannot speak for itself. It can be tempting to play fast and loose with the facts, selecting for emphasis only those that conveniently fit our preconceptions. Still, history is our best teacher. John F. Kennedy believed this. The past must be made usable, or it will become merely ornamental, an ivory tower profession and a hobby for the leisure classes. It is, we believe, just as irresponsible to refuse to bring history to bear on issues of the day as it is to cherry-pick history for proof of our favorite theories, ideologies or policy prescriptions.

As this paperback edition goes to press, the issue of the day for anyone concerned about U.S. foreign policy is: *What will Barack Obama do about*

Afghanistan? Many have already concluded that Obama's presidency will be chiefly defined, at least in regard to foreign policy, by his success or failure in the struggle against the Taliban and al-Qaeda in Afghanistan and neighboring Pakistan. In this preface we ask: Does the new documentation on JFK and Vietnam bear on the situation Obama faces in Afghanistan? Can virtual JFK "speak" via us to President Barack Obama regarding his predicament? Does Kennedy's approach to the question of escalating the war in Vietnam, especially during his first year in office, 1961, resonate with Obama's dilemmas in dealing with whether (or how much, or in what way) to escalate the war in Afghanistan?

We believe the answer to these questions is "yes."

Kennedy uniquely offers Obama a heuristic mindset for thinking about the fateful decisions he will be called on to make all during at least his first term in office, and beyond, if he is reelected. Of course, he needs to meditate at length on Lyndon Johnson's descent into the tragic quagmire that, for Americans, defines the American experience in Vietnam. He certainly will not want to repeat LBJ's mistakes. But what *should* he do? What questions should he be asking of his advisers every step of the way? That is, we believe, where an accurate understanding of JFK's mindset can be helpful to him. In other words—with apologies in advance to our historian friends—we think it would do Obama some good to meditate on the way Kennedy approached Vietnam during his presidency. And we believe even more emphatically that it would do him a *lot* of good to consider what virtual JFK would have done about Vietnam if he had survived Dallas in November 1963 and been reelected.

1. Will Obama's Afghanistan = LBJ's Vietnam or JFK's Vietnam?

This book, written as the Bush administration's Iraq war reached its crescendo of violence and devastation, contains many comparisons between the U.S. war in Iraq and the U.S. war in Vietnam. The first chapter and epilogue are given over almost entirely to the comparison. In general, we take the view expressed in 2004 by the late Senator Edward Kennedy, quoted in chapter 1, that the war in Iraq was "George Bush's Vietnam." By "Vietnam," we mean, as Senator Kennedy did, "Lyndon Johnson's Vietnam"—an unnecessary war; a war of choice, not a war of necessity. These wars were driven by the ignorance and arrogance of U.S. leaders, especially the respective presidents, Johnson and Bush. We believe, therefore, that the legacy of these wars, and that of the presidents who chose to wage them, will continue to be harshly judged in the court of history.

Curiously (in retrospect, as we write this preface to the paperback edition in November 2009), reference to the war in Afghanistan, which began nearly a decade ago in late 2001, is entirely absent from the book, except for one throwaway reference to it on p. 156 in which it is simply lumped with the war in Iraq as "Bush's wars." Afghanistan had faded from the top tier of concerns of most Americans during our drafting of this book. We did not realize it, but just as we were submitting the manuscript in mid-2008, things were about to change fundamentally. The hardback edition was published just a week before Barack Obama was inaugurated as the 44th president of the United States in January 2009, just before evidence of the resurgence of the Taliban in Afghanistan began to creep back toward page one of the newspapers. Two months later, in March, Obama began to elaborate on his campaign characterization of Afghanistan as a "necessary war," as opposed to the war in Iraq, which he opposed as a senator and which he labeled Bush's unnecessary "war of choice." Most of Obama's senior advisers agree with his characterization of the effort in Afghanistan as a necessary war, including Secretary of State Hillary Clinton, Secretary of Defense Robert Gates, and Chairman of the Joint Chiefs of Staff Michael Mullen. Obama's choice as U.S. commander in Afghanistan, General Stanley McChrystal, also shares this view. In other words, while Obama inherited a war in Afghanistan, he chose to embrace the U.S.-led NATO effort there as his own. Ever since he ordered approximately 20,000 additional U.S. troops to Afghanistan in the spring of 2009, the war against the Taliban and al-Qaeda in Afghanistan and Pakistan has been known as Obama's war.

Since the end of the Second World War, Americans have tended to refer to the countries or regions in which they intervene militarily not as sovereign countries or collections of countries, but simply as wars, as events, or as occasions for the U.S. to take notice of otherwise unimportant, far-away, somewhat exotic locales. Korea, Vietnam, the Persian Gulf, Iraq and Afghanistan—to most Americans, these do not refer to sovereign countries or peoples, but rather to violent events in which Americans participated and sometimes died. Applying this classically American narrative line to Afghanistan, the following question arises: *Will "Barack Obama's Afghanistan" more closely resemble "Lyndon Johnson's Vietnam" or "John Kennedy's Vietnam?"* Will Obama, like Johnson, take the advice of his senior advisers and propel America ever deeper into a war and occupation? Or will he, like Kennedy, ask hard questions of his advisers who urge him to deepen and broaden the war? If he does, will he conclude (as Kennedy did, regarding Vietnam) that the phased withdrawal of U.S. forces from a foreign conflict, despite its political costs in the United States, is the best course to follow? What advice might virtual JFK, the JFK whom we believe would *not* have taken the United States to war in Vietnam, offer Obama on Afghanistan?

2. "Kennedy's Vietnam" by November 1961

In this book, we attach great significance to JFK's decisions in 1961 because we believe that, by mid-November 1961, Kennedy was already leaning decisively toward avoiding a U.S. war in Vietnam. His November 15, 1961, showdown with his advisers over whether to send U.S. combat troops to Vietnam is the principal subject of chapter 3 in this book. Having carefully and repeatedly examined the recommendations of his advisers throughout 1961 to commit large numbers of U.S. combat forces to the conflict, JFK seems to us from the available evidence to have decided that an American war in Vietnam made no sense. He acceded to his advisers' requests for more U.S. advisers and equipment. But he refused to send *any* combat troops to Vietnam.

Here, in three bullet points, are the elements of "Kennedy's Vietnam":

- JFK's reluctance about escalating to a U.S. war in Vietnam becomes clear when some of his other major foreign policy decisions in 1961 (but not only 1961) are taken into account, as we do in this book, and as Koji Masutani does in the companion film.
- JFK decided not later than November 1961 that he was not going to take the United States to war in Vietnam. The new documents and audiotapes lead us straight to this conclusion.
- JFK was right to want to avoid an American war in Vietnam. Our previous research on the war, and the research of many others, shows conclusively that the war was unwinnable at any level of violence short of genocide committed against the Vietnamese population.

The phrase "Kennedy's Vietnam" is thus something worthy of a Kurt Vonnegut novel: a non sequitur, a virtual non-war, a virtual non-tragic, nonhappening in American history. To repeat: we believe Kennedy reached this view by November of his first year in office.

3. Kennedy the Cautious Gambler: Is the Game Worth the Candle?

Before there was a Las Vegas or a Monte Carlo, and long before gambling became re-packaged as wholesome family entertainment, there were dimly-lit backrooms and basements where professional gamblers plied their trade and took their chances by candlelight, having been forced into hiding by authorities charged with preventing them from practicing their putatively sinful and parasitic profession. The proverbial bottom-line question for any gambler in those long-gone days was thus: Am I likely to emerge from this game with at least enough winnings to pay for the candle needed to illuminate the proceedings? If so, then maybe I will get in the game. But if not, then I will not, because the game is literally not worth the candle.

Many scholars and journalists have written over the years that President John F. Kennedy was a gambler. Most meant this to be a devastating criticism, a thorough condemnation of putatively reckless behavior and a retrospective repudiation of a president who, they believed, made decisions without carefully considering the facts and likelihoods in the most dangerous situations of all—those involving U.S. national security. This view of Kennedy was once dominant. Kennedy's critics believed, for example, that he recklessly brought on the Cuban missile crisis and then, in a mad gamble, took Nikita Khrushchev, the Soviet Union, and the world to the brink of nuclear war before Khrushchev breathlessly backed down in the nick of time. We now know that this account is wrong in every important respect.

Many of these critics also believe that the U.S. war in Vietnam should be thought of as "Kennedy's war," not "Johnson's war" or "Nixon's war." It was Kennedy, they emphasize, who greatly increased the number of U.S. advisers to the Saigon government during his presidency from several hundred to more than sixteen thousand. This so-called "micro-escalation" under Kennedy was thus seen as initiating the process that led seamlessly to an American war under Johnson, with the tragic last act having been played out under Richard Nixon and Gerald Ford. But since key declassified documents and secret audiotapes from the Kennedy White House on the missile crisis and Vietnam have become available, the view of Kennedy's gambling proclivities has taken something of a U-turn. In fact, the characterization of Kennedy as a reckless gambler has become untenable. It is now clear to us from the available documentation that JFK's caution and skepticism about the use of military force was actually the essential element in keeping the United States *out* of war during his presidency. Earlier historians, having little declassified documentation to counterbalance their preconceptions and hunches, got Kennedy all wrong. We now know that the JFK who soared to the presidency on his Cold War rhetoric is worlds apart from the skeptical, cautious decision-maker he became in the White House.

Yet while not a reckless decision-maker in matters of war and peace, Kennedy himself would not have objected to being called a gambler. He believed any decision, from the trivial to the cosmically significant, involved a roll of the dice. He worried constantly (some of his hawkish advisers thought he worried obsessively) about a constellation of possibilities that fall under the umbrella concept of *inadvertence*—unintended and unwanted consequences of a decision and its implementation due to misunderstanding, miscalculation, and misperception. Kennedy himself preferred some variant of the term *screw-up* when speaking about the phenomenon of inadvertence. From his extensive reading in diplomatic history, and from his indelible personal experience of the horror and the absurdity of World War II in the Pacific, JFK understood that things seldom turn out as planned by the "brass hats," as he referred to military leaders. He was skeptical of grand plans, grand theories, and grand visions.

Kennedy brought this hard-earned skepticism about the use of military force to the White House when he became president. As a decision-maker, he knew he was often groping in the dark, with misleading or just plain false information about an adversary, and with no clear sense of how much time was available to arrive at a decision before events would become unmanageable. When he became president, he already possessed keen awareness of human fallibility and the virtually limitless capacity for self-delusion. Once in office, he soon realized that he must now add to these malevolent factors a chaotic and muscle-bound U.S. national defense bureaucracy that was entirely unable, as Kennedy saw it, to meet the demands of conflict and crisis prevention in the modern world. To Kennedy, the distinguishing feature of the nuclear age was that it was now possible that a screw-up, or a series of screw-ups, might lead to the destruction of civilization in a matter of minutes.

So deciding, to Kennedy, was always a gamble, and a gamble on the use of military force was *always* a bet against the odds that the outcome would be as rosy as the advisers predicted. Thus, Kennedy's bottom lines in foreign affairs were: try to keep the risks of making a bad decision down; try to "lengthen the fuse" of available time to decide; don't decide until you have to decide, because if you take your time you might learn something important on the way to making a decision; and in the application of military force, assume that something will always go terribly wrong. This was the mindset of the newly-elected occupant of the Oval Office in 1961. The issues and events with which he was confronted that year, and throughout his presidency, confirmed his fears in spades.

Virtual JFK would want President Obama to understand, if he is not already convinced, that every presidential decision is a gamble.

4. LBJ's Vietnam and Obama's Afghanistan: The Controversy

At the moment (November 2009), a cacophonous controversy rages among journalists, scholars, and (increasingly) ordinary citizens over the validity of an analogy between the U.S. war in Vietnam in the 1960s and the war in Afghanistan now. Some argue that the comparison is apt, and that the lesson of Vietnam is that President Barack Obama should do what Presidents Lyndon Johnson and Richard Nixon did *not* do in the 1960s and 1970s: give the U.S. military whatever they say they need to achieve victory in Afghanistan over the Taliban and their allies in the al-Qaeda terrorist network. In other words, *pursue victory, whatever it takes!* Others argue that the comparison is apt, but the lesson they draw is that President Obama should do *now* what Johnson and Nixon did belatedly in Vietnam, which is to begin the withdrawal of U.S. forces from Afghanistan immediately, because winning that war is impossible, eventual defeat is assured, and prompt withdrawal will reduce the eventual costs in blood and treasure to the American people. Their advice: *get out now, before your sunk costs make it even more difficult to do so!* Still others argue, with equal enthusiasm, that for various reasons the analogy is fatally flawed and that whatever President Obama decides to do in Afghanistan, his decision should not rely on any so-called "lessons" derived by journalists or scholars or his advisers from their understanding of the Vietnam war. There is no valid analogy. Their recommendation: *whatever you decide, forget Vietnam!*

We think it is important to emphasize one largely unnoticed feature of this controversy: in each case, no matter what the stated view of the analogy, the comparison is to *Lyndon Johnson's* Vietnam—the tragedy known to history. The advice is either to "pursue victory as Johnson timidly did not," or "don't aggressively escalate the war as Johnson did," or "ignore what Johnson did or did not do, and get on with business in Afghanistan." It is perhaps understandable that the comparison is to Johnson's war, which is a historical reality, after all, whatever one's views on it may be. But the newly available information strongly suggests that "Kennedy's Vietnam war" and "Johnson's Vietnam war" do *not* represent a seamless continuum of escalation. In other words, the implied hybrid president invoked by these commentators on the analogy—"KennedyJohnson's Vietnam"—never existed. Sometimes we are compelled to radically revise our view of history to take account of newly available information. That is indeed the case with JFK and Vietnam. We argue throughout this book that it is now necessary to make a clear distinction between LBJ's Vietnam and JFK's Vietnam.

It is of course as important as ever to understand Johnson. We should study LBJ's Vietnam war as a case study of a president determined to lead his country into a war of choice, a war favored by his advisers, but ultimately a war fully authorized by Lyndon Johnson. But we should also henceforth study JFK's Vietnam war as a case study of a president who, after considering the unanimous and fervent entreaties of his senior advisers to take the country to war in Vietnam, concluded that the game in Vietnam was not worth the candle.

We cannot conclude from a study of JFK and Vietnam that the game is never worth the candle. Kennedy was no pacifist, and neither are we. But we know that JFK believed it did not make sense to transform the conflict in Vietnam into an American war, and we know that he was right. We need to understand the mindset of the president who kept us out of war, at least as completely as we understand the mind of the president who led us into disaster. We need to know what questions Kennedy asked that Johnson did not ask. What were the key criteria for the escalation of a war that JFK (but not LBJ) believed Vietnam did not satisfy?

5. LBJ's Vietnam and Obama's Afghanistan: The Analogy

Mark Twain famously said that while history may not repeat itself, it does sometimes rhyme. LBJ's Vietnam and Obama's Afghanistan resonate like an early Bob Dylan lyric, with line after line ending in often weird but suggestive rhymes. The analogy is as complete as two discrete historical events, from two different historical eras, are ever likely to get. Of course, there are differences. A rhyme is not a repetition. Communism is not Islamic fundamentalism. A jungle is not a desert. And so on. But these differences are superficial; the similarities are profound—eerily profound. Here they are, in outline, as they appear to us near the end of President Obama's first year in office:

- *The Mission: Nation-Building.* The United States *then* sought to build in South Vietnam an independent, democratic, viable, pro-Western government and society in Saigon that would provide a bulwark against the spread of communism in Southeast Asia. The United States *now* seeks to build such a government and society in Afghanistan to prevent the spread of Islamic fundamentalism and terrorism directed at Western countries.

- *The Threat: Falling Dominoes.* The United States *then* cared little for the intrinsic value of South Vietnam, a poor country half a world away, but had come to believe that if the South Vietnamese "domino" fell, all of Southeast Asia would soon "fall" like a row of dominoes, perhaps leading even to the loss of Japan, the key U.S. Cold War ally in the region. The United States *now* is uninterested in either Afghanistan or its people, but many Americans have convinced themselves that if the Afghan "domino" falls to the Taliban and their al-Qaeda allies, nuclear-armed and fragile Pakistan may be the next to "fall," leading perhaps to the acquisition of Pakistani nuclear weapons by terrorists, or even to a nuclear war in the region involving Pakistan and arch-rival India—a war that would inevitably involve the United States and possibly other nuclear powers with interests in the region.
- *The Solution: Military Intervention and Counterinsurgency.* The United States *then* believed the South Vietnamese would, on their own, collapse, and thus become a fallen "domino." Massive military intervention was thus necessary—making it an American war—as was an equally massive effort to win the "hearts and minds" of the Vietnamese people by building a civil society conducive to Western values. The United States *now* believes the Afghan people, tribal and mutually suspicious, cannot organize successfully for their common defense against the Taliban insurgency, so U.S. forces must do it for them, while U.S. military advisers train an Afghan army and police force, and U.S. civilian advisers try to develop the infrastructure of a Western-oriented civil society.
- *The Partner: Corrupt, Arbitrary, Incompetent and Illegitimate.* The United States *then* installed and propped up the government of Ngo Dinh Diem and his brother, Ngo Dinh Nhu, in Saigon. The Ngo brothers became progressively so corrupt, unpopular, and uncooperative that the United States authorized a coup to remove them, in which the military Junta that succeeded them killed both. The United States *now* supports the government it installed after the Taliban were driven from power in 2001–2002, led by Hamid Karzai, who rules unofficially with his brother, Ahmed Wali Karzai, a drug lord, election-fixer, and sometime retainer of the CIA. Recently, the Karzais essentially stole the presidential election, which Washington nevertheless implicitly treated as a legitimate victory.

On January 27, 1965, McGeorge Bundy and Robert McNamara presented LBJ with the famous "fork in the road" memo (discussed in chapter 5; excerpted in Appendix A). The gist of the memo was: we cannot go on like this. The war is going badly. We must go in big, Americanize the war, and pursue a military victory, or begin to get out, while we search for a negotiated settlement that will provide a fig leaf of cover for our abandonment of the effort in South Vietnam. Bundy and McNamara told LBJ they favored getting in big and pursuing victory. LBJ was predisposed toward the same conclusion and took their advice. The same advisers gave Kennedy the same advice in November 1961; JFK rejected it as comprehensively as LBJ embraced it.

The question in our minds is not, "Is LBJ's Vietnam analogous to Obama's Afghanistan?" It *is* analogous. The comparison is, we believe, self-evidently meaningful and potentially instructive. The question of moment is: which way will Obama go? In like LBJ, or out like JFK? America is unlikely to support a long, drawn-out, ambiguous, inconclusive war of attrition, as LBJ discovered too late to save his failed presidency. Obama, it appears, will be forced to choose: in big or out in stages. Will Obama conclude that the game in Afghanistan is, or is not, worth the candle?

6. Virtual JFK's Advice for Obama: Adopt Three-Dimensional Skepticism

We recommend that Obama adopt Kennedy's skeptical view as he considers the advice he is getting from most of his advisers to expand the war in Afghanistan—in effect, to go for victory in Afghanistan. We have "translated" JFK's skepticism into three canonical questions, which we recommend Obama ask and re-ask as long as he is confronted with the possibility of expanding the war in Afghanistan.

It may seem fanciful or presumptuous for us to undertake such a "translation." How do we know, it might be asked, what Kennedy asked behind the scenes, for example during that crucial month of November 1961, as he was deciding to refuse advice to send U.S. combat troops to Vietnam? We have two responses. First, we know more about Kennedy's decision-making style behind the scenes than we do about that of any other president, and perhaps more than any other figure, in U.S. history. This is due in part to the availability of declassified documents, of course. But the key "documents" bearing on this point are the secret audiotapes of Kennedy's meetings with his advisers on Vietnam, during the Cuban missile crisis, and on many other events. These are real-time, fly-on-the-wall recordings, and they are very revealing. The Kennedy on these tapes bears no resemblance to the supposedly hawkish Kennedy of rhetoric and legend.

Second, the "translation" of Kennedy's skepticism into the three questions that follow in this section fits with the recollections of our late colleague, co-author and friend, Secretary of Defense Robert S. McNamara. In fact, Bob McNamara often said that Kennedy's fear of wars getting out of control—his gut feeling that wars are not controlled by anyone, not even U.S. presidents—was Kennedy's distinguishing feature as a national security decision-maker. Kennedy really *did* give copies of Barbara Tuchman's *The Guns of August* to McNamara and his other senior foreign policy advisers. He worried that he might be asked to get involved in a war that, like the one initiated by the European leaders described so vividly by Tuchman, spiraled quickly and catastrophically out of control. McNamara added that Kennedy had a tendency to interrogate his advisers on how they could be so sure that the application of military force would lead to a happy ending, and that this tendency infuriated the very people in the Pentagon whose management was McNamara's job. But Kennedy, as far as McNamara could remember, never backed down—he never accepted on faith the outcomes predicted by those recommending the use of U.S. military force, in Vietnam, during the Bay of Pigs invasion, over the Berlin Wall, over Soviet activity in Laos, or during the Cuban missile crisis.

Kennedy's skepticism is important because, in the light of history, we know that it was justified. We now know, on the basis of the available historical data, that these crises carried a very high risk of spiraling out of control. We know a lot about what various adversaries were up to, what they were willing to do, how they would have responded, and what the ultimate outcomes probably would have been. Each retrospective judgment is grim. And with regard to Vietnam, estimation is unnecessary. We know, because of what happened, that JFK was right and LBJ was wrong.

We believe Barack Obama ought to adopt JFK's three-dimensional skepticism about the use of military force in Vietnam as he gears up for years of difficult decisions about the U.S. commitment to the war in Afghanistan. To witness Kennedy in action vicariously, interrogating his advisers about their hawkish advice, consult pp. 281–283 in this book—the notes of the November 15, 1961, showdown on Vietnam in the White House. The following bullets represent our effort to transpose Kennedy's questions about Vietnam to Obama's situation in Afghanistan:

- **Falling Dominoes?** Is it true that the dominoes will fall? Is it true that if Afghanistan falls to the Taliban, then the risk to the U.S. homeland will increase unacceptably? If Afghanistan falls to the Taliban, will Pakistan come apart? If Pakistan collapses, will the Indians invade to protect themselves preemptively from the possibility that some of Pakistan nuclear weapons will be used against them? In short, is it true, as many believe, that a triumph by the Taliban in Afghanistan will threaten the strategic interests of the United States?

- **Prevention?** If it is true that a Taliban victory will threaten U.S. strategic interests, is it also true that the United States can prevent it from happening? Is a military victory, perhaps in combination with a variant of counterinsurgency and nation building, in the cards? Can an indigenous, resourceful, committed insurgency be defeated by a Western power, half a world away? What is the evidence that the United States can prevent a Taliban takeover and whatever else may follow?

- **Cost and Risk?** If the dominoes in the region will fall following a Taliban victory over the U.S.-backed Kabul government, and if in principle the United States can prevent this from happening, at what cost to the United States will the dominoes remain standing? What will be the cost in American lives lost or ruined by such a war? What will be the cost to the U.S. image in the Islamic world of a protracted U.S. war and occupation of a Muslim country? How much collateral damage will the Afghans and Pakistanis tolerate before even those in the region initially hospitable to the U.S. intervention begin to oppose the war and occupation? What will be the financial burden borne by the American people in order to prevent the fall of the presumed dominoes? And how do these costs, taken together, compare with the cost of another major terrorist attack on the United States whose perpetrators may be traced to training camps in an Afghanistan re-conquered by the Taliban, following a hypothetical decision by Obama to begin to withdraw U.S. forces from the region?

These are, we believe, the queries consistent with JFK's skepticism about the application of U.S. military force that President Obama should be asking with respect to Afghanistan.

James G. Blight
janet M. Lang
David A. Welch

The Balsillie School of International Affairs
University of Waterloo
Waterloo, Ontario
November 18, 2009

by Fredrik Logevall

It's the most controversial what if in the history of American foreign policy: What if John F. Kennedy had lived? What would he have done in Vietnam? The question resonates and tantalizes because of the costs of the war—so immense to the U.S. in so many ways—but also because of the timing and circumstances of Kennedy's death. His departure came at a particularly important moment in the Vietnam saga, a mere three weeks after a U.S.-sanctioned coup d'etat in Saigon caused the overthrow and then murder of South Vietnamese leader Ngo Dinh Diem, and only about a year before Lyndon B. Johnson initiated large-scale war. And Kennedy died suddenly, without leaving a clear statement of his intentions regarding Southeast Asia. Then, too, there is the contradictory nature of his decisions on Vietnam. On the one hand, he expanded U.S. involvement dramatically, and he approved a coup against Diem. He showed scant interest in seeking a negotiated settlement and voiced periodic support for the domino theory. On the other hand, despite the periodic urgings of top advisers JFK refused to commit U.S. ground forces to the struggle. Over time, he became increasingly skeptical about South Vietnam's prospects and hinted that he would seek an end to the American commitment.

Just what a surviving Kennedy would have done in Vietnam can never be known with certainty, of course, which is why many authors are reluctant to probe the matter in depth. Professional historians, in particular, are likely to be dismissive of such "counterfactual" theorizing—following E. H. Carr's lead, they see it as a mere parlor game, worth a few throwaway sentences, perhaps, but no more. Deciphering actual history is difficult enough, these skeptics say, never mind the history of what might have been. Hypothetical history is unscholarly, since it leads away from the real and verifiable to the imaginary and unprovable; as such, it should be left to the poets and novelists.

This book challenges this view head-on, and rightly so. James Blight, janet Lang, and David Welch (none of them, I note, a professional historian) understand that when properly done, the investigation of unrealized possibilities, of roads not taken, provides critical insight into why things turned out the way they did. As such, thinking about unrealized alternatives is indispensable to students of history—we can judge the forces that prevailed only by comparing them with those that were defeated. Such comparison also helps protect us against what political scientists refer to as hindsight bias, reminding us that to the policymakers of the past, the future was merely a set of options. What's more, whenever we write about the past and make claims of cause and effect we are engaging in speculation and envisioning alternative developments, even when these alternatives are not stated explicitly.

Blight, Lang, and Welch refer to their approach as "virtual history," to distinguish it from what they see as highly fictionalized, nonrigorous "counterfactual history." Fair enough, though I would say that what they advocate is merely counterfactual history properly done. Whatever the preferred name, the case of JFK in Vietnam is especially conducive to fruitful examination of this kind because of the massive amount of archival material now available; because of the short period of time between Kennedy's murder and the moment of truth in the decision making (in my view, about fifteen months); and because of the small number of likely changes in other key variables. Through careful examination of the unrealized alternatives on Vietnam during these months in 1963–1965, this book persuasively suggests, we can better understand the options that U.S. leaders of the time had or did not have, the choices they did or did not possess. We can come closer, in other words, to that Rankean ideal of understanding "how it essentially was."

To get at these issues, the three authors utilize to great effect a method they pioneered in earlier work on the Cuban missile crisis. They call it "critical oral history," and it involves the sustained interaction, in a conference setting, of former officials and scholars who have before them declassified documents (plus, in this case, tape recordings) relevant to the issue at hand. In April 2005, Blight, Lang, and Welch gathered a group of us together at Musgrove on the Georgia coast to discuss Vietnam if Kennedy had lived. I had read with deep interest the results of their work on the missile crisis, but had not been involved personally in that project; this would be my first direct experience with critical oral history. I made sure to prepare. Though I was familiar with much of the documentary material sent to us—in an enormous package—in advance, I read it carefully before departure and on the flight. Though I knew most of the other participants,

I took time to read up on those I would be meeting for the first time. I rehearsed the essentials of the critical oral history method as I understood them.

What followed was a series of marvelously stimulating discussions spread over three days. Frequently the exchanges continued during coffee breaks and over meals and during walks in our idyllic surroundings. Documents were passed back and forth across the table; audiotapes were played and replayed. Disagreements were frequent and sometimes heated, as could be expected with people who in the past had staked differing positions on the core questions under discussion. Were many minds changed? It is hard for me to know. I came to the conference believing that a post-Dallas Kennedy most likely would have avoided Americanizing the war (but also that he had made no firm decision prior to Dallas to withdraw from Vietnam); I left still adhering to that position. But I came away with a better grasp of the opposing arguments and (I like to think) a better appreciation of them. From the policymakers in attendance I learned again how difficult it can be for those who hold minority positions to make themselves heard, and how tempting it can be to go along with the dominant view.

Iraq, of course, was never far from our minds at Musgrove. Two years had passed since the invasion, and the insurgency raged. Troubling questions were being raised in the media about the circumstances in which the Bush administration had taken the nation to war, and about whether America had become mired in "another Vietnam." Whatever the ultimate utility of the Vietnam analogy to the calamity that is the Iraq War, the evidence is overwhelming that these were both wars of choice, not of necessity, and were understood as such by senior officials from the start. Alternatives to the use of military force existed in 1965 and 2003, not merely in the superior vision of hindsight, but in the context of the time. It is this, more than anything, which makes this such a powerful and instructive book.

Department of History
Cornell University

"Was this catastrophic war necessary?"

Whither Vietnam, If Kennedy Had Lived?

The American war in Vietnam was among the bloodiest conflicts of the last half of the twentieth century. Over 2,000,000 Vietnamese and more than 58,000 Americans were killed, and many times these numbers were wounded, displaced, and imprisoned. In the course of the war, North and South Vietnam were nearly destroyed as functioning societies, while American society was torn apart over issues related to the war.

It is ironic that *both* the U.S. and Vietnam achieved their principal goals: communism did not spread in Southeast Asia, and the Vietnamese unified their country under the leadership of the communist government in Hanoi. In light of this outcome, the question inevitably arises: Was this catastrophic war necessary? Was so much death and destruction required between two countries that have subsequently established full normal political relations (in July 1995) and trade relations (in July 2000), even though both adversaries retain their individual systems of governance that seemed so important and antithetical during the war? The U.S. two-party system of democracy, with its capitalist underpinning, still contrasts starkly with the stronghold the Communist Party retains throughout Vietnam, yet relations between the two countries are "normal."

Might the U.S. and Vietnam have achieved their goals at far less cost in blood and treasure? If so, how? Which aspects of this tragic history would have to have been different for the war to have been avoided?[1] In this book, we examine the most famous variant of this question—a variant with obvious and powerful resonance to the situation in which the U.S. finds itself now in Iraq. The question is this: if John F. Kennedy had lived and been reelected in November 1964, would he and his administration have initiated, escalated, and prosecuted the war in Vietnam more or less as did his successor, Lyndon B. Johnson, or would JFK have withdrawn U.S. forces from Vietnam, effectively ending direct U.S. involvement there and thus avoiding the Vietnam War?

This is the most debated and controversial what if in the history of American foreign policy. We tackle the question in a way that maximizes the dependence of our answer on empirical evidence—on declassified documents, oral testimony of former officials, and the analysis of top scholars of the war in Vietnam. Our research is based on a new approach to historical what if questions called virtual history, an approach that avoids the fictional excesses of so-called counterfactual history—fantasies about the "history" of what did *not* happen.

Our understanding of history is that it is a product of an ongoing argument, based on access to only a small proportion of the possible evidence in any matter of consequence, and that it is powerfully driven by factors having nothing to do with history itself, such as who is making the argument, the climate of the times in which the argument is made, and the audience to which the argument is addressed. But our understanding of history is not, or at least need not be, arbitrary. The evidence matters. The strength of the argument matters.

Some historical arguments, and the understanding deriving from them, are better than others. But "better" should never be confused with "certain." Convictions of certainty in historical matters are dangerous, in addition to being illusory, because a certain mind is not an inquiring mind, and without renewing our historical understanding by serious inquiry at every opportunity, we are apt to lose our history. We lose our way. We forget. We especially forget just how costly historical misunderstanding can be, how what we did not know hurt us. The American war in Vietnam is, we believe, the most tragic certainty-driven episode thus far in U.S. history. However, the current fiasco in Iraq, also driven by delusions of certainty, is far from over, and its ultimate consequences are still unclear. It is possible that someday the certainties that led the U.S. into Iraq will be regretted as profoundly as those which led to the quagmire in Vietnam. In some quarters, they already are.

Alas, the historical literature on the war in Vietnam, especially as written and interpreted in America, is, to a regrettable degree, a literary and psychological swamp infested with certainty. In this book, we seek to battle those who are certain that they understand why, and at the order of whom, the war in Vietnam escalated to catastrophe. Mainly, certainty is used to buttress accusations as to who is to blame for the war in Vietnam. This book is not about blame. We offer instead an *argument* about Vietnam if Kennedy had lived. It is an argument shaped and moved forward by the improvisational, the unpredictable, and even the occasional surreal insight. This argument, which fills chapters 3–6 in this book, was carried on face-to-face by nearly two dozen extraordinarily qualified people who had a wide range of experience and informed views on the issue of Vietnam, if Kennedy had lived. It was an argument spread over three intense days. In addition, although this is a book about the Vietnam War, we would be pleased if we also delivered significant discomfort to some who are certain they fully grasp the connections between the wars in Vietnam and Iraq.

Prepare vicariously to pull your chair up to that conference table and join the argument.

HANOI

BAGHDAD

"Great is the guilt of an unnecessary war."—John Adams to Abigail Adams

CHAPTER 1

Why Kennedy, Johnson, and Vietnam? Why Now?

The Relevance of the Vietnam War: "Great Is the Guilt of [Another] Unnecessary War"

Why, really, should we care about Vietnam if Kennedy had lived? Until very recently, there seemed to be no great urgency. The what if character of the question made any answer largely speculative prior to (roughly) the mid-1990s, when important new sources on the Kennedy presidency began to be declassified. But even if the question had yielded a confident answer, the war in Vietnam has seemed to many for quite some time to be something long ago and far away, hardly relevant to the conduct of U.S. foreign policy today, in the early twenty-first century. Until recently, Americans too young to remember the war had a lot in common with the daughter of the protagonist in Tim O'Brien's celebrated 1990 novel of the war in Vietnam, *The Things They Carried*. He is a Vietnam veteran who has returned to Vietnam to show his daughter some of the places he frequented during the war. She is unimpressed and uninterested. He finally remarks, "The war was as remote to her as cavemen and dinosaurs."[1]

For most of the nearly half-century since JFK's assassination on November 22, 1963, the debate over this issue has more closely resembled a contest of zealots mainly interested in scoring points against those with opposing views than a dispassionate search for historical truth. There are two principal reasons for this. First, a lot of relevant information has, until quite recently, been unavailable. Archives have been sealed. Admiring memoirs published in the wake of JFK's death by his closest associates lacked endnotes and references entirely, which prevented others from checking on the accuracy or even the plausibility of their claims.[2] To some, these laudatory books confirmed their positive image of JFK as president. But to others, the heavy reliance in them on privileged information led to the strong suspicion that JFK's proclivities regarding Vietnam, as well as other issues, had been systematically whitewashed by Kennedy loyalists. Only in the last decade or two have some of the most revealing documents and audiotapes been declassified, deciphered, and analyzed, allowing outsiders to form independent judgments.

Second, to a degree scarcely imaginable to Americans under the age of fifty, the U.S. defeat in Vietnam polarized an entire generation, hell-bent, so it has sometimes seemed, only on assigning blame for this greatest foreign policy disaster in U.S. history, rather than on trying to understand how it happened and how it might have been avoided. With the collapse of Saigon and the end of the war in April 1975, the collective American effort to assign blame for the disaster began in earnest and has continued apace ever since. Even President Ronald Reagan got caught up in the Vietnam blame game. For the venue of his November 11, 1988, Veteran's Day address, Reagan chose the Vietnam Veterans Memorial in Washington, D.C. In that speech he called the war a "noble cause," legitimizing the search for culprits who had allegedly perverted or denied its presumed nobility.[3] Who were the villains? Who was responsible for the dead, for the wounded, for the missing, and for ruining America's reputation by actually losing a war to Vietnam, an adversary President Lyndon Johnson liked to call "that little pissant country"? Was John F. Kennedy to blame? Lyndon B. Johnson? Robert McNamara? General William Westmoreland? Richard Nixon? Our feckless South Vietnamese allies? The U.S. Congress? The peace movement? The military-industrial complex? All too seldom were the Vietnamese communists given much credit in America for winning the war.

Writing in 1985, the American journalist Gloria Emerson, who reported on the war from Vietnam for more than fifteen years, captured the psychological turbulence, the swirl of highly contradictory emotions that the war generated for many Americans who lived through the Vietnam era.

> In our country Vietnam is not the name of a small nation with its own rivers and mountains, its little vegetable gardens with lettuce and peppers, its splendid beaches and rice fields, its children learning arithmetic, and the old men who love the roses they grow. There were orchards once, and cattle once, and flowers whose names I did not know.
>
> Now Vietnam is our word, meaning an American failure, a shorthand for a disaster, a tragedy of good intentions, a well-meaning misuse of American power, a noble cause ruined by a loss of will and no home front, a war of crime, a loathsome jungle where our army of children fought an army of fanatics.[4]

The disaster in Vietnam became, to many Americans, all about us, a kind of multipolar family feud about who is to blame for this terrible blot on our otherwise spotless reputation. Within the family, therefore, the term *Vietnam* should almost always be placed within quotation marks, to denote the metaphor it has become for us.

Our own students, now all born long after the war in Vietnam was over, have a favorite word for the way their elders have typically characterized the war to them, filled with powerful, only half-verbalized emotion, and often devoid of factual information about what actually happened. Their favorite assessment: "weird." All that emotion. All that blaming. So few facts. The former *New York Times* reporter Joseph Lelyveld succinctly captured the essence of this phenomenon: "When we talk about Vietnam, we are seldom talking about the country of that name or the situation of the people who live there. Usually we are talking about ourselves. Probably we always were."[5]

On March 19, 2003, the U.S. invaded Iraq. The invasion was only the initial act in a tragic drama still to be played out in full, but which for many already seems eerily to mimic the disastrous war in Vietnam. If the U.S. adventure in Vietnam were still a historical oddity, as it was prior to the invasion of Iraq—a one-time thing, a failure whose lessons have been learned, a mistake never to be repeated—then interpreting the meaning of the war in Vietnam could safely be left to two groups: those who lived through it and still feel compelled to fight the old battles all over again, and historians specializing in one or another aspect of the war who make a living trying to make sense of it. In that case, the need to inquire into Vietnam if Kennedy had lived, which is the purpose of this book, would itself be much less compelling. And it is doubtful whether, if the Vietnam War were still considered "only" historical, scholars such as ourselves—none of us is a professional historian—would have tried to tackle this particular historical what if?

But it is now obvious that in some rough but meaningful sense, the formerly unthinkable is happening again, this time in Iraq. This is not the place for a lengthy disquisition on why this is so—why, for the second time in the lives of many Americans, the U.S. has blundered, like déjà vu, into a foreign policy disaster of immense proportions. Iraq echoes the disaster in Vietnam. But it is worth asking, "Why is the U.S. afflicted with this apparent 'learning disability'?" Is it because it is difficult to learn valid lessons about our history when the history itself is shunted aside as, in effect, much less important than winning the blame game? Is it because in talking ceaselessly about ourselves, we become oblivious to potential and actual adversaries, the way we are regarded by adversaries, and important features of their societies that may be very different from our own? Is it because we as Americans are so self-absorbed with regard to the war in Vietnam, so awash in our strong but inarticulate emotion, that we appear not only "weird" to younger generations, but have also been unhelpful in imparting useful lessons as to how to avoid such tragedies in the future? In a recent essay, Marilyn Young, the distinguished historian of the war in Vietnam, cites Gloria Emerson's famous comment that Americans have "always been a people who dropped the past and then could not remember where it had been put." Then Young adds a comment, full of portent and heavy with condemnation of those responsible for the decision to invade Iraq, the vast majority of whom lived through the Vietnam conflict. "This time," she writes, "they've put it in Iraq."[6]

For this reason, the current generation of young Americans has already begun to bear a burden not unlike that borne by those who came of age during the Vietnam era. This is occurring even before the U.S. withdraws from Iraq, as one day it must, leaving it in a mess, following which the historical accounting for who is to blame for this foreign policy calamity will no doubt begin in earnest. Senator Edward Kennedy has said, "Iraq is George Bush's Vietnam."[7] Whether or not one fully endorses Kennedy's analysis, it becomes clearer what Bush is being accused of if, in the two paragraphs cited above from Gloria Emerson, one simply substitutes the word *Iraq* for *Vietnam* in each paragraph, and the word *desert* for *jungle* in the second.

Of course there are differences. The scale of the Iraq War has, so far, not reached that of the war in Vietnam. Equally, the post–Cold War, post-9/11 Middle East differs in many respects from Cold War Southeast Asia, and so on. But the differences seem increasingly less important than the similarities. Well over 650,000 Iraqis may have died since the March 2003 U.S.-led invasion of Iraq, and more than 4,000 Americans have been killed in action.[8] There is currently no end in sight to the horror. Saddam Hussein's Iraq, one of the world's most brutal police states, has been transformed via the American intervention into something even worse: an anarchical hell on earth, a desert apocalypse. America has once again become one of the world's most hated nations in many parts of the world. And lest we leave out the linchpin that, for Americans, will likely forever entwine Vietnam with Iraq: the U.S. will leave Iraq eventually, and no matter what the politicians and spin doctors find to celebrate as the last American soldier leaves Iraq, we will understand that, once again, America has *lost*—has been both humiliated and vilified in the eyes of the world.[9]

This leads us to the regrettable but inescapable conclusion: Vietnam if Kennedy had lived is not and can no longer be an idle historical curiosity, an obsession of pro-Kennedy and anti-Kennedy zealots, about events of nearly a half-century ago remembered, if at all, as little more than a series of grainy black-and-white images of JFK that appear reliably on television with every anniversary of his assassination divisible by five. The U.S. war in Iraq—"a disaster, a tragedy of good intentions," in Gloria Emerson's (once only descriptive, but now also prophetic) phrase—that quagmire in the desert, has changed all that.

As the disaster in Iraq continues to unfold, and as the analogy with Vietnam becomes more arresting and multidimensional, we inevitably begin to ask, with renewed urgency, how the war in Vietnam, that earlier disastrous "war of choice," might have been avoided. A comment by John Adams, America's second president, was sometimes invoked in the 1960s by opponents of the war in Vietnam. "Great is the guilt of an unnecessary war," Adams wrote to his wife Abigail in May 1794, when he was George Washington's vice president and pressure to go to war with France was building.[10] Was the war in Vietnam an unnecessary war? If so, would JFK have avoided it? Do the answers to these questions provide clues as to how the war in Iraq might have been avoided and, indeed, how future unnecessary wars might be avoided? What kind of president stands the best chance of avoiding such unnecessary wars in the future? These are some of the questions that contribute to the unprecedented urgency of what would have happened in Vietnam if Kennedy had lived.

Actual JFK: Avoiding War Over the Bay of Pigs, Laos, the Berlin Wall, and the Cuban Missile Crisis

We had been circling around this issue, Vietnam if Kennedy had lived, indirectly for more than twenty years before we decided to try to tackle it head-on. Our research on the foreign policy of the Kennedy administration, beginning in the mid-1980s, provided us with the background for the research reported in this book. We began our work on the Cuban missile crisis in the mid-1980s hoping, at most, to add a footnote here or there to what was already known about the crisis. But unexpectedly, the Soviet Union under Mikhail Gorbachev began to open its long-sealed foreign policy archives. By the late 1980s we, along with colleagues from several research institutes in the U.S. and abroad, were beginning to obtain information revealing how the Soviet leadership made its decisions before, during, and immediately after the missile crisis. Then the Cold War came to its unexpected climax in November 1989, when the Germans began dismantling the Berlin Wall. The breakup of the Soviet Union followed at the end of December 1991, just weeks before our own, surreal U.S.-Cuban-Russian conference in Havana, Cuba, with such participants as Cuban President Fidel Castro; JFK's secretary of defense, Robert McNamara; and Russian General Anatoly Gribkov, who in 1962 had been the mastermind who planned the Soviet missile deployment to Cuba.[11]

The end of the Cold War and the collapse of the Soviet Union changed almost everything for those of us doing research on the recent history of U.S. foreign policy. Instead of having to read between the lines of biased memoirs of sometimes dubious authorship, we were suddenly flooded with relevant primary documents. Just as suddenly, we could talk to officials and use the documents to anchor our discussions in the real world as it was, rather than as some might like us to believe it was. We joined with scholars from all over the world to exploit the unprecedented opportunities to understand the era and events that had to that point shaped our lives. In this heady atmosphere, we carried out research on the failed April 1961 Bay of Pigs invasion (in the U.S., Russia, and Cuba); the Laos crisis of spring 1961 (in Vietnam); the Berlin Wall crisis of the summer and fall of 1961 (in the U.S., Russia, and eastern and western Germany); the October 1962 Cuban missile crisis (in the U.S., Russia, and Cuba); and the escalation of the U.S. war in Vietnam in the mid-1960s (in Vietnam and the U.S.).[12]

We were far from the only scholars who took advantage of these new possibilities for research.[13] Yet we had begun our Cold War studies fortuitously with a reevaluation of the Cuban missile crisis, which was the first major Cold War event on which significant declassified documentation and access to top officials became available. We had been frankly surprised, given the dominant image in the 1980s of JFK as a hawk, by the composite picture of Kennedy that began to emerge from our study of the missile crisis. This "new" JFK was a far cry from the Kennedy who in his inaugural speech famously called on Americans to "pay any price, bear any burden" in the fight against Soviet communism. On the contrary, JFK in action during that supremely dangerous crisis appeared cautious, fully in charge, willing to run political risks to avoid war over missiles in Cuba, and highly skeptical of the hawkish military advice he got from many quarters. It was with this image of JFK as a cautious, war-averse decisionmaker in the missile crisis that we began. We wondered: Was Kennedy's performance in the missile crisis uniquely cautious, perhaps because of the unprecedented danger of the event? Or was Kennedy always like this when it came to making decisions in matters of war and peace? With these and similar questions in mind, we set out to reexamine some of the other pivotal crises of Kennedy's presidency, episodes when war and peace seemed to be on the line and when the president's choice—whether or not to step over the line that divides crises from shooting wars—seemed so heavy with significance. Indeed, in more than one of these crises, to borrow a phrase made famous in the 1980s, "the fate of the earth" seemed to many to be hanging in the balance.[14]

JFK's foreign policy education was of course continuous, over the roughly thousand days of his presidency. Yet in those darkest days of the Cold War, the bulk of his education in foreign policy occurred, we believe, in relatively short, explosive bursts. These crises seemed to occur suddenly, sometimes without warning, and they appeared to JFK (though often not to his advisers) to be very dangerous. In response to these crises, his top national security aides provided Kennedy with advice that was often hawkish in the extreme, seemingly heedless of America's military vulnerability to the threat of Soviet nuclear forces, but also oblivious to the international political fallout that would, in JFK's view, be a likely consequence of the introduction of U.S. military force into conflicts in the developing world. Here, in outline, are some of the principal lessons we now believe "actual JFK" learned from Cold War crises we investigated before deciding to tackle the issue addressed in this book.

- *April 1961, the Bay of Pigs debacle.* Just before taking office, JFK is told that he has inherited from Eisenhower, his predecessor, a CIA scheme for regime change in Cuba, using 1,200 Cuban exiles as an invasion force that, according to the CIA, will incite a popular uprising against the Castro government. JFK is told before the invasion that the operation will almost certainly succeed. Then, as it is failing miserably, he is told that it can still succeed if he agrees to use U.S. air power and to send in U.S. Marines, who are positioned on U.S. ships almost within site of the Bay of Pigs. His advisers at the CIA and at the Joint Chiefs of Staff are almost apoplectic with disbelief when he refuses their request to bomb Cuba and invade the island.

  The lessons: Do not trust your intelligence bureaucracy to come clean on the costs and risks of the invasion of another country. Do not trust the rosy estimates of the military brass on important aspects of a foreign military adventure.

- *Winter/Spring 1961, the Laos crisis.* JFK is told that the Soviet resupply of communist insurgents in Laos must forcibly be stopped using U.S. regular forces, but possibly also by using tactical nuclear weapons. He is told that if he fails to Americanize the conflict, the communists will overrun Laos and threaten all of Southeast Asia. Kennedy neither orders U.S. troops into Laos nor does he authorize the use of U.S. air power against Soviet assets in Laos. He is appalled at the thought of using nuclear weapons in Laos or anywhere. Instead, he works with Soviet leader Nikita Khrushchev to resolve the crisis via a political compromise: a neutralist government for Laos.

The lessons: Do not be intimidated by military brass, not even General Dwight Eisenhower, your predecessor and a military hero (who told Kennedy to do "whatever is necessary" to save Laos from the communists). Do not believe advisers who tell you that just because the communists appear to make gains, the sky is about to fall or, in any event, that a military intervention against Soviet forces can be undertaken anywhere at acceptable cost and risk.

- *August–October 1961, the Berlin Wall crisis.* JFK is told, as the Wall goes up in Berlin, that he must threaten the Soviets with both conventional and nuclear weapons until they capitulate, tear down the Wall, and refrain from harassing U.S. personnel in East Germany en route to and from Berlin. Kennedy refuses to intervene or risk a military engagement between U.S. and Soviet forces in Berlin. As a result, he encounters stiff public criticism and bitter internal dissension from his hawkish advisers. Nevertheless, Kennedy tells his representative in Berlin, former General Lucius Clay, to back off, and Khrushchev reciprocates. The Wall goes up and stays up, tragically closing off the principal route for East Germans to escape to the West, but a war in the heart of Europe is avoided.

  The lessons: Retain strict civilian control of military operations in any direct confrontation with the Soviet Union. Never forget what many military and civilian advisers seem not yet to have grasped—that nuclear weapons are not usable weapons, but rather are little more than doomsday devices.

- *October 1962, the Cuban missile crisis.* JFK is told point-blank by most of his civilian and military advisers that the U.S. must bomb Soviet missile sites in Cuba and invade the island as soon as possible in order to ensure that Soviet military capability on the island is destroyed and the Castro government removed. Kennedy personally restrains his U.S. military advisers, who are aghast at what they take to be his timidity and cowardly reluctance to use the deployment of Soviet missiles as a pretext to destroy the Cuban Revolution. But JFK works out a compromise with Khrushchev and, we now know, is ready to absorb enormous political heat rather than risk war with the Soviet Union.

  The lessons: Escalation to an all-out nuclear war between the U.S. and the Soviet Union is possible, and in this crisis may even have been likely, even though none of the involved leaders wished for it. Thus, do everything possible to avoid a direct confrontation with the USSR and begin to seek a new basis for relations between East and West because, as the missile crisis proves, the Cold War confrontation is too dangerous to be sustainable.[15]

If we had to choose a single word to characterize the actual JFK who has emerged over the twenty years during which we have become retrospectively acquainted with him, it would be *skeptical.* JFK arrived at the White House mistrusting slogans and easy answers as well as servile and self-serving advisers. He was bored and irritated by yes-men. He seems to have been almost instinctually skeptical of immediate, emotional responses to crisis situations. But after the humiliation he brought on himself and his administration by allowing the Bay of Pigs invasion to go forward, he seems to have become an even more skeptical exemplar of a principle of leadership attributed to one of his historical heroes, the French diplomat Maurice Talleyrand: "Above all," Talleyrand proclaimed, "no zeal."[16] Over the past twenty years, as we have listened to the Kennedy tapes, read the written record of decision making during the Kennedy administration, and cross-examined those who served in it, we have become struck by how clearly Kennedy the skeptic appears over and over again. He is a president who often asks the toughest questions and whose skeptical proclivities often stand out in sharp relief from the Cold War boilerplate often served up to him by his advisers.

In claiming that JFK was a war-averse decisionmaker, a skeptic on the overt use of military force, we are not endeavoring to recruit Kennedy retrospectively into the ranks of pacifism. That would be silly. He had been a patrol boat commander fighting the Japanese in World War II. Kennedy was no pacifist, but he was a serious student of history, especially diplomatic history. He knew from his study of history, and also from having his patrol boat cut in half by a Japanese destroyer in the Pacific, that war is unpredictable, and that those who initiate it usually vastly underestimate its costs in blood and treasure. Kennedy was immersed in the history of war. One of the most eloquent statements of the value to public officials of immersion in history comes from the Brown University historian of the American Revolution, Gordon Wood.

History does not teach lots of little lessons. . . . [I]t teaches only one big one: that nothing ever works out quite the way its managers intended or expected. History is like experience and old age: wisdom is what one learns from it . . . [chiefly] skepticism about people's ability to manipulate and control purposely their own destinies. By showing that the best laid plans of people usually go awry, the study of history tends to dampen youthful enthusiasm, and to restrain the can-do, the conquer-the-future spirit that many people have. Historical knowledge takes people off emotions and gives people a perspective on what is possible and, more often, what is not possible.[17]

This fits JFK to a "T." It's not pacifism. It's skepticism, derived from his study of history and his personal experience, and his skepticism drove his approach to foreign policy when war and peace were on the line, especially after it was so powerfully reinforced by his humiliation at the Bay of Pigs.

And so we return at the end of this section to where it all began for us: to the Cuban missile crisis, and to a single example of JFK's particular kind of skepticism and caution that seems to us to have characterized all his foreign policy decision making, as it has been revealed to scholars in the Kennedy tapes and other documents. On what turned out to be the final weekend of the crisis, Kennedy's principal task was to try to force his exhausted, frustrated advisers, many of whom were increasingly belligerent, to face a supremely unpleasant and inconvenient possibility. The tape recordings of those fateful discussions reveal that on several occasions and in a variety of ways, JFK explained to his advisers that were he to accept their advice and order an air strike and invasion of Cuba, the U.S. might find itself in a catastrophic nuclear war with the Soviet Union. In retrospect, it is remarkable, given the stakes, that most of his advisers, though not all, do not seem to "get it." As a consequence, and with only partial success, JFK spends many hours trying to explain to his advisers the facts of life in the nuclear age.

Here is the scene. It is early in the evening on October 27, 1962. JFK and his advisers have been meeting for nearly twelve hours on this, day twelve of the now famous thirteen days. Kennedy has been told what he must and must not do: he *must* order the attack on Cuba before the Soviet missiles become operational, before they become capable of being launched against U.S. targets, and he must *not* publicly trade NATO missiles in Turkey for the Soviet missiles in Cuba, as Khrushchev has suggested in a message of earlier that day, because agreeing to such a public trade might cause the Turks to quit NATO, leading to the collapse of NATO altogether. JFK listens patiently. He leads the discussion of how to respond to Khrushchev. JFK clearly believes that the idea of a missile trade is logical, even reasonable, and will be so judged by clear-thinking people everywhere, especially if the alternative is a war that could involve a nuclear exchange. He leaves the room briefly one last time to encourage a more open exchange of views among the advisers than is possible with the president in the room. He returns just before the group will break for dinner. It is clear immediately from the discussions that the majority of his advisers simply cannot bring themselves to endorse a public missile trade. Psychologically, the trade seems to them to connote needless capitulation when, as they see it, the U.S. has overwhelming military superiority in the Caribbean and also overwhelming nuclear superiority, and ought to use its power to force a favorable resolution. When news reaches the group that a U-2 spy plane has been shot down over Cuba and its pilot killed, many in the group want to attack immediately. They are angry. They want to punish the Soviets and their Cuban hosts. But JFK's reluctance to resort to military force is palpable.

It is at this point on the audiotape of that critical meeting that one can hear Kennedy comment almost off-handedly with the cosmic irony of which he was capable in moments of supreme crisis, but which in this case, given the circumstances, can also send shivers down the spine. JFK tells his advisers that should the U.S. attack Cuba, and should escalation to nuclear war occur, a war that could have been avoided by publicly trading missiles, "I don't see how we'll have a very good war."[18] Here is a portion of the exchange.

> **President Kennedy:** We can't very well invade Cuba, with all the toil and blood it's going to be, when we could have gotten them [the Soviet missiles] out by making a deal on the same missiles in Turkey. If that's part of the record, then I don't see how we'll have a very good war.
>
> **Vice President Johnson:** It doesn't mean just missiles. He takes his missiles out of Cuba, and takes his men out of Cuba, and takes his planes out of Cuba. Why, then your whole foreign policy is gone. You take everything out of Turkey: 20,000 men, all your technicians, and all your planes, and all your missiles. And crumple.
>
> **Unidentified:** Especially if you take the men out.
>
> **Vice President Johnson:** It won't. It won't . . .
>
> **President Kennedy:** How else are we going to get the missiles out of there, then? That's the problem.
>
> **Rusk:** Well, last night, he was prepared to trade them for a promise not to invade. Now he's . . .
>
> **Vice President Johnson:** Somebody told him to try to get a little more. Every time we send him a message . . .
>
> **President Kennedy:** We already sent him one.
>
> **Vice President Johnson:** Well, send him another one, then. . . .
>
> **Rusk:** No, but I mean we—
>
> **President Kennedy:** I don't think we can get it.[19]

As can be seen from the transcript, the advisers don't seem to think JFK's comment is funny, or possibly even relevant. And only one of them, Secretary of State Dean Rusk, knew then what we now know: that Kennedy had already made up his mind not to go to war over missiles in Cuba, even if he had to trade missiles publicly with the Soviet Union to avoid it. In the end, the Soviets settled for a *secret* trade of missiles, in addition to terms of the *public* bargain: the Soviets removed their missiles, and the U.S. pledged not to invade Cuba.[20] This recorded exchange, at the height of tension and danger in the missile crisis, embodies the actual JFK we had come to know before we decided to investigate "virtual JFK." He was not a pacifist, certainly, but he was also very far from a knee-jerk cold warrior, as many formerly believed. Kennedy was instead a skeptical realist whose decisions revealed surprising caution to those of us who initially knew him only via his often stirring but sometimes bellicose Cold War rhetoric.

But what about that "other" crisis, the conflict in Vietnam, the escalation of which JFK's successor, Lyndon Johnson, depending on one's reading of the evidence, was either unable or unwilling to avoid? For a tantalizing clue to this what if puzzle, we urge readers to take another look at the above October 27, 1962, exchange, this time with the coming crisis over Vietnam in mind. It is possible to catch a glimmer, we believe, of one of the key differences between JFK and the adviser who would on November 22, 1963, become his successor, Lyndon Johnson. We are, in effect, "flies on the wall"—witnesses to a rare, recorded exchange between the once and the future presidents that reveals a good deal about how each thought about political risk in a crisis, when a decision must be made that might lead the nation into war.

First, JFK.

President Kennedy: I don't see how we'll have a very good war.

Kennedy has been considering some of the possible, dire consequences of the war that the majority of his advisers are pleading with him to initiate. He doesn't like what he sees when he imagines it. The war could escalate to catastrophic dimensions. Yet he also knows that by deciding not to take the country to war he should anticipate a tremendous amount of political heat: from many of his advisers, from influential members of Congress and journalists, and from certain elements in the American public, especially the rising and increasingly virulent right wings of both major political parties. Of course, if successful, he will be able to say that he avoided a disastrous war, even though many of his advisers are convinced, as he is not, that the Soviets will be too intimidated to go to war with a U.S. whose nuclear forces greatly outnumber their own. But if this is the headline coming out of the crisis, JFK knows his political future may be at risk. He will leave himself open to charges of cowardice, of timidity, of being insufficiently tough in the face of the communist threat, of not having had the guts to have gotten a better deal—charges he has faced almost daily since becoming president. But he is willing to run that risk.

The question is: why? The answer, we believe, is as simple as it is profound: the alternative is too dangerous. He feels viscerally, he knows from personal experience, he has learned from his education and from deep, lifelong immersion in political history, that it is easy to start a war, but often impossible to control it or stop it before it reaches catastrophic proportions. JFK knows that he will eventually have to explain all this convincingly to the American people and to the world if he is to survive the missile crisis politically. He will have to bring them around to his point of view after the fact, just as he is in this very meeting on October 27, 1962, trying to bring his advisers around. Apparently, he is confident, at this critical juncture, in his ability to do just this. And why not? He had, after all, just the previous year explained with considerable success why *not* attacking Cuba when the invasion at the Bay of Pigs was failing was the right thing to do. Now, a year and a half later, he is not going to war when he can avoid it with a trade of missiles, even a public trade that, according to his advisers, will strike a humiliating, and possibly fatal, blow to the NATO alliance.

Now consider LBJ's response to the same situation.

Vice President Johnson: You take everything out of Turkey . . . and crumple.

Johnson is concerned above all, it seems to us, with maintaining the appearance of winning, or at least the appearance of not losing—of not appearing to "crumple," as he puts it in a typically vivid, Johnsonian formulation. The audiotape is even more vivid; were we to transcribe it phonetically, it would sound something like this: "Yuh take ever'thin' aht a TURR-key . . .'n *CRUMP'l!*"—the last word spoken with what seems like disgust. It brings to mind crushing a wad of paper in your hand just before you toss it in the trash. All the top military brass have said there is no need to stoop to "crumpling" in a public missile trade with the Soviets. LBJ seems to see no need to quarrel with their advice. They are, after all, the experts who ought to know about these matters—when to go to war, how to fight a war, how to win a war. We get the impression, therefore, that LBJ, were he sitting in the president's chair at that moment, would have asked a question utterly different from Kennedy's implied query: how are we going to have a good war, if we could have avoided it with a public trade? As president, Johnson would want to know: what do we have to do so people won't say we had to "crumple"—to appease the communists?

This is one of only a small handful of exchanges of which we are aware between JFK and LBJ on the Kennedy tapes. We first became aware of the exchange in the summer of 1987, while working with JFK's and LBJ's national security adviser, McGeorge Bundy, on the declassification and editing of Bundy's path-breaking transcription of the discussions between Kennedy and his advisers on the climactic day of the missile crisis, October 27, 1962.[21] At the time, we read the October 27, 1962, transcripts with tunnel vision, focused almost exclusively on the missile crisis. We scarcely noted LBJ's interventions in the instance just cited, or anywhere else for that matter. The vice president seemed to play only a very minor role in the deliberations of JFK's advisory group during the missile crisis. In many of the meetings at which he appears to have been present, he did not speak at all. He almost never spoke when Kennedy was in the room. His forceful disagreement with the president in this instance is therefore quite remarkable.

After we began to think about the question of Vietnam if Kennedy had lived, we also began, for obvious reasons, to pay much closer attention to Johnson wherever we might find evidence of his tendencies with regard to matters of war and peace, including on the Kennedy tapes. For Vietnam if Kennedy had lived must be seen against the background of what actually happened in Vietnam after Kennedy died. The JFK who emerges from the transcript is familiar to us. But what does this tell us about Vietnam and about LBJ? Were we seeing, in miniature, not only JFK staring down his hawkish advisers in the missile crisis, but also a harbinger of the way he would have resisted pressure to commit U.S. combat troops to Vietnam to prevent the Saigon government's collapse? And in addition, is it possible to derive, again in miniature, a little foretaste of Lyndon Johnson as commander in chief, who would by early 1965 decide, also under considerable pressure from his advisers—almost exactly the same advisers who counseled Kennedy—to Americanize the war in Vietnam?

Of course, one must be careful not to read too much into a single exchange. We can only make an educated guess, at this historical distance, about the sense that JFK and LBJ may have had at the time about what they said to one another in that particular situation, specifically regarding the possibility of publicly trading missiles with the Soviets. And we should have even less confidence in our ability to extrapolate accurately from this "miniature" exchange over missiles in Cuba to each man's approach to whether U.S. combat troops should be sent to South Vietnam. But to us, the exchange is suggestive. Call it a hypothesis. It looks to us as though JFK and LBJ have deeply incompatible bottom lines. We now know that JFK was willing to absorb whatever political consequences might follow from his effort to avoid a war over missiles in Cuba that he was not confident he could control once he initiated it. JFK's bottom line was: it's too dangerous, therefore no war. LBJ, on the other hand, seems unwilling to countenance the appearance of military defeat. His metaphor, "crumple," speaks volumes about his approach to the crisis. LBJ's bottom line was: it's too important, therefore no defeat.

We knew, in initiating this research, that we would have to educate ourselves in the history of what actually happened with regard to the war in Vietnam—a history that is now varied, rich with details derived not only from public pronouncements, but also from declassified documents, audiotapes made by both JFK and LBJ, and oral testimony by former officials. That would establish a factual baseline within which we would hope to pose the question that really interested us: would Kennedy have avoided the escalation to an American war that left much of Southeast Asia in ruins and several million people dead?

While becoming familiar with the vast literature on the war in Vietnam is a formidable task, it can be accomplished, more or less, by hard work and commitment. But the issue of Vietnam if Kennedy had lived goes beyond history. We wondered: Would we be able to investigate the question *empirically*, in a way that would be taken seriously commensurate with its potential historical and political significance, rather than as some kind of parlor game based on fantasy? Might we look into this question in a way that would permit us actually to *learn* something about the real world—a world in which war breaks out when peace fails, in which individuals, groups, nations, and even entire human generations can now be destroyed? If so, what might we learn? With these questions in mind, after more than twenty years of research on the Kennedy administration's foreign policy as our background, we took the plunge to try to determine how JFK would have dealt with the crisis that became America's longest war and its bitterest foreign adventure.[22]

Actual JFK and Actual LBJ: The U.S. in Vietnam Before the Assassination and After

Students of the Kennedy presidency who have focused directly on the conflict in Vietnam have written thousands of pages on what Kennedy *actually* did, or decided, and what Johnson *actually* did, or decided, with regard to Vietnam. It is not our purpose here to review this immense academic literature dealing with Kennedy's and Johnson's decisions regarding Vietnam.[23] Relevant aspects of this literature come up at various points in chapters 3–6 in this book. Here, we want merely to suggest some of the fault lines in the debate about these two presidents and that war, and show how they informed our own approach to the topic.

Scholars have been fascinated by the apparent link between what JFK did regarding Vietnam and what they believe the evidence suggests JFK might or might not have done if he had survived Dallas and been reelected. The link between the two—what JFK did and what he might have done—is fascinating because, to many, it constitutes one of the most unusual and revealing naturally occurring quasi-experiments in the history of U.S. foreign policy. Take November 22, 1963, the day JFK was murdered, as the watershed date when the Kennedy administration *became* the Johnson administration. We believe it is important to remember that, in regard to issues of national security, the Johnson administration did not, in any meaningful sense, *replace* the Kennedy administration. For although of course Johnson replaced Kennedy as president, LBJ retained every significant member of Kennedy's national security team, most of whom had been chosen by Kennedy without so much as consulting, or even informing, his vice president. In other words, the resulting situation, looked at retrospectively, appears to many to closely resemble a natural "experiment." When the transition occurred, everything remained the same, except for one factor, one "variable," to continue the metaphor of a scientific experiment, and that is the identity of the occupant of the White House.

Thus, so goes this line of thought, it ought to be possible, at least in principle, to determine if that factor—the personal transition from Kennedy to Johnson—is what, in effect, caused the American war in Vietnam. It ought to be possible, in principle, to determine whether that ghastly, humiliating, brutal, foreign policy disaster was *Kennedy's* war, which Johnson merely continued, or whether it was Johnson who fundamentally transformed the U.S. commitment in Vietnam into the massive war it ultimately became, thus making it unmistakably *Johnson's* war. This helps to account for the intensity of the debate among historians and journalists over the years as to what both JFK and LBJ did and/or did not actually do or decide with regard to Vietnam. The enormity of the disaster, coupled with the appearance of something that seems close to a surefire means of determining whether Kennedy or Johnson is culpable, has made this topic irresistible to many. It has also caused the debate to be framed in a particular way. To an unusual degree, the debate has re-sembled a courtroom trial, the purpose of which is to determine which president is guilty and which one is innocent in the matter of the war in Vietnam.

In practice, however, the task of assigning historical responsibility for the war in Vietnam has proven to be far more complicated and controver-sial than the above outline might at first suggest. Understanding history, alas, is not much like conducting an experiment in a laboratory, regard-less of whether one uses the lingo of historical causes, effects, and vari-ables. A quick glance at just one of the relevant questions illustrates this. It is an apparently simple question. One might conclude, therefore, that the answer should ultimately be either a plain "yes" or "no," once the relevant facts are known. Here is the question: did JFK significantly *escalate* the war in Vietnam, thereby establishing his "ownership" of the war?

At least the question is simple, right? Wrong. What do we actually *know?* We know that in the approximately three years Kennedy was presi-dent, the number of U.S. advisers in South Vietnam increased dramati-cally, from several hundred to around 16,000. During the same period, the U.S. also substantially increased its commitment in equipment and financial assistance to the struggling Saigon government. That is a fact, and for some, it is the absolutely essential fact to bear in mind about the president we are calling "actual JFK." For some, this counts as a signifi-cant escalation of the war—no ifs, ands, or buts. Many would say that acceptance of this "fact" is the price of admission into the club whose members are permitted to wade into the murky, epistemological swamp of what might have happened in Vietnam if Kennedy had lived. For schol-ars inclined toward this view, the question of what Kennedy would have done is thus a no-brainer: of course he would have *continued* to escalate to war; he would have *continued* to do whatever was necessary to avoid losing to the communists in Vietnam. He would, in other words, have done more or less what his successor, Lyndon Johnson, did after Novem-ber 22, 1963. It is not coincidental, these scholars believe, that Lyndon Johnson declared time and again in his public pronouncements that he was *continuing* Kennedy's Vietnam policy, rather than departing from it. Of course, Johnson *continued* the escalation, according to adherents of this view. But the policy of escalation was due to Kennedy, they say, a policy that he bequeathed to Johnson, who carried it out as best he saw fit. So the Vietnam War, in this view, was Kennedy's war.

Not so fast, say others. Yes, JFK increased the number of advisers the U.S. had in Vietnam, and yes, he approved other sorts of assistance, but it means almost exactly the *opposite* of the conclusion reached by those described in the preceding paragraph. For in fact, it is pointed out, when pressured by most, and sometimes all, of his senior national security aides to send *U.S. combat troops*—not just advisers, equipment, and money—to save the failing government in Saigon, Kennedy said "no" over and over again. So, say these scholars, forget about everything except U.S. combat troops. The absolutely fundamental tasks, they say, are to compare the number of U.S. combat troops in Vietnam when Kennedy assumed office, and the number there when he was assassinated, on the one hand; and, on the other hand, to compare the number of U.S. combat troops in Vietnam when Johnson assumed office with the number there when he left the White House in early 1969. Here are the relevant facts, when the question is posed this particular way: there were *zero* U.S. combat troops in Vietnam when JFK took office, and *zero* when he was killed; there were *zero* U.S. combat troops in Vietnam when Johnson took office and more than *500,000* when he left the White House. To scholars inclined to frame the question in this way, therefore, the answer is equally a no-brainer: of course, Johnson *discontinued* Kennedy's policy of no U.S. combat troops; of course it was Johnson—who replaced Kennedy while retaining all of his senior advisers—who was responsible for the war in Vietnam. With Kennedy, it was, and always would have been, the South Vietnamese government's fight, not America's, whereas Johnson discontinued Kennedy's policy of aid but no combat troops, wrested control of the war from the Saigon government, and made it a U.S. war. The Vietnam War, in this view, is obviously Johnson's war.

Now we come to an odd feature—at least it initially struck us as odd—in this often ferocious debate: as in the example just mentioned, those who believe LBJ continued JFK's policies, and those who believe he reversed them, can often agree on which historical facts are decisive in determining "ownership" of the war. They disagree, obviously, on the meaning they believe should be attached to the facts. Moreover—and even more interesting to us—there also tends to be relatively little disagreement about which historical episodes one must consider when addressing the problem of actual JFK and actual LBJ.[24] Here are the episodes, in condensed form, with detailed analysis to follow in chapters 3–5.

- *November 1961, the internal showdown over Vietnam.* JFK is told by all his foreign policy advisers that the U.S. ally, South Vietnam, is collapsing under pressure from the communist insurgency, and that the U.S.-backed government can only be preserved via the introduction of U.S. combat troops. Kennedy refuses to send any combat troops, but sends more U.S. advisers and equipment instead. All of JFK's military advisers, and most of his civilian advisers, are unhappy with this decision, because they believe South Vietnam's viability is at risk, and that if it fails, the "dominoes will fall" in Southeast Asia, endangering friendly governments from Indonesia to Japan. In fact, however, 1962 becomes a relatively good year for the Saigon government, during which the communist insurgency grows at a slower rate than it did in 1961.

The lessons: At issue is what Kennedy learned from the showdown with his advisers—his refusal to send the combat troops coupled with his authorization of many additional advisers, new equipment, and increased aid. Do his decisions prove he concluded that the war in Vietnam was unavoidably unconventional, an insurgency that cannot be defeated with even a large U.S. Army, which must eventually leave, since the U.S. has no traditional imperial ambitions? Or do his decisions prove that uppermost in Kennedy's mind was avoiding a defeat in Vietnam, and that he must do whatever is necessary to avoid defeat? (See chapter 3 for a more detailed discussion of these issues.)

- *October 1963, the McNamara-Taylor mission and preparations for the coup in South Vietnam.* From May through early autumn, South Vietnam is in turmoil, and the government of South Vietnamese President Ngo Dinh Diem looks doomed. The insurgency has once again made substantial gains, and many Americans in Saigon and Washington fear an imminent communist takeover. The Diem government has repeatedly embarrassed its American sponsors with its brutal treatment of dissidents, rampant corruption, and general incompetence. JFK is bombarded with proposals from many advisers aimed at preventing a complete collapse in Saigon, focused on replacing the Diem government. After months of discussion and some last-minute indecision, in August he authorizes, and his advisers set in motion, a coup by South Vietnamese officers that does in fact remove the elected government. (Diem and his brother, Ngo Dinh Nhu, were murdered on November 1 at the order of the junta that overthrew them, ushering in not stability, as JFK had hoped, but chaos.) JFK begins finalizing a plan to withdraw U.S. forces from Vietnam. Defense Secretary McNamara and Chairman of the Joint Chiefs of Staff General Taylor return from South Vietnam in early October with a report calling for the U.S. to begin withdrawing training units from Vietnam, stating that their training mission has been fulfilled.

The lessons: At issue is what Kennedy learned regarding Vietnam in the final months of his life. Recently declassified and deciphered tapes and transcripts reveal new evidence about Kennedy's approval of the McNamara-Taylor guideline for withdrawing 1,000 Americans by the end of 1963 and most of the rest by the end of 1965. Yet the question remains: was the withdrawal contingent on whether or not the U.S.-backed Saigon government was winning? Would JFK do whatever was necessary—that is, escalate to an American war—to *win*? Or would he do whatever was necessary—that is, order a complete pullout of U.S. personnel—to *avoid* an American war in Vietnam? (See chapter 4 for a more detailed discussion of these issues.)

- *January–July 1965, decisions to begin the air war and ground war in Vietnam.* In the days following JFK's assassination, President Lyndon Johnson tells several of his key aides that he wants to "win the war" in Vietnam, whatever it takes to do so. Key questions are: Is this what LBJ believes JFK's policy really was—to "win" in South Vietnam? Or does LBJ issue this command more or less without reference to whatever he may have thought JFK wanted done, or would have done? Or—yet a third option—does LBJ feel trapped, as president, by pressure from various advisers who tell him that the situation is desperate in South Vietnam, and of course President Kennedy would never have allowed the communists to take over? Or is some combination of these three alternatives decisive in LBJ's decisions during the first half of 1965? These decisions include the February decision, following insurgent attacks killing several dozen Americans at two bases in the Central Highlands of South Vietnam, to authorize initiation of the air war against North Vietnam, the principal supplier of the communist insurgents in South Vietnam, and his decisions in June and July to grant the request of the U.S. field commander in South Vietnam, General William Westmoreland, for more than 175,000 U.S. ground combat troops by the end of the year.

  The lessons: At issue is what Johnson learned from his advisers—what did they tell him about JFK's intentions with regard to Vietnam? Did they provide him with realistic options for countering the rapid deterioration of the situation in South Vietnam following the November 1963 coup, *other than* the way Johnson ultimately chose to deal with it, by Americanizing the war? What did LBJ's inherited foreign policy advisers think about their new boss—regarding, for example, his inexperience in foreign affairs and his insecurity when dealing with military men, his unwillingness to jeopardize his domestic agenda by appearing to "lose" Vietnam, and his tendency to personalize the war in Vietnam? And did their perceptions of the differences between JFK and LBJ affect the advice they provided to Johnson? (See chapter 5 for a more detailed discussion of these issues.)

Scholars agree that these are the three critical episodes. This gave a clue as to how to proceed. Might it be possible, we wondered, to convene some of the leading advocates of both positions—the *continuity* view and the *discontinuity* view—to jointly discuss the evidence for and against each view, and to get them to agree to a no-holds-barred cross-questioning of one another? We realized that the outcome of such a discussion could be quite predictable, in one sense: former officials and scholars who have lived with these issues much of their lives are unlikely to change their minds at this or any single meeting just because others present take views contrary to their own. But we also thought the conversation might be quite unpredictable in another sense: we wondered what would happen, how might the specialists respond when pressed to really engage with—to *empathize* with, though not necessarily to agree with—the views of others? What might that encounter be like, between those believing the war in Vietnam was, in the end, John F. Kennedy's war, and those believing it was Lyndon Johnson's war? Would they find it possible to put themselves vicariously in one another's shoes? And if they did, how would they individually and jointly resolve the issue on the table: Vietnam if Kennedy had lived.

We began sorting through and collecting what seemed to be some of the most important declassified evidence bearing on the issues. We got in touch with leading figures in the field and shared impressions with them of JFK and LBJ as decisionmakers. In the end, keeping an open mind about whether LBJ continued or reversed JFK's policies regarding Vietnam was easier than might be imagined. This was because proponents of both sides of the argument happily argued their often mutually incompatible positions to us with cogency and voluminous supporting evidence, and they were not shy about explaining what it all meant. They knew we had a certain view of Kennedy. We soon learned that each of them did, too. Together with this dedicated and highly competent band of expert collaborators, each profiled in chapter 2, we decided to try to assemble the pieces of the puzzle—the former officials, declassified documents, and top scholars—in a common space and time and to see what would happen.

The Method: Critical Oral History

Declassified documents and transcripts on these three clusters of events—presidential decision making on Vietnam in November 1961,

October 1963, and January–July 1965—would provide the roughly 1,000-page empirical core of a briefing notebook that all participants in our discussion would, as the price of admission, be required to digest prior to the meeting. Then, according to a plan we worked out over the course of approximately a year, the former officials from the Kennedy and Johnson administrations and top scholars of the war in Vietnam would bring their briefing notebooks to the table and the face-to-face discussion would begin. This method of attempting to resolve historical issues is called *critical oral history*. This book is based on that discussion.

Critical oral history is a method we pioneered in our research on the Cuban missile crisis. Critical oral history requires the simultaneous interaction, in a conference setting, of three elements: former officials, declassified documents, and top scholars of the events and issues under scrutiny.[25] The philosophical core of critical oral history is captured succinctly in an 1843 journal entry by the Danish philosopher and theologian Søren Kierkegaard: "It is perfectly true, as philosophers say, that life must be understood backwards. But they forget the other proposition, that it must be lived forwards."[26] We scholars study a historical event already knowing the outcome. That is usually why we study it in the first place: the outcome is important, or at least seems important to us, and we want to explain why it happened. We work backwards from effects to causes in search of understanding. But the decisionmakers who helped produce the outcome of interest worked forward, in a fog of highly imperfect understanding, burdened with many misperceptions, hoping for the best, and bracing themselves for the worst. The reliance on declassified documents provides something of a level playing field on which the scholars and decisionmakers can have a useful discussion, a place to begin to develop a more comprehensive point of view that incorporates the chronological precision and analytical acuity that is possible when looking backward, yet also includes the dynamism, creativity, uncertainty, and tension that emerge in the memories of former officials of moving forward into the unknown, of endeavoring to make history, without the benefit of knowing the outcome.

Critical oral history provides a "free market" for historical propositions. Advocates of deeply irreconcilable points of view—including both the former officials and the scholars—present evidence for their interpretations from documents and/or experience, and then cross-question each other with reference to whatever evidence they believe bears on the issues under investigation. Each participant typically moves into, and withdraws from, a figurative "time machine" many times during the exchanges as the discussion moves back and forth from retrospective immersion *in* the forward movement of the historical events (this *happened*), to the retrospective analytical interpretation *of* those events (this is the *meaning* of what happened). For readers, the transcript in chapters 3–6 provides a second-order time-machine experience. Chapters 3–5 are focused on what happened from 1961–1965, as JFK and LBJ made decisions regarding the U.S. role and commitment in Vietnam. Chapter 6, on the other hand, is focused mainly on the meaning of the evidence discussed in the first three chapters—what would have happened in Vietnam if Kennedy had lived. As the participants in the critical oral history process periodically relive some of the events of the Kennedy and Johnson administrations, framed by their personal experiences and/ or reference to key documents or tape recordings, readers are offered a figurative seat at the table as data and interpretations are put forward, criticized, and defended.

This is what happened in April 2005 when former officials and scholars from all across the spectrum met to discuss Vietnam if Kennedy had lived. We issued invitations to Musgrove with an eye toward balance—some from each extreme and some from the middle of the continuum. The participants, profiled in chapter 2, are grouped in part according to their own well-known predilections regarding Vietnam if Kennedy had lived. We also invited people who varied widely regarding the *strength* of their convictions—on how sure they were that they were right about Vietnam if Kennedy had lived. As we believe chapters 3–6 attest, we succeeded in assembling a group of participants whose deep and varied knowledge of John F. Kennedy, Lyndon B. Johnson, and Vietnam was matched by the profundity of their disagreements.

We had no interest in the question "Who won?" We tried to play it straight, as honest brokers between factions. This is represented in our choice of participants, but also in the choice of documents, the organization and agenda of the conference, and the selection of which participants would lead off particular discussions. In each case, we consulted with the participants about every inclusion or exclusion, with the single exception of who finally was invited to the conference. (With the exception of two elderly prospects who were forced to decline owing to reasons of health, everyone we invited accepted the invitation.) The "honest broker" role is one we have endeavored to play many times before in critical oral history exercises involving groups who strenuously disagreed with one another: for example, Americans, Soviets, and Cubans regarding the missile crisis. Confidence in our honest brokerage, built up over our past research and in the run-up to the Musgrove conference, is an important reason why people with apparently irreconcilable views on issues of great mutual interest agreed to come to the table in the first place.

This is also why, in a critical oral history exercise, this question "Who won?" is irrelevant. The study of history is not like soccer or baseball or a TV reality show. History is above all a collision of arguments, passages in a conversation that continues as long as the issues under scrutiny are of interest. "History," as Dutch historian Pieter Geyl famously wrote, "is an argument without end."[27] We wanted to know which arguments could best withstand empirical scrutiny and which could not. We were especially interested in the dynamic of the conversation between advocates of opposing views. What happens when, instead of "preaching to the choir" in the usual fashion of people with strong views on polarizing issues, the participants' feet are held to the fire by people across the table whose views are incompatible with their own? How do they defend themselves and their positions? Viewed from our standpoint as the organizers, we wanted to know: how has our understanding been enriched? We are greatly indebted to this dynamic mix of documents and former officials and scholars, who all had an intense and long-standing interest in Vietnam if Kennedy had lived, for agreeing to journey with us into history and beyond.

What might have happened with a different cast of participants? Certainly, many things would have been different, depending on their personalities, specific interests, and experiences. But, assuming roughly the same spectrum of views would have been covered by an alternative group, would the overall outcome have been fundamentally different? Possibly. But as we believe chapters 3–6 reveal, advocates of each of the positions put forth forceful, cogent, well-documented arguments. The former officials spoke confidently about their experience with both Kennedy and Johnson and their inner circle of senior advisers. Within the bounds of civility, each discussion was a no-holds-barred exchange. "How do we know," asked a colleague who was not involved in the project, "that this *actual* virtual JFK group is better than any *virtual* virtual JFK group that we might have assembled?" The correct answer is, "We don't know." But we believe the group we did assemble acquitted itself brilliantly.

See for yourself. We encourage readers to look closely at our data—the document-rich and experience-rich discussion and cross-questioning at the Musgrove conference. Familiarize yourself with the documents and with chapter 2, "Who's Who at the Musgrove Conference." Pull your figurative chair up to the imaginary conference table, take your notes (virtual or actual), and decide for yourself whether you believe there would have been, or would not have been, an American war in Vietnam if Kennedy had lived. And decide for yourself whether your own conclusions usefully inform your understanding of U.S. foreign policy, especially our choice of president, at this tumultuous, dangerous moment in our history.

The Approach: Virtual History, Not Counterfactual History

The method of critical oral history provided us with a necessary but insufficient condition for tackling the problem of Vietnam if Kennedy had lived. We needed, in addition, an approach to what if history that is not counterfactual—does not involve us in elaborate accounts of hypothetical causes and effects that are contrary to historical fact. We needed a way to defictionalize the analysis of the what if.

For nearly a half-century, the debate between those who believe JFK would or would not have Americanized the war in Vietnam has been no debate at all, in the proper sense of the term. Instead of debating one another's arguments and the facts used to buttress them, the structure of the exchanges over the years has more closely resembled a cafeteria food fight. Take a Kennedy partisan, typically wistful and wishful, and let the individual describe in loving detail how much different, how much better, the world would have been if Kennedy had lived to avoid the American war in Vietnam. Let this individual revel unashamedly in *counterfactual* history—in the narration of events, strung together in elaborate causal chains, all deriving ultimately from Kennedy's safe return from Dallas in November 1963. If they gravitate toward details, the partisan may say, "Lyndon B. Johnson did this, but John F. Kennedy would surely have done that," and so on ad infinitum. This is a narration of events that are contrary to fact, stories of events that never happened. This is fiction.

To many historians, these stories of what we might call "counterfactual JFK" are rubbish, maybe even worse than rubbish, because collectively they are what might be called *motivated* rubbish. Their purpose seems to skeptics to be transparent: to preserve an idealized picture of a president who never existed, except as a product of the vaunted Kennedy spin machine. This sort of counterfactual exercise is regarded by the skeptics as proof of nothing more than a pathetic, childish need to preserve an image of JFK as a hero, cut down by an assassin just as he was allegedly preparing to prevent America from making its fateful mistake in Vietnam. This counterfactual JFK is often regarded as not just fictional; he is a fabrication of a vast, quasi-conspiratorial effort to obscure the real JFK and what these critics take as the self-evident conclusion that Vietnam if Kennedy had lived would have differed little if any from what actually happened.

In response to the JFK partisans, the canonical response of the critics is some variant of, "Johnson did this, and Kennedy would have done more or less the same thing." These scholars tend to see themselves as anti-counterfactual vigilantes—as proponents of the avowedly *factual* and enemies of the counterfactual.

Readers of chapters 3–6 will vicariously see (and we hope even feel) some of this tension between the participants in the Musgrove conference. Yet here, at the beginning of the book, we feel a little like the *Miami Herald* humorist Dave Barry who, whenever he feels his "reporting" is about to strain his readers' credulity, writes, "I am not making this up." So we feel obliged, in laying out the origin and development of the book in this first chapter, to provide at least one example of the terms of the debate—evidence that we too are "not making this up." Can a controversy between scholars over Vietnam if Kennedy had lived really have been this acrimonious? Yes, it can, and it still often is. In what follows, we provide one example of each pole of the controversy.

In a 1987 article, "JFK and the Might-Have-Beens," Boston journalist Jack Beatty provides an account of the very different (and, in his view, obviously *better*) America, from 1963–1987, if Kennedy had lived.

> Nearly a quarter of a century after his death, John F. Kennedy remains our unfinished president, still presiding over an America that might have been. The Vietnam war never happened in Kennedy's America. . . . If the Saigon regime could not stand on its own, he would cut our losses in Vietnam once the 1964 election was behind him. . . . Inflation never got started in that America, because there never was a massive unfunded military buildup in Vietnam. Richard Nixon never captured the White House; and Ronald Reagan, with no Berkeley student rebellion to run against, never became governor of California.
>
> Kennedy might have redeemed his promise . . . and kept the country out of the Vietnam war. If he had, then tens of thousands of our bravest young men might have lived to grow old in Kennedy's America.[28]

You may ask: what is wrong with engaging in this kind of alternative history of "Kennedy's America," a history without a war in Vietnam, a history in which two controversial Republican presidents, Nixon and Reagan, evaporate into thin air? Sure, it is speculative. But what is the harm, after all, in imagining a "Kennedy's America" of the past (nearly) half-century, in which not only JFK but many others lived longer, fuller lives than was possible in the circumstances that actually transpired? Historian Diane Kunz, writing on behalf of the vast majority of her fellow historians, has the answer. Pay attention, especially if you found "Kennedy's America" inspiring, because you are about to be scolded. According to Kunz:

The Cold War is over, and the statues of Marx and Lenin have fallen to the ground—but John F. Kennedy's image, though tarnished, remains fundamentally intact. In the years after his death, a legend of Camelot on the Potomac took root. According to this myth, propagated in large part by the Kennedy family and court, John F. Kennedy was a kind of King Arthur in modern dress. His advisers were modern Knights of the Round Table and Jacqueline Kennedy his noble Guinevere.

Not surprisingly, no aspect of the Kennedy legend has proved more durable than the notion that, had he lived, the United States would never have become mired in the Vietnam conflict. . . . How nice it would be to believe that the Vietnam debacle was not the result of ill-timed and ill-conceived American ideas but rather the fault of one man: Lee Harvey Oswald.

Fairy stories are necessary for children. Historians ought to know better. In fact, John F. Kennedy was a mediocre president. Had he obtained a second term, U.S. actions in Vietnam [would have been] no different from what actually occurred. His tragic assassination was not a tragedy for the course of American history.[29]

We asked ourselves: How do we get beyond the food-fight atmosphere, which pits advocates of the counterfactual against defenders of the factual? Is there an alternative approach that permits us to address Vietnam if Kennedy had lived in a way that permits open-minded people to come together and discuss it, according to the empirical requirements of critical oral history?

There is. It is called *virtual history*. The term and its theoretical development are due to Harvard historian Niall Ferguson, in a 1997 book of that title.[30] Virtual history is discussed at some length in the introduction to chapter 6. But here in brief is a set of principles we found helpful in applying virtual history to Vietnam if Kennedy had lived.

- First, begin with Kennedy, not with Johnson. Do not begin with a survey of all or some of Johnson's individual decisions on Vietnam, with the objective of comparing what Johnson did with what you think Kennedy would have done in each case. Johnson's decisions created his own realities. No one knows the details of the successive realities JFK's decisions would have created if he had not been assassinated on November 22, 1963. (This is absolutely critical, but may at first seem counterintuitive. But stick with it.)
- Second, build a figurative "model" of JFK as president on matters of war and peace. When Kennedy is pressured to commit U.S. military forces to escalate a crisis or conflict, what does he do? Call this composite decisionmaker *virtual JFK*. (This is not as difficult as you might imagine.)

- Third, consider in as much detail as the evidence will allow what the *actual* JFK decided with regard to Vietnam. Focus on what he did, not on what his supporters and detractors report JFK told them he was going to do. (This is not as easy as you might imagine.)
- Fourth, "simulate" what virtual JFK would have done regarding Vietnam, had he lived and been reelected. Would JFK have gotten in, gotten out, or something in between? (This is not as difficult as it may appear, though achieving unanimity of opinion on this emotional issue may be challenging.)
- Fifth, *stop right there*! Read the first point again. Make your retrospective "prediction" about Vietnam if Kennedy had lived. Do not yield to the temptation to fill in the unknowable, counterfactual details that might follow from your prediction, such as, "JFK did this, and then he did that, and then he did the other thing. . . ." (The temptation to create a counterfactual JFK may be great. But if you yield to it, you will have entered the realm of historical fiction.)
- Sixth, draw whatever lessons seem appropriate from your analysis of the difference, whatever it may be, between the decisions made by JFK and his successor, Lyndon Johnson. (This is tricky, but we believe necessary, in light of the remarkable similarities between Vietnam and Iraq.)

In other words, counterfactual history and virtual history differ in the following respects. In counterfactual history, a good deal of creativity is invested in creating fiction. The prevailing ethos of counterfactual history seems to be that of a game: have fun, go wild, try to top *this* one! The ratio of known or accepted fact to invented fiction is low. Virtual history, on the other hand, begins with a targeted question, is severely constrained by data, and is no more speculative than any other kind of historical inquiry. In virtual history, the ratio of fact to fiction is roughly the reverse of counterfactual history. If done rigorously, we believe, there need be no fiction in virtual history at all, in the sense of something "made up" that never happened.

This may seem a little abstract at this point, prior to your entry into the argument that takes up the bulk of this book. For now, we suggest you think of the alternatives this way.

The counterfactual history assignment:
What happened with regard to Vietnam, if Kennedy had lived? It's an essay exam. Be as creative as you like. Tell a good story, or at least a strange or arresting story, and don't neglect to include a few facts with

the fiction, to appear historically "credible." Don't worry whether people actually believe you or not, because no one can prove you're wrong. Don't take it seriously. After all, it's only a game.

The virtual history assignment:
Would there have been an American war in Vietnam if Kennedy had lived? True or false? Why or why not? Argue your case only with reference to the evidence. Be prepared to defend and/or amend your argument, with reference to what is known or believed that bears on the issue, and in response to cross-examination from your peers. The exercise is serious and possibly important, so be careful.

A good deal turns on this distinction in chapter 6. Here is a brief synopsis of one aspect of that chapter. The participants in the argument have now done their "homework," having for the better part of two long days dug into some deep pockets of the relevant history of actual JFK and LBJ. At last they are urged by us, the organizers, to tackle the subject of Vietnam if Kennedy had lived. We have a good deal to say in chapter 6 about what happens next, when the discussion, according to the agenda and by previous agreement, moves to a consideration of the what if. Some appear to believe that what they have been asked to do is play a counterfactual game, and they are not happy about it. Their interventions suggest rather strongly that they believe they have been given what we just called "the counterfactual assignment." Their probable reasons are interesting and understandable, given this understanding of the assignment: the subject matter is tragic, absolutely serious, concerned with the responsibility for a horrible disaster, and should therefore not be trivialized by giving it a game format. So they resist. They think it inappropriate to speculate about what JFK would have done if he had been forced to face the crises over Vietnam that plagued LBJ between the assassination and the Americanization of the war.

But some of the other participants clearly, so it seems to us, are operating in a different paradigm. They make an effort to respond to what we are calling the "virtual history assignment." They seem not to feel the need, for the most part, to discuss LBJ at all. They are focused on JFK as they understand him. For these participants, the discussion of Vietnam if Kennedy had lived seems to follow almost seamlessly from the previous two days of historical sleuthing of the documents, transcripts, testimony, and analyses of Vietnam while Kennedy was, indeed, alive and in the White House.

"Former officials and scholars are not playing a game. They are engaging in an argument about a subject that is supremely serious: war, humiliation, arrogance, ignorance, regret, and responsibility."
Top: Chester Cooper. Bottom: Bill Moyers.

CHAPTER 2

Who's Who at the Musgrove Conference

The Musgrove Conference Center: "Camp David South"

The face-to-face argument over Vietnam if Kennedy had lived presented in this book occurred from April 8–10, 2005. Nineteen people gathered around a long, narrow, makeshift conference table. The room in which the conference occurred is the main living room of Musgrove Plantation, the vacation compound of the Bagley family, who founded and still run the Arca Foundation, located in Washington, D.C. When not in use by the Bagley family, the living room and the other buildings in the compound become the Musgrove Conference Center. It is rustic, but not *too* rustic for people used to modern amenities. The view of the wetlands off St. Simons Island, Georgia, where Musgrove is located, is serene. It is so isolated and off the beaten path that it can be difficult to find, especially at night. The "driveway" is well over a mile long, and it winds through dense semitropical vegetation.

On two previous occasions, we have found this peaceful atmosphere a useful antidote to the sometimes heated discussions that occur when former adversaries discuss events in which they were involved. When the heat from a conversation begins to overwhelm the light shed on the issues, it has been a relief to take a break among the fragrant gardens and the ubiquitous Spanish moss outside. We have done this at critical oral history conferences at Musgrove on nuclear arms control (Soviets and Americans) and on the Bay of Pigs invasion (Cubans, Cuban exiles, and Americans). The occasional alligator has been known to appear in the channel that borders the property, momentarily disrupting the serenity of strolling conference-goers unused to them. But conference participants are told by the staff upon arrival, with a wink and a grin, that the alligators are "hardly ever" successful in actually getting past the sea wall and onto the estate itself. The staff prepares and serves food that is robustly southern. For all these reasons, Musgrove seems to exist in a space and time utterly different from what most of us are used to, or have ever experienced. This is why it is a marvelous venue for the discussion of controversial subjects, such as the issue we were concerned with in April 2005: Vietnam if Kennedy had lived.

Musgrove is said by others with the appropriate experience to bear some resemblance to the compound of "cottages" at the presidential retreat in Camp David, Maryland. In fact, Musgrove, too, has a presidential connection. It has strong ties to former President Jimmy Carter and many members of his inner circle. The first meeting of Carter's incoming cabinet occurred at Musgrove in December 1976. You are reminded of this as you enter the living room and look sharply right. There on the wall hang two Andy Warhol originals—portraits of Jimmy Carter. In one of the portraits, Carter seems to be out of focus. Either that, or there are several concentric Carters in the portrait, each a caricature of Carter's famously oversized grin. On the long weekend of our conference, one other feature of Musgrove was Camp David–like. Each participant arrived bearing a huge briefing notebook, containing roughly a thousand pages of declassified documents, which they had received a month beforehand. As one of our senior people stepped off the shuttle bus that had brought him from the Jacksonville, Florida, airport to Musgrove, he quipped, "The airline let me carry my luggage onto the plane, but they made me check the notebook because of its weight!"

Collectively, the participants represent a "Who's Who?" of the subject we had gathered to argue about. Obviously, a different, equally distinguished group of former officials and scholars might have been convened. But our group was high-powered. They were also a management challenge, but in the best sense: they all had important things to say on nearly every topic that came up but, with only a little encouragement from the chair, they also proved to be patient listeners. We and they were looking for an argument that made sense of the evidence, especially the recently declassified evidence—an argument that stretched our minds in productive directions. We believe that is exactly what we got. We are greatly indebted to all the participants, who are listed and described in this chapter.

Vietnam: A Liberals' War

One way the war in Iraq differs from the war in Vietnam is this: the war in Iraq was conceived, supported, and implemented mainly by neoconservatives on the right wing of the Republican Party establishment, while the war in Vietnam was a liberals' war, a war directed, protested, regretted, and later explained chiefly by liberals with formal or informal ties to the left wing of the Democratic Party. The deeply conservative elements within the Republican Party were decimated in the 1964 election. The Democrats increased their majority in both houses of Congress. Lyndon Johnson, a southern liberal committed to social justice and racial equality, had roared into the White House with one of the biggest electoral victories in the history of the country. The 1964 election was not about Vietnam, which to the American public was still just one of many Third World hot spots in the global Cold War. The election was about hard-core liberalism versus hard-core conservatism, focused on the Democratic side mostly on domestic issues such as education, civil rights, and government programs for the poor and the elderly. The Democratic landslide provided a mandate for the ambitious federal social programs that lay at the heart of the liberal agenda Lyndon Johnson had fervently embraced throughout his career as a congressman and senator.

Yet seemingly without warning, only weeks after Johnson's inauguration on January 20, 1965, Vietnam became the central and divisive issue it would remain for the next decade. In February, the U.S. began bombing North Vietnam. In March, the first U.S. Marines landed. The U.S. war in Vietnam was on. Thus, to a degree that, in retrospect, seems almost schizophrenic, the Johnson administration became utterly devoted to two causes simultaneously: the "Great Society" program designed to help Americans who most needed assistance—those who were denied the opportunity to vote, or denied a decent education, or denied equal pay—on the one hand, and, on the other, blasting the Vietnamese communists half a world away to smithereens until they surrendered.

This dissonance between the liberal domestic agenda and the liberals' war in Vietnam helps to account for the frequent expressions of incomprehension and regret from the former officials at the Musgrove conference. The subtexts of many of their interventions might be summarized this way: how did we go astray in Vietnam? Or where did we go wrong, and why did we not act in our foreign policy according to the liberal values we held, and which were the heart and soul of LBJ's domestic programs? Note throughout this book the way these comments are usually formulated: where did *we* go wrong, not where did *they* go wrong. These are liberals reexamining a liberals' war. In her diaries of her White House years, Johnson's wife, Lady Bird, captured this irreconcilable conflict for liberals, and the anguish it produced in her husband. On February 7, 1965, the day LBJ had authorized the sustained bombing of North

Vietnam, she wrote: "In the night, we were waiting to hear how the attack had gone. It came at one o'clock [a.m.], and two o'clock, and three, and again at five—the ring of the phone, the quick reach for it, and tense, quiet talk. . . . It was a tense and shadowed day, but we'll probably have to learn to live in the middle of it—not for hours or days, but years."[1]

Four days later, on February 11, she confided to her diary: "While Lyndon and Hubert [Humphrey] were talking, I was rather startled to hear [Lyndon] say something I had heard so often, but did not really expect to come out of his mouth in front of anyone else: 'I'm not temperamentally equipped to be Commander-in-Chief. I'm too sentimental to give the orders.'" Lady Bird then added, "Somehow, I could not wish him *not* to hurt when he gives the orders."[2]

*   *   *

Here is the line-up from this "Who's Who?" of Vietnam if Kennedy had lived, beginning with the former officials, each of whom served in various capacities in *both* the Kennedy and Johnson administrations. For each former official and scholar, we lead off with a brief summary comment describing roughly where we believe they stood on the issue of Vietnam if Kennedy had lived *before* their participation in the Musgrove conference. We leave it to you to decide for yourself whether you think they evolved in their thinking during the conference. Participants in all three groups—former officials, scholarly skeptics, and scholarly radicals—are listed in alphabetical order within each of the categories.

The Former Officials

For the three former officials, there was far more at stake at the Musgrove conference than, as one of them put it during one of the coffee breaks, "playing Trivial Pursuit with a bunch of Vietnam War geeks." The discussion was foremost about responsibility: their own and that of the people for whom they worked. It was about coming to grips with the ghosts of the disastrous debacle known in shorthand in the U.S. simply as "Vietnam." It was about three men in their seventies and eighties staring into the historical abyss in an effort to understand the catastrophe that had consumed so much blood and treasure, so much liberal optimism, and so much of their own personal lives.

CHESTER L. COOPER

He came to the Musgrove conference agnostic on Vietnam if Kennedy had lived. He distrusts people who are convinced that Kennedy would have, or would not have, Americanized the war in Vietnam. He doubts Kennedy knew what he was going to do.

Chet Cooper was a representative of the Office of Strategic Services in China during World War II. He became a Central Intelligence Agency analyst for Southeast Asia, 1953–1963. During that period, he was a participant in the Geneva conferences on Vietnam in 1954 and on Laos in 1961. After his return from Geneva, Cooper joined the staff of the National Security Council, where he was special assistant for Vietnam affairs to McGeorge Bundy, the national security adviser. Cooper admitted to having been awestruck by his boss's intelligence, his remarkable ability to synthesize vast quantities of information and to formulate concise options for both Kennedy and Johnson. Yet Chet Cooper also assisted Bundy, as they flew back to Washington from Vietnam in early February 1965, in the drafting of the memorandum that recommended to LBJ that he begin intensive bombing of North Vietnam—a relentless, destructive bombing campaign called ROLLING THUNDER that would go on for years and kill countless people to no good end [**Document 5-5**]. Later, after Bundy left the government, Cooper worked as a deputy to Assistant Secretary of State Averell Harriman. His job was to find a way to terminate the U.S. bombing campaign he had been instrumental in initiating. But he never found a way. The bombing went on year after year. When Chet Cooper spoke at Musgrove, he spoke as one who deeply regretted his own role in creating the Frankenstein's monster that the war became. This is a lot for a liberal's conscience to bear. The written transcript alone does not convey the anguish in his voice during some of his interventions.

Chet Cooper had previously been a key participant in our earlier critical oral history project on the war in Vietnam, a joint U.S.-Vietnamese investigation of the escalation of the war in the 1960s. He brought to the earlier project, as to this one, deep and broad firsthand knowledge from, as he often said, "deep in the belly of the beast" of policy making. He had a detailed knowledge of the way policy was made and implemented, insights into the major personalities involved with Vietnam over the nearly half-century during which he was involved in Southeast Asian affairs, and a very dry wit, which frequently is in evidence. To an unusual degree, Chet Cooper remembered not only decisions that actually were made, but also was often able vividly to recall decisions that were considered but not made, or which were made, but not implemented. While involved in the project on the escalation of the war in Vietnam, Chet Cooper became a proponent of the idea that numerous opportunities were missed in the 1960s to avoid or cut short the war in Vietnam.

You will find Chet repeatedly questioning other participants at the Musgrove conference who seemed to him just a little too sure of themselves. He was especially fond of needling academics who, fresh from reading a document or listening to an audiotape, might breathlessly proclaim that they had at last found *the* document, *the* paper trail, maybe even *the* truth, about a given historical episode. At such moments, Chet Cooper typically put up his hand to get in line to speak, indicating that he had a very relevant, very short comment on exactly what was being said at that moment. When his turn came, he would say, in the thick accent of Roxbury, Massachusetts, where he was born and raised, something like, "Gee, Professah, that's a very clevah, very fascinating theory. Really, I never thought of it that way. Alas, nobody else did eitha, as fah as I know. Nice theory, but wrong. Bettah luck next time." All this was done with a twinkle in his eye that made the medicine from Chet's corner of the real world go down a little easier with the "professah" to whom the comment was directed.

Chet Cooper was also a kind and gentle soul who helped we three "professahs" over the years in countless ways. We are grateful for his participation at Musgrove. He is the author of *The Lost Crusade: America in Vietnam* (1970), a scholarly memoir of the war, and an autobiography, *In the Shadows of History: 50 Years Behind the Scenes of Cold War Diplomacy* (2005). Chester Cooper died in October 2005 at age eighty-seven. We miss him.

THOMAS L. HUGHES

He believes JFK did not want to get involved in a war in Vietnam, but he came to the Musgrove conference believing that Kennedy was not sufficiently in charge of his hawkish advisers to rein them in, and also that Kennedy's authorization of the November 1963 coup in Saigon led to sufficient chaos that even Kennedy probably would have sent in the U.S. Army in 1964 or 1965, rather than "lose" South Vietnam.

Tom Hughes is a graduate of Carleton College in Minnesota, a Rhodes Scholar at Oxford University, and a graduate of Yale Law School. He became involved as an adviser during the 1950s to several senior Democratic Party politicians. These included Chester Bowles of Connecticut and Hubert Humphrey from his home state of Minnesota. When Bowles became chief foreign policy adviser to presidential candidate John F. Kennedy during the campaign of 1960, Hughes became Bowles' principal assistant. He followed Bowles into the Kennedy State Department when Bowles was named undersecretary of state for political affairs. Following

Bowles's departure in November 1961, Hughes succeeded Roger Hilsman as director of Intelligence and Research (INR) at the State Department, where he remained until 1969. He later became president of the Carnegie Endowment for International Peace in Washington, D.C.

As director of INR, Tom Hughes and his small coterie of analysts remained fiercely independent of the much larger group of specialists involved in the CIA's intelligence gathering on Vietnam. Under Hughes's leadership, INR produced credible estimates on Vietnam that were relentlessly pessimistic from 1963 onward and which often contradicted other intelligence estimates from within the U.S. government. In retrospect, INR seems to have gotten things right most of the time. Interest in INR was high at the Musgrove conference due to the occurrence of a major milestone the previous year for scholars of U.S. decision making on the war. Released under the Freedom of Information Act on May 6, 2004 was a top-secret, 596-page retrospective study of INR's intelligence assessments on Vietnam covering the years 1961–1968. The study was commissioned by Tom Hughes toward the end of his tenure at INR. He also worked with scholars to obtain the release of the report. In news accounts of the release, the INR study was often referred to as "the State Department's Pentagon Papers." Portions of this study were included in the briefing book for the Musgrove conference.

After becoming director of INR, Hughes maintained frequent contact with his fellow Minnesotan, Hubert Humphrey, while Humphrey was in the Senate and after Humphrey accepted Lyndon Johnson's invitation to become his vice president in the summer of 1964. It was in connection with his close personal relationship with Humphrey that Tom Hughes made an unexpected and significant contribution to the Musgrove conference. He brought with him copies of a memorandum from Humphrey to LBJ dated February 15, 1965, that represented Humphrey's last valiant effort to explain to LBJ why he should not, as planned, transform the conflict in Vietnam into an American war. Hughes was a full partner with Humphrey in the drafting of the document, one of the most extraordinary memoranda of the entire war. In it, Humphrey explained "the politics of Vietnam" to Johnson with a mixture of shrewd political analysis and Jeremiah-like warnings of the total disaster an American war in Vietnam might become [**Document 5-6**]. The memorandum was prophetic. When one changes the tense from future to past, it reads like a summary of what actually came to pass. For his efforts, Humphrey was spurned by Johnson—more than spurned, he was humiliated and ostracized by LBJ for what he took to be his vice president's disloyalty. Instead of heeding the warnings in the Humphrey-Hughes memorandum, LBJ made the decisions in the spring and summer of 1965 that began America's downward spiral into the tragic quagmire the war eventually became.

Tom Hughes is also a world-class raconteur. His account in chapter 5 of a meeting with LBJ during the Tonkin Gulf affair of August 1964 led to a brief unscheduled but absolutely necessary coffee break, because in listening to Hughes tell the story, the participants had become almost incoherent with laughter. We don't want to spoil the surprise, but we think you will enjoy his vivid account of LBJ turning the screw and exerting a perverse kind of control over his new chairman of the Joint Chiefs of Staff, General Earle Wheeler. The general, a large and forceful man, was nicknamed "Bus"—as in "I almost got run over by a bus." But Bus was no match for LBJ. For this anecdote, for the INR study, for the Humphrey memo, and for his knowledgeable and thoughtful contributions at Musgrove, we are very grateful to Tom Hughes.

BILL MOYERS

He said at the Musgrove conference that he is "not a very speculative person" himself, but that he is also fascinated by the educated guesses of people who are speculative. Yet at Musgrove he did speculate aloud, along with the others, siding most of the time with those who doubted JFK could have found a way to avoid the war that consumed his boss, LBJ.

Bill Moyers was born in Hugo, Oklahoma, and raised in the east Texas town of Marshall. His education proceeded on a dual track: he became an ordained Baptist minister, but he also pursued studies in journalism and, as a teenager in Marshall, he was already working as a reporter for the local newspaper. A distinguished television journalist with CBS and later with PBS, winner of more than thirty Emmys for series on a vast array of topics (ranging from poetry to religion to history to politics), he was the absolutely indispensable man for President Lyndon Johnson from LBJ's very first day in office. Moyers stood beside the new president as he took the oath of office on November 22, 1963, aboard Air Force One on its return from Dallas, Texas, to Washington. In 1963 at age twenty-nine, he had already been working for Johnson off and on for nearly a decade. He had first gone to work in LBJ's Washington office as a college intern in the summer of 1954 as a mail sorter. During the 1950s he rose to become LBJ's unofficial chief of staff, despite his youth. He served President Johnson in several capacities until, irreconcilably at odds with Johnson over the war in Vietnam, he resigned as presidential press secretary in December 1966. He is also the author of more than a dozen books on a diverse set of topics, including several best sellers. He remains one of America's best-known journalists and a champion of an independent press.

Bill Moyers was privy to many presidential decisions made by Lyndon Johnson, yet he has over the years said and written relatively little in general about his former boss, and almost nothing about LBJ and the war in Vietnam. Yet no one, with the possible exception of Lady Bird Johnson, had equivalent access to LBJ and the process by which he made his decisions. So it was something of a surprise when Bill and his wife, Judith Davidson Moyers—host and producer of so many PBS specials—agreed to participate in the Musgrove conference. In critical oral history, as in just about everything else, timing is everything. The invitation reached them in January 2005 just after they returned from a month-long getaway celebrating their fiftieth wedding anniversary, during which they had discussed the possibility of doing something—a television show, a series, perhaps a book, or maybe all three—on the 2008 100th anniversary of the birth of Lyndon Johnson (born August 27, 1908). Bill and Judith Moyers told us they thought that the conference being planned at Musgrove would provide an excellent opportunity to bring themselves quickly up to speed on the latest thinking on the war in Vietnam during the tenures of the presidents Bill had served. (He was deputy director of the Peace Corps during the Kennedy administration.) Bill Moyers warned us, however, that he had no direct responsibility for Vietnam policy, so what he would try to offer instead would be some insights into the two presidents, whom he knew well, and the principal advisers to them on Vietnam: McGeorge Bundy, Robert McNamara, Dean Rusk, Walt Rostow, and others. That is exactly what he did as he spoke for the first time at length and on the record about LBJ and Vietnam. That he was willing to do so while surrounded by a room full of specialists on the war in Vietnam attests to his courage as much as to his curiosity.

Bill Moyers sat at the conference table. Judith Davidson Moyers, who also knew the two presidents and their advisers, sat just to one side, taking copious notes. Both were willing throughout the conference to make themselves available to our small but inquisitive horde of participating scholars. As Bill and Judith Moyers told us during the conference, they felt a little odd at Musgrove because they were participating in order to learn what they could about Kennedy, Johnson, and Vietnam, yet the moment each session ended they were surrounded by the scholars, asking questions of them about their experience.

As the debate on the war in Iraq has heated up since the Musgrove conference, Bill Moyers has not been shy about urging his television audience to think about the analogy. His style is typically indirect; he encourages those in his audience to make their own connections and draw their own conclusions. For example, on June 1, 2007, he played an excerpt on his weekly PBS show from an audiotaped May 1964 telephone conversation between LBJ and McGeorge Bundy, his national security adviser. At this time, as Moyers pointed out while introducing the clip, Vietnam was "just a small dark cloud on the horizon." LBJ tells Bundy on the recording, "I just thought about ordering . . . ordering those kids in there . . . and what in the hell am I ordering them out there for? It's damn easy to get into a war, but it's . . . going to be harder to ever extricate yourself if you get in. . . ." Moyers follows with this comment: "That was May 1964. Two hundred and sixty Americans had been killed in Vietnam by then. Eleven years and two presidents later, when U.S. forces pulled out, 58,209 Americans had died, and an estimated three million Vietnamese."[3] Later that night, a woman who identified herself as "[The Other] Katharine Harris" and who had just seen the show posted a comment that gave poignant voice to the mystery that, we suspect, remains the fundamental question for Bill Moyers about LBJ and the war in Vietnam. "Wow, heartbreaking stuff," she wrote. "What happened to change his mind? How, from being so right in the analysis shown here, did LBJ go so far wrong?"[4]

The Scholarly Skeptics: Vietnam If Kennedy Had Lived Would Have Differed Little From LBJ's War

THOMAS S. BLANTON

He believes that while in certain of his moods JFK opposed an American war in Vietnam, fundamentally Kennedy would have done that which was advantageous politically in the short run—which would have been to send in combat troops to prevent the collapse of South Vietnam.

Tom Blanton is director of the National Security Archive, George Washington University, in Washington, D.C., known to historians of the Cold War simply as "the Archive," and whose scholars are widely known as "the docu-hounds." Blanton and his associates are expert in prying loose classified documents from the U.S. government, sometimes via the Freedom of Information Act (FOIA—or "FOY-ya"), sometimes via lawsuits. But since the end of the Cold War, the Archive has also been at the forefront of institutions acquiring documents from former communist countries and in educating scholars around the world in the fine art of getting documents declassified within their own countries. The Archive has been in charge of document collection for each of the nearly two

THE FOREIGN POLICY EDUCATION
OF JOHN F. KENNEDY

Bay of Pigs, Cuba, April 1961

JFK's lesson: do not trust the rosy estimates of the CIA or the military regarding a foreign military adventure.

Laos, March 1961

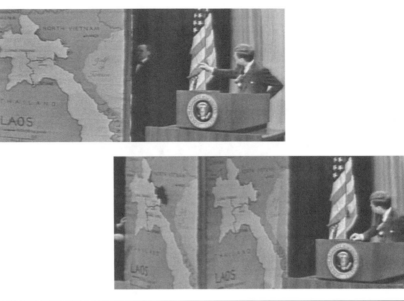

"These three maps show the area of effective Communist domination as it was last August . . . and now next, in December . . . and now . . . near the end of March, the Communists control a much wider section of the country. . . . Soviet planes, I regret to say, have been conspicuous in a large-scale airlift into the battle area. . . . It is this new dimension of externally supported warfare that creates the present grave problem." [Presidential news conference, March 23, 1961]

JFK's lesson: do not believe advisers who tell you that a military intervention against Soviet forces can be undertaken anywhere at acceptable cost and risk. [Images taken from *Virtual JFK: Vietnam If Kennedy Had Lived*, a film directed by Koji Masutani]

Berlin, August 1961

JFK's lesson: retain strict civilian control over military operations in any direct confrontation with the Soviet Union.

"combat forces"

"grave concern"

"If we move without ambiguity-
without the sickly pallor of our
positions in Cuba and Laos-...there
is a better than even chance that
the Communists will back down ....
This we should cheerfully accept."
(Asst. National Security Advisor to Kennedy, November, 1961)

"necessary immediate military actions"

"The President repeated
his apprehension"

JFK's lesson: a president is not bound by the advice of others.

Cuban Missile Crisis, October 1962

JFK's lesson: remain skeptical of seemingly simple military solutions.

October 31, 1963 ". . . we would expect to withdraw a thousand men from South Vietnam before the end of the year . . . "
[Images taken from *Virtual JFK: Vietnam If Kennedy Had Lived*, a film directed by Koji Masutani]

dozen critical oral history conferences we have organized over the past twenty years, as well as dozens of other events organized by the Archive's scholars. Tom Blanton is a native of Mississippi and a graduate of Harvard College, where he worked as a reporter for *The Harvard Crimson* and was a member of the debate team. He also attended the June 1997 conference in Hanoi on the war in Vietnam, which we organized. He has a special interest in the war and has supported scholarly work on the war at the Archive throughout his two decades there. He is a documentary zealot, in the sense that he never met a declassified document he didn't like, and his enthusiasm at Musgrove for interpreting documents was infectious, as always.

FRANCES FITZGERALD

She is extremely skeptical about the claims made about Kennedy and Vietnam over the years by members of JFK's inner circle. She does not believe that Kennedy would have been able to restrain the U.S. military and civilian hawks who eventually convinced LBJ to Americanize the war in Vietnam.

Frankie FitzGerald is well known as the author of one of the most influential books ever written about the war in Vietnam, *Fire in the Lake: The Vietnamese and the Americans in Vietnam*. It was published in 1972 and hailed as something extraordinary, a book by an American who seemed fully informed about U.S. decision making in both Washington and in Saigon and also with the totality of the Vietnamese reality, both communist and non-communist. For *Fire in the Lake*, Frankie FitzGerald was awarded the Pulitzer Prize for writing on contemporary affairs, a National Book Award, and the Bancroft Prize for Historical Writing. The book remains one of the most scathing indictments ever written of U.S. policy in Vietnam. She has written for *The New Yorker*, *The New York Review of Books*, *The Nation*, *The New York Times Magazine*, and *Rolling Stone*. She is also the author, more recently, of *Way Out There in the Blue: Reagan, Star Wars and the End of the Cold War* (2000); and (with Mary Cross) *Vietnam: Spirits of the Earth* (2002). She also has a family connection to our subject. Her father, Desmond FitzGerald, was deputy director of the CIA and a specialist on Southeast Asia. She is a reader and speaker of the Vietnamese language. She possesses a slightly unnerving investigative manner: she is unfailingly civil and polite, on the one hand, but she is also highly focused when trying to get to the bottom of a story. Both these traits were evident at the Musgrove conference, as she pursued the story of Vietnam if Kennedy had lived.

JAMES G. HERSHBERG

He doubts that Kennedy could have let the Saigon government collapse, as it was inevitably going to do sooner or later. He does not doubt JFK's intention to avoid an American war, but he believes his intentions would have been no match for the political realities facing a president accused of having "lost" Vietnam.

Jim Hershberg is associate professor of history and international relations in the Department of History and the Elliott School of International Affairs, George Washington University. He is the author of *James B. Conant: Harvard to Hiroshima and the Making of the Nuclear Age* (1995). He was also a founder of the Cold War International History Project (CWIHP) at the Woodrow Wilson International Center for Scholars and the founding editor of the project's *Bulletin.* At CWIHP, he championed the efforts of scholars from former communist countries to get their new governments to declassify and release Cold War–related documents and to publish their analyses of the documents in the *Bulletin.* As a scholar of the Cold War, he is a genuine polymath, having published articles and chapters on the Cuban missile crisis, the war in Vietnam, the war in Afghanistan, and dozens of other disparate topics. Inside the circle of scholars of the Cold War, he is sometimes known by his well-earned nickname, "Flypaper," so named because every detail from every document and piece of oral testimony he has ever encountered sticks to his brain and can be retrieved at a moment's notice. Jim Hershberg is also known as one of the most generous scholars working on the Cold War, eager to share his vast knowledge of the documentary evidence or to assist foreign scholars with editing and translating and getting their work published in English. At Musgrove, his intensity was fully on display in his frequent and spirited interventions and in his friendly but comprehensive interrogation of the former officials between sessions.

TIMOTHY NAFTALI

He believes that Kennedy would probably not have been willing to absorb a defeat in the Third World on the scale of having "lost" Vietnam to the communists, and thus that JFK would have felt compelled to send in U.S. combat troops to prevent the collapse of the Saigon government.

Tim Naftali became, on October 6, 2006, the first director of the Richard M. Nixon Presidential Library and Museum, Yorba Linda, California. From 1999–2006, he was associate professor and director of the Presidential Recordings Program at the University of Virginia's Miller Center of Public Affairs. The Presidential Recordings Program has proven to be a gold mine for scholars of the Cold War. Presidents Eisenhower, Kennedy, Johnson, and Nixon all, to one degree or another, secretly recorded telephone conversations, meetings, and other conversations and personal ruminations. The program that Naftali directed took the lead in declassifying, deciphering, transcribing, and disseminating the recorded documentation from these Cold War presidencies. The program's website, http://millercenter.org/academic/presidentialrecordings/, remains a vital resource for scholars of the Cold War and the presidency and their students. He is also the author of many books and articles on the Cold War, including (with Aleksandr Fursenko) *"One Hell of a Gamble": Khrushchev, Castro & Kennedy, 1958–1964* (New York: Norton, 1997); and (also with Aleksandr Fursenko) *Khrushchev's Cold War: The Inside Story of an American Adversary* (New York: Norton, 2006). Although not a specialist on the war in Vietnam, Tim Naftali knows as much as anyone alive about the Kennedy administration's foreign policy. He is also a document enthusiast: he is familiar with a vast array of documentation, including on the Russian side (he is a fluent reader and speaker of Russian) and, in words and gestures, he is brilliantly theatrical—arms flailing in the air, voice rising with the approach of the punch line—in his ability to make the past come alive as it is revealed in the documents. Anyone who believes discussing documents from the past is necessarily tedious has clearly never encountered Tim Naftali.

JOHN PRADOS

His view on Vietnam if Kennedy had lived goes considerably beyond mere skepticism regarding JFK's ability to avoid escalation of the war; he believes Kennedy did escalate the war significantly and repeatedly before his assassination when he authorized increases of U.S. advisers, equipment, and financial support to the Saigon government.

John Prados is an independent scholar and a Research Fellow on National Security Affairs, National Security Archive, George Washington University, Washington, D.C., where he is also director of the Archive's Vietnam Documentation Project. In addition to his work on contemporary national security issues, John Prados is one of the most prolific scholars now writing about the war in Vietnam. Among his books on the war are (with Ray W. Stubbe) *Valley of Decision: The Siege of Khe Sanh* (Boston: Houghton Mifflin, 1991); *The Hidden History of the Vietnam War* (Chicago: Ivan R. Dee, 1995); *The Blood Road: The Ho Chi Minh Trail and the Vietnam War* (New York: Wiley, 1999); and *Lost Crusader:*

The Secret Wars of CIA Director William Colby (New York: Oxford University Press, 2003). For a peek at another of John Prados's interests, visit the website www.boardgamegeek.com/game/2904. There you will find advertised his board game, *Third Reich*, and links to his many other historical, military, and/or political board games. His Vietnam Documentation Project at the National Security Archive was the principal source for the declassified documents included in the 1,000-page briefing notebook that was required reading for the participants in the Musgrove conference. He and his assistants have combed through dozens of document collections in presidential libraries, the Library of Congress, the National Archives, personal papers, and other sources to provide a kind of "one-stop shopping" for scholars of U.S. decision making in Vietnam. It is a phenomenally valuable resource. Prados also has a well-earned reputation, both in print and in person, as a blunt, cut-to-the-chase inquisitor. At Musgrove, he lived up to his advance billing and was exceptionally valuable as a provocateur. And because of his view that before his assassination Kennedy had *already* escalated the war in Vietnam to an American war, Prados was destined to clash with another Musgrove participant, Jamie Galbraith, who is equally blunt and provocative, but believes just the opposite—that before the assassination Kennedy had *already* decided to withdraw. The Prados-Galbraith axis provided a great deal of intellectual fireworks.

MARC SELVERSTONE

He believes that while JFK did in fact authorize the withdrawal of 1,000 U.S. military personnel from Vietnam in October 1963, the audiotapes of the relevant discussions suggest that Kennedy would only have gone ahead with a more comprehensive withdrawal if the U.S.-backed Saigon government appeared to be winning the war on its own. Otherwise, he believes Kennedy would have been forced to escalate the war, just as Johnson did.

Marc Selverstone is an assistant professor in the Presidential Recordings Program at the University of Virginia's Miller Center of Public Affairs. At the Miller Center, he has been the coordinator of transcribing and annotating the audiotapes of John F. Kennedy and Lyndon B. Johnson. Several of these tapes were played at the Musgrove conference, along with their accompanying rolling transcripts projected onto a screen. Just before departing for Musgrove, Selverstone was shocked to learn that the Musgrove Conference Center is aggressively low-tech, as some believe might befit a true family getaway, and therefore did not have a connection to the Internet. He had just enough time to recover from his shock to copy all the presidential recordings he needed at Musgrove onto a CD before leaving for the conference. The transcript of JFK's meeting on Vietnam of October 2, 1963, 11:00 a.m.–11:55 a.m., began the second session of the Musgrove discussions. That discussion is in chapter 4 of this book.

MARILYN B. YOUNG

She believes that the decision of Lyndon Johnson and his advisers to escalate the war in Vietnam derives, in the end, from their hubris and lack of interest in what many specialists, including herself, predicted at the time would be the tragic result of such a war. She is inclined to think Kennedy would have done no better, but is not sure of this and, given the parallels between Vietnam and Iraq, she believes the question is too important to ignore.

Marilyn Young is a professor of history at New York University (NYU) and the author of many works on the Cold War, including several on the war in Vietnam. She is a former director of the NYU International Center for Advanced Studies and has been codirector of NYU's Tamiment Library Center for the Study of the United States and the Cold War. Marilyn Young's book *The Vietnam Wars, 1945–1990* (New York: Harper, 1991) is a magisterial synthesis of the literature from many sides of the war, including the American, North and South Vietnamese, Chinese, and Soviet perspectives. She was among the first historians of the war to include in her narrative the historical and cultural features of Vietnam and the Vietnamese people, including the viewpoint of the Hanoi government and the communist insurgency in the South, the National Liberation Front. Several years after publishing *The Vietnam Wars*, she coedited (with Marvin Gettleman, Jane Franklin, and H. Bruce Franklin) a companion book that also became a classic in the field, *Vietnam and America: A Documented History* (New York: Grove Press, 1995). More recently, Marilyn Young has explored the uses and abuses of the analogy between the wars in Vietnam and Iraq. She was among the first historians to predict, and later to document, the ways the use of the analogy mirrors the ideological purposes and blinders of those making the comparison. She recently edited (with Lloyd Gardner) *Iraq and the Lessons of Vietnam: Or, How Not to Learn From the Past* (2007). Marilyn Young is a graduate of Vassar College; she earned her PhD in history from Harvard University. She taught at the University of Michigan from 1969–1979, where she was a leader among the faculty on that tumultuous campus in protesting the war in Vietnam. Marilyn Young, both as a scholar and as an activist, is unusual in that she can be a fierce, eloquent, and devastating partisan for causes she feels are just, while remaining remarkably open-minded and ready to consider alternatives the evidence seems to her to indicate. At the Musgrove conference, she was both: fierce and occasionally devastating, but also intensely curious about Vietnam if Kennedy had lived.

The Scholarly Radicals: No American War In Vietnam If Kennedy Had Lived

JAMES K. GALBRAITH

He believes that JFK had already decided by the time of his assassination to withdraw U.S. advisers from South Vietnam and that this process would probably have been completed in late 1965. He believes these conclusions follow unmistakably from evidence found on Kennedy audiotapes regarding Vietnam and also in newly available documentation from Pentagon sources.

Jamie Galbraith is the Lloyd M. Bentsen Professor of Government and Business Relations, Lyndon B. Johnson School of Public Affairs, University of Texas, Austin. He is a graduate of Harvard College and earned his PhD in economics from Yale University. He is a well-known liberal economist who has written widely on economic policy for both economists and for the general public. He writes a popular column, Econoclast, for *Mother Jones* magazine. He is also the coauthor of two highly successful textbooks in economics.[5] But Jamie Galbraith's presence at the Musgrove conference had little to do with his considerable reputation as an economist. It is due instead to a series of provocative articles he has published, stemming from what he describes as a "discovery" in Robert McNamara's 1995 memoir of the war in Vietnam, *In Retrospect: The Tragedy and Lessons of Vietnam*. In that book he encountered a claim he had never read in any of the standard histories of the war. He regards that discovery as a revelation with significant consequences for our understanding of how and why the U.S. commitment to the war in Vietnam actually happened. It also launched Jamie Galbraith on a (by now) more than decade-long avocation as a historian. Here is the phrase from McNamara's book that astounded Galbraith: ". . . President Kennedy's decision on October 2 [1963] to begin the withdrawal of U.S. forces. . . ."[6] In a series of subsequent pieces published in late 2003 and early 2004, around the time of the fortieth anniversary of the assassination of JFK, he advanced the radical thesis that by the fall of 1963, Kennedy had decided—not that he *would have* decided, but that he had *already* decided—to withdraw from Vietnam.[7] He buttressed his claim with declassified Kennedy audiotapes, Pentagon documents, and the memories of his father, John Kenneth Galbraith, who had been JFK's economics professor at Harvard, Kennedy's ambassador to India, and a member of the Kennedy inner circle. Although he was the lone economist among the historians and former officials at Musgrove, he was not intimidated. In fact, because of the boldness with which he advanced his radical views on Vietnam if Kennedy had lived, his interventions were bound to attract the attention of John Prados, an equally bold scholar whose views on Vietnam if Kennedy had lived are incompatible with Jamie Galbraith's.

GORDON GOLDSTEIN

He believes that JFK made an ironclad distinction between U.S. advisers in Vietnam and U.S. combat troops in Vietnam and that Kennedy decided, probably as early as November 1961, never to send combat troops into a war he regarded as an insurgency, the outcome of which could not be affected significantly by the introduction of U.S. military force, even massive military force.

Gordon Goldstein is senior vice president for global affairs, D. B. Zwirn & Co., New York, New York. He is a graduate of Columbia University, from which he also received his PhD in international relations. Like Jamie Galbraith, Gordon Goldstein's "day job" (as a financial manager) has nothing to do with his participation in the Musgrove conference. Goldstein's involvement with our subject, Vietnam if Kennedy had lived, began in 1994 when he agreed to become coauthor, with former National Security Adviser McGeorge Bundy, of a memoir Bundy planned to write on Kennedy, Johnson, and Vietnam. The principal focus of their book was to be a comparative assessment of decisions on the war made by the two presidents for whom Bundy had worked. In the process of collecting material for the book, Bundy uncovered a good many long-forgotten personal papers, diaries, and other documents. The collaboration was well underway when, in September 1996, Bundy died unexpectedly of a heart attack. Gordon Goldstein, as Bundy's collaborator, had full access to all of the new material, as well as more than forty hours of tape recordings containing Bundy's recollections and reflections on the war, often in response to questions posed by Goldstein. In a public lecture given at Yale in 1993, Bundy spoke of having been surprised by two findings as he got deeper into the documents: first, his own hawkishness on the war in Vietnam, under both JFK and LBJ; and second (he thought this was even more astonishing), what seemed to him to be JFK's firm determination to avoid sending U.S. combat troops into Vietnam under any circumstances.

That Bundy did not live to complete his memoir is tragic. But, as will become evident from the outset of the Musgrove conference, Gordon Goldstein has thought long and hard about JFK and LBJ as he and Bundy discussed them intensively over the two years during which they collaborated. The views Goldstein put forth at the Musgrove conference are his own, though they can also be taken as consistent in essential respects with McGeorge Bundy's views at the time of his death.

FREDRIK LOGEVALL

He believes an argument can be made that Kennedy would have escalated the war in Vietnam, much as Johnson did, but that a better argument is that Kennedy would not have done so, because the most important features of LBJ's personality that drove him to escalate the war were alien to JFK. He thus finds it difficult to imagine JFK making the decisions on Vietnam that Johnson made, which ultimately led to an American war in Vietnam.

Fred Logevall is professor of history, Cornell University, where he is director of graduate studies in the History Department. A native of Sweden, he grew up in Canada and is a graduate of Simon Fraser University in Burnaby, British Columbia. He received his PhD in history from Yale University. He is cofounder of the Center for Cold War Studies at the University of California, Santa Barbara, and is the recipient of many awards, including the 2001 Kuehl Book Prize and the 2003 Bernath Lecture Prize of the Society of Historians of American Foreign Relations. His path-breaking 1999 book, *Choosing War: The Lost Chance for Peace and the Escalation of the War in Vietnam,* has had a remarkable impact on the way historians think about Kennedy, Johnson, and Vietnam. In *Choosing War,* Fred Logevall argues that we need to imagine a continuum, which he calls "the long 1964," stretching from August 1963, through the assassination of JFK, past the initiation of heavy bombing of North Vietnam in February 1965 and the sending of U.S. combat troops to South Vietnam the following July. In Logevall's analysis, many decisions taken by U.S. leaders during the "the long 1964" were unnecessary, imprudent, and tragic. Had it been otherwise, he argues, the American war in Vietnam need not have occurred. His argument, put forth in careful and subtle but compelling prose, buttressed with voluminous documentation from a global array of archives, has two principal components. First, he argues that in order to understand decisions leading to what *did* happen in Vietnam, we must consider what did *not* happen with regard to the war. So-called what if history, often demeaned by historians, is not only acceptable, he believes, but mandatory. Second, he argues that if we take the full measure of Presidents Kennedy and Johnson, we notice that Kennedy lacked almost completely the characteristics that drove his successor to escalate the war, such as LBJ's relatively simpleminded understanding of foreign affairs and his unwillingness to listen to advice from those who disagreed with him. In *Choosing War*, Fred Logevall brought both ideas out of the closet into which historians of U.S. foreign policy had stuffed them. He legitimized what if history and he challenged his colleagues to rethink Vietnam if Kennedy had lived. By the time of the Musgrove conference, this courteous, gregarious historian had already caused a mighty ruckus among historians—and once at Musgrove, he continued to provoke and challenge them.

FRANCIS X. WINTERS

He believes that the question of Vietnam if Kennedy had lived must be understood with reference to JFK's overriding concern: getting reelected in 1964. He believes Kennedy's authorization of the coup against President Ngo Dinh Diem in Saigon was part of a strategy to eliminate Vietnam as an issue during his campaign for reelection because, politically, Diem and South Vietnam were losers. He believes JFK would have withdrawn as soon as possible, possibly in early 1964, a strategy LBJ either did not understand or did not endorse.

Frank Winters is professor of ethics and international affairs, Edmund A. Walsh School of Foreign Service, Georgetown University. Originally a specialist on the ethical and moral issues associated with nuclear deterrence, he was a senior adviser to the U.S. Conference of Catholic Bishops during the research and drafting of their highly influential 1983 Pastoral Letter on War and Peace. During the late 1980s and early 1990s, he carried out a series of interviews with many former officials from the Kennedy administration and from the House and Senate regarding the decision to authorize the November 1, 1963, coup in Saigon against South Vietnamese President Ngo Dinh Diem. His findings were published in a 1997 book, *The Year of the Hare: America in Vietnam: January 25, 1963–February 15, 1964*. Subsequent research by Winters and others has tended to confirm his view that at the heart of the tragedy of America in Vietnam is a contradiction: that JFK was not going to Americanize the war in Vietnam, yet it was in part the chaos that followed the coup in Saigon that made it almost impossible for his successor, LBJ, to do anything other than to try to avoid "losing" South Vietnam. At the Musgrove conference, Frank Winters encouraged his colleagues to consider the intrinsic ethical implications of JFK's authorization of the coup and its link to our understanding of Vietnam if Kennedy had lived.

Warning: An Argument, Not a Game

Yes, we have summarized the basic positions of the former officials and scholars on Vietnam if Kennedy had lived. Yes, we have subdivided the scholars into "skeptics" and "radicals." And we have even foreshadowed a few of their quirks and proclivities. We hope these shorthand devices encourage you to figuratively pull your own chair up to the Musgrove conference table and get involved in the argument. But none of these shortcuts into the Musgrove discussions is meant to trivialize the proceedings by implying, even subtly, that the participants were selected to be on "teams," or that they understood their role to be as team members competing against the players on an opposing team. They are not playing a game. They are engaging in an argument about a subject that is, to them, supremely serious. Yes, disagreements arise, sometimes vividly, and there is little to do at the end of some of them other than to agree to disagree. Yes, there is humor. There is even the occasional frivolous anecdote. But humor and even frivolity were simply compelled by the burden of our subject: war, humiliation, arrogance, ignorance, regret, and responsibility. After all, Hamlet is sometimes hilarious and Romeo and Juliet are often frivolous. But at the end of each play, the stage is littered with corpses.

The war in Vietnam was a tragedy and Shakespeare is the poet laureate of the tragic. But Shakespeare's tragic figures are kings and queens, princes and princesses. With the war in Vietnam, the "princes" under scrutiny—JFK and LBJ—are long dead. But there was more than enough tragedy to go around, to affect anyone who was involved with the war. In his 1966 play *Rosencrantz and Guildenstern Are Dead*, the British playwright Tom Stoppard fashioned a tragedy a little closer to the one to which the former officials at Musgrove give voice. In Stoppard's play the two title characters, who have minor walk-on parts in Shakespeare's *Hamlet*, are given the lead roles, while Hamlet and the others who figure centrally in Shakespeare's original are relegated to the background. Rosencrantz and Guildenstern wander confusedly throughout the play, ordinary men caught up in events they can neither understand nor control, headed toward a tragic end they can't quite see and will not be able to avoid. Any of our former officials—Chet Cooper, Tom Hughes, or Bill Moyers—could easily have uttered the lines Stoppard gives to Guildenstern toward the end of the play:

> There must have been a moment, at the beginning, when we could have said "no."
> But somehow we missed it.[8]

Was there such a moment? Could they have said "no"? Would LBJ have listened if they had? Would JFK have missed the moment too, or would he have seized it?

"the inner conviction of your
Vice-President, your Secretaries
of State and Defense, and the two
heads of your special mission"

"We must insist"

"United States forces
defend South Viet-Nam"

"Combat Forces"

"The President ... questioned the
wisdom of involvement in Vietnam"

*"The 1961 proposal leaves Kennedy encircled by his most senior
national security officials, who all support the deployment of ground
combat troops to South Vietnam."*

CHAPTER 3

What JFK Decided: November 1961

Gordon Goldstein: No U.S. Combat Troops for Vietnam, Neither Now nor Later

The first session of the Musgrove conference is initiated by a provocation from Gordon Goldstein, an international relations scholar who worked closely with McGeorge Bundy, national security adviser for JFK and LBJ. Goldstein and Bundy collaborated on a writing project during the two years prior to Bundy's sudden death from a heart attack in September 1996. The book Bundy envisioned at the outset of the project was in some ways an analogue to the controversial 1995 memoir of Robert McNamara, In Retrospect: The Tragedy and Lessons of Vietnam.[1] Bundy, who had been a hawk on Vietnam when he served under Kennedy and Johnson, had, by the time he and Goldstein began their collaboration, turned nearly 180 degrees. Having read the available documentation and having reflected on the proclivities of President Kennedy, Bundy seems to have reached two conclusions as rendered in the following provocation by Goldstein: Kennedy very definitely was not going to Americanize the war in Vietnam; and Lyndon Johnson very definitely, from the moment he succeeded Kennedy, was going to do whatever it took to "win the war" in Vietnam, including sending U.S. combat forces in large numbers, if that is what it took to "win." Some of the key evidence, according to Goldstein, is contained in JFK's response to the Taylor-Rostow Report, given to President Kennedy following a fact-finding visit to South Vietnam in late October 1961 by Kennedy's special military representative, General Maxwell D. Taylor, and Walt Rostow, the deputy national security adviser.[2] Taylor (somewhat hesitantly) and Rostow (enthusiastically) were inclined to recommend the introduction, as soon as possible, of several thousand U.S. combat troops, but ultimately, in all probability, tens of thousands.

While Goldstein's views expressed in what follows and throughout the conference are his own, he developed them in the course of dozens of conversations with Bundy, and they can be taken as consistent with the views Bundy held when he died. Goldstein's conclusion, like Bundy's, is radical and unequivocal: if JFK had lived, the American war in Vietnam would not have occurred. Kennedy was not, in their view, going to send in the U.S. Army in an attempt to rescue the Saigon government. By implication, history would thus have been profoundly different, arguably profoundly better, if JFK had lived and been reelected.

JAMES BLIGHT: In this first session, we're focused on late 1961. The question is, "What did Kennedy decide in November 1961?" Gordon?

GORDON GOLDSTEIN: From early 1995 until his death in September 1996, I engaged in a close collaboration with McGeorge Bundy to produce a retrospective historical study of the Vietnam War. In the remarks that follow I will revisit that collaboration and discuss the key themes of our work together. You can assume the remarks that follow represent my best effort to accurately and precisely capture the essence of his views and our joint study of the period between 1961 and 1965, which was the period of greatest interest to Bundy. I will not quote from the draft passages of that completed work; it is not necessary to do so to convey the core arguments we were exploring. I want to make it very clear that I am not here as a posthumous spokesman for Bundy, nor am I here to speak as his defender—and I am certainly not here to speak as his critic. I'm here as a student of the Vietnam War, as someone who had the very good fortune of collaborating with Bundy in the last years of his life as he grappled with a question of great historical importance: why did the tragedy of the Vietnam War play out as it did, and what are the lessons that we can learn from it to guide us in the future?

Here's my agenda: in the limited time available to me I'm going to address the following questions.

- What was proposed and decided in 1961? And what is the historical significance of President Kennedy's decision to reject the deployment of ground combat troops to South Vietnam?
- What is the relationship between Kennedy's Vietnam policy of 1961 and his later policy directives of October 1963?
- Finally, what does the '61 policy tell us about the broader what if of how the Vietnam crisis would have been managed by Kennedy if he had survived Dallas and had served a second term?

I will try to answer these questions briefly with a sequence of related propositions, each of which has a substantive basis in the research and analysis I conducted with Bundy prior to his death.

The autumn '61 recommendation is nothing less than a proposal to Americanize the war. It is a recommendation to shift from a strategy of providing arms and advisers to South Vietnam to a strategy in which American combat troops will play a direct role in fighting the insurgency and prosecuting the war on behalf of South Vietnam. Kennedy recognized that this was a proposal for a fundamentally different policy: a shift from a mission of providing military support and training to a mission of combat operations against the communist insurgency.

This is not a proposal for 8,000 combat troops; it is a proposal for more than 200,000 troops. The architects of the autumn '61 proposal state, clearly and repeatedly, that the United States must make the first installment of a combat troop commitment that could grow to six divisions, totaling more than 200,000 troops. They advise, clearly and repeatedly, that the commitment, although enormous, is necessary. To quote the November 8th draft memorandum from McNamara to the president, which is also endorsed by the Joint Chiefs and Secretary of State Dean Rusk: "The fall of South Vietnam to communism would lead to the fairly rapid extension of communist control or complete accommodation to communism in the rest of mainland Southeast Asia and in Indonesia. The strategic implications worldwide, particularly in the Orient, would be extremely serious. The chances are against, sharply against, preventing the fall of South Vietnam, by any means, by any measures, short of the introduction of U.S. forces on a substantial scale" [**Document 3-1**]. The proposal then notes that the struggle "may be prolonged," that China and the Soviet Union may intervene, and that six divisions, or 205,000 troops, may be required. The proposal concludes by recommending to the president that "we commit the U.S. to the clear objective of preventing the fall of South Vietnam to communism and that we support this commitment by the necessary military actions."

In discussing the 1961 proposal, some commentators have conflated the meanings of an advisory mission and a combat mission. As the McNamara memorandum makes clear, and as Mac Bundy pointed out repeatedly, the distinction cannot be confused. Ground combat troops means Marine forces, or U.S. Army forces organized in combat units, infantry, artillery, armor, or airborne, in companies, battalions, regiments, and divisions. These are not supply forces, these are not air forces, these are not forces assigned to advise, train, or assist South Vietnamese combat troops. These are fighting forces; these are combat forces.

The 1961 proposal leaves Kennedy encircled by his most senior national security officials, who all support the deployment of ground combat troops to South Vietnam. There is a formidable bureaucratic coalition aligned behind the proposition that the United States should deploy combat troops to South Vietnam. Various formulations of the proposal are raised at least five times by the spring of 1961, and then several additional formulations of the proposal follow, culminating with the recommendation the president must eventually address in November.[3] Over time, the loose coalition in favor of deploying combat troops includes, among others, McNamara, the secretary of defense; Rusk, the secretary of state; Bundy, the national security adviser; Walt Rostow, the deputy national security adviser; Maxwell Taylor, the president's special military adviser; Lionel McGarr, the chief of the Military Assistance Advisory Group in Vietnam; Edward Lansdale, the Pentagon assistant for special operations; and all members of the Joint Chiefs of Staff. All of them support it—whether as a symbol of determination, as a deterrent, as a defense for U.S. bases (the rationale that ultimately prevails in March 1965), or under the rather transparent ruse of so-called "flood relief." The president is surrounded. And with the exception of Undersecretary of State George Ball and a few other advisers of significantly lower rank, the president is alone.

The president slams the door on the combat troop deployments to South Vietnam proposed in 1961, and that door remains firmly shut. For the duration of Kennedy's presidency, the no-combat-troop policy is never revised. It is never reversed. It is never challenged. There is no record of the national security bureaucracy replicating the consensus and intensity of support for combat troop deployments as it does throughout 1961. The president has made it clear to his senior advisers that this is not an option he favors. As General Taylor remarked about the proposal he and Rostow presented, the president was "instinctively against [the] introduction of U.S. forces."[4]

The greatest significance of the no-combat-troop policy is ultimately reflected in casualty figures. For the duration of Kennedy's presidency, when a no-combat-troop policy prevails, the total number of U.S. troops killed in Vietnam is 108 and the total number of military advisers on the ground rises to roughly 16,000. The number of Americans killed in Vietnam remains sharply limited following Kennedy's death, as Johnson adhered to a no-combat-troop policy though all of 1964 and into March 1965. As we all know, the reversal of the no-combat-troop policy and the cascading Americanization of the war eventually results in the deployment of more than 500,000 troops and the deaths of 58,000 American soldiers. In sum, when we contrast the American advisory mission with the American combat mission, we observe a significant difference in the configuration of forces, a significant difference in the number of forces deployed, a significant difference in the mission of these forces, and, finally, an astronomical difference in the number of soldiers killed. Those analysts who dismiss these differences as simply different positions along a so-called continuum of military involvement are guilty, I think, of a simplification that is extremely misleading and untenable.

Kennedy's refusal to deploy ground combat troops is based on a series of mutually reinforcing and internally consistent determinations. He was deeply skeptical of his military advisers and simply did not trust the Chiefs. He was burned at the Bay of Pigs and the Chiefs never regained their credibility. The disarray over Laos in '61 further illustrates the flaws in their recommendations for regional intervention with ground combat forces. Kennedy is mindful—always mindful—of the disastrous French colonial experience in Vietnam and the lessons it suggests for the United States. He cites these lessons frequently. Kennedy did not perceive Vietnam to be a conventional conflict amenable to resolution by conventional war. He believed counterinsurgency required significantly different tools, and to the extent there was a Kennedy military strategy in Vietnam, it was based on unconventional forces and strategies. It is difficult to imagine he would have abandoned this conviction in favor of Westmoreland's blunt nonstrategy of forty-four battalions to be deployed more or less as the general saw fit.

Although the historical record demonstrates that a no-combat-troop policy prevails for the duration of Kennedy's presidency, that policy is never explained. While Kennedy tells Walter Cronkite and others that the Vietnamese must win the war themselves, he never formally sets a limit precluding the deployment of combat troops.[5] It is not part of the declaratory policy. The result is that the policy that is not acknowledged is easily reversed. After the assassination, the no-combat-troop policy is an evanescent thing; it evaporates. One what if we should consider is this: what if Kennedy had publicly established a clear upper limit on the scope and form of U.S. military assistance; would that declared U.S. policy have inhibited Johnson's choice to send the first Marines ashore in March 1965?

Two final points. First, the 1961 no-combat-troop decision is completely consistent with Kennedy's pledge in NSAM [National Security Action Memorandum] 263 (in 1963) to conclude the advisory mission in South Vietnam by the end of 1965 [Document 4-6]. But that consistency does not depend on the premise, which we will discuss and debate tomorrow, that NSAM 263 is the beginning of Kennedy's extrication strategy. At the very least, the October 1963 decisions confirm Kennedy's commitment to an advisory mission, not a combat mission. And it further confirms Kennedy's desire and intent to wind down the advisory program at the earliest possible date. The October '63 decision, even interpreted conservatively, underscores the character of the Kennedy program of action in South Vietnam. Advisers, yes; combat troops, no.

Final proposition: had he survived Dallas and served a second term, Kennedy, just like Johnson, would have collided with the limits of the no-combat-troop policy. He then would have faced the dilemma of escalation or withdrawal. How he would have managed that dilemma is of course the great what if question we are left with. As you know from the materials Jim and Janet distributed, Bundy strongly believed that Kennedy had profound doubts about the prudence and viability of Americanizing the war. If that is true—and the evidence seems to strongly support it—the question then becomes whether Kennedy would have been somehow forced, or compelled, to deploy combat troops? And to answer that question we must ask, forced by what interest? Or compelled by what influence? If Kennedy can stand his ground in '61, can he not do so again in '65, even if it means a messy endgame in South Vietnam? Many assert that the Diem coup deepened the U.S. obligation to South Vietnam. But for Kennedy, wouldn't the protracted instability that follows the coup in 1964 and early 1965 simply reaffirm the dismal prospects for holding on in Vietnam? Wouldn't this undeniable mess substantiate all that he feared? And wouldn't Kennedy then have great latitude to maneuver? He has no Great Society program to push through Congress, he has tamed the Chiefs ever since the debacle of the Bay of Pigs, he is the champion of the missile crisis, and he is personally liberated from politics. He will never face another election again. As Bundy notes, he can define the national interest irrespective of his own personal political interest. Thus history could have been profoundly different if Kennedy had lived.

Thomas Hughes: No U.S. Combat Troops Yet, but Probably Later

The counterprovocation by Tom Hughes questions many of Gordon Goldstein's major conclusions. Tom Hughes was throughout the period during which the war in Vietnam escalated director of Intelligence and Research (INR) at the State Department. He counters Goldstein's reading of the declassified documents with an insider's knowledge of how decisions occurred, but also with a scholar's familiarity with the documentary record. Hughes says he would like to believe that Kennedy made a decision once and for all in November 1961 to avoid an American war in Vietnam, but he just can't buy it. He points out that many senior officials in the administration continued to argue, through and beyond November 1961, for the introduction of U.S. troops into Vietnam, more or less as if Kennedy had made no decision at all. For example, he mentions Walt Rostow, the deputy national security adviser, a thoroughgoing hawk on Vietnam throughout his entire eight-year service in the Kennedy and Johnson administrations. Rostow, Hughes points out, persisted in writing his ultra-hawkish memoranda as if Kennedy still had an open mind on the issue of sending U.S. combat troops to rescue the Saigon government from the communist insurgency. Rostow's ideas included, for example, serious consideration of "going North"—that is, mounting an American invasion of North Vietnam with as many as 1,000,000 U.S. troops—a proposal that, if implemented, would have represented the antithesis of what Goldstein and McGeorge Bundy believe JFK decided in November 1961. Many others believe likewise, according to Hughes.

Thus, he is inclined to call what Kennedy did in mid-November 1961 in response to the Taylor-Rostow Report a "so-called decision." Whatever Kennedy may have thought he was doing, according to Hughes, officials throughout the administration carried on as before, with some clearly assuming that a massive introduction of U.S. troops was virtually inevitable, because that was what it would take to achieve what most seem to have regarded as the ironclad objective of preventing the fall of the Saigon government in South Vietnam to the communist forces of the National Liberation Front (or "Vietcong") underwritten and directed by the government of Ho Chi Minh in Hanoi.

*Importantly, Hughes notes what he understands to be JFK's way of dealing with difficult issues on which his senior advisers disagree either with each other, or with Kennedy's views, or both. Hughes asks us to pay close attention to the way Kennedy lets one or two senior subordinates know, in some fashion, how he ultimately wants the issue to be resolved. JFK would then, according to Hughes, expect his adviser (for example, he says Defense Secretary Robert McNamara often played this role when issues of national security were involved) to argue the case forcefully while in the presence of other members of the administration who were known to disagree with the president. In this particular case, Hughes says that McNamara became, so to speak, a kind of "stalking horse." Hughes points out that this occurred only after the defense secretary withdrew his hawkish response of November 8, 1961, to the Taylor-Rostow Report [**Document 3-1**] and replaced it with an November 11 draft more in keeping with Kennedy's skepticism with regard to the troop question. If Hughes has correctly described Kenne-*

dy's approach to resolving controversy inside his administration, the president had in McNamara an ideal candidate to be his point man. Few U.S. officials in the post–World War II period combined the three essential traits required by Kennedy's strategy: first, exquisite sensitivity to the wishes of the president; second, supreme loyalty to the boss; and third, a powerful personality and ability to dominate the policy process on the president's behalf. Having McNamara argue JFK's own case while the president feigned neutrality on whatever issue was under discussion thus raised the odds that JFK could bring along recalcitrant members of the administration without overtly having to strong-arm them himself—which Kennedy preferred not to do.

JAMES BLIGHT: Thank you, Gordon. I'd like to turn the floor over to Tom Hughes.

THOMAS HUGHES: Thank you very much, Jim.

I would like say from the beginning that I would like to believe that Kennedy decided in 1961 to withdraw as clearly and as permanently as Gordon has indicated. I wish I could believe that, but I'm afraid I just can't. I think it overstates matters to say that doors were slammed in November 1961 and were never opened again. It is a reach to say that the combat troop issue was never again challenged. And just to prove I read the huge briefing book, let me refer to the pertinent documents that discuss the November 1961 situation. These all pertain to the question of the quality of the decision that Kennedy presumably made.

It is true that the advisers were unanimously proposing the decision to commit whatever was necessary in Vietnam, and that six divisions may have been on the horizon. It is true that Kennedy refused to accept this part of the recommendation, although he agreed to some other things, including counterinsurgency training. But what is fascinating about these documents is that they show that once this "decision" was made, everyone and his brother come back as though it hadn't been made, and as though the issue were still wide open.

For instance, Walt Rostow persists immediately in writing memos about military actions against North Vietnam [**Document 3-2**].[6] Mac Bundy tells the president on November 15th, 1961, ". . . I am troubled by your most natural desire to act on other items now, without taking the troop decision," by which Bundy means not the decision *not* to send in troops, but the decision *to* send in troops [**Document 3-3**]. He has an inverted reference to the decision, and the decision that is haunting Bundy is the president's temporary (at least) refusal to go along with the unanimous recommendation. He talks about the decision in these inverted terms and says, "Whatever the reason, this has now become a sort of touchstone of our will." This is November 15th, a couple of days after the so-called decision. When is a decision a decision? Rusk continues to say a couple days later, we must meet Khrushchev in Vietnam [**Document 3-4**].[7] Hilsman is preparing a memorandum in INR to support Rusk's recommendation for troops: this is still in November, the same month as the so-called decision. Hilsman agrees with Bundy that we still need more combat troops, that 8,000 isn't going to be enough.[8] Rostow suggests in addition to planning a contingency for a coup, that we have to look at our major objective, the unalterable objective of preventing the fall of South Vietnam to communism [**Document 3-2**].[9] The JCS is immediately back into action and General Lyman Lemnitzer writes memos saying "go back to May when we said we are not going to lose Southeast Asia to communism, go back and re-read our last recommendations."[10]

The point is that all over town people are continuing to write memos within days of this so-called decision that don't reflect the fact that any decision has been made. One could ask what we mean by a decision. Of course there are temporary decisions, there are tentative decisions, there are revisable decisions, there are decisions that last for a while and then can be reviewed when circumstances change. But to state, or overstate, that a decision was made that was in some sense unalterable, and that it henceforth governed the behavior of the president and the rest of the administration, does a disservice to the complexity that surrounds this issue.

The memo prepared by McNamara and later coordinated by [Deputy Undersecretary of State] U. Alexis Johnson is interesting as well. Johnson emerges as one of the key figures in this whole operation: he is the link between Rusk and the Pentagon, and is a major drafter of the troop introduction proposals. One sees in this whole situation a pattern in President Kennedy's behavior. The draft memorandum is apparently withdrawn by McNamara when he finds out that Kennedy is not going to go along with it. This is one of the early examples of what becomes a commonplace feature in the Kennedy administration: private agreements with the president are reflected in a decision presumably taken by the subordinate, but at the president's instigation, from which the president distances himself. We see that in McNamara's behavior more than once. And perhaps we can see it in [NSC adviser] Michael Forrestal's behavior in the Diem coup telegram [**Document 4-2**].[11] This is presidential suggestiveness so contrived that somebody else will implement it. This is a feature of Kennedy's modus operandi that is not repeated under Johnson.

Documents are another question. Documents are related to instructions, and the president gets directly involved in this instruction business. Taylor and Rostow go off to Vietnam only to have the instructions, which Taylor has written for himself, changed by Kennedy in the direction that Gordon Goldstein suggested: take the troop issue off the table. This is fascinating. [John Kenneth] Galbraith says, "The president sent me to Vietnam because he knows I don't have an open mind."[12] Well, there were other people who didn't have open minds either, and Kennedy was sending them too. They didn't represent Galbraith's position either, for example, Taylor and Rostow. That presidential technique comes through again.

It's not quite as bad as John Newman says—that there was deception within deception; that the military were deceiving the advisers; that the advisers were deceiving the president; that you had the president sometimes deceiving all around him. But that you had occasional three-way deceptions going on is undeniable.[13]

Finally, one thing that Kennedy learns from this whole exercise is that there is going to be a phalanx in town against him. If in fact all the advisers are lined up against him, what is he going to do about it? He takes very specific steps to disperse the phalanx, to create wedge problems, to isolate the JCS, to get the JCS to fight with itself internally, to exploit McNamara and Taylor vis-à-vis the JCS. These are gentlemen that were not highly regarded by Lyman Lemnitzer or Curtis LeMay.[14] He deliberately appoints Roger Hilsman, assistant secretary of state for the Far East, after looking at him for two years in April in 1963. Hilsman—champion of continuing to stay in Vietnam, with counterinsurgency, guerrilla warfare, and so forth. He annoys the JCS. Rostow annoys the JCS. So there are splintering operations going on. The president is very much in charge of that and uses it as a technique to dismantle the phalanx. Kennedy is quite successful in doing it.

Yes, JFK Was Reluctant to Send U.S. Combat Troops, but Would He Have Had a Choice?

Much of the declassified documentation that has recently become available on JFK and Vietnam strongly suggests that Kennedy was skeptical, at the very least, about inserting U.S. combat troops into South Vietnam. In fact, throughout these documents and deciphered audiotaped discussions of Vietnam (made by the president without the knowledge of his advisers), Kennedy seems very much the same cautious decision maker who is revealed in the so-called Kennedy tapes made during the Cuban missile crisis

*of October 1962, which have been publicly available for more than a dec-
ade. In the following conversation, however, several conference participants suggest that while presidential caution may have been a necessary
component of avoiding an American war in Vietnam, it was still not sufficient. Jim Hershberg, in particular, stresses this point: yes, it is now clear
that Kennedy didn't want to Americanize the war. But Hershberg also
points out that Lyndon Johnson didn't want to do that either, though he
ultimately did so. What is the difference? According to Hershberg, Kennedy
did not have to face the imminent collapse of the U.S.-backed government
in Saigon as Johnson did. If Kennedy had faced such a looming disaster, it
seems clear to Hershberg that Kennedy would have had little choice but to
do what Johnson did in 1965: begin with air strikes against North Vietnam
followed by the introduction of U.S. Marines to protect the planes and
associated equipment and finally the deployment of tens of thousands of
U.S. Army combat troops.*

JAMES BLIGHT: Thank you very much, Tom. I will keep a list of people
who wish to speak. Please stick to the one finger–two finger rule: put up
two fingers if you want to jump the queue and comment on exactly the
point under discussion; raise one finger if you want to take the discussion
in a different direction. And please, there is no need to put up both hands
(and feet). I will be keeping two lists, and will call on you as soon as I
can. First I have John Prados.

JOHN PRADOS: I actually draw two different overarching perspectives;
maybe our former officials can comment. The first is the vision of policy
as a war of the officials against the president. The officials are out there
all the time boxing in the president; they are not accepting the decisions
that were made; they are pushing; they are coming back for the same
decision again. This has been mentioned in other places—Herb Schandler argues very much this same point. He says every time the Joint
Chiefs were asked for an opinion on Vietnam, they came back with the
same list of six things.[15] They are doing exactly what you are talking
about, Tom. But on the other hand, you're giving us this vision of the war
of the president against the officials: he's running around splintering
them all by pulling these maneuvers. Can we have some discussion of
this? What is the reality of the policy making here? Is the development
of a coherent and consistent policy possible under these conditions?

JAMES BLIGHT: What was really going on, Chet?

CHESTER COOPER: I don't know the answer. There are a few other
things that I think affected Kennedy. One was his experience in Vienna

very early in his administration. I was in Geneva at the time, too [for the Laos negotiations].

THOMAS BLANTON: You mean the June [1961] summit with Khrushchev?

CHESTER COOPER: Yes. I think that Kennedy was licking his wounds after that meeting, and he had a sense that he had to make a stand someplace to show that he had guts. Certainly what was going on in Laos was not going to be a test of American determination. The people we were supporting in Laos were feckless and hopeless. I remember a briefing we got from a colonel, part of the American delegation from the Defense Department. He comes in to tell us things are better in Laos because, although the soldiers we are supporting in Laos ran away again, this time they took their weapons with them. So things were looking up! [Laughter.]

I had a feeling the [South] Vietnamese delegation to Laos was a very good one—outspoken, smart. One of them became ambassador to Washington. I know I and many others took a look at these guys and said if we have to make a stand in Southeast Asia, better we try to do it in Vietnam than in Laos.

Another thing that I think had a role in this—but I'm not sure—is McNamara. I've gotten to know McNamara very well; he's a neighbor of mine. McNamara had absolutely no combat experience when he took over. His rank was Air Force colonel, but basically all he was doing was working on bombing rates over Japan and Germany.[16] I had more experience than he did, and I was just a staff sergeant. But here he was confronted, within twenty-four hours of taking over, with a war—a tough war—that he as the secretary of defense would now have serious responsibility for. I think it took McNamara about two years before he could really come to grips with some of these issues.

JAMES BLIGHT: Chet has become our "McNamara mole."

JAMES HERSHBERG: I just want to put on the table a few propositions to disagree somewhat with Gordon Goldstein about the significance of the fall 1961 decisions. I don't think there's any question, in reading over the records, that Kennedy shows both an acute reluctance to Americanize the war and a certain tenacity of character in terms of being willing to overrule Rostow and the other advisers. On the other hand, Lyndon Johnson was also not eager to Americanize the war either, as some of those taped conversations, especially with [Senator Richard] Russell in

'64, have shown.[17] The question, though, for our purposes, is: how relevant is that to the issue of whether he would have escalated?

I would suggest that it is of fairly dubious relevance, because he did not face the imminent collapse of the Saigon regime. He was not presented with an either/or proposition. And I think the tendency of any president, including JFK, when faced with a difficult, troubling decision that you don't have to make at that moment, is to punt it down the road. Kennedy was not told, "You have to do this or else South Vietnam will go down the drain." He saw a series of half measures, partial measures, that could possibly keep the situation afloat. So I'm not sure that his decision making in the fall of '61 necessarily tells us what he would have done when he came to the crossroads of having to choose between South Vietnam going down the tubes and escalating. His advisers then, and Johnson's advisers later, would have told him, "If you do this, this has a chance to save the game." Would he then have taken the chance to bite the bullet? It would have depended on a constellation of factors in early '65 that are impossible to predict. But it certainly does not seem, even though he was not inclined to escalate, that he had taken an ironclad decision. Preparing an option he'd prefer doesn't mean that decision could not be changed according to circumstances.

What Did LBJ Think of JFK's Decisions in November 1961?

Bill Moyers, who served as deputy director of the Peace Corps in the Kennedy administration and who became an indispensable aide to LBJ after he succeeded JFK, is clearly perplexed by what he is hearing. The problem, roughly, is this: if, on the one hand, JFK was really very skeptical about sending U.S. troops to Vietnam, and if he actually made a decision not to do so as early as November 1961, as Gordon Goldstein has argued, then, on the other hand, why didn't LBJ understand this when he assumed office? Moyers asks this because, as he will reiterate throughout the conference, LBJ really did try earnestly to "continue" JFK's policies, and of course he even retained most of Kennedy's senior advisers. So, Moyers asks in his perplexity, why didn't Johnson try to "continue" JFK's policy of not sending combat troops to South Vietnam, rather than doing precisely the opposite?

There are several possibilities: Did Johnson for some reason not understand what JFK's Vietnam policy actually was? Or did LBJ understand what JFK was up to, but secretly disagreed with Kennedy's skepticism and caution on Vietnam? In that case, would Johnson have consciously reversed, rather than continued, the course Kennedy had set as early as November 1961? Fred Logevall gives a lengthy response in which he tells Bill Moyers that the Kennedy decisions of November 1961 reflect both JFK's skepticism regarding the recommendation of his advisers to send combat troops to South Vietnam but also, and somewhat paradoxically, JFK's willingness to go along with their requests to greatly increase the size of the U.S. commitment to the Saigon government of President Ngo Dinh Diem—in advisers, equipment, and overall financial investment. In other words, according to Logevall, what LBJ would have observed in JFK's decisions on Vietnam in November 1961 (or, in the case of the critical November 15 meeting, read from the minutes, which were provided to him after the fact by his military attaché, Colonel Howard Burris) contained genuine contradictions that would make it difficult for Johnson to determine exactly how he should proceed in order to continue Kennedy's policies.

BILL MOYERS: May I ask a question? When you look at the records of this discussion about the November 1961 proposal, was the vice president in any of those meetings? Does the record show that?

GORDON GOLDSTEIN: The vice president goes to South Vietnam, doesn't he?

BILL MOYERS: I know that, but was he in the meetings discussing the specifics of the '61 proposal?

JOHN PRADOS: He was in some of the meetings, but not all.

JAMES HERSHBERG: There is a memo from November 15th about his travel complications.[18]

THOMAS BLANTON: He's not at the November 11th meeting, either.

BILL MOYERS: But he would not be unaware of these meetings in 1965—I am referring to the meetings in late '61?

THOMAS BLANTON: A quick note on that point: the last person listed on the November 15th meeting is Colonel Howard Burris, Air Force military aide to the vice president.

JOHN PRADOS: I will tell you that I went through Howard Burris's files—his daily reporting memos to LBJ—and they cover the waterfront in terms of national security subjects. They were often less detailed than you will see in these decision documents, but I think the purpose of them was different: they were intended to serve as simple briefings to LBJ on a level with agenda notes, things to deal with—sort of like the things that Busby used to do for him in the fifties when he was in the Senate.[19] But, yes, LBJ was aware of these issues.[20]

JAMES GALBRAITH: There is no question that LBJ was very capable of being informed by Colonel Burris, and the vice presidential security files reflect that very effectively.

JAMES BLIGHT: Bill, behind this question, I take it, there is another question, which is: when LBJ arrives unexpectedly at the presidency in November '63, what did he think the policy actually was? What did he think had been decided that was supposed to be carried forward? Is that what you are asking?

BILL MOYERS: No, I wouldn't put it quite that way. I think he would have known what the policy was. What we don't know is what he *thought* of the policy—his opinion of it. I did remember him saying that he used to sit in on meetings—I don't know if those were these meetings—and he said, "I had just decided to say nothing." So I don't know what he thought about the November 1961—

THOMAS HUGHES: Well, LBJ certainly opposed the anti-Diem coup in '63.[21] And he was shocked that McNamara had discussed withdrawing troops. He thought it was a bad public statement to make.

MARILYN YOUNG: He said explicitly, "I sat silently even though I thought it was a bad idea, but I didn't say a word." But that's later; that's in '64, in a discussion with McNamara about the withdrawal [**Document 5-2**].[22]

JAMES BLIGHT: Fred Logevall.

FREDRIK LOGEVALL: I concur with those of you who have said that the vice president, when he becomes president, shows in some of the tapes in '64, and some of the other materials we have from both '64 and '65, that he is better informed about the nature of the policy making in the Kennedy years than some authors have suggested. He even makes a reference or two to the fall '61 decisions. This leads me to my point: I think it may be possible to reconcile Gordon's opening provocation with Tom's response. It seems to me that the reluctance—the heartfelt opposition—to sending ground troops is there, and I concur that is highly important, certainly in terms of the what if and also in general terms of understanding what happens. I also think, however, that as Tom was suggesting—or at least what I want to suggest—what emerges from November '61 is very important in terms of later policy making. NSAM 111, which you have in your briefing book, is a very important document [**Document 3-5**]. Notwithstanding McGeorge Bundy's suggestion that we ignore memoranda, this one, dated 22 November 1961, seems to mark a major escalation of U.S. involvement in the war. The British caution the Americans on this. It marks a clear and wholesale violation of the Geneva Accords in terms of what was allowed. Arguably, the United States and the North Vietnamese had already violated those accords many times in other ways. What emerges from NSAM 111, and what comes out of the November meetings, is a very important expansion of the war.

Interestingly enough, as most of you know, because of what is in NSAM 111, we see improvement in ARVN's performance on the battlefield in 1962.[23] But of course, arguably, it also ties Kennedy's hands. It makes later decisions, depending on how you look at it, either easier to take, or more difficult to take. So many of Gordon's points are well taken, but it is also important to note that we have an important escalation of the war and of U.S. involvement in November.

JOHN PRADOS: NSAM 111, the document Fred is referring to, is Kennedy's formal response to the Taylor-Rostow recommendations.

Why Does Vietnam Become an Important Issue in the Fall of 1961?

It is important in a critical oral history conference to have scholars at the table who approach the events under scrutiny from widely varying perspectives. It was therefore useful to have Tim Naftali involved even though he is not a scholar of the war in Vietnam. He is instead a well-known scholar of U.S.-Soviet relations, of the relationship that evolved between Kennedy and Soviet leader Nikita Khrushchev, and of the high politics of arms control and the mutual U.S.-Soviet concern, in the early 1960s, over the possibility of a crisis between them leading inadvertently to a catastrophic nuclear war. Because of this background, Naftali has long suspected, as he reveals in the following segment, that the U.S. concern over Vietnam during the first year of the Kennedy administration was a decidedly secondary matter, almost a sideshow to the "main event"—U.S.-Soviet relations. So he asks the other participants, many of whom specialize in the war in Vietnam, a question from his perspective: why did Vietnam suddenly seem so important in November 1961? To Naftali, this doesn't quite make sense. The deeply dangerous Berlin crisis was ongoing, the rhetoric regarding the nuclear arms race was heating up, and Castro's Cuba was becoming a tremendous problem in U.S.-Soviet relations. Compared to these problems, Naftali says, Vietnam was not centrally important.

Naftali gets many different answers as the Vietnam War specialists respond: JFK had gone through a very rough first year, and needed to do something positive and tough; he didn't want the "dominoes" to fall in Southeast Asia; the situation was getting very grim very quickly in South Vietnam and needed attention; and having compromised by agreeing to a neutral solution in neighboring Laos, Kennedy needed to show a more forceful response in South Vietnam.

These varied responses provide plenty of perspectives for Tim Naftali to assimilate. But in addition, Jamie Galbraith intervenes to disagree with the entire tenor of the discussion, arguing instead that his father, Ambassador John Kenneth Galbraith, JFK's envoy to New Delhi, was pressed into service by Kennedy to go to South Vietnam as the November 1961 decisions were being made. Why? Specifically, according to Jamie Galbraith, to provide Kennedy with cogent arguments for keeping Vietnam on the back burner and for keeping combat troops out of South Vietnam, and in general to give the president breathing room to deal with issues that (as Galbraith reports his father's story) were both more important and potentially much more tractable than continuing to help the essentially helpless, brutal, corrupt, and incompetent Saigon government fight the Vietcong insurgency. In effect, therefore, Galbraith tells Naftali and the other participants that JFK and his father agreed with Naftali's implied assessment of the salience of the Vietnam issue in November 1961: it really wasn't a top-drawer problem compared, say, to Berlin or Cuba. At least not to Kennedy, though clearly many of his advisers believed it was.

DAVID WELCH: It is worth recalling that none of the principals involved in these decisions thought any of these were good options. Everyone was trying to identify the "least bad" option. I think this was probably also true of Kennedy: he was agonizing over which was the least bad option. Gordon is probably exactly right that, at that particular time in '61, Kennedy does not think that Americanizing the war is the least bad option. He thinks something short of that is less bad. At least provisionally, that was a decision he made. Would he have revisited it? Possibly yes. He did like to wait as long as possible before making hard decisions; that was his style. He was capable of making hard decisions, but he didn't like to do it quickly.

I would like to ask a more general question to help fill in the background: just what portion of Kennedy's time and energy was being spent on Vietnam at this point? Where did this rank on his agenda in '61? Was it so far down on his list that he didn't feel he had given it the time, energy, and attention to make a hard decision yet?

THOMAS HUGHES: I think it was also a case of last resort in 1961. That was a whole year of bad luck, if not failure, for Kennedy: the Bay of Pigs, the Vienna summit, the Berlin Wall. As he was talking to people, he was saying, "I can't take any more defeats this year." That was the rationale for staying with Vietnam.

TIMOTHY NAFTALI: I would argue that shutting the door was never a characteristic of John F. Kennedy's decision making. That doesn't mean that he couldn't make a decision, but he always waited until the last possible moment to make a decision. You name the crisis, and I can give you the example.

I'm interested in why Vietnam is on the table in November 1961. I read in the documents that there is a crisis in September 1961 in South Vietnam.[24] I'd like to know why Taylor was sent in the first place, because what is so odd in this period is that at the same time that the United States is increasing its involvement in South Vietnam, the Soviets are actually backing away. In September 1961 the Soviets are meeting the Pathet Lao and the North Vietnamese. The Pathet Lao and the North Vietnamese are complaining to Moscow that they are not spending enough money to help, and the Soviets are looking for a way out of the Berlin crisis. Someone asked about the percentage: the percentage now I bet is about ten percent on Vietnam in foreign policy at the most, because of Berlin. The Berlin crisis is not over.

FREDRIK LOGEVALL: Which month, Tim?

TIMOTHY NAFTALI: I argue it doesn't matter until '63. You have the 22nd Party Congress, where Khrushchev takes the ultimatum off the table for the moment, but the rhetoric doesn't change.[25] They're still interested in revising Berlin. The Berlin crisis does not end with the Berlin Wall; but that is a different story and conference. Berlin is what's on his mind. [Roswell] Gilpatric has just made the speech to say there is no missile gap . . .

JAMES HERSHBERG: It favors us.

TIMOTHY NAFTALI: Yes, it favors us, but we are still scared enough of the Soviets, and we want to make that clear. This speech, I would argue, was primarily for American consumption, but it certainly had an impact on the Soviets.[26] The Berlin crisis is not yet resolved; Laos is stable for the moment; so what put Vietnam on the table? In the period from September to November 1961, the Soviets are trying to reengage in détente. Khrushchev is sending pen pal letters to Kennedy—private letters. For the first time in history, a Soviet leader is personally writing an American president: "Let's talk about a test ban; let's talk about joint space technology." Why is Vietnam on the table? Why are they making this decision now? The reason the door is left ajar is that Kennedy's mind is on bigger more strategic issues—much more than his advisers.

JOHN PRADOS: Going back, I have to agree with Chet. I think he is exactly right to raise the Vienna summit and then punctuate it by the crisis that reemerges in Berlin and invigorates itself in the fall. Here is Kennedy worried about the Russians, and they are worried about him. He wants to be tough, and here's Vietnam, which started out as this sort of experimental laboratory where they can test their counterinsurgency techniques. He saw it as an opportunity early in his administration where he could put Gilpatric in charge of a committee to come up with new options. They come in with a whole series of new options, and he actually spends most of the year putting new committees back on this issue, expanding and reexamining the options. Gilpatric comes in with a set of recommendations, then he gets the economic advisers with Eugene Staley to come up with economic recommendations for Saigon.[27] In the middle of this, Rostow raises the issue about a bigger and stronger military response, so he sends Taylor and Rostow out to South Vietnam, and they are the ones who come back with the set of recommendations. That is what in fact sets up the set of decisions that he makes in NSAM 111 [**Document 3-5**]. The context is that he's been developing these recommendations all year—not necessarily spending a lot of time on it himself, but it's been coming up repeatedly. There is also the Russian threat expressed in Vienna, and concretized in Berlin. What is the American response going to be? I think that is really the context here.

JAMES BLIGHT: I have a note here from Chet in response to Tim Naftali's question, "why Vietnam in late 1961: Vietnam = Dominoes."

JAMES GALBRAITH: [John] Newman's thesis is that the hyping up of the advisers in South Vietnam in the fall of '61 is tied to the military's failure to successfully insert forces into Laos. This is the context in which Kennedy feels the pressure to put forces somewhere in Vietnam. That is Newman's argument.[28]

FRANCES FITZGERALD: In the context of what was just talked about—this is what surprised me most when I first read the Pentagon Papers in 1971: McNamara calling for 205,000 troops. Now, nobody in the press would have ever thought that the estimates were that huge in 1961. It was just amazing to us. If you look back at it, can you imagine

Kennedy, or any president, saying, "Okay, now we're going to send 200,000-plus troops to Vietnam"? Vietnam? Nobody had ever heard of Vietnam in the U.S. at that time. The military situation was getting worse, but Saigon was not about to fall. There was simply no preparation for it. Why did all these advisers fight for all these troops? Where did that come from, and why did the JCS feel so strongly about this? Normally what the JCS do is say, "Look, you've made a decision: you want to hold on to South Vietnam. This is what you can do about that." But you don't read that in the documents that we have. You hear them saying, "We have to save South Vietnam in order to save Southeast Asia, and this is what we are going to need to do it." They're not giving their professional military advice about options given the strategic situation in Southeast Asia. They are simply saying we need this. Why would they expect that Kennedy would take this? He'd have to be nuts.

JAMES GALBRAITH: That leads directly to the main point I wanted to make. I think the possibility exists that McNamara knew very well that Kennedy would not accept the recommendation for 205,000 troops. 50,000–25,000 might have been negotiable; 205,000, clearly not.

The problem I have with Gordon's thesis is in the suggestion that there was complete unanimity from the advisers, which is clearly not the case. There was a certain adviser who was strongly opposed, as evidenced in the 21 November 1961 cable from New Delhi to JFK in the briefing book.

A time of crisis in our policy on South Vietnam will come when it becomes evident that the reforms we have asked have not come off and that our presently proffered aid is not accomplishing anything. Troops will be urged to back up Diem. It will be sufficiently clear that I think this must be resisted.

Our soldiers would not deal with the vital weakness. They could perpetuate it. They would enable Diem to continue to concentrate on protecting his own position at the expense of countering the insurgency. Last spring, following the vice-president's promise of more aid, proposals for increased and reform [sic] taxes which were well advanced were promptly dropped. The parallel on administrative and political reform could be close.

. . . It will be said that we need troops for a show of strength and determination in the area. Since the troops will not deal with the fundamental faults—since there can't be enough of them to give security to the countryside—their failure to provide security could create a worse crisis of confidence. You will be aware of my general reluctance to move in troops. On the other hand I would note that it is those of us who have worked in the political vineyard and who have committed our hearts most strongly to the political fortunes of the new frontier who worry most about its bright promise being sunk under the rice fields. . . .[29]

That adviser was not in Washington, he was in New Delhi, but his position was very clear: (1) the situation in Vietnam was untenable and (2) troops could not repair it. That adviser was the adviser that Kennedy had known the longest, and with whom he had the most enduring investment of trust. He was the adviser who recommended Robert McNamara for the Defense Department, as McNamara says in his own memoirs.

This cable of 21 November 1961 reflects repeated discussions, including during [Indian Prime Minister Jawaharlal] Nehru's visit earlier that year, as Richard Parker's biography of my father discusses.[30] It is indicative that, when Kennedy responds the next day with NSAM 111 [**Document 3-5**], there are a lot of things in it, but combat troops are not among them. It seems to me, Gordon, that if you would withdraw the presumption of unanimity, or the Beltway bias, it would be a more accurate argument.

GORDON GOLDSTEIN: I may have made too subtle a distinction. I was referring to senior national security advisers. Arguably the ambassador to India was serving in that role, but I was looking at the core group . . .

JAMES GALBRAITH: And I would argue that he was serving in that role.

GORDON GOLDSTEIN: Fair enough.

JAMES BLIGHT: Let's declassify the name of this adviser: it is John Kenneth Galbraith.

MARILYN YOUNG: I would just like to briefly introduce into the discussion the analysis that Gareth Porter has made in his new book. He argues that the military imbalance in favor of the U.S. was so decisive, and so known to the national security bureaucracy, that it permitted a confidence in the ability to take risks. The Soviets were backing away, but that didn't mean that you didn't act: that meant you could act *more*.[31] Keep that in mind as we sort through these issues.

JAMES BLIGHT: Frankie?

FRANCES FITZGERALD: The Soviets may have been backing away, but the Chinese were still there.

MARILYN YOUNG: China was freaked by the possibility of serious American intervention.

FRANCES FITZGERALD: Quite so, but again the issue is, why was the military so anxious to get in there after Korea?

JAMES BLIGHT: I have Fred and Tom Hughes and Jim.

FREDRIK LOGEVALL: This is in response to Tim's question, "Why Vietnam in the fall of '61?" John's answer got to it, but I want to underscore that the main reason is simply that there is growing evidence things are going south. The insurgency is succeeding in a way it hasn't before. That certainly helps to explain why you have a high-profile mission, and why NSAM 111 [**Document 3-5**] is then passed. Fundamentally the answer to your question of why is this on the agenda now in November '61 is that the Vietcong are growing stronger, there are increasing problems with ARVN, and it looks grim.

THOMAS HUGHES: Kennedy, of course, benefited from the missile gap. It is true that he found out after he got into the office, if he didn't know before, that it didn't exist. Nevertheless, on this whole business of maintaining a reputation, Kennedy knew he had something going for him with the missile gap, and he rather enjoyed that. So did his friend Joe Alsop, who kept writing through this whole period how wonderful it was to have this tough president, and Kennedy thought this was terrific.[32]

Kennedy is full of doubts about many courses of action. He is a positioner, and he positions himself equidistantly, frequently, on any number of issues. To weigh against Galbraith on the one hand you've got Alsop, you've got the toughness, the whole disposition towards counterinsurgency. The macho image is there for sure. Kennedy isn't about to relinquish those political assets. He begins 1961 with recommending that everyone in the administration read the Khrushchev speech about wars of liberation, and Rusk, for example, goes around the room and asks, "Where are we going to prove that we are fighting these wars of liberation?" Kennedy regarded the Khrushchev speech as Khrushchev's answer to his own inaugural.[33]

Then it turns out next year there is a new kind of required reading, Barbara Tuchman's *The Guns of August*, which has quite a different message.[34] Kennedy starts seeing miscalculation as the worst thing you can possibly do. So whatever he does, he isn't going to miscalculate. This is an idea he has in his mind. He carried the Munich analogy and anticolonialism in his mind simultaneously, even though they are not very compatible; nevertheless they are there concurrently, and every week or so one or the other comes up.

He wasn't quite as heavily forested on the inside as Franklin Roosevelt was supposed to be, but there were antithetical things in the mental makeup of JFK, and even in his phraseology—that we won't negotiate out of fear, but we won't fear to negotiate, was a typical balanced Kennedy couplet.[35]

JAMES HERSHBERG: Tom's comment about JFK's internal balancing segues precisely into what I want to emphasize. This is also a partial response to Tim's question about "Why Vietnam?" but it also addresses Jamie's and others' questions about why there were demands for such strong action.

We need to keep in mind the parallel track in Laos—not only in '61, but as we move forward—not for the importance or lack of importance of Laos, but for the alternative or the lack of an alternative of neutrality or neutralization, which is always going to be supported by de Gaulle and various other intermediaries. The interesting thing in 1961 is that the only thing JFK and Khrushchev were able to agree on in Vienna is neutrality in Laos. JFK was willing to give that a shot. In terms of his internal relationship within the administration, as well as domestic politics, he had to compensate for that by being willing to be tougher in Vietnam.

THOMAS HUGHES: It was a trade-off.

JAMES HERSHBERG: Exactly, and therefore it is not that mysterious. The people (especially in the military) who were frustrated, who wanted to escalate in Laos, said, "Okay, we have to extract our price for that."

MARILYN YOUNG: Jim, is that right? They wanted to go more into Laos? I remember seeing a document a long time ago in which Roger Hilsman comes home and tells his wife what had happened that day, and he says, "God, we really could go into Laos, but the damn military is scared to do it."[36]

JAMES HERSHBERG: The alternative, Sorensen would say, is that Cuba saved us. The JCS would have been delighted to go into Laos, and they explicitly said, "Well, if the Chinese come in we can get them with nuclear weapons." And Kennedy, as quoted by Sorensen, said, "This was what they were selling me, but after the Bay of Pigs I knew better."[37] I think that internal dynamic is going on, and it is something to keep in mind for future sessions, even as late as Johnson in '65–'66. Is neutrality going to be politically acceptable? Of course, in retrospect, and later on, they would have loved to have gotten it. But at the time, neutrality in Laos is something Kennedy is willing to try in '61, but the eventual and progressive failure of the Laos agreement undermines optimism for neutrality in Vietnam later on.

JAMES GALBRAITH: Just to underscore Jim's point: the danger in Laos was that we would get into a position where we would have to use nuclear weapons to protect ourselves. It seems to me that as soon as Kennedy knew—which he would have known from CORONA in August 1960—that the Soviets did not have an effective deterrent force for our intercontinental ballistic missiles, the nature of the nuclear equation changes.[38] The real danger becomes one of stumbling into a military situation—something that almost happened in Korea—where you have to use nuclear weapons on your own first initiative in order to avoid military disaster. That is part of the discussion over Laos, and it is a constant through the Kennedy and Johnson years. This is absolutely central to Johnson: the care and limitation in the prosecution of the eventual war. He was keen that we not provoke the Russians or the Chinese and put ourselves into a situation where our only recourse is the use of nuclear weapons.

Gordon Goldstein Responds: JFK Decides, the Advisers Resist

Gordon Goldstein now responds to his critics around the conference table who remain unconvinced that JFK had decided once and for all by November 1961 that under no circumstances was he going to send U.S. combat troops to South Vietnam. His response involves reversing the traditional version of the JFK what if on Vietnam. Traditionally, one asks, "Would Kennedy, had he lived and been reelected, been capable of resisting the pressure from his advisers (and the Congress and perhaps even the electorate) to Americanize the war in Vietnam?" Goldstein, however asks the following question, "What conceivable circumstances would have led Kennedy, having already decided decisively in November 1961 against sending U.S. combat troops to South Vietnam, to reverse this decision later on?" (Jamie Galbraith also argues along these lines in this chapter.)

*Goldstein also reports that McGeorge Bundy, when confronted with the key documents from November 1961 bearing on JFK's decisions regarding U.S. combat troops in Vietnam, had no recollection whatever of JFK having been pressured by his advisers to the degree evident in the documents. As Goldstein says, this is quite remarkable, given that Bundy himself was one of the advisers seeking to convince JFK to send at least an initial contingent of several thousand U.S. troops, and eventually to be prepared to send tens of thousands [**Document** 3-3]. Why, one might ask, might Bundy have* *obliterated from memory the discussions of November 1961? Is it because he came down on the opposite side from the president, lost the battle, and would rather not recall the substantial disagreements he continued to have with his boss on Vietnam? Or might Bundy have been more inclined to want to forget the ultimate outcome of LBJ's escalation of the war, which Bundy finally came to support with enthusiastic hawkishness, producing arguably the worst U.S. foreign policy disaster in the history of the country? For whatever reason, as Goldstein reports, Bundy read the documents pertinent to the November 1961 discussions and decisions almost with disbelief.*

Jim Hershberg is, in any event, unconvinced by Goldstein's reversal of the traditional form of the what if. He reasserts his belief that, while JFK clearly was skeptical about an American war in Vietnam, it seems doubtful, when push came to shove as it did for Johnson in late 1964 and early 1965, that even Kennedy could have resisted the push toward a major American war in Southeast Asia. Hershberg does not claim to be absolutely sure JFK would have escalated the war more or less as LBJ did, but he clearly leans toward that conclusion.

In the midst of the Goldstein-Hershberg face-off, Marc Selverstone and Jamie Galbraith clash over the role and importance of the initial pretext suggested by some of Kennedy's hawks for sending the first 8,000 combat troops to South Vietnam: allegedly, to assist the South Vietnamese in their efforts to provide humanitarian relief in the wake of seasonal flooding. Galbraith suggests that, even on this seemingly obscure issue, JFK specifically asked his father, John Kenneth Galbraith, to provide him with arguments as to why it was not necessary to send troops under the guise of flood relief. The elder Galbraith, as it happens, got his start as an economist working on just such problems at the intersection of agriculture and economics. In the passage from the memo from John Kenneth Galbraith to JFK, quoted by Jamie Galbraith, Kennedy is told that such flooding as has occurred in Vietnam is normal, is in fact necessary to fertilize the soil, is something that the Vietnamese have been living with for millennia, and that the president can and should therefore stop thinking about flood relief for South Vietnam altogether. The Vietnamese neither need it nor want it, according to Galbraith, even though the hawks surrounding Kennedy have yet to understand this.

GORDON GOLDSTEIN: Two comments, one in regard to doors being shut or left slightly ajar, and one to return to Fred's important observation about NSAM 111 [**Document 3-5**].

On what JFK decided: there are two aspects to it—what Kennedy decided, and how his advisers respond to it. Was the door shut for JFK? I would grant, theoretically, of course he could take a different position in 1962 or '63, or any time in his presidency. One can't argue that he would not; it is an unknowable. The question I would ask you or others who entertain the possibility that he would have reversed his very pronounced resistance and skepticism is, "Do you know of any evidence in the record to show that he viewed the application of ground combat forces in South Vietnam in a significantly more favorable light at any other point in his presidency?" If that evidence exists I'd like to know about it, because I haven't seen it.

The second point on the advisers goes to Tom's observations: I'm not surprised they don't accept it. They are really pissed off about this, and they are going to whine about it and push back. They continue to do that in the weeks after Kennedy has made his decision, because Kennedy deliberately doesn't want to communicate it, since it is very closely held. He doesn't want this in the press. When the report comes back from Saigon during the Taylor-Rostow mission that they are prepared to make a recommendation to send in combat troops, he instructs Mac Bundy to send them a cable to say, "Zip it up; I don't want to read about this in the papers. I don't want to be pushed into this decision." He is making a conscious effort to contain this and not discuss it. If anyone knows of a comparable lobbying effort among these senior figures—the secretary of defense, the secretary of state, the national security adviser, the Joint Chiefs of Staff—around a combat troop proposal in '62 or '63, I'm interested to know about it. I don't think it exists in a comparable fashion.

On the question of NSAM 111 [**Document 3-5**], I do not dispute Fred's observation that it marks, in a substantive sense, an important escalation of American military operations in South Vietnam. I would make two further observations, however. One is from a realist position: one could predict that President Kennedy, or anyone in his position, would take very robust measures to try to support the independence of a non-communist South Vietnam. They would use a series of measures to arm them, to train them, to give them more dynamic fighting tactics, to reform economic and political administrative issues—you would do anything you could to prop up that government. I think you see that reflected in NSAM 111. What is significant about that directive, however, is what it does not include: the combat troop provision. I believe that Kennedy was prepared to accept several measures to prop up the government, provided that he could maintain the effort below the level of sending in ground combat troops.

Remarkably, Mac Bundy had no recollection at all of the 1961 proposal. He had no recollection of this memo. When I showed it to him, he asked, "What the hell is this swimming pool memo? The other day you asked me in the swimming pool what do I think about sending troops into Vietnam? I think it is a really good idea, let's send in 20–25,000 when needed, and let's get going" [**Document 3-3**]. It is a very glib recommendation to the president about a very serious question, and Bundy was retrospectively appalled at the superficiality of his guidance to the president at that point. He became fascinated with the question of 1961, and then he did what I did—we did it together—we went and we revisited the documentary evidence, and we saw that, coming from multiple angles, there was this powerful, emerging, and ultimately very inclusive consensus to send in ground combat troops to Vietnam in 1961. He had no recollection of this, and that was remarkable to him. He retrospectively ascribed great significance to it, because he saw at that point that he and McNamara and Rusk all thought the odds were against—"probably sharply against"—holding on to South Vietnam without a substantial military deployment [**Document 3-1**].[39]

MARC SELVERSTONE: Responding to Gordon regarding any case in which the issue of ground troops might have been raised again, at least as far as the tapes are concerned: there is nothing that we've been able to detect from '62 to the October decisions in '63, but what is interesting from these tapes is Kennedy's real commitment to winning the war—so much so that you hear him playing with the wording of various memos, putting things in various places, to make it crystal clear that this war needs to be won. Bundy says flat out that the president wants words to make it absolutely clear that our objective is to win the war, first and foremost [**Document 4-4**].[40]

Second, regarding October–November 1961 and the crisis that was confronting the South Vietnamese that Fred and Jim have alluded to, three factors are in play. One is the apprehension that does stem from Laos that they're going to be compromised because of the negotiations. Second is the success of the Vietcong that Fred alluded to, which seems to suggest, in General Taylor's words, that they were outstripping the ability of the ARVN to deal with them. But then you have the third element, which really seems to be the proximate cause for sending Taylor out in the first place: the flooding of the Mekong River. Here there is an element of chance and accident. Were it not for the flood, I'm not sure whether the decision, which resulted in NSAM 111, would have been made. It seems to me that they actually looked to this as an excuse to send Taylor, and for Taylor then to propose the numbers he proposes. It is really this variable that no one could have counted on that forces their hand.

JAMES GALBRAITH: This is on the question of the flood: Kennedy had an agricultural economist who had worked on this subject (I am quoting again from the 21 November 1961 cable to JFK from New Delhi).

> I come now to a lesser miscalculation, the alleged weakening emphasis of the Mekong flood. Floods in this part of the world are an old trap for western non-agriculturists. They are judged by what the Ohio does to its towns. Now as the flood waters recede it is already evident that this flood conforms to the Asian pattern, one repeated every year in India. The mud villages will soon grow again. Some upland rice was drowned because the water rose too rapidly. Nearer the coast the pressure on the brackish water will probably bring an offsetting improvement. Next year's crop will be much better for the silt.[41]

There was no senior adviser in Washington who had that level of expertise.

MARC SELVERSTONE: No, but this wasn't just an economic problem, it was a political and military problem, too. [Ambassador Frederick] Nolting reported hundreds of thousands of people left homeless by the flood, and Rostow, who was concerned about the infiltration problem, saw this as a very, very serious situation . . .

JAMES GALBRAITH: But they did not have degrees in agricultural economics.

MARC SELVERSTONE: No, but they were sensitive to other issues . . .

FREDRIK LOGEVALL: The perception is what matters, rather than the reality.

MARC SELVERSTONE: Galbraith's wasn't the final word that Kennedy heard on this matter.

JAMES HERSHBERG: I want to briefly respond to Gordon; he asked for any evidence we can point to that demonstrates Kennedy's proclivity for sending in ground troops in '62 and '63. Obviously he had none, but that isn't the issue. There is no question that he didn't want to do that. But he also took progressively stronger actions to deepen the American military, political, and economic stake in Vietnam, fully aware, as an intelligent politician, that it would implicate American prestige and progressively make it more difficult to extricate under conditions of what would be obvious international humiliation. In turn, that would enhance the pressures to Americanize. It is ultimately unknowable, because we will never know what Kennedy would have faced in '65.[42] I don't think there is any question that he wouldn't have Americanized before the election. But he took actions, as Fred mentioned, that escalated involvement. He did not send combat troops—he didn't want to send them—but he knew it would be harder to reject that advice later on given the deepening American stake there.

JFK, Counterinsurgency, and the Conflict in Vietnam

In the early 1960s, leaders in Washington began exploring the possible uses of what came to be known as counterinsurgency doctrine. Direct military confrontations between the nuclear-armed superpowers had become, in the minds of many, just too dangerous to pursue, or even to tolerate, as an instrument of foreign and defense policy. This situation was often described as "mutual assured destruction," or "nuclear deterrence." By whatever name, the new reality to be faced was this: each side could absorb a first strike from the other and still deliver a devastating retaliatory strike against the other, resulting (presumably) in the destruction of both societies, and perhaps most of human civilization as well. This unprecedented situation contributed to making the Cold War cold—that is, preventing a shooting war between the forces of the U.S. and the Soviet Union, such as was widely feared shortly after the end of World War II, when the U.S.-Soviet confrontation began in earnest. (Chet Cooper, in the following segment, reminds the participants that this fear of nuclear war was palpable during the Kennedy and Johnson years.) While seeking to avoid a catastrophic nuclear war, the two sides still bitterly opposed each other on a wide range of issues, including who would be dominant in the newly emerging countries that had formerly been colonies of the European powers. This became known in the U.S. as the struggle for the "hearts and minds" of the people, leaders, and fledgling governments of the "Third World" that were not yet capitalist or communist.

It is against this background that we must appreciate JFK's interest in counterinsurgency doctrine. The new wars, in his time, tended to be fought in the Third World by new, postcolonial governments, often allied with the U.S., who struggled to put down communist-inspired insurgencies. Kennedy saw the conflict in Vietnam primarily as a war of this new kind—an irregular conflict involving hit-and-run tactics, political persuasion and co-ercion of the population, and insurgents often fanatically devoted to one or another variant of Marxism-Leninism. Equally important, members of these movements were often funded, even trained, by Soviet and/or Chinese specialists in insurgent warfare.

*John Prados opens the discussion of this topic by arguing that what NSAM 111 [**Document 3-5**], the decision document of November 22, 1961, actually did was to significantly raise the level of commitment of the U.S. to the counterinsurgency efforts already underway in South Vietnam. Prados reminds the other participants that counterinsurgency warfare, whatever else it may involve or imply, is war and it is bloody. Moreover, according to Prados, the Americans advising the South Vietnamese counterinsurgency fighters were killed and wounded in increasing numbers as a result of the November 1961 decisions formalized in NSAM 111. The discussion that follows is driven by an effort to understand whether Kennedy felt the U.S. counterinsurgency advisory effort would suffice to allow the government in Saigon to defeat the communist insurgents. This question, as Marilyn Young points out, will become especially important in 1963, when it becomes clear that the answer is "no"—that the government of President Ngo Dinh Diem will collapse without an infusion of a large number of U.S. combat troops.*

JOHN PRADOS: I want to focus on the larger issue of what are we talking about in NSAM 111 [**Document 3-5**]. We're not just talking about 8,000 troops versus no 8,000 troops, or 8,000 troops versus 205,000 troops, or that the escalation theme was rejected or accepted. In fact, there is an escalation here, and the escalation does involve both combat and U.S. combat troops. NSAM 111 provides for U.S. combat service support to the South Vietnamese Army. That means air assault companies and combat helicopter units. American combat helicopter units arrive in South Vietnam in January 1962. The spike in U.S. combat deaths in South Vietnam starts then. That's when our casualties begin to rise and the number of American advisers in South Vietnam goes from 685 in January 1961 to 2,000 in January 1962 to 11,000 in January 1963. In other words, the effect of NSAM 111 is to put at least as many American combat troops in South Vietnam as were recommended under the Taylor-Rostow recommendation for 8,000 troops. And those Americans are involved in combat. The Joint Chiefs of Staff issue rules of engagement for American combat involvement in South Vietnam in January 1962. We're engaging in combat, not only with these helicopter units, but often with aviation in the form of covert Air Force counterinsurgency units. The effect of NSAM 111 is escalatory. That's its concrete impact.[43]

While I'm at it, let me also talk about the flood. The recommendation was to send 8,000 troops who were supposed to be engineers. One of the arguments raised was, "If we are going to do this at all, why do this silly thing of putting in these engineers that have no real combat value? Let's do something that has real impact." And I think you see that reflected in what happens in NSAM 111.

JAMES BLIGHT: Thank you, John. It is interesting how we are weaving between what was decided, and what may have been decided later on. Chet Cooper next.

CHESTER COOPER: I have three disparate observations. First, on the recommendation by Rostow and Taylor: Jamie, your father, with all due respect, was not the only one who thought it was a scam. It was a transparent ploy. It was never taken very seriously.

JAMES BLIGHT: What was the scam?

CHESTER COOPER: The business that if we sent troops over there, the guys would actually be helping with the flood.

Second, I think we should recognize that the domino theory was taken very seriously by an awful lot of people. Laos is for all practical purposes out of the action now. If Vietnam is next, then comes Thailand, and it goes all the way to Malaya—and some people would say Singapore, and Italy, and then NATO would be in danger. [Laughter.] I know, I know, it seems funny now, even to me. But back then, this was considered very serious stuff. They—we—actually *believed* a lot of these things.

Third is a more general point. As we talk about what Kennedy is thinking about and what is recommended to him, we should remember that this is at the height of the Cold War. People were building bomb shelters in my neighborhood. People were really scared. Most of you people here are too young to remember this. I can remember talking with some of my colleagues in the CIA about what would happen if you knew there was going to be a nuclear war, how would you spend your last two days? This was lunchtime conversation. I can remember emergency drills. I was locked up in a cave in the West Virginia hills for four or five days. That was the atmosphere.

MARILYN YOUNG: What? You were locked up in a cave?

CHESTER COOPER: Not locked up, exactly . . .

MARILYN YOUNG: No, but you were in a cave? Doing what?

THOMAS BLANTON: It was an exercise in emergency preparedness.

FRANCES FITZGERALD: He was an important guy. Only the important ones were allowed in the caves. [Laughter.]

CHESTER COOPER: Important? Hardly. The point is that what we've been talking about was done against a background of great concern and worry. These decisions weren't made under an ordinary set of circumstances. If something happened in the Soviet Union that was good, we worried. If something bad happened there, we had a good day. It was that kind of climate. And I think these discussions have to keep in mind the context of the kind of concerns that people in Washington and across the country had at the time.

TIMOTHY NAFTALI: I want to get a sense of the point when push comes to shove on the Vietnam issue for Kennedy. Is November '61 a period when push comes to shove? That's why I ask, "Why then?" Did he have a sense of crisis on Vietnam? Is that why he sends Taylor to Vietnam? I ask this because I think we are going to find tomorrow, and when we deal with the later period, that we're going to have to ask ourselves how much of a crisis Vietnam is for Kennedy, and try to understand his terms of reference. Gordon raised an important point about the nature of this struggle. Is Kennedy primarily seeing this as a counterinsurgency problem, or as a conventional warfare problem? When I read these memos, it seems that Taylor is describing this as a counterinsurgency problem: Khrushchev is using a new kind of aggression. McNamara seems to think of this as more of a conventional issue. He says it wouldn't be enough to send just an intelligence team and 8,000 men; we have to really start thinking about six divisions. Where is Kennedy in this? Does Kennedy see Vietnam as a test of a new kind of warfare for the United States? I don't know, but I think it is worth thinking it through, because the implications of a counterinsurgency strategy are different from the implications of a conventional warfare strategy. Are we seeing here the birth of a counterinsurgency test case, with Vietnam as the central piece in the fall of '61? When we get to '63, we have to ask if we've succeeded in this new venture, and it may be time to think about conventional forces, because we're not doing too well. I don't know. I'd like to hear from others who know more about this. To what extent is Vietnam a test case for counterinsurgency? To what extent has Kennedy signed on to it, and to what extent does he see a crisis in Vietnam? How wobbly does he think the Vietnam domino is in the fall '61?

I can tell you based on everything else he's doing he's really more focused on Berlin at this time. I'm a little skeptical that this matters that much to him.

JAMES BLIGHT: Thank you.

CHESTER COOPER: Don't forget that the Green Berets were JFK's baby.

TIMOTHY NAFTALI: Yes, I think he believes in counterinsurgency. I'm just wondering how much Vietnam mattered to him in the fall of '61.

THOMAS HUGHES: I was in contact with Roger Hilsman throughout this whole period. Hilsman gets to know Kennedy very well in 1961, well before Vienna.[44] Kennedy is calling on the phone frequently, talking about guerrilla warfare and Burma. Roger goes to the White House and Kennedy is so impressed that he sends him out to Vietnam in early '62. Kennedy is personally involved; he is fascinated with the whole idea [of counterinsurgency], and I think he thinks of it as a way to get out of these other problems with the JCS and the big troops issue. It keeps him in the military framework.

Bobby is already keeping a green beret on his desk in Washington at this point. Bobby emerges as the president's foreign policy confidant during this period. He is involved in Cuba operations as well, so he is full of counterinsurgency. I think it is real. I think JFK took time out from Berlin. I think he compartmentalized his life and took time out for lots of different things.

TIMOTHY NAFTALI: Some presidents—Eisenhower, for example—used covert action as a way of getting away from the tough questions of using force. Kennedy sees counterinsurgency as another way around.

THOMAS HUGHES: Covert action as well.

JAMES HERSHBERG: This is exactly the same week that he is getting going with Operation MONGOOSE.[45]

TIMOTHY NAFTALI: MONGOOSE, yes, with [General Edward] Lansdale.

JAMES BLIGHT: On the importance of counterinsurgency, I have Frankie, Fred, Marilyn, and Jamie.

FRANCES FITZGERALD: First of all, in some sense there is no difference between counterinsurgency and conventional warfare, because you have to use conventional troops in order to fight the insurgency, whether the troops are Vietnamese or American. We're doing the same thing in Iraq right now. Secondly, what interests me is what Kennedy really thought about the effectiveness of his advisers, and also about the longer-term prospects of winning the war. I think Marc brought this up. Kennedy is talking about winning the war, and so on, but he's been told by the JCS that it will take 205,000 troops—so why is he so optimistic at this point? It is an important question if we are going to talk about what he might have done.

FREDRIK LOGEVALL: In answer to Frankie's last question, I think the measures he agreed to on November 22nd [Document 3-5] that led to the escalation that we are taking about did show some signs of success in the first half of 1962, and into the summer. As a result, there is a period of relative optimism in the spring of 1962. This is something we will come back to tomorrow in talking about the origins of the withdrawal idea. The lesser measures he agreed to in the fall of '61 do allow him to believe that this is not only something that we need to win, but something that we *can* win, even without using regular ground troops.

Just quickly on Tim's first question about the importance of Vietnam to Kennedy in the grand scheme of things: my sense from looking at the agenda items, and also from looking at what is actually discussed at the highest levels of the administration, is that Vietnam becomes important in day-to-day terms in July–August 1963, and it will be for the next ten years. What you have before then—including in November '61—are periods of attention. For a week or two it is big, but I think otherwise you are quite right, it is not as important as some of the other issues.

TIMOTHY NAFTALI: I want to know why it spiked in November.

FREDRIK LOGEVALL: The spike is in part because the situation is dire. You have a high-profile team out there, they come back, and they've got a recommendation. But I think only in the summer of '63 does it become a consistently high-profile issue.

JAMES BLIGHT: Thank you. Marilyn?

MARILYN YOUNG: Maybe that's the issue: it is going badly in Vietnam in 1961:

On counterinsurgency: although I agree with you, Frankie, fiscally, there is a difference between big unit warfare and the kinds of things that are approved in NSAM 111, which amount to an increase in counterinsurgency efforts. There is a brief moment where it goes well, and then by '63 things really go sour. Then the question of conventional troops comes up, because the counterinsurgency isn't working. It's not that it is not tried or considered, it's just not working. At least, it's not working at the level of commitment necessary, and I don't think it would have worked anyhow. But that's not the point. It wasn't working. There is a sense of crisis that there will have to be something more—and then the Buddhist crisis comes into all this as well.[46]

Combat Troops Versus Advisers in Combat: A Firebreak for JFK?

Did JFK believe the war in Vietnam could be won by the South Vietnamese with training, equipment, and other counterinsurgency-related assistance from the U.S.? Jamie Galbraith and Gordon Goldstein do not think so. In the conversation that follows, each declares his belief that Kennedy perceived the difference between military advisers and combat troops as an absolute firebreak. This was why, they believe, Kennedy was willing to support that part of the Taylor-Rostow Report of November 1961 that called for a substantial increase in many aspects of the U.S. "training function" in South Vietnam—advisers and equipment, including helicopters and attack aircraft—while at the same time he was also seemingly unequivocal in his opposition to the sending of regular U.S. combat troops. According to Galbraith and Goldstein, JFK was simply determined not to head down that slippery slope of escalation leading ultimately to a takeover of the war by the U.S. armed forces.

*Their views, however, are not unanimously endorsed by the other participants, some of whom mount their own version of an insurgency against the view that Kennedy believed that an impenetrable firebreak divided advisers from combat troops. The problem is described by John Prados: the document that Kennedy signed—NSAM 111 [**Document 3-5**]—gave a green light to all sorts of operations involving combat for U.S. personnel, no matter what label one might wish to apply to the U.S. forces in South Vietnam. They were flying combat missions. They were taking casualties in increasing numbers following, and because of, what was approved by JFK in NSAM 111. The disagreement is pointed and very sharp. In fact, much rides on one's view of this issue. For if JFK believed a firebreak existed, more or less as described by Goldstein and Galbraith, and JFK also believed the war must be won or lost within the confines of counterinsurgency warfare, then it is obvious that if Kennedy had lived, he would not have authorized anything like the massive escalation of the war that occurred under Johnson. If, however, one believes that the distinction between advisers and combat personnel was not ironclad in Kennedy's view, then it is possible to imagine Kennedy moving incrementally, much as Johnson would do in 1964–1965, to an authorization of large-scale combat units as the Saigon government neared collapse and as the communist insurgency seemed on the verge of conquering the whole of South Vietnam.*

JAMES GALBRAITH: I don't believe there is any convincing evidence that Kennedy is at any point persuaded that the training missions would be successful by themselves. He is pessimistic about this all the way through. That pessimism is rooted more than a decade earlier. The passage to read is [Daniel] Ellsberg's discussion with Bobby Kennedy in the mid-1960s, when Bobby makes the point that Jack would never have put in combat troops, and Ellsberg asks, "Well, what makes you so smart?" and Bobby says, "Because we were there in the early 1950s." Kennedy came away from that, having met with the American officers and French officers, persuaded that this was not a war you won by military means.[47] And he did not change that view. His willingness to do certain things, or to concede the training missions, was his way of holding short of his self-imposed limit, his bedrock assumption: no combat troops. Later, for Johnson, it was no nuclear weapons.

MARILYN YOUNG: Can we just underline John Prados's point that there may not have been combat troops, but there were American troops who engaged in combat? You can read David Marr about this.[48] The U.S. was flying helicopter missions, using napalm, and killing people in South Vietnam in this very period where nothing is supposedly going on.

GORDON GOLDSTEIN: But the number killed only amounted to 108.

MARILYN YOUNG: I'm not talking about American dead, I'm talking about who we were killing out there. I just want you to remember that.

GORDON GOLDSTEIN: I'm not making light of that. In terms of evaluating the American commitment, one very powerful measurement is the number of American casualties, and putting aside John's statement—

JOHN PRADOS: It is a qualitative statement. The question is, "Are men fighting?" Is combat taking place? Yes it is. End of story. The question of casualties is secondary.

JAMES GALBRAITH: No, I think the issue has got to be, is there a qualitative distinction between a combat mission and a training mission? The answer to that is very clearly yes. We have to make that distinction.

MARILYN YOUNG: [to Galbraith] You think they weren't fighting?

JOHN PRADOS: The answer is right here in NSAM 111 [**Document 3-5**]: engaging in combat service support. Let's have someone who served in these administrations comment.

MARILYN YOUNG: You can read the memoirs of the men who were fighting at this time.

FRANCES FITZGERALD: Read Neil Sheehan; read David Halberstam.[49]

MARILYN YOUNG: Read David Marr.[50]

GORDON GOLDSTEIN: To put it differently, if Kennedy had continued along that course, limiting the American commitment to the types of activities that were prescribed in NSAM 111, how would the war have turned out at that point? You would have confronted the same question about whether in '65 he is going to escalate with ground combat troops or whether he is going to withdraw. I just don't see how this type of support is really meaningful to the distinction.

JOHN PRADOS: Listen, I quite agree with you, Gordon, that our casualty rate would have remained low and would have continued to rise at a low level, but as a matter of military practice—as a matter of engagement—you ask any officer of the U.S. Army if he was flying a combat mission when he was flying helicopters to insert South Vietnamese troops into a combat zone for combat operations, and he would tell you yes. As a matter of functional reality, he would be right: this was a combat mission. We called it a training function, but our labeling of this as a training function in 1961 and 1962 was for public consumption.

JAMES GALBRAITH: No, it provided a very important firebreak between what Kennedy was prepared to do and what he was not prepared to do. Yes, he was prepared to have some American soldiers engaging in combat—usually alongside the South Vietnamese, as you said, although perhaps not always. But he was not prepared to have the introduction of the large-scale combat units that would have conducted the fighting by Americans alone. This is a clear distinction that Gordon made.

JOHN PRADOS: Wait a minute . . .

JAMES GALBRAITH: The fact that the foot soldiers were doing some fighting and taking some losses cannot obliterate that distinction. It continues to be treated right up through 1963 and after as a training mission, because fundamentally that's what it was.

DAVID WELCH: You are *all* correct!
   Of course Kennedy sees a "firebreak" between advisers and combat troops. His problem is trying to get the Vietnamese to win their war. He can't have Americans look like they are doing the actual fighting. He wants ARVN to be on the pointy end of the stick. But to train the Vietnamese, and get them to win their war, he has to let "American advisers" push them, pull them, get them in the field, tell them what to do, and sometimes be the pointy end of the stick themselves.

THOMAS BLANTON: And provide the high-end firepower.

DAVID WELCH: Right. So of course Kennedy represents it as a firebreak. But from the perspective of the U.S. military, it's not so clear.

Soldiers are volunteering for assignment in Vietnam because they see it as a combat opportunity. In the field, it's just not a significant distinction. So different groups have different perceptions on this issue.

Trying to Read JFK's Mind in November 1961

The discussion of November 1961 concludes with a fascinating series of exchanges responding to janet Lang's invitation to the participants to try to "read Kennedy's mind" with regard to what the president thought he was doing by affixing his signature to NSAM 111. Broadly speaking, the conversation is really about whether it is conceivable that President John F. Kennedy approached the responsibilities of his office strictly in pragmatic, situational terms, with virtually any sort of decision being at least theoretically possible, on the one hand; or, on the other, whether with regard to the possibility of U.S. combat troops being sent to South Vietnam Kennedy had, for various reasons, reached a firm negative decision, based at least as much on deeply held principles as on an assessment of the particular situation he confronted in South Vietnam. janet Lang mentions the multilateralism and foreign-policy minimalism displayed by Kennedy in his public address in Seattle on November 16, 1961, the day following the showdown with his advisers over the issue of sending U.S. combat troops to South Vietnam [Document 3-6]. The implication she draws from the speech is that the individual giving that speech is highly unlikely to intervene in a Third World country to anything like the extent desired by his advisers. Gordon Goldstein, in addition, finds abundant evidence in the minutes of the November 15 National Security Council meeting to support the view that Kennedy already had worked out a detailed argument as to why large-scale U.S. military intervention in South Vietnam would be self-destructive [Document 3-4].[51]

Scholarly reactions to the minutes of what appears to be that decisive meeting on November 15, 1961, mirror those among the participants in the Musgrove conference—the principal fault line is between those who see Kennedy as merely temporizing, putting off a decision, and seeking to avoid political difficulties, on the one hand; and, on the other, those who see in the minutes of the meeting a reflection of Kennedy's mindset on Vietnam, and his willingness to stonewall even his most hawkish advisers on Vietnam policy. For example, the American military historian Robert Buzzanco has written that Kennedy's "critical ruminations amounted to little more than devil's advocacy,"[52] *a claim strenuously disputed by British historian Sir Lawrence Freedman. Buzzanco's interpretation, according to Freedman, "ignores all the corroborative evidence on Kennedy's thought processes and is best seen as what happens when an implausible thesis meets an unpalatable fact.*"[53] *According to Buzzanco's interpretation, therefore, the minutes fail to provide evidence that Kennedy would not have Americanized the war in Vietnam. They tell us merely that Kennedy didn't want to decide if he didn't have to. Freedman, on the other hand, believes those minutes give us as clear a picture as we are ever likely to get of Kennedy's real intention, which was to not commit American combat troops in an effort to "save" South Vietnam.*

Jim Hershberg agrees with Buzzanco. In his view, neither Kennedy nor any president likes to make decisions that are simply unalterable, period, independent of the particular circumstances he faces. Hershberg says that he cannot imagine Kennedy simply ignoring Saigon collapsing, South Vietnam being overrun with communist insurgents, and U.S. politicians calling for a forceful military intervention—all of which, according to Hershberg, JFK would have faced not later than early 1965. Hershberg believes that in such circumstances, JFK would not have stood by idly and done nothing simply because he had made a certain decision in the fall of 1961 not to intervene. As usual, Jamie Galbraith disagrees more or less completely with Jim Hershberg. Galbraith hints here at something he will emphasize at length later on: he believes JFK has made exactly that decision that Hershberg cannot imagine him making, and he believes Kennedy has articulated that decision to his colleagues in the November 15 meeting referred to in this conversation by Gordon Goldstein and in the Seattle speech emphasized by janet Lang. This does not mean, however, that the advisers listened carefully to what Kennedy told them. As we have noted, McGeorge Bundy, a notable hawk before, during, and after the November 15 discussions, could not even remember years later that such a discussion had actually occurred.

A very short summary of that principled perspective and ironclad decision postulated by Galbraith might go something like this: the problem in South Vietnam is a communist insurgency; this type of conflict cannot be decisively affected by the insertion of a foreign army, no matter how large or well-trained; the government of President Ngo Dinh Diem is incapable of winning its battle against the insurgents, and any successor is also likely to be unsuccessful; therefore, the U.S. will do what it can to assist the South Vietnamese in what is almost surely a lost cause, but it will not, under any foreseeable circumstances, take over the fight from the South Vietnamese. That is more or less the view of Galbraith and Goldstein. But did Kennedy, in November 1961 or later, actually reach such an irreversible determination of what was to be done and what was not to be done with regard to Vietnam? If he did, was his determination strong enough to withstand the

*domestic political pressure that would surely have been applied in the di-
rection of intervention, of "saving" South Vietnam, if he had returned un-
harmed from Dallas in November 1963? These are key issues that carry
from this discussion of November 1961 over to the discussion of October–
November 1963, which follows in the next chapter.*

jANET LANG: I just want to pick up on what David said. I do think the
issue is, what did Kennedy think he was doing at that point? But to me
the idea of clear distinctions is a first cousin to the tooth fairy. I don't see
clear distinctions out there. This is really complicated, and it is fluid.

One of the things I would like to get our group to think about, and to
share, is related to the sensibilities of Kennedy. I was absolutely struck
by some of the memos Mac Bundy writes to him, not only in tone, but
in substance. He writes one right before the meeting on November 15th
where he basically says, "I don't think you are taking this seriously;
you're not putting enough time into this. Let me remind you, Mr.
President . . ."—and he really keeps coming at him [**Document 3-3**].
Certainly that tells me something interesting about Kennedy. He toler-
ates this. He doesn't say, "Mac, you send me another one of those
memos and you're back at Harvard." Ken Galbraith's letters to him are
just as phenomenal.[54]

You have a guy who, at a minimum, is comfortable with opposing views
and internal debate. He doesn't take account of who's on either side of
the debate. He's happy being the minority who overrules everybody. That
is interesting to me. I'd like to know if you think that changed over the
course of his presidency.

Finally, on that November 15th meeting, the buildup to it with the
memos, the meeting itself, and the aftermath: to me that speech he gives
on November 16th at the University of Washington in Seattle is striking
[**Document 3-6**]. As Gordon pointed out, he is very clear with his associates about what he wanted reported in the press. This whole issue of
what Kennedy decided and what other people knew about it is really
key—but here in this November 16th speech in Seattle, he touches on
some interesting ideas about multilateralism and who we're fighting. On
the insurgency as terrorism, Kennedy says, "We're fighting a terrorist
enemy, but we can't use the same kinds of tactics they do; that might
mean in the short run it looks like we will lose, but you have to have
confidence that in the long run we will win" [**Document 3-6**].[55] That is
all out there for the public. So it's no secret that Kennedy's approach to
foreign policy generally, and the problem of communist insurgencies—
like the one in South Vietnam—is far from hawkish. It is a complex mix
of considerations of national interest, history, and even ethical issues.

So as we're concluding this session, I wonder if I could get some of you to help us "read Kennedy's mind" a little bit.

GORDON GOLDSTEIN: In the November 15th NSC meeting we have Kennedy on the record saying exactly how he summarizes the situation. This is the quote from the notes in the meeting; Kennedy is comparing the Vietnam War with the Korean War, and he says this: "The conflict in Vietnam is more obscure and less flagrant. . . . [I]n such a situation the United States needs even more the support of allies in such an endeavor as Vietnam in order to avoid sharp domestic partisan criticism as well as strong objections from other nations of the world. The President said that he could even make a rather strong case against intervening in an area 10,000 miles away against 16,000 guerrillas with a native army of 200,000, where millions have been spent for years with no success. . . . The President compared the obscurity of the issues in Vietnam to the clarity of the positions in Berlin, in contrast of which could even make leading Democrats wary of proposed activities in the Far East" [**Document 3-4**].

jANET LANG: I forgot to comment on Jamie's point about Bobby Kennedy's conversation with Ellsberg about what JFK thought, in which Bobby claims that JFK learned from the French experience in Indochina. I don't know; I remain agnostic about that. But I do think it is important to appreciate the difference between Kennedy and his advisers. Early in the Kennedy administration, Mac Bundy—not the dumbest adviser a president has ever had—has some correspondence with his father, who tells Mac something like, "I'm getting really nervous about all this stuff with Vietnam. This is bad. Are we really in jeopardy? What about what Bernard Fall has said?" Bundy writes back something like, "Yes, I've read Bernard Fall, but that's the French; we're the Americans." So Mac Bundy, at least, is not seeing the relevance of the French experience that his boss evidently did.[56]

GORDON GOLDSTEIN: And Mac says to Kennedy in a memo that Laos after 1954 was never really ours; Vietnam is, and wants to be [**Document 3-3**].

JAMES HERSHBERG: Whether there was a firebreak in Kennedy's mind is something I have worked on. Since the essence of this conference is about what if speculation, I think we need to tackle the nub of the issue, which is to project a situation in which Kennedy lives in November '63. There is a natural progression of the advisory mission to maintain the status quo at least through the '64 election, and then at some point in '65 Kennedy has to face the day when there is collapse of the South Vietnamese government's authority and a military collapse. Kennedy would be faced with the question of what to do. Do you simply let it happen? Or, since you need to introduce additional American forces to cover a withdrawal, do you respond to the desperate appeals of those South Vietnamese anti-communists who are willing to put up a last-ditch effort? Does he let it all go down the drain, or does he say, "We've seen this in our own lives in multiple disaster situations; we have to put in people to cover withdrawal anyway, so let's let them back it up." Think of the dynamic of a South Vietnamese collapse; I think Kennedy would have to approach that on its own terms at that time. He wouldn't just say, "I made this decision in '61, so that's that."

JAMES BLIGHT: Fred Logevall.

FREDRIK LOGEVALL: The only thing I would say to Jim is that I like the way the conference is set up. It seems that what is most helpful is if we try to avoid the what if now. What is helpful is to talk in terms of '61 and what it means at that time. I think we should discuss the implications to some degree, but maybe we should not go to the what if yet.

JAMES HERSHBERG: But the question is whether a decision was made and existed in Kennedy's mind that was unalterable. It was a decision he didn't need to make, so why would he make it?

JAMES GALBRAITH: There is nothing desperate in Vietnam in '61. The South Vietnamese government is not in imminent danger of collapsing, but even if it was, the consequences are not desperate from the American point of view. We are perfectly willing to entertain the possibility that, for example, the South Vietnamese government would just strike a deal and Ho Chi Minh would respect it. There is not a large North Vietnamese army in South Vietnam at that time. There is a substantial South Vietnamese army, it is possible that something could have been worked out that could have provided Kennedy with a political cover that he might be willing to accept. So it is not at all clear that leaving at that point is as costly as some think.

JAMES HERSHBERG: We'll come back to that in '63 when that becomes a possibility.

JAMES BLIGHT: There was a comment made about Diem; we have at this table a personal acquaintance of Diem's named Chet Cooper.[57] Chet, what did Diem think was going on?

jANET LANG: Did he perceive that there was a difference between combat troops and advisers?

CHESTER COOPER: I don't think he made one. Diem wouldn't have known the difference: American troops were there. To some extent he wanted them there, and to some extent he didn't.

JAMES BLIGHT: And on that note we're out of time. A good start! We will meet for dinner at seven, and then reconvene tomorrow to consider what, if anything, Kennedy decided in 1963.

"Action: The Secretary ... stated that the phase out of U.S. personnel is too slow and that we should try to get U.S. numbers down to a minimum level earlier than FY '66"

(Secretary of Defense Conference, May 1963)

"It should be possible to withdraw the bulk of the U.S. personnel by that time [the end of 1965]."

(Report to the President on the Situation in South Vietnam, October 1963)

". . . in the autumn 1963, Robert McNamara and Max Taylor come back from Vietnam with a certain date of when we were going to withdraw troops. Six months later [when Johnson is president], the same two went to Vietnam and come back saying we needed more troops."—Chester L. Cooper, Musgrove conference

CHAPTER 4

What JFK Decided: October–November 1963

Marc Selverstone: JFK and His Advisers on Tape, October 2, 1963

In the period immediately following the flurry of activity in November 1961, Vietnam diminished in importance as an issue in U.S. national security. One reason was that the measures authorized by JFK in NSAM 111 on November 22, 1961, produced a temporary turnaround in the fortunes of the Saigon government [**Document 3-5**]. *In fact, 1962 was a year of relative optimism in Washington about the prospects for South Vietnam, even though Vietcong attacks continued and the insurgents continued to grow in numbers via recruitment in the South and via infiltration from North Vietnam.*

There were also other reasons why Vietnam receded from page-one significance between November 1961 and the late spring of 1963, when it returned with a vengeance. In 1962, the Cold War was heating up faster elsewhere than it was in Southeast Asia. The dangerous issue of the status of West Berlin, and the new fact of life, the Wall dividing East Berlin from West Berlin, produced periodic crises requiring the full attention of JFK and his advisers. Berlin was supremely dangerous. Within several hundred kilometers of Berlin in West Germany was a substantial portion of the tactical nuclear arsenal of NATO. (The nuclear warheads, according to the terms of the NATO treaty, could only be released from storage bunkers and mated with their launchers on the authority of the U.S. president.) Within roughly the same distance eastward from Berlin were several million members of the Soviet Red Army and the armies of Moscow's Eastern European allies. In effect, Germany, East and West, were still unofficially occupied countries, even though World War II had ended nearly two decades before.

Any war beginning within the confines of Germany would almost certainly, therefore, become catastrophic in short order. For while the massive Soviet conventional forces would presumably overwhelm the tiny NATO contingent in Berlin almost immediately, NATO commanders had at their disposal hundreds of tactical and theater nuclear weapons that they believed they could count on using to avoid defeat in Central Europe.[1]

As it happened, of course, the most dangerous crisis of 1962, and of the entire Cold War, did not derive from the Berlin tinderbox but from an unexpected source: the secret and deceptive Soviet deployment of nuclear missiles to their new ally, Fidel Castro's Cuba, in the summer and early autumn of that year. For many months, the Cuban missile crisis was the number one issue for the senior U.S. national security advisers to JFK.

Then on May 8, 1963, Vietnam rose once again to the top of JFK's foreign and defense policy agenda. The Saigon government led by President Ngo Dinh Diem and his brother, the head of secret police Ngo Dinh Nhu, ordered the police to break up a gathering of Buddhists in Hue, in the northern sector of South Vietnam. The Buddhists had gathered to observe the birthday of the Buddha. Diem and Nhu, fervent Roman Catholics, had forbidden the celebrants in Hue to fly Buddhist flags. When the flags were spotted by the police, they moved in to break up the celebration. In the mayhem that followed, seven people were killed by an explosion, and the event made headlines all over the world. JFK was disturbed that a U.S. ally—indeed, virtually a U.S. dependent—would act so brutally and brazenly to massacre innocents in Hue, an act that implicated Washington in the eyes of much of the world.

The situation went from bad to much worse the following month, when Buddhist monks began a series of highly publicized ritual suicides via self-immolation to protest the regime of Diem and Nhu. On June 27, Kennedy replaced his ambassador in Saigon, foreign service officer Frederick Nolting, who had been a strong supporter of Diem, with a major political figure, Republican presidential hopeful Henry Cabot Lodge. Kennedy dispatched Lodge to Saigon with instructions to bring the deteriorating situation, and Diem and his family, under control. But things got worse, not better, through the summer and into the fall of 1963. Various rumors circulated in Saigon, some involving a possible coup against Diem and Nhu, others suggesting that Nhu, with Diem's approval, was seeking to cut a deal with Hanoi for some sort of coalition government in Saigon that would order the U.S. out of South Vietnam (and, in effect, cede control of all of Vietnam, North and South, to Hanoi). Officials in the State Department and in the CIA station in Saigon began discussing the possibility of sponsoring a military coup against Diem and Nhu.[2] *And in late September, Kennedy sent*

Defense Secretary Robert McNamara and General Maxwell D. Taylor, the chairman of the Joint Chiefs of Staff, to South Vietnam with orders to report back to him in early October with their findings and recommendations [**Document 4-3**].

Some of the post-Saigon discussions between Kennedy, McNamara, and Taylor, along with several other senior officials, were secretly audiotaped by JFK, and have only recently been deciphered and made available to scholars. The discussion of the pivotal events of fall 1963 are introduced below via one such audiotape from the morning of October 2, just after the McNamara-Taylor group has returned to Washington. At least seven voices can be identified in the conversation: JFK, McNamara, Taylor, National Security Adviser McGeorge Bundy, his brother Assistant Secretary of Defense William Bundy, CIA Director John McCone, and Director of the Bureau of Management and Budget David Bell. A surprise awaits anyone who may have hoped that the existence of Kennedy audiotapes on Vietnam would clarify, once and for all, the mystery regarding JFK's intentions for Southeast Asia. They do not, as is demonstrated by the vigorous, sometimes volatile, discussion at the Musgrove conference that follows the recording. In particular, the following questions dominate the discussion: Is Kennedy determined to win the war against the communist insurgency in South Vietnam or not? Is McNamara trying to force his proposal on JFK to withdraw 1,000 U.S. service personnel by the end of 1963 or not? Are McNamara and Bundy lined up against each other or not? And if they are, with whom does the president seem to side?

The tape is introduced by Marc Selverstone of the Presidential Recordings Project of the Miller Center at the University of Virginia (UVA).

MARC SELVERSTONE: The date that we are going to flag is the morning of October 2nd. General Maxwell Taylor is briefing the president on the war.[3] We also have transcripts of the conversations from the morning and evening of 2 October, when they are trying to decide on the wording of the statement that [Press Secretary] Salinger is going to read to journalists following the NSC meeting that night.[4] We also have material from October 5th, when they're deciding on what instructions to send Ambassador Lodge in Saigon. To reiterate: the following conversation occurred on October 2nd, 1963, 11:00 to 11:55 a.m.

> **President Kennedy:** Do you think this thousand reduction can really . . .
>
> **McNamara:** Yes, sir. We—
>
> **President Kennedy:** Is that going to be an assumption that it's going well, but if it doesn't go well [*unclear*]?

McNamara: No. No, sir. One of the major premises—two [*unclear*] we have. First, we believe we can complete the military campaign in the first three corps in '64 and the fourth corps in '65.[5] But secondly, if it extends beyond that period we believe we can train the Vietnamese to take over the essential functions and withdraw the bulk of our forces. And this thousand is in conjunction with that and I have a list of the units here that are represented by that thousand.

President Kennedy: Bob, have they—

McGeorge Bundy: What's the point of doing it?

McNamara: We need a way to get out of Vietnam. This is a way of doing it. And to leave forces there when they're not needed, I think, is wasteful and it complicates both their problems and ours.

President Kennedy: Why can't the North Vietnamese continue to just supply? Do you think there's a real limitation on their supply—?

McNamara: Yes. And as the [South] Vietnamese patrol the countryside and shut off the food supply of the Vietcong it becomes more and more difficult for them to live. This is particularly true in the north.

Taylor: And this is a costly, painful operation for them. They must be getting [*unclear*].

President Kennedy: Viet [*unclear*]—you mean the North Vietnamese?

Unidentified: [*Unclear*] why is it so costly?

Taylor: Simply because of the losses they're taking and the fact that they're—

McGeorge Bundy: Their losses are locals.

Unidentified: Yes.

Taylor: Their strategic hamlets are building up and the recruiting locally is running out, at least [*unclear*].

McNamara: Well, when you say "costly," it's not necessarily costly to North Vietnam in terms of money. But it's costly to the Vietcong.

William Bundy?: Oh yes, I understand that.

McNamara: In terms of lives.

William Bundy?: [*Unclear*] was not clear it was costly to the North Vietnamese.

Taylor: Well, I think that the ability to get any of them to come down to [*unclear*].

Unidentified: Yeah.

Taylor: We could find very little proof of infiltration, except the farms. We found in the Delta [*unclear*] heavier weapons are coming in.

McGeorge Bundy: Where are they coming?

Unidentified: [*Unclear.*]

Taylor: [*presumably pointing to a map*] Down the Mekong [*unclear*], over by [*unclear—*"C"/ the sea]. [*Unclear*] that's here.

McGeorge Bundy: Right.

John McCone: [*Unclear*] the bayous, they get down into the Delta, into the bayous [*unclear*].

Taylor: They do. And we're seeing [*unclear*] caliber machine guns and recoilless rifles and things of that sort.

McCone: It's hard to do the strategic hamlets down there because there isn't very much land down there.

Taylor: [*Unclear.*]

McCone: They're all strung up and down the [*unclear:* valley].

Taylor: That's the construction problem.

McCone: Right . . .

McGeorge Bundy: The question that occurs to me is whether we want to get publicly pinned to a date? [*Unclear*] 6a.[6]

McNamara: Well, that goes back to paragraph two, Mac.

McGeorge Bundy: Yes, it does. It's . . .

Taylor: Well, it's something we debated very strongly.

McNamara: Yeah.

Taylor: I think it is a major question. I will just say this, that we talked to 174 officers, Vietnamese and U.S., and in the case of the U.S. [officers] I always asked the question, "When can you finish this job in the sense that you will reduce this insurgency to little more than sporadic incidents?" Inevitably, except for the Delta, they would say "'64 would be ample time." I realize that's not necessarily . . . I assume there's no major new factors entering [*unclear*]. I realize that—

President Kennedy: Well, let's say it anyway. Then '65 if it doesn't work out [*unclear*] we'll get a new date.

Taylor: '65 we'll [*unclear*].

McNamara: I think, Mr. President, we must have a means of disengaging from this area. We must show our country that means.

   The only slightest difference between Max and me in this entire report is in this one estimate of whether or not we can win the war in '64 in the upper [*unclear:* three] territories and '65 in the [*unclear:* fourth]. I'm not entirely sure of that. But I am sure that if we don't meet those dates, in the sense of ending the major military campaigns, we nonetheless can withdraw the bulk of our U.S. forces, according to the schedule we have laid out, worked out, because we can train the Vietnamese to do the job.

To illustrate the point: we have two L-19 squadrons over there.[7] These are very important. They're the artillery observers and the fire control observers. But it's very simple to train Vietnamese to fly L-19s. Now, why should we leave our L-19 squadrons there? At the present time we set up a training program to give them seven weeks of language training, four months of flying school, three weeks of transition training with L-19s, and they can go out and do L-19 work. And we've set it up in Vietnam. It's being run by U.S. officers. It's working very well. Now, I think we ought to do that for every one of our major elements. We've talked to [*unclear*]—

President Kennedy: How much does our presence there contribute to sort of stiffening—

McNamara: Very important. Very important.

Unidentified: Important [*unclear*].

McNamara: Very important. *But* this is at the battalion level. There are 90 battalions and 3 men per battalion are the stiffeners. That's 270 men out of 17,000. Now, we might well want to keep those there for an extended period. General [Tran Van] Don has told me three times that contrary to his first impression—he was rather cool for putting these U.S. advisers at the battalion level—the U.S. advisers were stiffening the backs of the Vietnamese officers and men, and frequently turned them into fire when they would otherwise have turned away from it. That's quite an admission from the head of their army.[8]

Taylor: I would think if we take these dates, Mr. President, it ought to be very clear what we mean by victory or success. That doesn't mean that every [*unclear*] comes [*unclear*] a white flag. But we do— we're crushing this insurgency to the point that the national security forces of Vietnam can [*unclear*].

McGeorge Bundy: It doesn't quite mean that every American officer comes out of there, either. [*Unclear.*]

Taylor: No. [*Unclear.*]

McNamara: We have about 3,500 left at the end of the period.

McGeorge Bundy: Right.

McNamara: We worked out a preliminary plan of how to do this.

President Kennedy: You want to word that "with the major U.S. part of the task"?

McNamara: Yes. Yes. I think so, Mr. President.

Unidentified: [*Unclear.*]

McNamara: It's not essential, but I think—

David Bell: Also wouldn't it be wise to put in there this training aspect? That's very important.

Unidentified: That's number—that's Arabic "2."[9]

Bell: Well, but as I understand it, 6A, B, C, and D are supposed to constitute a self-contained summary.

Unidentified: A public summary.

Bell: A public statement.

McNamara: All right, yeah.

Bell: Seems to me the training idea belongs in there.

McNamara: Yeah.

McCone: The difficulty is that this whole thing could be upset by a little greater effort by the North Vietnamese [*unclear*].

Taylor: I don't think so.

McNamara: Not on the withdrawal of U.S. forces. There's no reason to leave that [L-19] squadron.

McGeorge Bundy: You're really talking two different things. What— you're saying that the U.S. advice and stiffening function[s] you may want to continue but that the large use of U.S. troops, who can be replaced by properly trained Vietnamese, can end. I wonder if it isn't worth separating those two.

President Kennedy: Well, just say, "While there may continue to be a requirement for special training forces, we believe that the major United States part of the task will be completed by 1965," or "advisory forces."

McNamara: Yeah. Yeah. Yeah.

James Galbraith: Planning and Executing the Withdrawal, May–October 1963

Although the conference participants were obviously provoked by the tape recording (which was accompanied by scrolling transcript, projected overhead simultaneously, exactly as it appears on the website of the Miller Center), the discussion was held in abeyance, according to plan, until after the second provocation by James K. Galbraith. In late 2003 and early 2004, as the fortieth anniversary of the assassination of JFK was being observed, Galbraith published two controversial pieces on Kennedy and Vietnam. In the first piece, he argued that Kennedy had made an unequivocal decision by October 1963 to withdraw U.S. forces from Vietnam, and that the withdrawal was not to be contingent on whether or not the U.S. and its South Vietnamese ally were in some sense "winning" the war against the communist insurgency of the NLF. In the second piece, he attached documenta-

tion from Joint Chiefs of Staff and Department of Defense archives demonstrating, in his view, that objective evidence of the presidential decision to withdraw can be observed at least as early as a May 1963 meeting of U.S. military leaders in Honolulu [**Document 4-1**]. There was, in fact, a good deal of discussion at the Honolulu meeting of the implementation of the 1,000-man withdrawal, even though the plan was not formally authorized by JFK until October 11, 1963, when he signed NSAM 263 [**Document 4-6**]. Galbraith believes this and other newly available evidence prove that JFK was firm in his decision to exit Vietnam by the end of 1965, or perhaps slightly later if circumstances required it. All that would remain, according to the plan, were approximately 3,500 U.S. personnel serving in advisory roles.

Jamie Galbraith also mentions something that will become increasingly important as the discussion moves into the Johnson period, when the war in Vietnam escalated to an American war. Galbraith says that he regards much of the discussion of the traditional formulation of the Kennedy what if on Vietnam to be null and void because the basic traditional question—what would Kennedy have done if he had faced Johnson's dilemmas—is one that Galbraith regards as incoherent and inappropriate. Why? Because according to Galbraith, one of the greatest dilemmas, possibly the greatest, faced by LBJ was that of succeeding an assassinated president—something neither LBJ nor anyone else had ever imagined. Galbraith is obviously correct in asserting that Kennedy could not, in the nature of things, have faced this problem. But there is considerably less than unanimity among the conference participants as to whether, as Galbraith seems to imply in his introductory remarks, this issue—succeeding the murdered JFK unexpectedly—should be regarded as so decisive that, as Galbraith claims, "Johnson's legacy has nothing to fear from the truth on this particular matter." For it seems to some of the participants unconvincing to conclude, with Galbraith, that based on what we now know, LBJ escalated the war in Vietnam to catastrophic proportions mainly because Kennedy did not live to be reelected and serve out a second term. Galbraith seems almost to assert that no matter who succeeded the murdered JFK, the war in Vietnam would have escalated dramatically in ways, and to a degree, that (to him) are unthinkable under JFK. However one judges this particular issue, it is indisputable that this and similar propositions put forth by Jamie Galbraith were highly and usefully provocative not just in the "official" provocation that follows, but also throughout the discussions. Indeed, it seems that Galbraith provoked one or more of the other participants virtually every time he made a comment, and thus greatly enlivened and focused the discussion.

JAMES GALBRAITH: I'd like to say that I hope what follows today will not take on the customary coloration of a contest between the legacies of Kennedy and Johnson. This is particularly important to me personally, having spent twenty years at the LBJ School. My feeling is that Johnson's legacy has nothing to fear from the truth on this particular matter. My own involvement, and indeed my entire work as a historian, are limited to the three weeks of October 1963, essential matters pertaining to these issues, and peripheral matters surrounding this episode. This is not my principal occupation; it is a preoccupation. I got into it initially as a consequence of some teaching obligations in which I uncovered Newman's book, and the controversy surrounding it, which in 1993 led the publisher to cease selling it—a very strange phenomenon. It was only later that I began to realize the extent of my father's role in these events, through his mission to Saigon in November 1961 and his solicited advice to Kennedy in 1962, which is now part of the record and dealt with at length in Richard Parker's book on my father.[10] But I'm not going to deal with those issues today.

I want to pick up the story in the spring of 1963 and take it briefly through these decision meetings in October. My contention has been that the historical debate over whether there was continuity or discontinuity between Kennedy and Johnson's [Vietnam] policies has been one in which the large body of historical work has either passed over this episode in a rush or misstated the facts as we now know them. Secondly, the proper way to frame the relevant question about Kennedy is not what he would have done had he not been assassinated in 1963, but rather what he actually did do in the fall of 1963 with respect to Vietnam. That is to say: there was a decision to begin the withdrawal of U.S. forces from Vietnam. McNamara in his 1995 memoir uses that word precisely. He says Kennedy decided—he made a decision—to start the withdrawal. My contention is: that is a precisely correct statement.

A presidential decision, however, is not a causal thing, and its existence, I don't think, can be established definitely simply from comments made at a set of meetings. What there has to be for us to accept the judgment that there was a decision is a record of planning for that decision; there has to be discussion of that decision; and there has to be implementation of that decision.

Evidence for planning is very strong in the eighth SecDef conference in Honolulu in May 1963 [**Document 4-1**].[11] There is a plan to withdraw 1,000 U.S. military personnel by December 1963. General Paul Harkins and Secretary McNamara stated that this would have to be handled carefully due to the psychological impact.[12] However, there should be an intensive training program for ARVN to allow for the removal of U.S. units rather than individuals.[13] At this point, there is already in the record a plan in May 1963 to reduce U.S. forces to preinsurgency levels by fiscal year 1967, or about 1,600 men. In response to what General Harkins says, the secretary of defense stated that the phase out appears too slow. It is fair for us to say, I think, that between May and October 1963 the military was tasked to develop a plan that moved up the date by which U.S. forces would be reduced to preinsurgency levels from 1967 to the end of 1965.

Okay, let's move on to the October [1963] discussion of the withdrawal plan. In the tape Marc just played, you heard McNamara say we need a way to get out of Vietnam, and you heard him say that the only difference between him and Maxwell Taylor is that he is not entirely sure that we can completely contain the problem. But even if we cannot, we can withdraw the bulk of our forces according to the schedule laid out.

Moving on from that to the question of a decision: a formal decision occurs on October 5th, 1963 [**Document 4-5**]. It's in a short and somewhat unclear conversation in which McNamara asks for formal approval for the items in NSAM 263 [**Document 4-6**]. After a brief discussion about doing it in a low-key way without a formal announcement, Kennedy says, "Let's just go ahead and do it without making a formal statement about it."

Finally, there is implementation in the form of a memorandum dated October 4th, 1963 (following the October 2nd meeting) from Taylor to the JCS, and from the JCS to CINCPAC (commander in chief, Pacific). The first page of the memo states that on 2 October the president approved recommendations, and on the second page you have a passage that says,

> All planning will be directed towards preparing ARVN forces for the withdrawal of all U.S. special assistance units and personnel by the end of calendar year 1965. The U.S. comprehensive plan in Vietnam will be revised to bring it into consonance with these objectives and to reduce planned residual (post-1965) MAAG strengths to approximately pre-insurgency levels.[14] Execute the plan to withdraw 1,000 U.S. military personnel by the end of 1963 per your . . . July instructions, and as approved for planning by September. Previous guidance on the public affairs annex is altered to the extent that the action will now be treated in low key, as the initial increment of U.S. forces whose presence is no longer required because (a) Vietnamese forces have been trained to assume the function involved; or (b) the function for which they came to Vietnam has been completed.

My contention is that all the elements of a presidential decision are there in their entirety. We have the preparations for that decision, we have a record of the discussion leading up to the decision, we have the voice of the president making the decision itself, and we have a record of the moment that the decision was, in fact, implemented. Does that decision prove that the withdrawal would have been of every last U.S. soldier? No, it is clear that it would not have been. There would have been a military assistance unit left in Vietnam after 1965 totaling between 1,500 and perhaps 3,500 soldiers.

Does this analysis prove that Kennedy was inflexible as far as the December 31st, 1965, date is concerned? No, it doesn't prove that, because we already have him saying on the tape that he'd be open to extending that date if necessary. It is, however, worth noting that by the time you got to that decision, a certain part of U.S. forces present in Vietnam would have been withdrawn, and so the extension would have affected a much smaller number than the 16,000–17,000 that were there in October 1963. It would have been an extension for a part, not a whole, of the force. Does it prove that Kennedy would not have revised the decision in the wake of subsequent events if he had been exposed to what Johnson had been exposed to? No, we can't say anything about that. I'm going to be suggesting that it is very problematic to raise that issue in any coherent way, because Johnson faced circumstances that Kennedy could not have faced. Specifically, the fact that Kennedy was assassinated was a fact of life for LBJ and changed the circumstances under which he could make policy and present policy to the American public.

It seems to me that we have to deal with history as it was. But one aspect of that history is that Kennedy—always skeptical of the value of U.S. involvement in Vietnam—had made a decision to bring that involvement to an end over a period of time that would have extended past anticipated reelection in November 1964, and that would have gotten us out, all things being equal, by the end of 1965, for all practical purposes. I think that was the policy of the U.S. government in a formal sense as I look over the period from May to October 1963.

A Decision in Concrete, or a Situation in Flux?

The discussion is ignited immediately by Jim Hershberg, who reiterates his perplexity as to how Jamie Galbraith (and, by implication, Gordon Goldstein as well) can be so sure that Kennedy's decision to withdraw in October 1963 (if such a "decision" actually was made) would have been sustainable as the government in Saigon came apart at the seams and the communist insurgency came ever closer to victory. Hershberg restates his views in a terse intervention. Galbraith, equally terse, dismisses Hershberg's concerns:

there is plenty of evidence, according to Galbraith, that the withdrawal—both the initial 1,000-man pullout by the end of 1963 and the withdrawal of most of the others by the end of 1965—was not contingent on winning, or even the appearance of winning. To some of the participants, such a claim seems to violate the basic political wisdom one normally attributes to an elected official such as a president, and perhaps common sense as well, but it also seems, to Hershberg and to Fredrik Logevall, to violate the sense they get from some of Kennedy's actual remarks in the transcripts of the October 1963 audiotapes on Vietnam—evidence they put forward to support their case, which is seconded by John Prados.

Two veterans of these events, Thomas Hughes from the State Department and Chester Cooper from the National Security Council, have other objections to Galbraith's conclusion and his certitude regarding the firmness of Kennedy's decision. Hughes, with a bemused look down the table toward Galbraith, reminds the participants that the three-month period before Kennedy's assassination was crazy with planning and scheming about everything connected to Vietnam, especially the coup against Diem and Nhu. Officials during that three-month period, Hughes emphasizes, were not just involved in a few meetings about the withdrawal—meetings that happened to be captured on audiotape. Hughes, of course, was personally involved in a good deal of this activity as the chief intelligence officer of the State Department. Cooper, looking sideways from the other end of the conference table at Jamie Galbraith, asks for a little more humility in trying to guess, retrospectively, whether JFK would have pulled out of Vietnam. Cooper accompanied his boss, McGeorge Bundy, to Pleiku, South Vietnam, in early 1965, shortly after the U.S. facility was attacked by communist insurgents. He asks plaintively, "What would Kennedy have done in response to an attack like that?" Implied in Chet Cooper's remarks is the conviction that politics and policy making are inherently uncertain and improvisational, contingent on many factors, most of which are unpredictable. Even Kennedy, according to Chet Cooper, would not have known exactly what he would do a year or two down the road, a reality we need to consider, he says, when we are looking at events with the often misleading "wisdom" of hindsight.

But Galbraith refuses to budge from his initial position. Kennedy, he says, decided to withdraw. Period. This much, in his reading of the evidence, is obvious, and no alleged equivocation by Kennedy on the audiotapes, no speculation about what he might have done if he had faced the crises Johnson faced, matters, because Kennedy had made up his mind to withdraw from South Vietnam by the end of 1965, or a little later if necessary. Galbraith will say, at various points throughout the conference, that of course Kennedy might conceivably have chosen to reverse his decision to withdraw. That would have been his prerogative as president. Galbraith cannot himself imagine the circumstances that would have led Kennedy to such a reversal, but if others can, then they are welcome to state their views and any evidence they believe supports their positions. In other words, Galbraith is asking the other participants, in a particularly challenging way, to exchange the traditional what if regarding what Kennedy might have decided regarding Vietnam for the Galbraith variant, which is, "Having decided firmly to withdraw from Vietnam, what factors, if any, could have forced JFK to reverse himself?"

JAMES BLIGHT: Thank you very much. Those two presentations together form a serious provocation. Might the American war in Vietnam never have happened if Kennedy had survived his trip to Dallas? I can't think of anyone better than Jim Hershberg to leap into the middle of it.

JAMES HERSHBERG: A couple of points jump out from the tape. There is no question about the intentions and desires of JFK—and, for that matter, McNamara. But in analyzing the significance of this decision, two particular questions seem important. One, it all seems to be predicated on the idea that South Vietnamese troops can be successfully trained to do the job. We really need more rigorous analysis of how realistic that was. It would be good to have a specialist on ARVN such as Bob Brigham tell us how realistic that really was, given the second question that jumps out of the tape, which is McCone's: couldn't the North Vietnamese simply increase their effort?[15] We know from subsequent experience that they certainly could have, but what we can't really tell is if they would have increased the effort commensurate with a poor South Vietnamese performance, or whether they would have let the Americans pull out and *then* raised their effort. And would that have forced the U.S. back in?

JAMES GALBRAITH: I didn't mention the question of the efficacy of the training because it doesn't jump out at me as a central question. It seems to me pretty clear that when McNamara speaks of training, he is speaking (for example) of training South Vietnamese pilots to fly L-19s. That is a very clearly definable task. Asking whether a South Vietnamese can fly an L-19 is not at all tantamount to asking whether the military campaign that results will be successful. McNamara is focused on the completion of training missions in that sense. There is no suggestion here that the war would be won. McNamara stated explicitly that the war might not be won by the end of 1965; nevertheless, the South Vietnamese would be flying the L-19s by that time, and there would be no need to keep our units there.

One can go into the whole question of whether the withdrawal plans were predicated on victory, but the Taylor memo to the JCS is clear: it is not contingent on victory. It simply says that "all" planning—not "some" planning—will be directed at achieving this goal by this timetable.[16] If other plans were going to be implemented, that would be a change from this point forward.

JAMES HERSHBERG: The implication is broader than the South Vietnamese being able to manage the situation, which is a condition of our being able to withdraw the bulk of forces. But I'll let others continue the analysis.

THOMAS HUGHES: Jim mentioned the peripheral matters that surrounded the three weeks of discussion and decision. This is a crescendo period that we're taking about, and the peripheral matters include everything that happens in this three-month period—from the coup planning that begins on August 24th with the green light telegram [**Document 4-2**] to Kennedy's assassination on November 22nd. These are three very hectic months, and lots of things are going on at the same time. The discussion of the troop situation is bracketed by the coup planning, and the coup planning begins in earnest in August and drags on throughout this whole period until the final convulsion in Saigon on November 1st.

MARC SELVERSTONE: There was no expectation that things were going to necessarily turn around very quickly. They are saying all throughout this period that it is going to take two to four months before we see any kind of improvement in the military situation. They are fully expecting that whatever happens, it is going to be a while before they see any progress in the military effort.

CHESTER COOPER: I'm a little concerned about the certitude some of my colleagues here display about Kennedy's intentions. I'd be happier if there were some pretty hefty qualifications about the predictions here, which is basically what all this is. You don't know, and I don't know, and Kennedy didn't know what was likely to happen during late 1963 or 1964, nor did we have any idea before 1965, for example, that American troops were going to be attacked at Pleiku, or what the president's reaction to that would be. We don't know how public opinion is going to react to a significant—not tremendous, but a significant—amount of casualties, or to just pulling out. How are we going to justify pulling out if things are not going well? How is Congress going to react to all of this?

I'm a little concerned about what seems to be a feeling that there was this decision in concrete that this was going to happen. Decisions in Washington about future matters are not made in concrete. There's always plenty of resilience in such a decision. And in any case, even if you reverse a decision, there are very smart guys who are paid to put the best face on it, so it's not necessarily true that you are bound in 1964 or 1965 by a decision that you make in 1961 or 1963. You are *not* bound by it. I would like to hear more qualifications to these predictions.

FREDRIK LOGEVALL: I think Chet Cooper's point is well taken, and I would probably take it a bit further and suggest not merely that we are talking about a decision that is not really in concrete, but that we need to look at the three months as a whole, as opposed to simply October. I agree with Tom about that. The conclusion I draw from close examination of those three months is this: Kennedy leaves for Dallas on that fateful day in late November still committed to the war and still undecided about what he's going to do. This is something I'm going to address tomorrow morning, in terms of the what if. You know he's a good politician and he wants to leave his options open. I think the transcripts that Marc and Tim have provided are quite interesting, and I want to draw your attention to one that we didn't talk about, but you have seen. This is the 6 o'clock meeting on the 2nd—

TIMOTHY NAFTALI: When they talk about winning the war?

FREDRIK LOGEVALL: I was struck by the comment—well, I may have a different version actually, but it is—

BILL MOYERS: 6:05 to 6:30?

TIMOTHY NAFTALI: Yes, there are two sections with 6:05 to 6:30, and they both begin with McGeorge Bundy.

FREDRIK LOGEVALL: Here's the thing that I found interesting, where Kennedy says, "My only reservation about it is that it commits us to a kind of a . . . if the war doesn't continue to go well it'd look like we were overly optimistic on it." That's often the line that's quoted, but I find the next part of it even more interesting: "I'd like to know what benefit we'd get out [of it] at this time of announcing one thousand" [**Document 4-4**]. It suggests to me that this is not something he has certainly decided on. It may even be the case that this is not something he's given a lot of thought to at this point.

The final point I'll make—and then I'll shut up—is that it seems to me that a president who has made the kind of decision that Jamie says he's made is going to speak less elliptically in public throughout these three months about his plans. I think he is going to be much more categorical than he is, including in remarks he had prepared to deliver in Dallas, but didn't get the chance, as he was gunned down. My own sense is that he's going to put off the difficult decisions; he's going to hope that the insurgency can be brought under control. If that can mean bringing home some troops—ultimately, all the troops—then so be it.

JAMES BLIGHT: Virtually everyone at the table is on the list. Let's try to be as concise as possible.

JAMES HERSHBERG: Fred and I just noted that making the point even more strongly in the transcripts that were circulated is on October 5th when Kennedy actually approves the 1,000 withdrawal [**Document 4-5**].

JOHN PRADOS: He *doesn't* approve it; it is unclear. "Mr. President, we would like to have formal approval of items 1, 2 and 3."

JAMES HERSHBERG: That's not the point. The point is that he says, "Well, I think the only thing is if it is going horribly, just from the public point of view a withdrawal would seem illogical."

JAMES GALBRAITH: That's just from the public point of view.

JOHN PRADOS: What do you mean "*just* from the public point of view"? The public point of view is critical!

JAMES HERSHBERG: Kennedy is acknowledging the dynamic.

Robert McNamara Versus McGeorge Bundy?

The discussion now moves to a consideration of the views of two of JFK's key advisers on Vietnam, Defense Secretary Robert McNamara and National Security Adviser McGeorge Bundy. The conversation provides a telling example of the way the Kennedy audiotapes deepen and enrich the perplexity of historians, rather than yield the kind of clear, unambiguous insights one might perhaps hope to derive from having the ability, retrospectively, to become a fly on the wall as historic decisions are being debated. Timothy Naftali opens the discussion by excitedly quoting at length from the transcripts of the October 1963 discussions. Tim Naftali believes the tapes reveal that a significant fissure existed within Kennedy's own inner circle of advisers—specifically between McNamara and Bundy. As Naftali reads the transcript of these tapes, McNamara seems to be trying to strong-arm the president—peculiar though it might seem for a subordinate to do so with his boss—into agreeing to the withdrawal plan. Bundy, on the other hand, seems dead set against it, according to Naftali, while JFK seems undecided, even a little confused, although from the evidence he sees in these taped conversations, it seems to Naftali that the president is inclined to side with Bundy. For his part, Bundy sounds in the transcript very much like the Bundy of the Johnson administration, concerned that American credibility is on the line in South Vietnam, that the U.S. must keep its commitments and stay the course, and so on. Chester Cooper sheds some light on one issue, that of whether to commit publicly to a hard and fast date for the withdrawal to be completed—the end of 1965. Cooper reveals that in meetings of Bundy's staff, he recalls arguing strongly for avoiding a commitment to an end point for the conclusion of the advisory effort in South Vietnam. Cooper says he worried that to establish a date and to publicize it would be to lay a trap for oneself if subsequent events required the continued presence of substantial numbers of Americans in South Vietnam.

It is worth noticing that Chet Cooper's remarks are predicated on what may at first seem like a self-evident assumption: JFK had not, and would not, make the kind of set-in-stone decision to withdraw that Jamie Galbraith believes he made. Cooper believed during the debates in 1963, and at the conference in 2005, that a crafty politician such as Kennedy would not, or at least should not, tie himself down in the way that McNamara recommends in the transcripts of the October 1963 discussions. (One gets the impression that Cooper has no trouble imagining the famously precise, quantitatively oriented McNamara believing that setting a date for withdrawal was a good idea.) As we know, Bundy and Cooper lost that argument. JFK did, as McNamara recommended, go public with the projected date for the conclusion of the withdrawal of U.S. forces from Vietnam. To Chet Cooper, this made no sense, because if Kennedy had lived and been reelected, he still might very well have had to eat crow later on—extending the duration of the U.S. advisory mission—in order to prevent the Saigon regime from collapsing. Chet Cooper's views must be taken seriously because he was there, in the midst of the discussions, in the role, as he says, of "Bundy's Vietnam guy."

But it is also possible that Cooper may have been wrong about Kennedy. Consider Kennedy's decisions in April 1961. As the members of the U.S.-backed Cuban exile brigade were being killed or captured at the Bay of Pigs in Cuba, Kennedy decided he would rather suffer a defeat than be dragged into a jungle war on the island. He publicly assumed responsibility for the disaster even before all the members of the exile brigade had been rounded up by Fidel Castro's forces. But rather than Kennedy taking a political beating, his popularity actually rose dramatically among the American body politic, according to polls taken at the time. He asserted his ownership of the disaster: "I am the responsible officer of government, and that is quite obvious," he told the press corps on April 21, 1961, and commenting wryly to them, he acknowledged that "defeat is an orphan, while victory has a hundred fathers."[17] He made these statements even though his administration had inherited the planned invasion from the Eisenhower administration and he could conceivably, therefore, have tried to shift the blame onto the previous occupant of the White House.

By facing the music so quickly and forthrightly during and after the Bay of Pigs disaster, JFK transformed a potential political catastrophe into a political victory because he was able convincingly to characterize as extremists those demanding an invasion of Cuba by U.S. Marines. This subject—Kennedy's ability to tolerate political heat in order to avoid intervening militarily—is one to which the participants will return later on. The salient question for skeptics of the position of Jamie Galbraith and Gordon Goldstein is this: having decided on accepting defeat rather than launching a U.S. invasion of Cuba, and having decided on taking responsibility for the defeat of the exile brigade on the beaches of Cuba, is it unreasonable to suppose that JFK might have done likewise over Vietnam? If he had lived and been reelected, might he have stuck firmly to his December 1965 date for the end of the major phase of advising the Saigon government on how to defeat the communist insurgency? Further, if he had decided to withdraw, might he have ordered a troop pullout even earlier, if the defeat of the U.S.-backed government seemed imminent before that date?

TIMOTHY NAFTALI: We've listened to a lot of conversation, and we've only given you a snippet of the tapes. In one sense that is unfair, because one could always quote out of context. What is absolutely clear coming from the tapes is a sense that McNamara is pulling in one direction—towards withdrawal—and Bundy is pulling in the other direction. The president seems to be moving towards Bundy. More often than not, Mc-Namara has to convince the president, and explain over and over again. We've cited a few examples, but the president is wondering why are we doing this, and McNamara says, "It's a good idea, what I am doing." Look again at 6:05–6:30, October 2nd [**Document 4-4**]. Go to where Bundy says, "The president himself wants to be sure the document as a whole reflects the notion that the object here is to win the war and he thinks putting the sentences in these orders . . . strengthens that proposition."

The president is out of the room at this point. Go a little further and you'll see that McNamara says, "Why did you say the president wanted to make clear, Mac, that the primary objective was to win the war?" This is what McNamara is asking Bundy. Bundy says, "He wanted the—he didn't want to have it said that we were just Pollyannas who couldn't stand a little authoritarian government, or that we were . . . to making these noises." That is exactly Bundy's speech; unfortunately, it is not terribly clear. But Bundy is saying to McNamara: "You've got to understand, the president wants to win this war" [**Document 4-4**]. That's what it's all about.

I leave it to other researchers to determine how McNamara and Bundy came to these positions here. This story is one of struggle within the administration, and as is so often the case, the president is in the middle. It seems to me, listening to this, that the president is closer to Bundy in this discussion than he is to McNamara. What Fred says is also true. If the president had made up his mind, he would not be speaking this way. It seems to me that this is a distracted president in these conversations— just the fact that he has to be reminded of what McNamara and Taylor are trying to do illustrates that.

So often we argue that Kennedy had this keen sense of politics, and that he did things because he understood the elections, and so on. In this case, the dates don't seem to matter a whit to him. They don't seem to matter. He's not focusing on the '64 campaign; there's no discussion of the '64 election. The most important thing to him is that they not commit to moving troops out of Vietnam unless the deed is done—unless the war is won, unless the tide has turned. Again and again he's saying, "If things go sour"—and he's always skeptical of military analyses—"we can change the date." But that doesn't sound to me like somebody who has an iron-clad proposal to get out of Vietnam. We can discuss what this is, but it doesn't sound to me like a plan to de-Americanize Vietnam.

FREDRIK LOGEVALL: That last week in August, and the first ten days in September that Tim's talking about, is a very important period. Just to underscore Tim's point: not only do you have the cable, but you have de Gaulle's advocacy on August 31st for neutralization, which scares the administration.[18] You've got the interview with Cronkite that Mac Bundy prepares the president for, and that has important implications for at least the public posture in Vietnam.[19] It is a very important couple of weeks.

CHESTER COOPER: In reference to Bundy: it sounds as if Bundy was alone in making these decisions. Bundy had a staff, and these types of questions were the subject of a lot of staff discussion. I can't find any papers about it, but it was this sort of thing. I was on his staff; I was his Vietnam guy. The question of a certain date in 1963 came up, and—I don't mean to seem immodest—but I made a nuisance of myself about not making a public date certain. It seemed to me that we would be laying a booby trap for the administration—for the president, for McNamara, and for Bundy. Who knew what was going to happen over a couple of years? You could fudge a bit with some adjectives and adverbs, but you didn't need numbers, because at that point in 1963 it didn't look as if things were going to be so hotsy-totsy. A little insurance would be useful. I was the one working on it.

McNamara, Hughes, and Military Intelligence

During the years of massive escalation to an American war under President Lyndon Johnson, 1964–1968, a good deal of controversy arose over intelligence purporting to indicate whether the U.S. and its South Vietnamese ally were "winning" the war or "losing." Much of the controversy in the Johnson years was connected to General William Westmoreland's decision to use "body count" as the index of choice for revealing objective progress or regress in the war effort. But bitter controversies over intelligence—who was winning and who was losing in Vietnam—did not begin during the Johnson administration. One such disagreement arose in the late summer and early fall of 1963. It involved Secretary of Defense Robert McNamara and the State Department's director of INR, Thomas Hughes. McNamara attacked Hughes and his bureau via Hughes's boss, Secretary of State Dean Rusk. McNamara asked Rusk henceforth to prohibit Hughes and his colleagues from interpreting military intelligence. McNamara sought to preserve the exclusive right to interpret military intelligence, such as who was winning or losing on the battlefield in South Vietnam, for the Pentagon, with input from the CIA. In a 1995 review of McNamara's Vietnam memoir, Hughes expressed lingering anger and amazement that McNamara would have used his bureaucratic leverage to stifle Hughes and his colleagues at INR. To what end? Was it all about bureaucratic control, which McNamara famously sought and often achieved? Or was something else involved?[20]

After studying the tapes and transcripts of the meetings of early October 1963 on the troop withdrawal question—discussions at which Hughes was not present—Hughes tells the other conference participants that finally, after all these years, he thinks he now understands why McNamara was so angry at him that he tried (unsuccessfully) to get Rusk to fire him. The State Department's reporting on the military situation was pessimistic—the

U.S., according to INR, was losing ground—while McNamara, as Hughes now sees it, demanded more optimistic scenarios in order to give credibility to his enthusiasm for the withdrawal option—which, as Hughes acknowledges, is quite evident in the transcripts of the early October 1963 discussions. In fact, Hughes now believes that optimistic reporting of the military situation must have been crucial, in McNamara's mind, as he prepared to make his case to JFK after returning from Vietnam with General Taylor. Frances FitzGerald comments in a follow-up remark that McNamara's excessive optimism—his tendency to "hope against hope"—became even more evident later on during the Johnson years as he tried to restrain his own military by arguing that some of the more drastic escalatory options they were recommending were excessive—not appropriate for the situation either because they weren't needed or because they had already proven to be ineffective at weakening their Vietnamese adversaries.

John Prados leads off the discussion with a comment to Jamie Galbraith about what he calls the "totality of the situation." According to Prados, yes, there is discussion of the withdrawal option on these audiotapes and, yes, it is interesting. But this discussion, Prados says, did not occur in a policy vacuum. In fact, according to Prados, the discussion of withdrawal should probably be understood as something of an outlier in the midst of many more discussions about Southeast Asia at all levels of the government as the U.S. prepared to escalate the conflict in Laos and, Prados believes, also in South Vietnam. Prados sees Washington's endorsement of those in the South Vietnamese military planning a coup in Saigon against Diem and Nhu as an integral feature of the escalation.

JOHN PRADOS: I want to reemphasize the point about the totality of the situation—not just to underline the question of the administration's relationship to the coup, and to the planning of the approaching coup, which obviously is critical, but also the totality of Southeast Asia. We are talking about a situation in a period of time in which the administration simultaneously makes a decision to escalate in Laos. It goes through a similar decision-making process. It issues the NSAM that provides for a phase 1/phase 2 program of escalating in Laos.[21] In addition, the administration has an intimately related initiative in South Vietnam trying to do something about Diem and Nhu. The missing element in explanations of the intention about the U.S. withdrawal is the intention of the U.S. government to do something about Diem and Nhu. One of the functions of that 1,000-man withdrawal is to put pressure on Diem and Nhu. The State Department almost simultaneously prepares an evacuation plan for all U.S. personnel in Saigon and explicitly links that intention to getting the South Vietnamese to do something about Nhu. The totality of the issue needs to be dealt with here. Jamie, you are talking about one thing alone, but there are other issues in play here that bear on it as well.

FRANCES FITZGERALD: The first point is there is a very great difference between saying we are going to take 1,000 troops out by the end of this year and the rest by '65, and saying we are going to attempt to train the South Vietnamese to take over the functions of these troops by these two dates. One is conditional, it seems to me. You can say the condition of the L-19s can be easily satisfied, but there are people in that room, on the first tape we heard—mainly McCone and Taylor—who are asking, "Can the other conditions be satisfied?" There is this argument going on. I believe Kennedy is saying that sort of thing too. If you look at the October 2nd 6:05 exchange between him and Bundy, Bundy says, "They reported back by the end of this year," and Kennedy said, "Let us say 'vigorously pursue'" [**Document 4-4**]. That's the point—vigorously. It must be clear to them at this point that, in essence, McNamara is talking through his hat, because the war is going extremely poorly. That is why Taylor was sent out there, and so forth. The political situation is going even worse; they are facing a real breakdown. This, to me, is McNamara's hope against hope.

I see McNamara doing this quite a lot. I think we see more of it in '65 where he is trying to rein in what is going on, but it is extremely difficult.[22]

THOMAS HUGHES: In the same month of October, the famous confrontation written about in several places took place between McNamara and the Joint Chiefs on the one hand, and INR and the State Department on the other, when McNamara tried to fire me.[23] All this came up right in the middle of all this troop discussion, and I didn't know at the time— actually, I hadn't fully appreciated until just now—that INR was innocently playing into the troop decision, undermining McNamara's rationale by saying that MACV was inflating its numbers, and by using MACV's own data to show that we were losing, not winning. No wonder there was such ferocity! The JCS and McNamara came back to us to say, "Keep the State Department out of military assessments!" McNamara was saying, "You're not supposed to be involved in military estimates," and we said, "We're not; we're using the military's own data to come to different conclusions from what MACV is coming to, and we do coordinate at the top," and so on.

The issue subsided two to three weeks later. McNamara and the JCS now agreed with INR, and the figures came out looking so similar it was

CRITICAL ORAL HISTORY IN ACTION

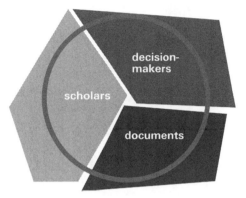

Top: *The three elements of critical oral history: decisionmakers, documents, and scholars.* Bottom: *The Musgrove conference table: up close and personal.*

Left: *Marilyn Young asks the others why Robert McNamara is so keen for the withdrawal from Vietnam in October 1963.*

Below: *Thomas Hughes describes the drafting of Hubert Humphrey's February 15, 1965, memo to President Johnson, as James Hershberg listens.*

Jim Hershberg

Left: *Bill Moyers speaks out on Johnson and Vietnam, with Timothy Naftali listening.*

Below: *Discussion continues through dinner for Chester Cooper, Bill Moyers, and James Hershberg.*

Top: *John Prados: the escalation of the war began under Kennedy.*
Bottom: *James Galbraith: no, Kennedy had decided to withdraw
from Vietnam.*

as if they were plagiarizing our estimates. Anyway, that comes right in the middle of all this discussion and helps explain why McNamara was so upset. Basically, we were undermining the rationale for his troop withdrawal proposal.

JAMES BLIGHT: I'm not going to ask you, Tom, if you're going to retract your *Foreign Policy* article, "Experiencing McNamara."

What Kind of Decision in October 1963?

James Galbraith tells his colleagues he believes they have strayed from the two basic points he tried to make in his opening provocation: first, a decision was made by JFK to withdraw from Vietnam, whether the Saigon government appeared to be winning or losing its effort to defeat the communist insurgency; and second, a detailed plan was drawn up to accomplish this objective, and it was already being implemented at the time of Kennedy's assassination. The conversation—which Galbraith believes has circled around his points, but not fully engaged them—must have seemed to him something of an oral replay of the scholarly situation in Vietnam War studies as he first encountered the field roughly a dozen years before. Back then, Galbraith, already a well-established economist but a newcomer to the scholarship on the Vietnam War, discovered that most of the major historians in the field did not seriously consider the possibility that JFK had decided to withdraw from Vietnam. There were exceptions, and Galbraith mentions some of them, just as during these conference discussions there are exceptions—Gordon Goldstein, for example, is in agreement with Galbraith on most points as was, we can assume, Goldstein's collaborator McGeorge Bundy at the time of his death in the fall of 1996. While denial of JFK's intention and plan to withdraw from Vietnam may have been justifiable to a degree back in the early 1990s, when evidence was thin and contradictory, this attitude is no longer tenable (as Galbraith sees it) in the face of the recent evidence he has cited.

As he chides the other participants, Galbraith makes a comment, just in passing, that should not be overlooked. He says, "The idea behind the withdrawal was to do this in a low key." As we look back with hindsight on the American war in Vietnam, we may find that this comment is hard for us to credit. After all, we know what happened: several years after these October 1963 discussions of a "low-key" withdrawal, the U.S. had more than 500,000 troops in South Vietnam, the U.S. bombing program represented the most awesome display of air power since World War II, and the carnage, particularly among the Vietnamese but also among U.S. troops, was horrific. "War in Vietnam" and "low-key" are phrases that are not, in retrospect, easily linked.

This is part of the difficulty in trying to imagine alternative courses of action with regard to Vietnam and throughout history more generally: we know what actually happened, and we can only with effort, and often with indifferent success, try to imagine the events unfolding in ways that are fundamentally at variance from what actually occurred. But if Galbraith's focus on the decision to withdraw and the planning associated with its im-plementation is correct, then we must assume that the way "Vietnam" looks to us now, retrospectively, early in the twenty-first century, is not the way it looked to JFK in the early 1960s. We should also ask ourselves: If JFK imagined a "low-key" withdrawal, did he believe that this approach to dis-engagement from South Vietnam would be roughly commensurate to its intrinsic significance (or really, its relative lack of significance)? Did he believe by the fall of 1963 that whether or not South Vietnam "went com-munist" or not was actually a second-tier issue, not at all comparable with reining in the arms race, beginning arms control talks with the Russians, defusing the Berlin crisis, banning the underground testing of nuclear weapons, as well as in the atmosphere? And would Kennedy have had the political skill required to convince the majority of the American people and the Congress of this view, in the face of predictable hand-wringing and finger-pointing from those accusing him of "losing" Vietnam?

Following Jamie Galbraith's renewal of his original provocation, a dis-cussion involving several of the participants ensues regarding the possible purposes of the withdrawal, the audiences with whom (presumably) Ken-nedy wished to communicate, and so on. In particular, Fredrik Logevall and Thomas Hughes remind the other participants of the possible salience in JFK's thinking of Senator J. William Fulbright, chairman of the Senate Foreign Relations Committee, a senior member of JFK's own party, who was already warning the administration publicly against getting mired in Vietnam.

JAMES GALBRAITH: I am very struck by the tenor of the reaction to my original provocation, which has essentially, so far, not addressed at all the central point I made in those brief few minutes. I would like to put this conversation back into the context in which I approached it when I first became interested in the issue roughly thirteen years ago. I wrote my paper, not as an exercise in history, but as an essay about the writing of history at a time when the overwhelming consensus—whether you were reading Gibbons, or Chomsky, or Karnow, or Hess, or Kai Bird—[24]

MARILYN YOUNG: Or me.[25]

JAMES GALBRAITH:—or any of a number of authors—was that there was essentially no withdrawal plan. At best, there was passing discussion of the issue. At most, there was discussion of Kennedy's comments to various confidants about what he would do after the election. In other words, the events we are talking about were essentially invisible, except to a handful of historians: Arthur Schlesinger, Peter Dale Scott, John Newman, and, later on, Howard Jones.[26] The efforts that have gone into this by those of us who believe there was a withdrawal plan have established that such a plan existed. The evidence of it is completely consistent through the phases that I just outlined.

BILL MOYERS: Jamie, is it conceivable to you that everyone could accept the factuality of what you say—agree with you that that is exactly the case—but that it is made irrelevant by subsequent events?

JAMES GALBRAITH: In some sense the plan was made irrelevant by Kennedy's assassination and the events that followed.

BILL MOYERS: I don't think anyone is challenging you on your facts.

JAMES GALBRAITH: Okay, good. I'm just pointing out that those facts were not established when I started on this process. What is being raised now is a very different set of issues—that perhaps Kennedy had some reservations or second thoughts; that was your position. Perhaps he was not completely committed; perhaps he was not set in concrete. We can discuss that. My view is that a presidential decision can be taken—and often is—by a president who is not 100 percent certain of the correctness of the view. The president does not have to be theologically committed; he just has to have the view that, on balance, it is the right decision to make at a particular time.

BILL MOYERS: With George Bush you have to be theologically committed.

JAMES GALBRAITH: Exactly. You can see the difference between Kennedy and Johnson and George Bush precisely in that, in making these decisions, the president we are talking about did not necessarily have a theological commitment to the exact correctness of his view. That, it turns out, is quite a healthy thing in a president. I do not think it speaks in any way against my case to allow for the possibility that Kennedy wanted to be very careful about the way in which the withdrawal took place and the way in which it was presented to the public, both for domestic political reasons and precisely so that the decision to withdraw

U.S. troops would not be seen in Saigon as contingent upon their performance. There was significant pressure to get them to reform—that is very clear; there was a significant simultaneous program, as you have pointed out—but withdrawal of the troops was not part of it. The idea behind the withdrawal was to do this in a low-key, get-the-guys-out-of-there manner. Does this mean that the U.S. would have been disengaged from Vietnam? No. There was a substantial aid program that would have continued.

The crucial thing that is established now is that there was a decision, as McNamara says, to withdraw with a timetable by the end of 1965. And it seems to me that the documentation on that is basically unequivocal. I want to emphasize the decision directive and the order that comes from Maxwell Taylor, which states, "All plans will be directed towards preparing ARVN forces for the withdrawal of all U.S. special systems units and personnel by the end of the calendar year 1965." If there was equivocation, it is not reflected in any document that I've seen. It is only reflected in people's views of what might have been Kennedy's state of mind. That gets into an area where, it seems to me, it is almost fruitless to go. Despite endless speculation, you cannot come to a conclusion, because, after all, there is no basis for a firm judgment in those areas.

DAVID WELCH: Jamie, I wonder if I could go back to your first comment that the evidence established a clear intent. I would say it establishes a clear desire. All other things being equal, Kennedy made a decision: he wants out. "Intent" is a bit strong, as it is very conditional—

JAMES GALBRAITH: Can I ask you why you just used the word "decision"?

DAVID WELCH: I'm getting to that in just a second. There are different kinds of decisions. There are decisions to fight, and there are decisions to lay the groundwork for a bigger decision. There are decisions to do something right now, and once it is done, it is done—there is no way to retract it. You have done us a terrific service by drawing our attention to the question of what Kennedy decided in this particular instance. But when I look at the evidence, I see that he "decided," in the strongest possible sense, to do only one thing: to authorize the withdrawal of 1,000 troops. I see a decision to plan a later possible date of withdrawal.

The whole episode reminds me of the debates about Operation MONGOOSE in Cuba. What did Kennedy decide to do with regard to Castro? He decided to authorize limited covert action, and he decided to lay the groundwork for later decisions about Castro. He was very, very restrained in what he was committed to doing.[27]

To me, the real decision here is to withdraw 1,000 troops. Throughout the period there is no backpedaling on the U.S. commitment in South Vietnam. So if everything fell apart in Saigon, I don't see that Kennedy had committed to the full withdrawal decision. There was nothing iron-clad, nothing he wouldn't have revisited if he had the opportunity to do so. That's how I interpret this decision. It was a decision to withdraw 1,000 troops.

By the way, it's an interesting question why he would do that. A thousand troops at this point doesn't make a whole lot of operational difference. It's a purely symbolic act. It signals something, but what's the signal? Who is he trying to impress? He could be trying to impress Diem. He could be trying to encourage the Vietnamese. He could be trying to send a domestic political signal. He could be trying to signal the Chiefs that he's just not interested in a larger American commitment. It was an inherently ambiguous signal. I would like to hear what others think he was trying to communicate with this relatively minor 1,000-man withdrawal.

FRANCES FITZGERALD: In particular, the decision whether or not to make it public, and whether to do it by individuals or by units.

MARILYN YOUNG: Which limits the signaling.

FREDRIK LOGEVALL: Part of the answer is domestic politics. There is already griping from Fulbright and others on the Hill, and this is a low-cost way of satisfying some of those concerns. It may also put pressure on Diem, as we've established, and it's very painless, because at least it could be done as a simple rotation. In fact, what happens, as we now know, is that the 1,000 men were withdrawn and promptly replaced [on Johnson's order]. But at least part of the answer is that this is a way to satisfy a number of different concerns, and to do so in a way that is not going to be very harmful to the other work to be done in Vietnam.

MARC SELVERSTONE: Those were all raised in the rest of the conversations, actually.

THOMAS HUGHES: I'd like to echo exactly what Fred just said. In fact, the Fulbright argument is one that McNamara himself uses and stresses [**Document 4-4**]. There's some evidence that Robert Thompson, the Malaysian guerrilla expert, went in to see Kennedy earlier, on—I forget the date—and said a token withdrawal of 1,000 somewhere along the line is going to pay big dividends politically, both at home and abroad. That figure seems to have stuck in Kennedy's mind. Certainly Hilsman had this notion.[28]

A JFK-McNamara Back Channel?

A pivotal moment in the conference occurs when Gordon Goldstein asks, in effect: who is this Robert McNamara on these tapes? Goldstein observes that the Robert McNamara represented in the transcripts of the early October 1963 meetings on Vietnam seems to be applying a good deal of pressure to JFK to get the president's assent to both parts of the withdrawal plan: pulling the first 1,000 advisers out within three months and the remainder (except for a small residual force of advisers) by the end of 1965. Goldstein asks his colleagues around the table for help in understanding what is going on. Why is it, he asks, that McNamara seems willing to push the president, almost to the point of lecturing him, to get him to agree to the proposals? Moreover, not only does McNamara seem to challenge McGeorge Bundy on the issue, it seems as if both Bundy and McNamara are genuinely flabbergasted that the other believes what he seems to believe. Why is this? Underlying the specific questions Goldstein asks about the "McNamara" in the transcripts is one that he doesn't ask outright, but is implied and is, in fact, inescapably on the minds of all those at the table. The question might be put as follows: how do we explain the fact that Robert McNamara, regarded by many as the principal architect of the escalation of the war in Vietnam under President Lyndon Johnson, is shown in the tapes and transcripts of the October 1963 meeting to have been a dove's dove, an advocate of withdrawal who seems willing to risk being rude to the president and his national security adviser to get his way? This is a McNamara who is surprising, in light of what happened later, a McNamara that needs some explaining.

Goldstein's query opens the floodgates as the participants offer their own perplexities about this "new" dovish McNamara they have discovered in the recordings. Marilyn Young says she has the impression that "McNamara changed." When Gordon Goldstein asks her if she has any idea where McNamara's fervor for withdrawal came from, and (later, under Johnson) where it went, she replies only, "It's really puzzling." Fred Logevall says he thinks McNamara was always a pessimist on Vietnam; at least he was pessimistic from a very early point after coming to office. As to Goldstein's question about why McNamara seems so different on these tapes than he seems later on—promoting and defending and, to a significant degree, actually designing the way the U.S. will escalate the war in Vietnam—Logevall

*says somewhat cryptically that whereas Kennedy was amenable to McNa-
mara's instinctual pessimism on Vietnam, Johnson wasn't: he didn't want
to hear about the difficulties or the risks, which seem to be the factors that
drove McNamara's pessimism. But the plot thickens considerably when
Frances FitzGerald and Tom Blanton both say that, actually, they see an
important point of continuity between "Kennedy's McNamara" (on the October 1963 audiotapes) and "Johnson's McNamara," well known to historians as a (privately) somewhat skeptical but (publicly) aggressive advocate
of the massive escalation of the mid-1960s. The similarity FitzGerald and
Blanton discern is this: Fred Logevall is right to insist that McNamara was
a pessimist about the ultimate outcome in Vietnam, but McNamara was
always something like an apostle of hope or "hoping against hope"—of
finding some kind of formula that would allow an escape from the untenable situation in Vietnam. This is the logic Frankie FitzGerald believes, for
example, is behind McNamara's "proposal" in November 1961 for JFK to
be prepared to send 205,000 combat troops to South Vietnam if the job is
to be done right. McNamara must have known that such a large number
would have been regarded as absurd by Kennedy, thus presenting JFK with
a kind of forced choice: zero combat troops or 205,000 combat troops.*

*The pivotal moment in the discussion arrives when James Galbraith at
last asks to comment. He says if the question is, "Why did McNamara do
and say as he did?" on the October 1963 tapes, then the answer may be
both obvious and extremely simple. In Galbraith's view, McNamara pushed
so hard for the withdrawal because that's exactly what JFK told him to do.
Jamie Galbraith draws on evidence shared with him by his father, John
Kenneth Galbraith, who told him that Kennedy often operated in exactly
this way. Suddenly, some pieces of the McNamara puzzle begin to fall into
place for Gordon Goldstein, who initiated the discussion with a simple
query about the sources of McNamara's enthusiasm for the withdrawal.
Goldstein now recalls that he once asked McGeorge Bundy why in November 1961 McNamara first espoused the introduction of U.S. combat troops
into Vietnam, then a day or two later withdrew his recommendation. Goldstein reminded Bundy that McNamara, in his 1995 memoir, said that he
withdrew it because he realized that he had been hasty and that his recommendation wasn't well thought out. Bundy's response was no. McNamara
would have reversed course abruptly on that issue for only one reason: Kennedy told him what he wanted. Goldstein then says that while he hadn't
thought about this before, the possibility of a Kennedy-McNamara "back
channel"—a confidential line of communication between them, scripted to
appear to other (possibly recalcitrant) JFK advisers present as if McNamara,*

not Kennedy, is the source. Goldstein says this is, to say the least, "a very interesting hypothesis."

GORDON GOLDSTEIN: A quick comment, and then a question regarding the comments made recently about the dynamics of how this decision was made. The comment is this: as we try to grapple with the evidence and arrive at some conclusion, I think it is important not to establish a criterion of confidence, or certitude, in analyzing the evidence that the evidence cannot sustain. And by that I mean we're dealing with a totality of evidence, and much of it is circumstantial in nature. Just as an attorney prosecuting a crime has to articulate the theory of the crime, we as analysts of this evidence have to articulate a theory of the policy.

To that end, we have to put the discussion of NSAM 263 [**Document 4-6**] into the context of all that we know about Kennedy's decision making about Vietnam, and all that we know about his views as expressed both in the formal documents and in the history of the period that come through in recorded conversations and in the research of scholars. I think what Jamie has established here can be interpreted at least in a conservative way as being entirely consistent with Kennedy's basic mindset about the war. It is consistent with what I see as his firm determination to maintain the level of U.S. engagement below that of combat troops. There seems to be at least a clear intent, if not a concrete decision, to wind this thing down in some foreseeable time frame in his presidency. I don't think we need to establish whether this is a decision that left no room for equivocation or no room for maneuver; I don't think that's a reasonable standard to attach to the analysis of the evidence. I think it is sufficient to say that it clearly establishes intent and a direction in which he was going, and that should be part of the discussion.

The question I have is for Chet and Tom Hughes. I'm really struck, listening to the tapes and reading the transcripts, by the insistence of McNamara. I've read in his book his partial recapitulation of this meeting, but when you see it in the full context, you really are struck by the fact that he is lobbying damned hard to make this thing happen.[29] I will accept Frankie's observation that he really is spinning the evidence to a degree, because maybe the war really isn't going well and he's making a stronger case than he is justified to make about the plausibility of this policy. My question is: Why is he doing this? Why is he pushing so hard? What is motivating him? What is going on in this particular period that is stimulating him to go against Bundy, and to really press the president to do this? What is the broader context?

MARILYN YOUNG: My sense is that McNamara changed. He's so insistent in these tapes at this point on having a way out, and then that seems to somehow disappear or change [after Johnson becomes president].

GORDON GOLDSTEIN: Do you have any insight into what inspires the fervor of his determination here, and then the dissipation of that fervor?

MARILYN YOUNG: It's really puzzling, and it's not something I have thought about previously. It's very interesting, and I would like to hear from Tom and Chet and Fred, too, on this.

FREDRIK LOGEVALL: I think—and I am in the minority view—that McNamara is a pessimist from an early point. I think he's already a pessimist, and we see it here. Some of the fascinating early phone conversations with LBJ in '64 indicate this. He tries to tell the president, "Things are terrible out there; I don't know what we can do to make it better." LBJ, in my opinion, is not very interested in listening to him [**Document 5-2**]. I think McNamara is a pessimist; I think he is ultimately, of course, an advocate for Americanization. That gets into the very fascinating subject of his loyalties—his loyalty to his position, to power—but I would simply answer by saying I think, in fact, he is not the superhawk that he is sometimes suggested to be, at least in terms of his faith. He's the supposed number cruncher, and I don't think he had all that much faith in his numbers.

TIMOTHY NAFTALI: In November 1961, as we saw yesterday, he was pushing for Americanization of the war [**Document 3-1**]. Does his opinion change?

THOMAS BLANTON: No, it's consistent.

JAMES BLIGHT: Let's spend a few minutes on McNamara's evolution.

FRANCES FITZGERALD: '61 is interesting, because you get that 205,000 troop figure, which the president is clearly not going to take. So why does it come up then? Someone was saying last night that this was a SEATO figure pulled out of the air; was it you, Chet?

THOMAS BLANTON: John Prados said it was a SEATO war plan for the sealing off of South Vietnam. You put 205,000 people across the Mekong . . .[30]

MARILYN YOUNG: Ah, they can hold hands. [Laughter.]

FRANCES FITZGERALD: So it is an absurd figure, and so are all the other figures, for that matter—the 8,000 troops, as McNamara actually says at the time. What is a small battalion going to do wandering around Vietnam? So you tend to think that's what he's doing. It's what [General Eric] Shinseki was doing in Congress that day when he said we need 250,000+ troops [in Iraq].[31]

THOMAS BLANTON: I want to bring this back to Jamie's question, which is about how we deal with this evidence. And I want to start dealing with Jamie's evidence by picking up on David Welch's point about Cuba. Because as I read all these documents, Cuba rang out to me; it's what I spent a lot more time on than Vietnam. The fundamentals of Cuba were that JFK had a schizophrenic, two-track policy. At the very same time he's sending people to kill Castro, he's also sending people like Lisa Howard to talk to Castro.[32] He was completely compartmented, as Tom Hughes has mentioned, both in his personal life and in his policy life, and when you, Jamie, say, as you said earlier, that there is no equivocation in any of the documents that you've seen about the withdrawal plan, I read them in exactly the opposite way. In every single document about the withdrawal plan I see equivocation, because every single document about the planned withdrawal is contingent on the South Vietnamese being trained. Every single one of them. Every transcript has some part of it that's about training the South. You've done an enormous service in putting on the table this extraordinary evidence, but to me the plan is totally hinged on a capacity issue that was the skunk at the garden party that never was realized.

The reason that McNamara keeps pushing for the withdrawal is that, in his own way, hoping against hope, he doesn't think the capacity is there from November '61, and all the way through, and yet the withdrawal is hinged on it. It is a classic form of the dilemma McNamara was pinned on throughout the entire Vietnam War. That's the counter. The equivocation is there all the way through, as I read it.

GORDON GOLDSTEIN: Do you think McNamara is just acting on his pessimism, and he sees this as an opening to contain this?

THOMAS BLANTON: I think he's trying to force the debate about getting out. He continually tries to put it on the table. He's trying to make Kennedy face up to it: "We're sunk here, we're in a trap." McNamara sensed it, felt it, and kept trying to push a clarity on it that never, never came.

JAMES GALBRAITH: Let me get into this.

JAMES BLIGHT: About McNamara? Sure, go ahead, Jamie.

JAMES GALBRAITH: Why is McNamara taking this position? Let me go back to my father's role. My father, as you know, was sent to Saigon in September 1961 by Kennedy in order to be equipped to render a negative assessment. That was the reason he was sent. Kennedy wanted a second opinion that he could use as a counter to Taylor and Rostow, and he got one. Kennedy instructed my father to prepare what I believe to be the memorandum in the briefing book. That was prepared on Kennedy's instructions.[33]

Kennedy sent my father to talk to McNamara. My father reported that he and McNamara saw the issues in the same way.[34] So I think the most likely explanation for McNamara's pressing this position is very simple: Kennedy told him to. Kennedy and he were agreed in advance that this was the course of policy that they were going to follow. That was a position they didn't share with anybody else, or with virtually no one else. They then imposed this, with McNamara playing the role of giving the argument he already knows Kennedy is going to accept, because Kennedy told him to do it.

This seems to be the most plausible explanation for McNamara's position.

MARC SELVERSTONE: In McNamara's memoir, he says that he makes the decision to begin planning for the withdrawal based upon statements Kennedy had made, and the statements of various Kennedy advisers. So this is McNamara's plan, fully consistent with Kennedy's intentions.

I believe that the two of them are working together, but it is *McNamara's* withdrawal plan, which is why Kennedy has to be led by McNamara in the October 2nd meeting. My question here is, when does Kennedy find out about the withdrawal plan? It's clear from the military documents that planning for this begins in May 1962. We can trace it all the way through 1962 and '63, but where is it in the White House documents? When is Kennedy briefed about these matters?

Supposedly, there is a conversation that takes place between Sullivan, Taylor, and McNamara on the trip back from Vietnam, and there is some question over whether to say something about the withdrawal. Initially they decide not to, and then Taylor said, "But we have to hold their noses to the grindstone"—and, in a fit of pique, he decides we have to put it in there. My understanding is that this is something new to Kennedy. I don't know if he's hearing about it for the first time, but I can't find any evidence predating this in White House memos. And, again, if you believe what McNamara says in his memoir, he is just kind of surmising that this is where Kennedy wants to go.[35]

Howard Jones will say there is an actual directive that Kennedy gives to McNamara, but there's nothing that can be found.[36] I've traced the documentary record, the footnotes—I don't see where it goes. Certainly there's no directive that we've uncovered.

JAMES GALBRAITH: One place where Kennedy has a direct private conversation with a figure he trusts on these matters is when my father accompanied Nehru to Newport in the late summer '61.[37] We are talking about channels that exist that Kennedy uses in part to form a judgment. He is clearly talking about these issues as far back as September '61—or earlier—with people he trusts.

GORDON GOLDSTEIN: This question of a Kennedy/McNamara back channel is really fascinating. I just want to augment Jamie's hypothesis with a hypothesis that Bundy had about the conversations between Kennedy and McNamara. In '61, we all know that there is this very mysterious recantation of McNamara's position. He says, "You know, Mr. President, we have to be ready to bite the bullet and send in more than 205,000 troops, and we have to make this decision now" [**Document 3-1**]. This is repeated in at least three iterations of that draft memo. And then within a three-day period, McNamara reverses himself: they scrap the proposal and the thing dies. He says in his memoir that he realized he was making a hasty decision and changed his mind after further reflection. Bundy thought that was total B.S. Bundy thought the reason McNamara changes his mind, when he is so rigidly focused on pushing the proposal, is because the president told him to. I think it is entirely plausible that there is communication that is not recorded in any documents. Somehow Kennedy communicates to McNamara, directly or through an intermediary. Kennedy could have expressed to McNamara, "You better back off of this thing, because I don't want to be pushed into a corner where I have to then reject your proposal." I think that's a very interesting hypothesis.[38]

The Significance of the Coup in Saigon

Thomas Hughes has pointed out earlier in the discussion that a three-month period of intense activity followed the August 24, 1963, so-called green light, or coup authorization telegram, sent from Washington to the

U.S. embassy in Saigon [**Document 4-2**]. *Some of this activity—a small proportion, according to Hughes (and John Prados)—was concerned with the details of the withdrawal. At the highest levels, however, much more effort went into trying to decide what to do with Ngo Dinh Diem and Ngo Dinh Nhu. Indeed, for many years, what little was known about the Kennedy withdrawal discussions and decision was thought by most scholars to be inextricably linked to the discussions about Diem and Nhu in the following sense: the 1,000-man withdrawal by the end of 1963, and the projected withdrawal of most of the U.S. advisers by the end of 1965, were believed to be a means used by the Kennedy administration to put pressure on the brothers in Saigon to begin to follow U.S. "suggestions" as to how to battle the communist insurgency and build a viable democracy. If the Ngo brothers did not agree to fall in line with U.S. requirements, then U.S. support would be withdrawn, presumably leaving the Saigon government helpless in the face of the strongly committed and well-supplied insurgents. The green light telegram of August 24, 1963, was consistent with this interpretation of what the pledged withdrawal schedule was really about. On that day, authorization was given to the embassy and CIA station in Saigon to contact senior members of the South Vietnamese military known to be interested in mounting a coup against Diem and Nhu and to inform them that if they succeeded in removing Diem and Nhu, they could count on quick recognition and support from Washington. Intrigue was always in the air in Saigon, but in late 1963, Saigon veritably reeked of plots and counterplots, secret deals, and even, as it turned out, assassination. The coup was carried out on November 1, and the Ngo brothers were shot dead shortly after they were captured.*[39]

Authorization of the coup in Saigon has long been seen by historians as perhaps the greatest mistake JFK made as president. After the coup, Saigon spiraled into ever-greater chaos. Those responsible for the coup were quickly deemed by their American sponsors to be, like Diem and Nhu, insufficiently attentive to the suggestions deriving from the U.S. embassy, and its viceroylike ambassador, Henry Cabot Lodge. Coup followed coup, with each successive general or generals seeming even less competent (in the eyes of the Americans) than those who preceded them. One of these, General Nguyen Khanh, actually cycled through the presidential palace several times over the next year or so, becoming a kind of "default" head of state, while the search was habitually reinstated for someone else to "lead" in Saigon. (The principal attribute of such a sought-after leader was, of course, his ability to follow U.S. suggestions.) As chaos and incrementally greater incompetence afflicted the U.S.–South Vietnamese effort to contain the communist insurgency, pressure mounted to introduce U.S. combat forces in large enough numbers to forestall a decisive victory by the insurgency.

The historian Howard Jones concludes his magisterial 2003 book, Death of a Generation, *this way:*

> President Kennedy's central tragedy lies in his ill-advised decision to promote a coup aimed at facilitating a withdrawal from Vietnam. His action set the administration on a path that tied the United States more closely to Vietnam, furthered the Communists' revolutionary war strategy by igniting political chaos in Saigon, and obstructed his plan to bring the troops home. No one can know, of course, what Kennedy would have done had he lived, but his assassination ended the waning prospect of withdrawal. Kennedy's legacy was a highly volatile situation in Vietnam that, in the hands of a new leader seeking victory, lay open to full-scale military escalation. President Johnson soon Americanized the war that resulted in the death of a generation.[40]

Timing, as usual, was everything. The timing of the coup and murders of the Ngo brothers in Saigon and Kennedy's murder three weeks later in Dallas inadvertently maximized the likelihood that the bitter, but still limited, struggle between the Saigon government and the NLF's communist insurgency would soon be transformed into a catastrophic nightmare for the entire region and for the U.S. The removal of Diem and Nhu left Saigon bereft of the only available leadership with any semblance of credibility in the countryside. It also fired enthusiasm among the insurgents and their ally in Hanoi to try to win the war—to escalate it—before the Americans could intervene decisively with U.S. combat troops. The removal of Kennedy, moreover, left the U.S. government without a leader who may well have used the occasion to intensify U.S. efforts to withdraw from South Vietnam in a "low key," but steadily. In other words, what occurred in November 1963 was the political equivalent of a perfect storm in which all the elements necessary for a disaster of epic proportions came together, ultimately giving rise to the American war in Vietnam, the worst foreign policy disaster in U.S. history, and an unmitigated disaster for Southeast Asia.

In the following discussion, the significance of the coup is debated with enthusiasm. Some, such as Francis Winters, James Galbraith, and Gordon Goldstein, argue that JFK, had he lived, would have come to regard the Saigon coup as a relatively minor perturbation. These scholars believe Kennedy was leaving Vietnam anyway, and he understood that Diem and Nhu couldn't last long in any event, so out of touch had they become from the reality on the streets of Saigon and in the South Vietnamese countryside.[41]

Others, including John Prados, Chester Cooper, Bill Moyers, and Marilyn Young, believe that the coup greatly deepened the U.S. commitment to South Vietnam, no matter who was president. They do not believe that the unfolding of events in 1964–1965 under Kennedy's leadership would have differed greatly from what happened under Johnson. Neither side converts the other to its views, but the debate and discussion illuminate the two poles of historical interpretation regarding the coup as well as several salient features of the situation that emerged from the coup against the Ngo brothers when combined with the assassination of Kennedy.

Finally, it is possible to detect in the late interventions of both Bill Moyers and Chet Cooper a trace of anger, in addition to the sadness anyone must feel when becoming immersed in the history of this tragic war. Bill Moyers and Chet Cooper were there, inside the administration, when these events occurred, and each is still trying to understand why, if JFK now seems to some to have been determined to withdraw from Vietnam and write it off as a lost cause, LBJ found it impossible to do so, even though Johnson's stated objective in Vietnam was "we shall continue" (with JFK's policies). Moyers and Cooper both settle on this hypothesis: some senior members of the Kennedy administration, having been frustrated (and ultimately defeated) by JFK in their efforts to convince him to escalate the conflict in South Vietnam to an American war, descended upon Johnson at their first opportunity and told the shell-shocked, inexperienced new president in no uncertain terms that he must not let South Vietnam fall to the communists. Thus began the pattern that would be repeated endlessly over the next several years. Johnson, unsure of himself in foreign policy and deeply insecure around all the Rhodes Scholars and Ivy League grads with whom Kennedy had stocked his administration, would stall, wring his hands, endlessly seek advice, but ultimately give his hawks a substantial proportion of what they said they needed to prevent a communist takeover in South Vietnam. The origins of that tragedy, according to Moyers and Cooper, lay in the unanticipated, traumatic transition from Kennedy to Johnson and the latter's inheritance of the mess in Vietnam in the wake of the coup, but not the experience or confidence to deal with it effectively.

MARILYN YOUNG: I don't think you can separate the coup from the withdrawal plan. That's always been the stumbling block to me in believing that Kennedy and McNamara just couldn't wait to get out. In early 1963, Jim Thomson comes and gives this talk and says, "Don't worry about a thing, Vietnam is going to be cool, because we are going to be invited out and we're going to be able to say, 'We did everything and you blew it; goodbye.'"[42] Terrific. They knew that Nhu and Diem were talking to Hanoi. If you want to get out, why do you have a coup? Because you have to have a stronger government before you leave? Then you're not leaving. Why do the coup? Maybe Diem and Nhu were fooling; they didn't really want to talk to Hanoi. Who cares? If you want out, you use them. If you have a coup, you're after something else. No one has ever explained to me—why the coup?

THOMAS BLANTON: It seems to me [we need] to keep in mind the dual track. Kennedy is proceeding with what is both a withdrawal plan and a massive escalation of U.S. commitment, and he was just beginning to pay attention to Vietnam. Fred mentioned yesterday that it was only in July/August of 1963 that Vietnam becomes a daily agenda item. That's an indication of the commitment, intention, and devotion of resources of the U.S. government at the highest level. The attention of the president is the scarcest resource of the U.S. government. At the same time, you have the planning to assassinate Castro *and* secret talks with Castro; you have the escalation of violence in Vietnam *and* the withdrawal plan. This is Kennedy's modus operandi. That is the context of this plan, and why I am not persuaded that it was serious.

jANET LANG: Similar points have been made, but on this issue of JFK and Bob McNamara, I want to acknowledge the point that Tom is making about Cuba, and use it as a way of trying to get some insight into Kennedy's thinking. I differ with Tom Blanton on a few points. Basically, if you think about the Cuban missile crisis, that was high drama, something that had everyone's focus. There are so many key places during the missile crisis where Kennedy is way ahead of his advisers. It's impressive to see Kennedy instructing his advisers on what he sees as the political realities of the situation they are in, and doing whatever he needs to do to bring them around.[43] He's not going to do the heavy hand, because that's not his style. It is very clear. We had some conversations with Mac Bundy about this, when he was first listening to the transcripts talking about that; he pointed out a few details. Kennedy in that situation is very much leading his advisers. I think something similar is going on with regard to Vietnam, but it is strung out over a long time, because (at least during the Kennedy period) it is not a time of high crisis. It is not a highly intense, concentrated moment like the missile crisis. It's spread out over months, even years. Berlin is also happening, and so on, so while Vietnam is on the radar screen, it blips in and out. It is a crisis in slow motion, and once again, Kennedy is out in front of his advisers, anticipating disasters and looking for ways to avoid them.[44]

The coup against Diem succeeded, but the coup was not a focused sort of thing: they kind of forgot about it, or just passively allowed it to go forward. Lodge is a little out of control. I don't think the president is an enthusiast for the coup. However, it doesn't speak well to his whole organizational system by any means, that he would just let it happen the way it did. But I don't think you can use the coup as an example that is parallel to the planning with regard to Castro and Cuba.

Chet, thank you for allowing me to cut in on your time.

CHESTER COOPER: Well, I'm getting older and wiser. [Laughter.]

JAMES BLIGHT: Chet Cooper.

CHESTER COOPER: First, I want to talk about people, not documents. The documents reflect to some extent what people were thinking about, but should not necessarily be the one and only criterion for piecing together what happened. Let me just give you a few examples. When you talk about McNamara in 1961, remember he'd only been in office for a matter of months. He knew nothing. He was in Detroit making automobiles. When he came to Washington, McNamara would probably have had a hard time figuring out where Vietnam started and Laos ended. Do you want to know why he changed his mind? He may have just discovered over the course of a couple of years what the realities of Southeast Asia were, which was something not very many people were aware of at the time.

The same thing is true with Kennedy, the Bay of Pigs, and the missile crisis. Kennedy got snookered into the Bay of Pigs. He was only in office for a couple of months, and he had these guys who threw him some bait, and I think he was eventually sorry he did it, but he grabbed at it. By the time the Cuban missile crisis came along, he worked it all out. He had been president for a year or two now; he knew these guys. He had some experience under his belt. But both McNamara and Kennedy, at first, were faced with a very difficult set of circumstances that they had literally very little experience to lean on when dealing with them.

On the issue of what was the rationale for the withdrawal, I remember the discussion. To some extent it wasn't only because we wanted to withdraw troops. We were having a hell of time with Diem and Nhu in Vietnam; we didn't know what to do with these guys. They wouldn't listen; they didn't care what we were concerned about. There was some reference in the fall that Diem wanted us out anyway. I think the withdrawal of 1,000—and I remember the discussion—was to get Diem and Nhu to concentrate on what we wanted to have happen, and to prove we were not absolutely hopeless and helpless in the face of their obstinate and corrupt approach. This, in a sense, was a warning signal.

It served another purpose, too: we did bring home some troops, and that helped put out a public message that this was not going to be a lengthy war.

I want to emphasize again, this was a cabinet that was faced with some very difficult questions. Kennedy was floundering around out there. The situation was very fluid.

JAMES BLIGHT: I'd like to call on Frank Winters to speak to these issues raised by the coup in Saigon. Frank, as you know, has studied and written about the coup against Diem and Nhu in some detail.

FRANCIS WINTERS: Thanks, Jim.

In response to a question from a very bright Vietnamese student at Georgetown—namely, "Why did you kill our president?"—which I thought was a pretty interesting question in 1972—I decided to read the literature. I found the literature less than forthcoming, not only about why we killed the president, or had that role in killing the president of Vietnam, but about the coup in general. It was not a major feature of the Vietnam war literature as far as I could see. So I decided to interview everyone who was still around. Chet [Cooper] was kind enough to see me twice during that period.

Things began to unravel in Saigon, I think, as soon as Kennedy understood that Diem was an improbable, and indeed an impossible, ally. Kennedy had great empathy for Diem's situation; he understood it better than most Americans, as far as I can see. He decided, as he says on the November 4th, 1963, tape, that Diem could never be made into a suitable ally for the United States.[45] I have a letter from [Senate Majority Leader] Mike Mansfield saying, "In response to your letter, I can tell you with great confidence that in March 1963 the president told me he was going to leave Vietnam after he was reelected, but not before, and that he would withdraw some troops in advance."[46]

Now, I know that most politicians have dim reputations and their word is not worth much, but I don't know that many people think Mike Mansfield was a liar. I feel quite confident, therefore, that President Kennedy intended by March 1963 to leave Vietnam after 1965. Whether he would have changed his mind is another issue, which is not of particular concern here. Charles Bartlett has told me the same thing.[47] JFK therefore needed somehow to get to a successful reelection before he could leave. He was also convinced that Diem was an albatross, that he had become isolated from the American press—in particular the *New York Times* and

David Halberstam. I suspect that Kennedy made a very calculated decision in which he thought that, if Diem didn't reform, he might lose the 1964 election to Barry Goldwater. He refused to lose the election. Charles Bartlett, who was a close friend of Kennedy, says that in any political conversation he had with him during the thousand days of his presidency, Kennedy would always talk about reelection. It was an absolute. Therefore, I believe he felt at this point that Diem was in the way and he would have to be a sacrificial lamb, in effect, to American public opinion. This is ruthless as far as I can see, but it was not unsympathetic. He just made a ruthless decision about his absolute value of reelection.

The facts were simple, thought [Ambassador Frederick] Nolting and some others thoroughly associated with the situation. If Diem goes, there will be chaos. LBJ was the most vigorous proponent of that side even though he rarely spoke in meetings, as I understand it. LBJ not only said that very bluntly to the president whenever he did speak, he also—and this is interesting—he continually told Nolting to speak up more. He said: "You're not being vigorous enough; this [coup] is a crazy idea. I can't speak, but you should speak more forcefully." Nolting did. Nolting finally said to the president: "Mr. President, this is a question of our honor. You have committed the United States not to intervene in the internal affairs of South Vietnam, which is exactly what you are doing. This is dishonorable."[48] How many people would say that to the president? Not many. I think Nolting was a hero of American diplomacy. So when Kennedy chose to get rid of Diem, he did it in full awareness of the high probability of chaos.

Now, how could that be? To my mind the explanation goes back to the same decision that Mansfield shared with me. He intended to get out, and therefore, as far as I can see, Kennedy could not have cared less what happened in Vietnam after 1965. He wasn't going to be there; we weren't going to be there; that was going to be somebody else's problem. This is obviously extremely ruthless, and in some ways not entirely admirable.

FRANCES FITZGERALD: On the coup against Diem: Kennedy did not have to precipitate it. A coup would have occurred within the next year. There is no question about it. Without a coup, Saigon would have fallen; things were that bad. So there's no question about keeping Diem in power. That's why Nolting was crazy for wanting to keep Diem. He adored Diem to such a degree that he couldn't see this. That's essentially why Kennedy needed to get him out of there, and Halberstam was right about that.[49]

My preference at that point would have been for Kennedy to say, "Too bad, this is Diem's fault, and there's nothing we can do about it; our guys out there have failed, and the only other answer was to put 205,000 American troops in the war, and we're not going to that." That was a possibility. But, practically speaking, there was no way to keep Diem.

FRANCIS WINTERS: The question is, who was responsible?

FRANCES FITZGERALD: Exactly.

GORDON GOLDSTEIN: I was very struck by Frank Winters's mention of the Mansfield letter; this is one of half a dozen pieces of anecdotal evidence that people keep returning to when we try to assess Kennedy's intentions in Vietnam.[50] What's interesting to me about this is the context you put it in. According to your theory, Frank, Kennedy had basically decided he was going to pull out, and he was prepared for there to be a real mess in the wake of pulling out of South Vietnam. I've always been very skeptical of what George Herring has argued in his book—that the Diem coup somehow left Kennedy obligated to stay longer in Vietnam.[51] Perhaps Kennedy should have felt that way, but to suggest that Kennedy was in fact more closely bound to the fate of South Vietnam after this to me always seemed like a very speculative proposition. I think he was prepared to be quite ruthless, as Frank has suggested, and this is consistent with that interpretation.

JOHN PRADOS: I liked a good part of what you had to say, Gordon, but I cannot let you get away with saying that whether or not the United States had supported the coup against Diem made no difference to the U.S. stake in Vietnam. I think this isn't just a theory that George Herring came to; this is the judgment of American historians. It's not just George Herring's opinion.

This brings into the open the fact that there's a contingent assumption built into the discussion of what might have happened: certain options just aren't possible unless the U.S. stake in South Vietnam remains completely unaffected by our support of the Diem coup. If you think that America's stake is immeasurably increased as a result of the Diem coup, as the consensus of historians has it, then whatever was or was not decided in early October 1963 is simply cancelled.

GORDON GOLDSTEIN: But what evidence is there that this constrained Kennedy in his thinking? How did it affect his thinking about what he was going to do? It seems to me there is an argument that it should have constrained him, but is there empirical evidence that it did constrain him?

JOHN PRADOS: I would say the major evidence that is on the table is NSAM 273 [**Document 4-7**].

JAMES GALBRAITH: Well, okay—

JOHN PRADOS: It's drafted just before Kennedy dies, and involves the next set of escalations in the U.S. program—another widening, in fact, of the U.S. involvement in South Vietnam.

JAMES GALBRAITH: I'd call your attention to page 2-61 of the briefing book, on which the change in NSAM 273 between the draft of November 21st and what Johnson was actually asked to sign on November 26th is spelled out. In the November 21st draft, there is a clear restriction to government of Vietnam resources behind what ultimately became OPLAN 34-A.[52] It is just incorrect to say that NSAM 273 [**Document 4-7**] represented a significant escalation of the war so far as Kennedy's policies were concerned. Whether or not the final draft represented a Johnson decision to escalate seems to me an open question.

BILL MOYERS: It was a decision put to Johnson by McNamara. McNamara sought the change in the document that Johnson signed on the 26th of November. It was not Johnson's change; he had no idea of it.

JAMES GALBRAITH: I accept that completely. And I'd further point out that if you look carefully at the implementation documents, the CIA sent guidance to their station the day before Johnson signed the decision saying, "This is what we're going to do." It seems to me that to turn this into a big policy change is on both counts, therefore, completely incorrect.

JOHN PRADOS: Well, I think you're conflating the issue, because the—

JAMES BLIGHT: John, can we just hold off—

JOHN PRADOS: Yes, after this. The push to eliminate the South Vietnamese role and move to a U.S. unilateral role is a CIA initiative. It's not a Kennedy initiative; it's not a Johnson initiative. It is a CIA initiative.

JAMES GALBRAITH: What? OPLAN 34-A?

JOHN PRADOS: The move to the U.S. unilateral approach, that's right.

JAMES GALBRAITH: Well, the use of speedboats that are CIA boats, that's true.

BILL MOYERS: We were getting close to something that I think historians should go back to. I believe Vietnam would have become a catastrophe whether Kennedy or Johnson, or whether Humphrey or Nixon, was in charge of it, given the realities on the ground.

Anyway, somebody chose, during the week of the funeral—at a time steeped in grief—to propose what subsequently became a major step in the escalation of U.S. involvement in Vietnam. Somebody chose to put it to the new president at that particular time, with inadequate briefing and inadequate preparation at a time of great uncertainty. I believe somebody did that deliberately. I don't think it's a conspiracy, but I do remember two principals standing in front of the president outside of the situation room after a rather procedural briefing and saying, "We have to do something in Vietnam; we have to act now." And the president responded, "Well, we should put that on the agenda to talk about."[53] How NSAM 273 [**Document 4-7**] got changed is something I do not understand, and I do not find any record to explain it.[54] But the effort at that moment to engage the new president in a profound change in a document and policy *was* a major change. Unilaterally taking over the covert operations against the insurgency was unintentionally a major change, perhaps, but in fact it was a powerful change, because it raised the stakes and affected what the new president felt he had to do. I'm not exonerating Johnson from this; I'm only saying something happened then bureaucratically, politically, or whatever, that changed the options he later came to see had been presented to him.

JAMES GALBRAITH: I accept that as well.

CHESTER COOPER: I agree with Bill that something happened between the two administrations that resulted in a tremendous change.

One thing that fascinates me is the fact that in the autumn 1963, Robert McNamara and Max Taylor came back from Vietnam with a certain date of when we were going to withdraw troops. Six months later, the same two went to Vietnam and came back saying we needed more troops. I don't understand that. The situation in Vietnam was not very good in April—not a whole lot different than it was in the autumn of 1963. All I can imagine is that McNamara and Taylor always felt we needed more troops and thought that Johnson was the man to convince the way they couldn't convince Kennedy. So they told Kennedy we should begin to withdraw in 1963 and move out in '65.[55]

THOMAS BLANTON: I just wanted to try to answer your question, how could they set a certain date for withdrawal and then say we needed more troops? It's because the date for withdrawal was totally contingent on the capacity of the South Vietnamese to take over U.S. functions. The documents said that over and over: "We're doing a withdrawal plan because we think we can achieve the training of the following corps in a certain sequence of time." The withdrawal plan was an illusion, because it was based on something—like so-called Iraqification now—that never happened. The later perceived change wasn't a change; it was dependent and contingent withdrawal. That Vietnamization didn't happen; the capacity got worse. So you have to add more American troops. It's coherent: it's not a change, it's not a flip; it's the fundamental flaw in the idea that there was a Kennedy withdrawal.

CHESTER COOPER: This happened over a period of six months?

THOMAS BLANTON: Yes, things were worse. The South Vietnamese training wasn't proceeding. McNamara is so optimistic in that tape recording with Kennedy: "We're going to do this in that order on this date. We'll be done with these three; the fourth will take longer."

JAMES GALBRAITH: No, no, no, you are conflating two things. One is completing the major military campaigns, and the other is the training mission. The training mission is a matter of training pilots to fly L-19s.

FREDRIK LOGEVALL: It is far more than that.

MARILYN YOUNG: It was a "for instance." The L-19s were a "for instance."

BILL MOYERS: Let's not forget that things were sufficiently bad for them to plan a coup against the man they put in office.

MARILYN YOUNG: That's right.

BILL MOYERS: I mean, it was not a static situation there; it was rapidly deteriorating. There was not an effective government to sustain an effort.

MARILYN YOUNG: May I read something from Jim Fallows? You'll see the relevance instantly. He's talking about planning ahead in Iraq: ". . . either because things are going well enough that U.S. troops can leave, or because they are going badly enough that the American troops have to go."[56] You pick it up and it could have been any year in the Vietnam War.

FRANCES FITZGERALD: And you can reverse those.

MARILYN YOUNG: Exactly.

JAMES BLIGHT: Thank you all very much, You have earned your break, which we'll take now.

"Johnson thought he was making the right choice. He knew more than anyone . . . what it was going to cost him. . . . It was his [choice] to make; no one made it for him."—Bill Moyers, Musgrove conference

CHAPTER 5

What LBJ Decided: The "Long 1964"

JAMES BLIGHT: As we witnessed in the first two sessions, these conversations can often raise many more issues than we can resolve in the limited time available. So we turn to LBJ's decisions without having reached agreement, to say the least, on what JFK decided regarding Vietnam.

John Prados: Was LBJ Fighting His Own Advisers?

Historians of the American war in Vietnam agree, more or less, on a rough timeline of the key events and decisions in the incremental U.S. escalation to an American war in Vietnam. The timeline begins with the November 1, 1963, coup in Saigon, the murder of the Ngo brothers, and Kennedy's assassination three weeks later. Most agree that almost from the moment when Lyndon Johnson took the oath of office aboard Air Force One, the subsequent progression of events regarding Vietnam unfolds like a Shakespearean tragedy, the end point clearly visible to us in the "audience"— that is, in the present—as it was not, alas, to the historical actors themselves.

Now we know that LBJ and his advisers are doomed. We know it is already too late for them to avoid catastrophe. Pick your favorite tragedy by The Bard and give Lyndon Johnson the starring role. Hamlet, perhaps? LBJ was certainly a leader who could never really decide whether to fully get in, or to fully seek a way to get out, of Vietnam. King Lear? Late in his presidency, Johnson walked the halls of the White House in his nightshirt, a glass of whiskey in one hand, the other hand drawn up in a Lear-like fist, the better to shake it at the gods above for cursing him with what he called "that bitch of a war."[1] Like any tragic figure, he is unquestionably culpable;

he made the decisions that brought doom to so many and so much, including his presidency, yet we in the audience cannot help but feel at least a twinge of sympathy for this man—manifestly the wrong man in the wrong position, conducting the wrong war at the wrong time against the wrong adversary.

The tragedy of Lyndon Johnson and "that bitch of a war" in Vietnam has the following elements.

Act I. *The assassinations of November 1963 signal the beginning of the tragedy. Thenceforth, key events unfold with the seeming inevitability of a drumbeat on the parade ground. Among the most important are these: increasing chaos in Saigon following the coup; rapid gains by the National Liberation Front (or "Vietcong") communist insurgents seeking to take advantage of the leadership vacuum in Saigon; the fruitless American search for a South Vietnamese leader who commands the respect of the population and is willing and able, more or less, to do Washington's bidding; and the dispatch of more U.S. advisers and the effort to recruit many more South Vietnamese into the armed forces.*

Act II. *There follow the events in the Tonkin Gulf in early August 1964, which have these results: the first U.S. air strikes on North Vietnamese targets; the first capture by Hanoi of a U.S. pilot shot down over North Vietnam; the passage through Congress of what became known as the Tonkin Gulf Resolution, giving LBJ authority to do whatever he deemed necessary to prevent the fall of the government of South Vietnam to the communists; and LBJ's landslide victory in November, in which he ran as a dove against the hawkish Barry Goldwater, even as his government was secretly preparing for massive escalation of the conflict in Vietnam— escalation involving the large-scale introduction of U.S. combat troops and a massive air war against North Vietnam.*

Act III, Scene 1. *In early February 1965, there are communist attacks on U.S. advisers and equipment at Pleiku and Qui Nhan in the Central Highlands of South Vietnam; also in February 1965, LBJ decides, in response to those attacks, to launch so-called "sustained reprisal" air attacks against North Vietnam and to send the first contingent of U.S. Marines to South Vietnam in March.*

Act III, Scene 2. *Finally, after months of anguish and equivocation, the president makes his decision to approve General William Westmoreland's request that approximately 175,000 U.S. combat troops be sent to South Vietnam. Historian Fred Logevall has usefully called this period from August 1963 to July 1965 "the long 1964." At the beginning of the long 1964, there was no air war and there were no U.S. combat troops in Vietnam. At the end of the period, the American war in Vietnam had begun, and it* *would not conclude until millions were dead, an entire region was in chaos, and the U.S. was torn apart by issues related to the war.*

John Prados, the outstanding military historian of the war in Vietnam, gives a dramatic opening provocation. He asks his colleagues around the table to consider the contrast between the several minutes of conversation about JFK's withdrawal decisions and plans on the recently available tape recordings, on the one hand; and, on the other, the many months of obsessive discussions between LBJ and all his relevant senior advisers regarding whether Johnson should Americanize the conflict in Vietnam. Using the formula suggested by Prados, we have approximately thirty seconds of tape-recorded discussion about JFK's withdrawal for every month that LBJ and his advisers discussed whether, how, and/or when to intervene massively during the long 1964. It really is astonishing. One gets the impression that this is one reason among several for Prados's skepticism regarding whether Kennedy would have found it possible to withdraw from Vietnam by the end of 1965 or to withdraw at all without first having to escalate the conflict to an American war, just as Johnson did during the long 1964. To Prados, as to other skeptics, the withdrawal in October 1963 may have been to JFK just one possibility among many, an adjunct to the strategy of putting pressure on Diem and Nhu to capitulate to U.S. demands. Prados asks: if LBJ and his senior advisers—virtually the same cast of characters who advised JFK—could not avoid the war in Vietnam with many months of intense searching, should we believe that JFK and his advisers would have fared any better? His answer is "no."

Prados concludes his provocation with a concise listing of LBJ's weaknesses as president when facing the question of what to do about Vietnam. He was dishonest with the American people and the Congress in not revealing what he had actually decided. He "stage-managed," as Prados aptly puts it, the debates among his advisers, often using Undersecretary of State George Ball as a bogus devil's advocate, primarily to provide the form and appearance of a serious and critical discussion, when in fact LBJ had already decided he was going to do precisely the opposite of what Ball was recommending. Finally, it seems to Prados that both LBJ and his advisers were so deceptive with one another on the Vietnam issue that the situation within the administration might almost be described as a "war" between a more-than-slightly paranoid president and advisers he never appointed. This was a group of ambitious, often confused advisers who were trying to read the intentions of a new boss who, to the Ivy Leaguers surrounding Johnson, seemed to have come from another planet called the Texas Hill Country—equal parts inscrutable hillbilly and ruthless Machiavelli. To the extent that the long, drawn-out, ultimately disastrous decision-making process of the long 1964 is attributable to the mismatch between LBJ and the JFK team he inherited, we might ask: might it be possible to imagine a better outcome, had Kennedy lived, been reelected, and surrounded by the team he had put together when he assumed the presidency? As we shall see, some, such as John Prados, think not, while others believe quite the opposite.

JOHN PRADOS: I would like to pick up right where we left off. I want to think that Kennedy would have withdrawn from Vietnam, and I'd love to think that Kennedy was going to withdraw from Vietnam, but I don't think, when you add up all the pieces, that it ends up that way. When I say that, that's my heart speaking, and not so much my analytical abilities, such as they are.

I'm going to focus primarily on the decision to intervene—the decision to commit ground troops in the summer of 1965. The contrast between scratching through hours of Kennedy tapes to find a net total of eight or nine minutes of discussion on this huge decision that supposedly occurred in '63 on the one hand, and what happens in the summer of 1965 when the U.S. government obsesses itself for several months over this similarly momentous decision, is so staggering as to be astonishing. As I understand it, the function of my position as provocateur is actually to provoke, so I really have just a few things to say about the summer of '65 decisions, on which I hope our former administration officials can comment.

Just to lay in the groundwork very briefly: as the U.S. moves into 1965, it responds to an incident that occurs in the Central Highlands of Vietnam by beginning retaliatory bombing of North Vietnam and by expanding that bombing into a regular campaign of bombing the North. Then it protects some of these air units that are on bases in South Vietnam by sending in a few groups, after which it comes to grips with recommendations from the American commanders in South Vietnam that would greatly expand that force. It gradually adds to the force, and then confronts another recommendation from the commander in South Vietnam [General William Westmoreland] to permit his American troops to engage in offensive combat operations. In that context, he asks to increase the force to a certain number of battalions. 175,000 troops is the number that is discussed in the summer of 1965. From late May 1965 to late July 1965 there is a succession of meetings of both the National Security Council as a whole and of Lyndon Johnson's more restricted Tuesday lunch group, which was LBJ's version of Kennedy's ExComm.[2] They mull over a succession of these decisions, and there are Pentagon-requested documents and planning documents similar to the documents we've been discussing. There are National Intelligence Estimates prepared by the CIA that comment on the possible responses by other countries if we do this thing we are thinking about doing. There are State Department commentaries about potential diplomatic consequences. There is even a momentary pause in the U.S. bombing of North Vietnam, which has now become a regular campaign, for the purpose of possibly ascertaining whether there's a diplomatic alternative to military action.[3] When it comes to just being around the table with Lyndon Johnson, there is a whole series of events wherein Johnson causes certain people around the table to do certain things at the meetings so that he can entertain discussions pro and con as regards doing these things that are being contemplated.

Among the things that happen—and this is apparent not so much from what is actually in the briefing book, but from the records of George Ball's telephone conversations; it arises in the context of this well-known idea that George Ball as the devil's advocate in these meetings about intervention in Vietnam is stage-managed debate—is that Johnson draws Ball out during the NSC meetings on the ground troop issue and says, "So, George, can you present to us your point of view?" And "Let's all listen to George."[4] On the sidelines, we have McGeorge Bundy sending memos to the president saying, "I think you should listen hard to what George has to say, and then reject it."[5] On the other side, behind the scenes, we have Lyndon Johnson talking to Bill Moyers, and Bill Moyers talking to George Ball. In fact, over a period of some days in July 1965, Ball's records suggest that you, Bill, very carefully maneuvered Ball to make a certain type of presentation at the NSC.

Secondly, two of the big mistakes that are typically assigned to Lyndon Johnson in the course of making these decisions are that he made them in secret—that is, by not telling the American people everything that was being done—and by not coming into the open. As part of that secrecy, he wouldn't go before Congress to ask for money to fund the war and pay the troops that were going to Vietnam. Both these things came back to bite them later on when people discovered the real costs of all of this. It turns out that the documentary records contain McGeorge Bundy memoranda to the president detailing, for example, "the eight reasons why you shouldn't go to Congress and ask for money." In another instance: "Here are a set of reasons why we should structure the revelation of what we are doing by talking about it." In fact, Johnson discusses this in telephone calls. "I'll reveal this much right now," he tells Richard Russell, "and then I'll talk later in the year about this much more that we're doing, and then later I'll give it in packets."[6] So they structure how they will reveal their decisions, and that also comes back to bite them.

All three of these issues raise a question regarding the role of advisers in all of this. Returning to the first point I made yesterday, in the opening of this show—doesn't it seem that simultaneously there exists a war of the president positioning himself among all these officials, and a war of the officials trying to sandbag the president in whatever direction they think the policy should be going? End of story.

Bill Moyers: JFK, LBJ, and Vietnam—Forty-plus Years of Perplexity

A much-anticipated moment arrives when it is Bill Moyers's turn to offer a provocation regarding Kennedy, Johnson, and Vietnam. He will note in these opening remarks and on several other occasions during the conference discussions that, despite the passage of forty years since the events under scrutiny, he has until now for the most part declined to speak for the public record about the two presidents he served specifically regarding the war in Vietnam. But Bill Moyers demonstrates immediately that despite forty-plus years of public silence on these presidents and this issue, he has nevertheless thought a good deal about them. And, happily, he is just as thoughtful and eloquent speaking informally from sketchy notes about events of decades earlier as he is on PBS.

As Bill Moyers emphasizes, he was never a major figure on either JFK's or LBJ's foreign policy team. (Under Kennedy, he was deputy director of the Peace Corps; under Johnson, he was a special assistant for domestic affairs until July 1965, when he became press secretary to the president, a position he held until his resignation in January 1967.) That said, he knew LBJ as well as any person who ever worked for him. With regard to the war in Vietnam, he admits to having been perplexed all these years by variants of a single issue: why did LBJ retain JFK's foreign policy team if he didn't intend to carry out JFK's intentions with regard to the conflict in Vietnam? One way he expresses his perplexity is as follows: if LBJ really knew that JFK intended to withdraw from Vietnam, then why didn't Johnson, consistent with his stated objective of continuing Kennedy's policies, also take steps to "continue" Kennedy's withdrawal from Vietnam? Moyers's perplexity also takes an alternative form: if in fact JFK intended to withdraw from Vietnam—as is suggested on the audiotapes and in some of the documents that Moyers has studied for the first time in preparation for this conference—why did he never hear McNamara or Rusk or McGeorge Bundy or

Walt Rostow ever tell LBJ that this was, in fact, what Kennedy intended to do? Moyers reiterates that he was not very involved in foreign policy, but, even so, he regards it as highly unlikely that he would not, at some point, have heard such conversations, or at the very least heard from LBJ about such conversations, if they had in fact occurred. But, he says, he heard nothing of the kind. Moreover, he has discovered in preparing for the conference that there is apparently no written record of LBJ having been informed by his senior foreign and defense policy advisers about any intention JFK may have had to withdraw from Vietnam, to say nothing of the detailed preparations for carrying it out described in the previous session by Jamie Galbraith.

Why not? Several answers suggest themselves, and each is addressed in the discussion Bill Moyers helps to provoke. Was it LBJ's fault? Was it because LBJ did not want to hear about any withdrawal plan—that he was in other words far more intrinsically hawkish on the issue of Vietnam than was Kennedy? Or was it the advisers' fault? Could it be that Kennedy's intention and plan to withdraw was exactly that—Kennedy's, and Kennedy's more or less alone, with his advisers going along and doing what they knew he wanted them to do but, being instinctively hawkish on the Vietnam issue, they did so without real conviction? If so, then is it possible that once LBJ succeeded JFK, the advisers were no longer constrained by the cautious president to whom they owed their positions in the government, and they thus gave LBJ the impression that Kennedy had been ready and willing to escalate the war? Or was the problem something like a clash of cultures between the homespun president and his elite, Ivy League–educated team of advisers? In his memoirs, George Ball, Rusk's principal deputy in the State Department, recalled his own feelings at the moment JFK was replaced as president by LBJ.

> President Kennedy was dead. He had been my friend and then my chief and the shape of the future was now obscure. I thought I had understood Kennedy. He resembled other men I knew well who had gone to good schools, were informed, literate, with a wry wit, and had a receptive ear for historical or literary allusions. . . . Rapport with Lyndon Johnson did not come so easily. He was of a breed I had known only from literature, legend or at a distance . . . I assumed I would never understand Johnson as I had John Kennedy, for he was, as I saw it, a man from a different culture. Lacking the tone and manners one expected of a President—with a breezy Texan tendency to oversimplify and overstate, overpraise and overblame—he would not, I thought, be easy to work with . . . I would never fully comprehend him.[7]

Unlike George Ball and most of the JFK holdovers in LBJ's administration, Bill Moyers was quite familiar with people like the new president, not only from "literature, legend or at a distance," but from real life. Like Lyndon Johnson, Bill Moyers was (though born in Oklahoma) raised and educated in Texas, and thus did not face the "cultural" hurdles faced by Ball and the other establishment figures Johnson had inherited from Kennedy. But as Ball suggests, these barriers were substantial and compounded by LBJ's deep feelings of inferiority when around these advisers, on everything from his diction, to his circle of friends, to his formal education, to his manners.[8]

In his preparation for the conference, it is clear that Bill Moyers's forty-plus years of perplexity have deepened as he has encountered new evidence for JFK's intention to withdraw from Vietnam. But search his memory as he might, he can recall no shred of evidence suggesting that LBJ himself was made aware of this by his inherited advisers. His provocation is highly personal, characteristically modest, and focused on that key moment when LBJ was unexpectedly thrust into the presidency and on Johnson's initial encounters as president with the JFK team.

BILL MOYERS: I haven't written or spoken on these issues very much, because I couldn't trust what I remembered, and I couldn't be sure what I thought at the time. When you are close to the center of the intense activities that engage any president, other people remember better than you do what was happening, because you move from one issue to another, you don't have time to make notes. Your memories merge, the days blur, and as time goes on the inventory of recollection piles up so high that it is like an attic, and you go up, look around, and decide—I'm never going to clean that thing out. I've never written or spoken much for those reasons, as well as for the fact that my heart, like so many others'—the hearts of everyone around this table who were born then—was broken on the 22nd of November 1963—broken by the tragedy that affected the country through the assassination of a president. Broken by the fact that my hero, John F. Kennedy, had been killed. I didn't know Kennedy well, personally, but he was a hero, because Judith and I sat in the cold of that inauguration and heard that famous speech that said we would bear any burden. He was a public man who moved me. He had appointed me deputy director of the Peace Corps when I was twenty-seven, a position requiring Senate confirmation, so I was deeply indebted to him.

I was also deeply indebted to my mentor and benefactor Lyndon Johnson, who had suddenly been thrust into an office he'd always wanted, under circumstances that he would never have wished for, and which he knew would cast an enduring historical shadow over whatever he did.

I revered both of these men. I'm saying this also for Jamie's benefit, because I've tried very hard—and still try very hard—not to articulate for either one at the expense of the other. These were two totally different men, joined only by their participation in the times. I revered JFK in no small part because I didn't know him personally, and revered LBJ despite knowing him personally. [Laughter.] I remember that I had just come into the room, once, at a particular moment when Johnson had called in Dean Acheson to seek some private counsel. Johnson was saying, "You know, Dean, I don't understand why people don't like me." And Acheson replied, "Well, Mr. President, maybe it's because you're not a very likable man." That was true. But I did revere him. I revered him because I knew what he wanted for the country. I was in awe of his prowess with different people, and his ability to get different people to set aside their own interests long enough to do what he wanted them to do.

I've been puzzled all these years, and the puzzle comes into focus in a session like this—puzzled as to why LBJ kept all these people who did not propose to him any change in the policy that Kennedy himself had been following. Never did I hear Johnson refer to Kennedy's plan to get out of Vietnam—or only once, and it was incidental, after [Vermont Senator] George Aiken had said we should declare victory and get out: Johnson was heard to say, "The time for doing that was eight years ago"—or six years ago, or some time before the stakes had increased so much. I've often asked myself: Why did I never hear LBJ refer to any option except the two that were on the table in '65?[9] Why did LBJ keep the Kennedy team if he didn't intend to continue the Kennedy policies?

I was on that plane back from Dallas. I was in Texas on the day of the assassination, because Kennedy had asked me to go down and help advance his trip. I was in Boston, flew to Dallas, came back, and I spent the next four nights at the Elms, which was LBJ's home as vice president, when Johnson decided, particularly and pervasively, that he was going to carry out the policies of the Kennedy administration. He did not talk about Vietnam; we talked about civil rights, economic policies, and the war on poverty. It is very clear he believed that his only way to gain credibility as president in the wake of the assassination was to make no changes in Kennedy's policies and to make no changes in personnel. Some of us argued that he should, for their sake; they were heartbroken and tragic.

I stood by Larry O'Brien and Kenny O'Donnell on the plane back from Dallas. They were totally heartbroken, but both said, "Mr. President, if you want us to serve, we will serve." Some of us thought that for their sake and for his sake, he should make some changes. But the president said no. He was going to continue the policies of John F. Kennedy [**Document 5-1**].[10] This is why he began his first address to Congress with very carefully chosen words, "Let us continue."[11]

I particularly puzzle over the role of a Kennedy man named Walt Rostow, because it was Walt who was theological about these things, and it was Walt who, when LBJ asked him to succeed McGeorge Bundy, kept telling Lyndon Johnson that John F. Kennedy had a deep commitment to the independence of Vietnam from which he would not have retreated. I do not remember him talking about a plan; I do not remember him talking about withdrawal, Jamie. I do remember Walt repeatedly talking about Kennedy's commitment to the independence of South Vietnam.

I meant to say yesterday that one of the most interesting moments in my young life was when I was deputy director of the Peace Corps. The White House sent around a speech that Walt Rostow had made at Fort Bragg in North Carolina—I forget the exact date; I think it was somewhere around the time we are talking about, the fall of 1961.[12] It was on wars of national liberation, and it was the theology of the time: the new administration, and the new frontier. I remember Walt when he became national security adviser [in February 1966] talking about that.

I puzzle over why LBJ didn't implement JFK's decisions, since the people who would be carrying them out would be the people that had recommended them to JFK. I do not remember it ever coming up. Granted, I was not a part of the foreign-policy apparatus, ever. I certainly was not during the period we are discussing. From 1963 to the buildup in '65, I was the coordinator of domestic policy. My job was to put together the task forces on the Great Society and present the findings to LBJ. It was only at the buildup that he asked me for a third time to become press secretary. I finally accepted on the day of the announcement of the escalation. The first time I said no, the second time I said no, and the third time I had to say yes. My shoulder is still dislocated from that handshake, but I did accept on that day. [Laughter.] I'll get back to that in a moment.

I puzzle over why there is no record of McNamara, Bundy, Taylor, or others urging LBJ to carry out Kennedy's plan. They never did in my presence. While I had nothing to do with foreign policy, LBJ, Jack Valenti, Joe Califano, and I were always around meetings that veered off into foreign policy, and I never heard that.[13] That doesn't mean it wasn't discussed, but I never heard it. Why, when things started to go badly again in '64, didn't LBJ see it to his advantage to implement Kennedy's plan and relieve himself from assuming stewardship of the war? He never considered that. He considered either escalating it to win it or continuing the status quo. It was never proposed to him in my sight or hearing that he do what he would have called "cut and run."

Going back for a moment to the impact of events on personalities, Johnson kept saying to me that every experience creates a new reality. It is a little mantra I have on the shelf in the office where Judith and I work. Every experience creates a new reality. It did on McGeorge Bundy. Gordon, I've always wanted to ask you this ever since I met you at Mac's funeral.[14] You know, McGeorge Bundy was a different man after Pleiku than he was before Pleiku. I guess it has something to do with when you hear the firing of the shells. When you are present, something happens to you. He was a different man after that [**Document 5-5**].[15] I'm not sure why, and I wonder if you have any comment on how that event changed him. I was actually in the room when Mac called from Pleiku and told the president that he had been there when the Vietcong attacked.

GORDON GOLDSTEIN: And did you sense a great depth of emotion in his recounting of those events?

BILL MOYERS: Yes. Mac and I were friendly. We were close. I had to fire him four times, because LBJ would send me over there to fire him every now and again. Mac would just say, "Oh, not again." [Laughter.] He was always crisp, collected, and composed, but there was a timbre in his voice that day on the phone. Granted, it was a military phone with poor reception, but I had never heard such emotion in his voice. I had never heard it, even after the assassination. When he came back, he had recovered, but he was different. I have never taken the time to try to figure this all out. As a matter of fact, as I said to you yesterday on the bus, one of the reasons I haven't talked about it is I think McNamara has talked too much about it.

McNamara thinks out loud. He did in meetings, in private, and in public. Look, we all think out loud, but you can talk so much in public and think out loud so much that you cease to be a credible oral witness. Mac never did that. I think Mac was trying to do what I will do if I ever write about this, and that is to control what I am saying so I can be certain that I can get it straight. That's why I think there was a tragedy in Mac's premature death. We would have gotten a book written in the precise way that Mac wanted us to understand the reality of what he had experienced at that time.

There was a strong continuity between the two presidents until events forced a break in the status quo. Dean Rusk kept arguing for the status quo: "Just stay with it and something will happen; we'll wear them down." Johnson did that until he felt that events had forced a change in the status quo, and that's when he made a decision to try to win the war. What do you mean by win the war? Preventing the North Vietnamese from taking over South Vietnam. He never pushed for bringing down the regime in North Vietnam. The only time I ever heard General "Bus" Wheeler say anything off of the briefing plan was when Johnson asked him, "What will it take to win?" Earle Wheeler said, "Well, it depends on what you mean by 'win.'" He then explained a scenario that began with the 205,000, but said, "If you really want to win—if you really want to stop them and prevent them from ever winning in South Vietnam—it will take a million men and five years." Johnson blanched. He never intended to do that. What he intended to do was to make the cost so severe that they would give up their plans in the South. That was winning, by his measure.[16]

I'm also puzzled as to why McNamara was always ambivalent about the war in his own mind. And he *was.* I had never heard these tapes before now, but there was ambivalence there, even when he talks about what he is good at talking about: figures. He was nonetheless ambivalent about the war. You can tell by listening to the tapes. Why was he always ambivalent about the war in his own mind, but often emphatic in his advice to the president? I think it goes back to what one of you were saying. McNamara was the original pessimist, and yet still selling Pintos. He was still putting it out there, until the public demand forced him to take the Pintos back.[17] I think it is a part of a deep ambivalence that a tragic man is still experiencing. I think he was often surprised by the consequences of his own recommendations, as you might expect of a businessman who puts a product on the line and then discovers the public doesn't like it. I don't know, but it all puzzles me.

Why, in listening for the first time to these October 1963 tapes, did I experience the same chill I had in listening to the same men talk in private in 1967?[18] The same degree of doubt and duplicity—honest duplicity, in the sense that they just didn't want to tell the public what might be the consequences of what was happening yet—you heard in '64 and '65. I don't think anybody ever believed it was going to turn out well. Nobody. And yet for psychological, political, and emotional reasons that I don't understand, we continued to pursue it. We were not theological the way Bush is, and that's a big difference. With theology you can turn yourself away from the consequences of your decisions, and in effect anaesthetize yourself. Johnson could never anaesthetize himself, even when he did what he did consciously. There was continuity in the fact that both men preferred to defer decisions until it was no longer possible to do so. That's true of every president. You can read the biographies of Roosevelt or Eisenhower—every president defers decisions as long as he can. I don't blame them for that, or for keeping options open. They are in the center of power struggles involving a variety of forces. It was always a struggle in our administration—the Kennedy/Johnson administration. It was never a real Johnson administration, not until Mac left [in February 1966] and McNamara went to the World Bank [in March 1968]. Until I also left [in January 1967], I was a Kennedy/Johnson man. I was from Texas and I loved Lyndon Johnson. I loved JFK too. I was a Kennedy/Johnson man. There was never a real Johnson administration until about 1968, which is why I have been so eager to hear those tapes—when, on his own, Johnson is weighing the very same things in 1968 that Kennedy did in 1961, seven years earlier.

Those are the things that puzzle me. I can't tell you exactly what Johnson decided in the summer of 1965, except that he couldn't keep on doing what we were doing. He took the next step to escalate the war, until he thought he could win it by preventing the North Vietnamese from taking over the South.

MARILYN YOUNG: Bill, before I start, I just want to say how much I wish you would write about this.

JAMES BLIGHT: Hear, hear!

MARILYN YOUNG: I said it privately; I want to say it publicly. Hearing you talk about this is more helpful to me than a lot of what I've been reading for the last thirty-five years. It's just so illuminating, and it makes such a difference, just as you have all along, politically. I would just like to urge you to do that.

jANET LANG: It is now adopted as a consensus.

Marilyn Young: Did "Faith-Based" Advisers Lead LBJ Into War?

The third provocation, from historian Marilyn Young, reminds us of the timing of the conference—April 2005—with her reference to a magazine piece by Ron Suskind that had appeared some months earlier.[19] The subject of that article is arrogance: faith in abstract ideas that form the intellectual foundation of the contemporary neoconservative (neocon) movement. According to these ideas, the U.S. in the post–Cold War era is said by Suskind's interlocutor to have become unambiguously an empire. According to many neocons, the lack of another global superpower to check U.S. ambitions means that it is more or less free to do as it pleases, to "create its own realities," to preemptively throw its weight around. Others—other countries, the United Nations, various other subnational groups—may not like American hegemony but, according to the neocon faithful, they will just have to get used to it. That was the position taken by the neocons during what history may come to judge as the brief, high tide of the sway of its ideas: initiating the U.S. global "war on terror"; endorsing the doctrine of preemption, according to which the U.S. government claimed the right to intervene militarily any where, any time it felt its interests were threatened; repudiating many international agreements and treaties, such as the Kyoto accords on the environment and the Anti-Ballistic Missile Treaty; and invading and occupying Afghanistan and Iraq. The November 2004 reelection of George W. Bush was interpreted by neocons as a referendum on the neocon agenda—the high tide of neocon confidence.

By the time of the Musgrove conference in April 2005, advocates of these ideas were having a difficult time explaining why the U.S. was becoming mired in a vicious and disastrous civil and sectarian conflict in Iraq, a conflict that was beginning to bear a startling resemblance to that other disastrous insurgent war, in the 1960s in Vietnam. Since the November 2006 midterm elections, through which Democrats gained control of both the Senate and the House chiefly on the strength of their opposition to the war in Iraq, things have gone from bad to worse for the neocons. To Marilyn Young, both colossal foreign policy blunders of her lifetime—the escalation and Americanization of the war in Vietnam and the invasion and occupation of Iraq—can be explained with reference to the arrogance of those whom Vietnam correspondent David Halberstam once called, ironically, "The Best and the Brightest."[20] This is the context of her remarks: once more, arrogant, well-educated, but unwise advisers have joined forces with an inexperienced, arrogant president to undertake a "war of choice," thus creating an unnecessary disaster on an epic scale.

In her remarks, Young refers to the transcripts of telephone conversations LBJ had with his informal circle of advisers, focusing on his former colleague in the Senate and fellow southerner Richard Russell of Georgia. The "script" of these conversations is played out in endless variations throughout the first year and a half of LBJ's presidency—"the long 1964"—during which the decisions to escalate the war in Vietnam took shape and were implemented. In these conversations, Johnson invariably tells his informal "adviser" that his formal advisers—chiefly McNamara, Bundy, and Rusk— are gung ho for war, that they say the communist insurgency in Vietnam can and must be defeated, and that they are convinced that the war can be contained inside Vietnam, leading to no wider war involving the Russians and/or the Chinese. LBJ then explains, in conspiratorial tones (the "adviser" is often given to believe this is the first and only time LBJ will have such a conversation) that he has his doubts about what McNamara, Bundy, and Rusk are recommending to him. This is the standard script, which LBJ then embroiders in riffs of astounding variety and a particularly southern form of homespun verbal virtuosity.

From such conversations as these, one can get the impression that LBJ feels trapped by the advice of his advisers, unsure of how to evaluate what they are telling him or how to respond to them, and suspicious that things are not as clear-cut as they make them out to be. No doubt this is exactly how Johnson did feel. He had inherited a job, a set of advisers, and a seemingly intractable problem, none of which had been chosen by him. Perhaps it should not be surprising, therefore, that several times during the long 1964 LBJ suddenly became mysteriously ill, often bedridden, hardly able to function, deeply withdrawn, and showing many of the signs of depression, whatever may have been the physical malady that had caused his absence from the duties of office.

Yet, as the discussion evolves in this session, the participants are urged by several colleagues not to take LBJ's complaints about his advisers at face value. They ask, for example: how confident should we be that Johnson's advisers told the president with confidence that the communist insurgency could be defeated at acceptable cost and risk? Robert McNamara, for instance, seems never to have believed this and never to have expressed it privately to LBJ, although publicly he projected supreme confidence that the U.S. would prevail in Vietnam, that South Vietnam would remain independent and non-communist, and so on. Perhaps we should ask, therefore, whether the situation in the U.S. leadership following JFK's assassination may have been more psychologically complex—not a straightforward case either of advisers duping their new boss, or the new boss turning a deaf ear to the inherited advisers. Is it possible that the advisers, their habits of advising having been well established under JFK, were in some sense still "looking for President JFK," putting forth views as if to a president of subtlety, confidence in foreign affairs, caution when it came to conflict, and with a hierarchy of priorities that helped prevent a Third World issue like Vietnam from rising higher than its intrinsic importance warranted in U.S. national security? And might it also be possible, conversely, that Lyndon Johnson, who had spent his entire adult life crafting deals in back rooms with colleagues, was searching in vain for someone— anyone—on the Vietnamese communist side with whom he could deal? Might LBJ, by force of long-established habits, figuratively have been "looking for Senator Ho Chi Minh," looking in vain for someone who would, as LBJ was always prepared to do, give a little to get a lot? Do considerations such as these, perhaps, underlie the remarks of all three provocateurs for this session—John Prados, Bill Moyers, and Marilyn Young—as they search for a way to understand how the disastrous decisions of the long 1964 came to pass?

MARILYN YOUNG: On Jim's advice, I did write something, and I will now offer it. It may also be a provocation as much as a response. You all know Ron Suskind's interview, which was in the *New York Times Magazine* last October. This is likely, in fifty or a hundred years from now, to become one of those anecdotes historians open with to capture the ethos of past times. It has already become iconic in the present. You remember how it goes: "The [Bush] aide said that guys like [Suskind] were 'in what we call the reality-based community,' which he defined as people who 'believe that solutions emerge from your judicious study of discernible reality.' I nodded," says Suskind, "and murmured something about enlightenment principles and empiricism. He cut me off. 'That's not the way the world really works anymore,' he continued. 'We're an empire now, and when we act, we create our own reality. And while you're studying that reality, judiciously, as you will, we'll act again, creating new realities, which you can study too, and that's how things will sort out. We're history's actors . . . and you, all of you, will be left to just study what we do.'"[21]

Reading through these 1,000 pages of interpretation and documents (most of them, anyway) I was struck by how little Johnson felt he could create new realities in Vietnam, and how hard he struggled to figure out what was real as the basis for what was possible. By contrast, it was his advisers—all of them inherited from his predecessor—who, in the documents, seem confident of the ability of the U.S. to impose its will on Vietnam through force of arms. A conviction? A faith? That seems almost to preview Washington today.

Although he frequently accused his critics of whining to the press about Vietnam, Johnson himself could whine with the best, and did so on the phone with some regularity. Over and over he talks his way around the same territory, clearly hoping one of his interlocutors will provide a better map, offering greater clarity about Vietnam and more reasonable choices for the U.S. In several long conversations in May and June 1964 with Richard Russell, Democratic senator from Georgia, Johnson complained that all his advisers—Rusk, McNamara, Bundy, [Averell] Harriman, and [Cyrus] Vance—want to "show some power and some force . . . they're kinda like MacArthur [sic] in Korea: they don't believe the Chinese Communists will come into this thing." Russell listened sympathetically and offered some Korean memories of his own when Johnson suggested that bombing the North might be a next step. "Bomb the North," Russell asks, "and kill old men, women and children?" No, Johnson reassured him, just "selected targets, watch this trail they're coming down." "We tried it in Korea," Russell protested. "We even got a lot of old B-29s to increase the bomb load and sent 'em over there and just dropped millions and millions of bombs, day and night . . . they would knock the road at night and in the morning, the damn people would be back traveling [sic] over it. . . . We never could actually interdict all their lines of communication, although we had absolute control of the seas and the air, and we never did stop them. And you ain't gonna stop these people either." But Johnson worries he'll be impeached if he just runs away from Vietnam. When Russell suggested the possibility that a South Vietnamese president could be induced to invite the U.S. to leave, Johnson sort of agreed but objected: "That's right, but you can't do that. . . . Wouldn't that pretty well fix us in the eyes of the world, though, and make it look mighty bad?" To which Russell said, "I don't know. We don't look too good right now."[22]

Johnson listened more closely to his Texan intimate, A. W. Moursund, than he did to Russell.[23] For Moursund, too, Korea was the touchstone. The conversation worried Johnson, who repeated it to Russell. "Goddamn," Moursund had told him, "there's not anything that'll destroy you as quick as pulling out, pulling up stakes and running. America wants, by God, prestige and power." When Johnson expressed his reluctance to "kill these folks," Moursund replied: "I don't give a damn. I didn't want to kill 'em in Korea, but if you don't stand up for America . . . [the fellows in Johnson City or Georgia or any other place], they'll forgive you for anything except being weak." Russell was not impressed. What Moursund urged would take a half-million men and the country would be bogged down for the next ten years. Sobering, Johnson agreed: "We never did clear up Korea yet."

Before the conversation ended, Russell came full circle: "As a practical matter, we're in there and I don't know how the hell you can tell the American people you're coming out . . . they'll think that you've been whipped, you've been ruined, you're scared, it would be disastrous." And just in case Johnson did not feel sufficiently stuck, Russell then observed that the American people weren't "so opposed to coming out. I don't think the American people want to stay there."[24] Back and forth, on all sides of the issue, their talk worries away at what is possible, what impossible, what Johnson must do, what he can't do.

Johnson's inherited advisers, by contrast, talk with confidence in their control of reality. Faced with a policy that seemed to have bogged down into inaction, Mac Bundy and McNamara addressed Johnson with great firmness on January 27th, 1965. Both were convinced that the current policy—waiting to establish a stable government in Saigon before taking further military action—was disastrous. The problem lay in the spreading conviction that "the future is without hope for anti-Communists." Good men and true were discouraged by "our own inactivity in the face of major attacks on our installations." They charged the U.S. with an unwillingness to take serious risks. Of course, Bundy hastens to say, given what the U.S. had done for the Vietnamese, and what more it would do if they would "only pull up their socks," this was outrageous [**Document 5-4**].[25]

But it seemed clear that the only way a stable government would emerge was for the U.S. to act. Two sorts of actions were possible: The first "is to use our military power in the Far East to force a change of Communist policy." The second was to negotiate and salvage "what little can be preserved . . ." Bundy and McNamara unequivocally urged the first course. They called it the "harder choice." The memo concludes with the somber warning that both of his principal advisers on Vietnam had come to the point where their obligations to the president did not allow them to continue to administer a policy they felt to be hopeless [**Document 5-4**].

Between January 1965 and the decision to give Westmoreland the troops he had asked for, the pressure on Johnson to escalate the war seems to me to have been relentless. In July, on the verge of full troop commitment, Johnson, feeling "pretty depressed," appealed to McNamara: assuming that the U.S. did everything it could "to the extent of our resources," was there any assurance it could win? "I mean, assuming we have all the big bombers and all the powerful payloads and everything else, can the Vietcong come in and tear us up and continue this thing indefinitely, and never really bring it to an end?" And was there sufficient domestic support for such a war? McNamara has a plan for dealing with the public, but he never answers Johnson's main question: can we be sure if we go all out that we will win? Then, too, faith-based policymakers won the day: Johnson took the country to war.[26]

The Tonkin Gulf Episode and the "Johnson Treatment"

On August 10, 1964, President Lyndon Johnson signed into law a bill called the Joint Resolution of the Maintenance of Peace and Security in Southeast Asia, which has been known ever since as the Tonkin Gulf Resolution.[27] The events leading up to the passage of the Resolution were portrayed by the Johnson administration as successive, unprovoked attacks by North Vietnamese patrol boats on U.S. destroyers in the Tonkin Gulf, just off the coast of North Vietnam (on August 2 and 4, 1964). In response, the U.S. Congress nearly unanimously voted (in the words of the Resolution) to "support . . . the determination of the President, as Commander in Chief, to take all necessary measures to repel any armed attack against the forces of the United States and to prevent further aggression."[28] LBJ would later claim to have gotten authorization via the Tonkin Gulf Resolution to launch a massive air war against North Vietnam and to dispatch hundreds of thousands of ground troops to South Vietnam. In short, with the approval of the Congress, Johnson received a "blank check" to carry on an undeclared war in Southeast Asia. Later, many senators and members of Congress felt they had been misled by Johnson. After the war bogged down and became unpopular with the American public, many claimed Johnson had led them to believe they were voting on a measure with a strictly limited scope and duration. For example, the chairman of the Senate Foreign Relations Committee, J. William Fulbright, said that, until his experience with LBJ and the Tonkin Gulf Resolution, he had no idea his own government, run by his own party, would lie to him.[29] Johnson was happy with the Resolution, however. As he is said to have quipped, "Like Grandma's nightshirt, it covers everything."[30]

The following discussion offers fascinating insights into the events surrounding the Tonkin Gulf Resolution by three people who were right in the thick of things. Tom Hughes describes in a sidesplitting anecdote the way LBJ responded to the news of the first attack on August 2 and the way Johnson used the occasion to work over General Earle "Bus" Wheeler, the new Chairman of the Joint Chiefs of Staff. LBJ gives the Army general the "Johnson treatment," as it was called, a technique Johnson used ubiquitously to establish control of discussions and to make people who made Johnson feel uncomfortable feel even more uncomfortable than he felt. Chet Cooper describes what it was like in the White House Situation Room when LBJ came asking: was there a second attack (on August 4) or not? And Bill Moyers suggests that the specific events in the Tonkin Gulf probably had little to do with the ultimate outcome—LBJ getting authorization for doing whatever he thought necessary militarily regarding Vietnam. Johnson, according to Moyers, was responding to yet further deterioration in the situation on the ground in South Vietnam and needed a fig leaf to cover the air attacks and military buildup that he was convinced would ultimately be necessary to deter the communist insurgents of the NLF in South Vietnam and their allies in Hanoi. The Tonkin Gulf Resolution provided that fig leaf.

It is now established that the first attack, on August 2, to which LBJ did not order military retaliation, did occur, whereas it is now virtually certain that the August 4 event was a phantom "attack" that never occurred, but instead was caused by some combination of technical failures and overzealous sonar men who were on edge and hypervigilant since the attack of two days earlier. With the 1964 party conventions and the presidential election on the horizon, the Tonkin Gulf—its actual and imagined events—and the Resolution were largely forgotten by the public until February 1965, when U.S. escalation began in earnest. But unknown to U.S. decisionmakers at the time, the air strikes against North Vietnamese targets, which Washington regarded as mere minimal, proportionate "pinpricks," were interpreted in Hanoi as providing certain evidence that the long-expected U.S. air war against North Vietnam had begun. Accordingly, many women and children were immediately removed from major cities in the North and taken to the countryside. Air raid shelters were dug. Soviet antiaircraft equipment was moved into place. Ho Chi Minh and his colleagues, along with their NLF allies in the South, were about to take on the U.S. of America in what was, from the Vietnamese point of view, a total war beginning in early August 1964. Henceforth, American actions in Southeast Asia would be interpreted by the Vietnamese communists, North and South, in this context and only in this context: not as efforts to coerce them or to bargain with them, but as attempts by the U.S. to destroy them.[31]

JAMES BLIGHT: Many thanks to John, Bill, and Marilyn for getting us started. I have Tom Hughes first on my list. Tom?

THOMAS HUGHES: I'd like to talk for a minute about the Gulf of Tonkin. At an earlier meeting at the LBJ Library in 1991, speaking from memory I gave the group a truncated account of the August 2nd briefing of Johnson.[32] I now look at some notes that I wrote right after that meeting. I didn't take notes in the meeting, of course, but shortly afterwards. I had to brief Humphrey for a television appearance later that day.[33] A few of us were still in town that Sunday, August 2nd. Everything always happens on the weekends in August, of course. I was called to Dean

Rusk's house at five a.m. We had an implausible group of Rusk, Vance, Ball, General Wheeler, and two guys on his staff.

JAMES BLIGHT: Did you say five in the morning?

THOMAS HUGHES: It was daybreak, as I recall, when the first reports of the attack had come in. We sat around trying to find the Gulf of Tonkin, how many miles from shore the destroyer *Maddox* was, who claimed territorial waters, where the islands were, and so on and so forth. 34-A operations were specifically mentioned [**Document 5-3**].[34] We went back to our respective offices for the latest intelligence and then went off to the White House to brief LBJ around eleven a.m. (I've been waiting for the tapes of this meeting, and I'm now told they don't exist. So this was not a taped meeting, and I guess my notes are the only ones that exist.) It was a session full of levity. Johnson began by saying, "Where are my Bundys? I know where they are; they're up at that female island of theirs, Martha's Vineyard." [Laughter.] "That's where you'll find them: playing tennis at the female island. What's the big emergency?" Someone pops up and says, "Well, Mr. President, one of our destroyers has been attacked." Johnson says: "One of our destroyers has been attacked? Now who would do a damn fool thing like that?" The Navy said, "Well, we think it's the North Vietnamese torpedo boats." "What more do we know about this incident?" "Well, that's about all we know at the moment, Mr. President, but as soon as we have more information we'll bring it to your attention right away." Johnson says after a pause: "We weren't up to any mischief out there, were we?" After another pause, Ball says, "Well, you remember, Mr. President, that you signed off on those 34-A operations last December, that were left over as recommendations to the previous administration" [**Document 4-7**].[35] "Now remind me what these 34-A operations do?" Ball explains that the American hand doesn't show, that they are disavowable, strictly run by the South Vietnamese themselves, etc. They sometimes blow up a bridge, capture a fisherman, or maybe light up the radar along the coast. "Light up the radar?" says Johnson, "so that if we just happened to have a destroyer in the vicinity, we could maybe map the coast electronically?"[36] "Maybe," the group agreed. "Would it have happened that any of those 34-A operations might have occurred recently?" There is another pause and then someone says, "Well, we're not sure if we keep exact track of these missions in Washington. That's CINCPAC's responsibility.[37] But it could be that something happened a couple of nights ago." "I see," said Johnson, "and that's all we know about it?" "Yes sir, that's all we know." "Well," said Johnson, "it reminds me of the movies in Texas. You're sitting next to a pretty girl and you have your hand on her ankle and nothing happens, and you move it up to her knee and nothing happens. You're thinking about moving a bit higher, and all of a sudden you get slapped. I think we got slapped." Then he left the room for a minute. [Laughter.]

I wrote a note across the table to Rusk that said, "Now that we know what happens in the movies in Texas, do you wish to continue to call this an unprovoked attack?" Rusk was not amused. He said, "We'll ask Cy Vance. He's our lawyer."[38] He turned to Vance and said, "This was an unprovoked attack, was it not, Cy?" And Cy, rising to the occasion with a wonderful non sequitur, says: "Of course. It happened in international waters." Then Johnson returns to the room and says, "Well, it seems a bit murky, and we won't have any retaliation, but we will warn them against doing anything further. Now, let's get on to something serious." Johnson now turns his attention to the Postal Pay Bill. He says to General Wheeler: "Now, General, you're my chief strategist, and this Postal Pay Bill is coming down Pennsylvania Avenue—it's already at 9th Street, going on 10th Street—and I'm going to be damned if I sign it, and damned if I veto it. You're my strategist. You tell me how to get out of this." [Laughter.] General Wheeler, who hasn't usually been called upon to discuss techniques of averting congressional pressures, is fumbling around, and Johnson gets impatient and says: "General, you're wasting time; the bill is already at 12th Street." The meeting ended in an uproar, and, as we were leaving, General Wheeler asked, "Is it always like this?" I think it was his first real experience of the Johnson treatment.[39]

And that was Act I of the Gulf of Tonkin at the White House. Johnson sized up the situation accurately and certainly acted with restraint and avoided escalation. Ironically, he ends up responding to a phantom attack two days later and sending his fateful resolution up to Capitol Hill.

MARILYN YOUNG: May I ask a question? Is there any record that Johnson was told about the doubts? Herrick's cables that McNamara read said, "We're really not sure what happened here" [Document 5-3].[40]

THOMAS HUGHES: About the second attack? Chet Cooper would know; he was right in middle of it.

MARILYN YOUNG: Was Johnson directly informed about the doubts surrounding the second attack?

CHESTER COOPER: The second attack was a source of great consternation. There was some queasiness about the whole thing. The sonar man was a young kid; the weather was bad; you could make a case that it was a false alarm. But I think most people, including McNamara, felt that the consequences of being wrong about the second attack—that is to say, the consequences for saying there was no attack—outweighed the consequences of the reverse.

THOMAS BLANTON: But was the president told about those doubts?

CHESTER COOPER: Yes, well. I was in the Situation Room when the president called and he said, "Tell me about the second attack." I said—now, remember this is within hours—"Well sir, we're waiting for further information, we really don't know." He said, "Well, is there or isn't there an attack?" I said, "Well, there are people who think there was, but we don't have assurance because we are waiting for CINCPAC, the Commander in Chief of the Pacific, and so forth, to get his views." In the end, he called the Pentagon and Sharp.

THOMAS BLANTON: Sharp had assured McNamara at that point?

CHESTER COOPER: Sharp said, "Yes, CINCPAC was sure at that point there was a second attack."[41] Of course there was no second attack. There are two aspects to this. One was: was there as second attack? It turns out there wasn't. The second was: who ordered these attacks—the first or second? The judgment at the time was the same judgment that was made at Pleiku.[42] It was a bum judgment, and we should have known better, but we didn't know enough. The judgment about the attacks was that no local commander would dare attack an American ship—or, in the case of Pleiku, American troops—unless he was ordered to or it was officially approved by the high command in Hanoi. That made the issues doubly difficult to avoid. If we had known it had just been some local commander, some trigger-happy captain, it would have been different.

BILL MOYERS: Here is the puzzling thing about that. It's been puzzling me a long time. There was a first attack; there was no second attack, although Johnson believed there probably was a second attack. We still acted too precipitously. I do not understand, even to this moment, why, with the doubts that Johnson held, as Tom Hughes just described it—his reticence to leap—why did he move so quickly to get the Gulf of Tonkin Resolution passed? People say that Johnson carried that around with him in his pocket. I don't think that was true—and this goes back to what Fred was saying. But he had asked for a way to get Congress involved in giving him support for what had earlier in the summer been detected as another deterioration in Vietnam.

Fred, I support your point about emphasizing periods, because the response to the Gulf of Tonkin Resolution was not prompted by the Gulf of Tonkin.[43] It was prompted by what was happening in Vietnam in May, June, and July.

THOMAS BLANTON: Here are Mac Bundy's own words at the White House staff meeting on August 5th, 1964. This is the record written by Bill Smith [of JCS] to Max Taylor, who wasn't there. [Donald] Wilson of USIA asks what evidence can be offered publicly about the second attack, and Bundy says, "Well, on the first attack, the evidence would be pretty good, on the second the amount of evidence we have today is less than we had yesterday." This resulted primarily from correlating bits and pieces of information and eliminating double counting. There must have been an attack; how many boats? How many torpedoes? This was all pretty uncertain, and it was of some importance since Hanoi has denied making the second attack. Now this is the morning staff meeting at the White House.

Douglass Cater happened to be sitting in on his first staff meeting as a brand-new White House staffer.[44] He raised the question about the congressional resolution. He hadn't thought it through completely, but the logic behind the resolution troubled him somewhat. How would an attack on U.S. forces specifically justify a resolution in favor of maintenance of freedom in Southeast Asia? Quote: "Bundy, in reply, jokingly told him, 'Perhaps the matter should not be thought through too far.' For his own part [Bundy's] he welcomed the recent events as justification for a resolution the administration had wanted for some time." This is Bundy to the White House staff, the morning after, referring to the president's meeting with the congressional "leadership." And the word *leadership* is in quotes. "Yesterday Bundy commented that 'leadership' was a funny word in this case in that there was little Congressmen could do in the way of leading in a situation in which the president's role was so primary." That's Bundy to the White House staff![45]

This sounds very familiar, doesn't it?—from what we know about decisions leading to the Iraq War.

CHESTER COOPER: That resolution, or a draft of it, had been written quite a while before that. I think Bill Bundy had written one. There was an itching—a scab that had to be picked—which was the need to find a way to justify unleashing a serious military effort. And if it hadn't been the Tonkin Gulf incident, it would have been anything else. Something would have come along.

The Key Moment: February 1965

Cornell University historian Fred Logevall's 1999 book, Choosing War, *is one of the most important analyses of the war in Vietnam to appear in a generation.[46] In the conversation that follows, Fred Logevall challenges his colleagues on two points. First, he argues that not all points along the timeline of the long 1964 are equally pivotal in producing the American war in Vietnam. His candidate for the most important month during the entire period from August 1963–July 1965 is February 1965. This is the month of the February 7 and 10 attacks on American personnel at Pleiku and Qui Nhan in South Vietnam's Central Highlands. It is also the period during which decisions were made by Johnson to launch the air war against North Vietnam and to send in U.S. Marines whose mission, at least initially, was to protect U.S. aircraft at the Da Nang airbase in northern South Vietnam. After that, according to Logevall, the American war becomes a fact, though how large a war effort it will involve is still momentarily an open question.*

*A second challenge Logevall puts to the other participants is this: that the much-documented meetings held by LBJ with his advisers in June and July of 1965 are largely a charade [**Document 5-8**]. By that time Johnson, Logevall says, has made up his mind. Johnson is a hawk who cannot by that point imagine any option other than a major escalation, however much anguish such a decision undoubtedly caused him to suffer, however much he may have regretted having to make that choice. But make it he did. LBJ chose war fundamentally because, according to Logevall, he lacked the imagination to see that other choices were still open to him, right up until the time he signed the order to send nearly 175,000 troops to South Vietnam to "win the war."*

Chet Cooper, who accompanied McGeorge Bundy on his fateful trip to Vietnam in early February 1965, agrees with Fred Logevall's nomination of February 1965 as the turning point for LBJ, beyond which there would be no turning back. "Pleiku," Cooper says, "ruined everything," because after that attack, anyone arguing for any approach other than escalation to an American war could not get a hearing at the highest levels. It is obvious to everyone that Chet Cooper speaks with deep regret. He helped Bundy draft the long memorandum written on the plane ride back to Washington from Saigon and signed by Bundy. It is a tough, no-holds-barred memorandum on the necessity of launching a program of "sustained reprisals" *against targets in North Vietnam [**Document 5-5**]. On a previous occasion, Chet Cooper has said that were it not for the unfortunate timing of the dramatic attack on Pleiku, he believes he could have drafted a very different memorandum on the plane ride home for Bundy to give to the president—a memorandum that would, in a phrase that would later become a mantra of the peace movement, "give peace a chance."[47] Many historians reject this. They believe the die was already cast, and even if a significant attack on Americans had not occurred while Bundy was in South Vietnam, ultimately some attack would occur, making inevitable, or so many historians believe, a response similar to that which Johnson ordered in February 1965.*

Chet Cooper expresses skepticism whenever one of the participants states confidently that JFK had decided to withdraw from Vietnam. Yet one of Cooper's remarks suggests that he may have had at least some sympathy with that view. He refers to the many informal meetings on Vietnam he had with Robert McNamara and Averell Harriman. (Harriman was Cooper's boss while he was working from 1966–1968 on trying to find a way to halt the war and move to the negotiating table.) According to Cooper, the three men met fairly often during this period to "bitch" about the war in Vietnam. Cooper, who had a reputation for pugnacity when he felt the situation required it, recalls telling his strong-willed superiors to take their concerns to LBJ, not just to some mid-level staffer like himself. But they wouldn't, or anyway they said they couldn't. The timidity, especially of the often confrontational and determined McNamara, is surprising. One is led to wonder: if JFK had survived Dallas and been reelected, might something like the "bitch club," as it is called by Tom Blanton in the following conversation, have met forthrightly in the Oval Office with JFK as a charter member, instead of furtively at the State Department, where LBJ couldn't hear them? If it had, might the "bitching" have surfaced much earlier than the 1966–1968 discussions recalled by Chet Cooper? One can find evidence of something like this atmosphere of wide-open give and take on some of the Kennedy tapes with regard to the war in Vietnam and also the Cuban missile crisis. A question to ponder is, "Would it have made a significant difference to the outcome of events in Southeast Asia if top-level presidential advisers had felt comfortable voicing their concerns, disappointments, even disagreements with courses of action ordered by their boss in the White House?"

FREDRIK LOGEVALL: I want to make a point about periodization. The point is that we have in the briefing book a large amount of material pertaining to June and July of 1965. John [Prados] phrased his comments in the context of June and July 1965. But I would like to suggest that the key period has by that point passed. I was struck by the fact that the briefing book does not have any documents on November and December 1964, an eight-week period that both I and David Kaiser in his book deem absolutely critical.[48] I think that if you were going to talk about a particular month—one that may be more important than any other month in the whole twenty-five-year-long U.S. involvement in South Vietnam—you'd have to speak in terms of February '65. I think that by the time you get into June and July, LBJ is trapped to some extent. The June and July discussions are important, of course, but whatever the outcome of the deliberations in June and July, we still have an American war in Vietnam. American troops have already been given the authorization to engage in offensive operations; the air war is proceeding apace. I think the options have been drastically limited and we have paid far too much attention to a series of deliberations in June and July. Johnson's handling of those conversations suggests that they are a little bit like a charade, I think (if I may be provocative) [**Document 5-8**].

In any event, in June and July you do not have the same range of options you have earlier on. That is a point about periodization. I think we have exaggerated the importance of those summer months, given that the key decisions happen earlier. LBJ speaks from a very early point, as I'm sure Bill knows, of feeling trapped on Vietnam. He says, "Whatever I do, I'm trapped."

I've been puzzled about something I find striking about LBJ in this period, even after all the work I've done on this issue: in '64 and '65, he invariably tends to frame his options in such a way that standing firm—which ultimately means escalation—is really the only choice. I find that very striking. He's a realist in many ways; he recognizes the problems in Vietnam in some cases before his advisers, but ultimately, it seems to me, he is a hawk. He is a hawk from an early point. I don't have any sense that he can imagine—for lots of different reasons we can discuss—any alternative to staying the course, and ultimately that always means escalation. "We can fight them in South Vietnam, or we can fight them in San Francisco." Ultimately, I don't think he can see any alternatives.

CHESTER COOPER: One of the disillusioning things about government for an innocent young man such as I was at the time was how you couldn't speak truth to power very easily. By '65 Harriman and McNamara were getting very leery about the war. McNamara used to go back to the Pentagon by way of the State Department in the evening, and he'd come up to Harriman's office and have a drink. Both of them would begin to bitch about what was going on in Vietnam.⁴⁹ They would begin to yell at me. Hell, I was a charter member of that club!

THOMAS BLANTON: The bitch club?

CHESTER COOPER: Yes! I kept saying, "Well, don't talk to me about it; walk up the street and tell Rostow, or tell the president." And they would say, "Well, we can't do that; we won't do that."

On another occasion—and this is also in response to the point on McNamara and counterinsurgency and Rostow—I thought I had something going in Norway. The Norwegian ambassador was going back to Hanoi. He had medical appointments in Oslo, and then he was going back. I got a call from the foreign ministry saying, "We have our ambassador here from Hanoi, and if Mr. Harriman has anything you want him to convey to Hanoi—but it better be something new—come over here fast, because he only has a few days." So I dashed off to Oslo, and in the meantime Bill Bundy and I put something together—a very rough version of what turned out to be this phase A/phase B thing. You know—we [the U.S.] agree to stop the bombing, if you [North Vietnam] first agree to stop resupplying the insurgents, or at least reduce it significantly, in one of our more desperate formulations.

I spent some time with the ambassador, and he said, "Well, we'll do it, but on one condition, and that is that you do not bomb while I am delivering the message. I don't want bombs to be falling while I'm waiting outside to deliver this message." So I said, "Of course, we'll suspend bombing. It would be stupid to send you on a mission like this with bombs falling." Okay. I came home, and I looked at the bombing schedule, and there on the very day that the ambassador was to land in Hanoi, a truck park adjacent to the airport was scheduled to be bombed. So I went to Harriman and I said, "We can't do that. You've got to call McNamara and call it off." Harriman said, "I can't do that." I said, "Well, call Rostow." He said, "Listen"—and keep in mind I love Harriman, he's like my uncle—he said, "I have political capital to keep."⁵⁰ He said, "*You* go over and talk to Rostow; you don't have any political capital." Well, he was right. So off I went to talk to Rostow, and, you know, I told Rostow the story, whereupon Rostow's response was a ten-minute lecture on the theory of counterinsurgency. That's all I got.

BILL MOYERS: Who did that?

CHESTER COOPER: Rostow. But God was with me and the ambassador that day, because the cloud cover was such that they couldn't send the bombers over, but it was okay to let the passenger plane land at the airport to deliver the ambassador. The visibility was not good enough to bomb the truck park.

BILL MOYERS: May I just say in response that your comment helps me connect the Pleiku incident with what was happening months before, even though it happened months after the Gulf of Tonkin Resolution. As Mac said, they come along all the time—the streetcars come along—and they were coming along in early September.

DAVID WELCH: I had a long conversation with Mac Bundy once about that, and he told me that he regretted ever saying, "Pleikus are like streetcars; if you miss one, another will come along shortly." He said it had been badly misunderstood. He didn't actually mean to suggest that the administration was actively looking for excuses to get into Vietnam, but rather that there were always perfectly good reasons to do it if you felt you should.[51]

CHESTER COOPER: Pleiku made a difference, though. The 27 January 1965 "fork in the road" memo listed three options: escalate, hold the course, or withdraw [**Document 5-4**]. Pleiku ruined everything because after the attack, no one wanted to discuss holding the course or withdrawing.

BILL MOYERS: There weren't many, though, who thought you could hold it together with the status quo. Johnson didn't. But he was equally scared of having it all fall apart, and of having a big war.

THOMAS HUGHES: And he was scared of Goldwater.

BILL MOYERS: Before the election, yes. Johnson was afraid of letting go before '64. But after '64, the man who really scared him was Nixon.

CHESTER COOPER: The thing you have to recall is that, after Pleiku, almost no one was recommending anything other than escalation.

Was Neutrality an Option for Vietnam?

In the exchange that follows, Bill Moyers provides insight into one of the dark corners of the mind of his former boss, Lyndon Johnson. In response to a query by Jim Hershberg about a "third option" of a neutral government for South Vietnam (verses escalating massively or getting out completely), Moyers says that LBJ fundamentally was not attracted to neutrality on any issue, domestic or foreign. He implies that LBJ's under-

*standing of neutrality in the Vietnamese context was at odds with that of
JFK. LBJ, says Moyers, felt he couldn't trust a devoted communist like
Ho Chi Minh to remain neutral, for example with regard to a coalition
government in Saigon containing communists and non-communists.
Johnson seemed to feel that the moment any "neutral" coalition was put
in place in Saigon, the Hanoi government would begin to undermine it.
Kennedy's thinking on the subject of neutrality was different. The question
he often put to his advisers was: can we put up some sort of neutral government that would ask us to leave Vietnam (something that, to Kennedy,
was inevitable) and would last long enough for the U.S. to carry out its
withdrawal without appearing to be abandoning an ally?*[52] *According to
Moyers, to LBJ neutrality was an end point, whereas to JFK it was just a
means to an end—withdrawal.*

JAMES GALBRAITH: To go back to late 1963 and the question of continuity: by 1964, if there had been a withdrawal, it would have been Johnson's withdrawal plan. The continuity with NSAM 273 [**Document 4-7**]
would have had to have been seamless for it to be seen as Kennedy's plan,
and that continuity was lost. The Tonkin Gulf really marked the end of
any real prospect of withdrawal. The only question at that point was
whether the United States would escalate partially, or go "all the way
with Curtis LeMay."

JAMES HERSHBERG: The fact is that Mac Bundy and McNamara
always claimed continuity. But they pushed Johnson towards war, and
then say Kennedy wouldn't have escalated. So which one is it?

I'm not sure there was no third way. There was the neutrality option,
the Laos-like solution. Why is there so little interest in exploring it at this
time?

BILL MOYERS: I never heard Johnson use the word *neutrality*. He
thought there was no such thing as neutrality on domestic issues, there
were only concessions, and to him domestic politics was the model for
all politics. But even if neutrality were something meaningful to him, he
wouldn't have thought you could trust the communists with neutrality,
because they didn't say what they really wanted. Johnson never would
have trusted Ho Chi Minh with neutrality.

How far could he go in the bombing program and not provoke China?
That was something that weighed on his mind very heavily. Goldwater
and LeMay and Nixon all scared him, because he thought they wanted
him to do things that would provoke a war with China. I don't know what

the sense is around the table here on that; maybe he worried about it more than he had to—

THOMAS HUGHES: Others did not worry so much. Rostow, for example, thought the Sino-Soviet split would keep China in check. Rusk, on the other hand, was paranoid about China.[53] But the other thing on Johnson's mind was his domestic program. He saw a very strong relationship between civil rights and Vietnam. Hanging tough in Vietnam was the price he had to pay to get what he wanted on civil rights.

BILL MOYERS: Yes, that's right, Johnson didn't want to kill the civil rights bill by looking like he was losing in Vietnam.

Was LBJ Afraid to Negotiate?

Just days after the U.S. began sustained bombing of North Vietnam in early February 1965, the Hanoi leadership began meeting in emergency session to develop a statement of its fundamental position with regard to eventual negotiations with Washington. Ho Chi Minh and his colleagues knew that they couldn't win an outright military victory over the Americans; therefore, they knew at a certain point negotiations must begin. Toward this end, the Hanoi leadership spent nearly two months hammering out what would become its famous Four Points. The Four Points represented a compromise between the needs of the forces in the South who were actually fighting the war against the U.S. and South Vietnamese armed forces, on the one hand, and, on the other, the views of the government of Hanoi, to which the war had suddenly been brought home in the form of American bombs. The southern communists of the NLF tended toward the radical position: no negotiations until all the Americans left the country—that is, they preferred demanding something very much like unconditional surrender prior to the beginning of negotiations, while the northerners, under whose aegis the country would presumably be united, wanted to spell out as clearly as possible at exactly what point negotiations could begin between Washington and Hanoi.

The Four Points were as follows.

1. Recognition of the basic rights of the Vietnamese people . . . the U.S. must remove its troops from South Vietnam; the U.S. must unconditionally stop the bombing of North Vietnam.
2. Pending the peaceful reunification of Vietnam, the military provisions of the 1954 Geneva Agreements on Vietnam must be strictly respected. All foreign troops must leave the country. There must

be no military alliances between either the Hanoi government or the Saigon government, and outside powers.

3. The internal affairs of South Vietnam must be settled by the South Vietnamese people themselves in accordance with the program of the National Liberation Front, without foreign interference.
4. The peaceful reunification of Vietnam is to be settled by the Vietnamese people in both zones, without foreign interference.[54]

The Four Points were approved on April 7, 1965, and made public the following day over Radio Hanoi. Ironically, also on April 7, 1965, LBJ gave a speech in Baltimore at Johns Hopkins University in which he pledged U.S. interest in "unconditional discussions" under any circumstances that might lead to a peaceful settlement.[55]

One might have been forgiven during those April days for being cautiously optimistic. Maybe—just maybe—the U.S. and the North Vietnamese governments could avert a bloody war after all. Of course, nothing of the kind happened. The question is, "Why not?" In particular, was Johnson serious about seeking negotiations at this early point in the hostilities or at any other point during the massive escalation? This is the rhetorical question put before the participants by Fred Logevall in the following discussion. He notes a U.S. intelligence study from July 1965 that noted increased flexibility on the part of Hanoi toward negotiations. It seemed to apply, for example, to Point Three, which the Johnson administration tended to see as little more than a formula for a communist takeover in South Vietnam. In fact, as many U.S. specialists believed even at the time, Point Three had embedded within it the expectation of some sort of coalition government, which would rule South Vietnam for a period of time extending perhaps to ten years or so following which the country would indeed be unified under the leadership of the government in Hanoi.

The intelligence alluded to by Fred Logevall was unequivocal: yes, Hanoi is interested in the initiation of talks with the U.S., but no, they will never do so in a way that smacks of compromise, and they will certainly not do so under the pressure of a bombing "pause" (with its contingent threat to resume the bombing if Hanoi doesn't respond in a manner, and within a duration, that Washington finds acceptable). For example, in mid-1965, INR made the following assessment.

After the announcement of Hanoi's Four Points in April 1965, INR scrutinized closely any variations in Hanoi's public statements, looking for indications that might suggest how interested in talks North Vietnam actually was. During the bombing pause in May 1965, INR estimated that Hanoi would not make concessions toward negotiations though it wanted the pause to continue; in general it believed that North Vietnam was interested in opening an exchange without signaling an interest in compromise. At mid-year [1965], INR judged that Hanoi was seriously interested in the possibility of bilateral contacts, but would make no concession for a bombing halt, and would reject a pause that was coupled with an ultimatum or a demand for reciprocity. INR estimated that an unannounced pause, if handled carefully, would be the most likely means of opening the way to substantive talks.[56]

On the basis of this and other studies and estimates from the time, Logevall argues that the information needed to proceed successfully toward talks between Washington and Hanoi was available—redundantly available— inside the U.S. government. It was available, but ignored by LBJ and his inner circle.

Was Johnson serious, then, about negotiating? Logevall argues from the declassified documents that the answer must be "no." Chet Cooper agrees, and he offers his personal experience to back up his conclusion. The tale told by Chet Cooper, who spent several years trying to initiate serious negotiations with Hanoi, is one of subversion by the White House of any effort toward negotiations that appeared to have the potential to succeed. At some point it became clear, Cooper recalls, that LBJ and his national security adviser (after February 1966), Walt Rostow, did not want Averell Harriman and Cooper to succeed; they actually preferred to escalate the war ever further rather than explore opportunities to move to the negotiating table. It is possible to hear in Chet Cooper's voice, recalling the most frustrating years of his life in government, both sadness and anger, having been sent on a fool's errand by a president and national security adviser who wanted him to fail.

FREDRIK LOGEVALL: There is an INR study that Tom and John know about that is referred to in the briefing book. In late July 1965 there is a memo—I don't think this is in the briefing book—but the memo asks, "Has Hanoi shown serious interest in negotiations?" The answer given is, "Yes, repeatedly." Then this memo proceeds to lay out what INR sees as increased flexibility in Hanoi, while Hanoi is still of course committed to the bottom line, which is the ultimate reunification of Vietnam under Hanoi's control. I think that's remarkable. It's interesting that several U.S. officials—including Mac Bundy and others—do see that the Four Points earlier that spring represent at least a possible opening if the U.S. wants to pursue it. The U.S. doesn't want to pursue it, and I think that's the most important theme throughout the Johnson years. In fact, the title of my dissertation years ago was *Fear to Negotiate*.[57] There was a fear to negotiate on the part of the United States. Opportunities existed along the way. The Chinese were always prepared to fight to the last Vietnamese. The Chinese were deathly afraid of an Americanization of the war if it would result in serious problems for them. For the Soviets, it was the wrong war in the wrong place at the wrong time. I think there are tantalizing what ifs, keeping in mind that they're going to drive a very hard bargain, and ultimately what we are talking about is a decent interval.

JOHN PRADOS: I wanted to bring the conversation back more towards the South and the North. You know, we have indications that at various times southern leaders approached northern leaders about negotiations—and look what happens. In the fall of 1963, Nhu talks to the North, and the Americans mount a coup. In the summer and fall of 1966, there are some feelers back and forth; they got chopped off. In the fall of '67, the South Vietnamese learned that the Americans are privately talking to the National Liberation Front. The South Vietnamese chop off that feeler. And then, of course, you have the actual opening of negotiations, which drag on for four years while the South Vietnamese consistently hold to a formula—just like Hanoi held to its Four Points. It was irreconcilable on both sides. The question is: how was a deal possible?

FREDRIK LOGEVALL: Just to piggyback on John's point, even though I'm not sure if it supports your ultimate question: what I find fascinating—and, Tom and Chet, you may remember this—is how, in the critical period of early 1965, there was an increasing American concern that some South Vietnamese might be talking to the NLF or Hanoi or both, and this adds a sense of urgency to American planners to begin the escalation of the war. There is an American concern about an internal Vietnamese settlement. That is extraordinary.

JAMES BLIGHT: Yes, Tom or Chet, would you like to comment?

THOMAS HUGHES: The fear was there; that's what Bundy and the rest were most worried about.

CHESTER COOPER: My own direct experience with negotiations began in April 1965, when the president made a speech in Baltimore. This has already been referred to.[58] The point was that someone—and I can't recall who—suggested, "Look, with all we've being doing in Vietnam, and all the press has been talking about is what we are doing militarily or in a paramilitary capacity, we need to point out that we are not just there for military purposes; we are there for a more noble purpose." Out of that came Johnson's second track, and out of that came statements such as, "I will meet the Vietnamese leaders at any time in any place and discuss this with them." In 1966, Harriman was appointed in the State Department as ambassador for negotiations. I've always suspected that Rostow and the president just wanted to keep Harriman busy, because there was very little support for Harriman during this period.[59] In fact, to some extent there was what I would call nonsupport. But Harriman and I spent two years running all over the world after every possible straw in the wind that might indicate that the Vietnamese would talk. The basic problem with the negotiations policy was the left hand/right hand problem. Every negotiation initiative required, by the Vietnamese, a halt in the bombing. But every negotiating initiative was regarded as so secret that only a handful of people at the Department of State, a handful of people at the Department of Defense, a few people in the White House—no more than a dozen to fifteen people—were aware of these negotiations. They were so secret they all had code names. Hanoi also wanted to keep these negotiations secret for their own reasons. In the meantime, we had the Air Force and the whole Defense Department geared up to bomb the hell out of Vietnam. We couldn't tell them to stop. There was only one occasion I remember when we were able to get them to stop: it was not about negotiations, it was the Christmas bombing halt.[60] You couldn't tell anyone to stop the bombing because we had one of these secret negotiations going on. As a consequence, we were never able, until the very end, to satisfy the one condition that Hanoi made to getting talks going, and that was an *unconditional* bombing halt.

It always all depended on whether the weather was okay. During one negotiation with the Poles about getting to the table, there was no bombing, because the weather was wrong. We said there was no bombing because we were holding it in order to talk to the Vietnamese. But as soon as it looked as if we were going to get together with the Vietnamese, the sun came out and the bombing started, and that was then end of that negotiation.[61]

I am telling you a tale of frustration, because that was basically what it was. We couldn't get anything going until the [January 1968] Tet Offensive, which was a disaster both for the Vietnamese and ourselves. The president decided the best thing he could do would be to indicate that he was not going to run again.[62]

All these documents that we talk about are extremely interesting, but this was all like a Greek tragedy. It was doomed to fail.

FRANCES FITZGERALD: Is tragedy the right word for it, or is it the lack of a presidential decision to pursue this?

CHESTER COOPER: Well, tragedy is a polite way of putting it. There was no interest—no real serious interest—on the part of the president. I blame Rostow for much of this. For much of the time that we were negotiating, the condition was unconditional surrender. We never said that, but that's what it was.

FRANCES FITZGERALD: Just stop doing what you are doing.

MARILYN YOUNG: That they should surrender.

CHESTER COOPER: Yes, sure.

MARILYN YOUNG: This whole process was governed by "Mad Hatter" reasoning, if I followed you correctly, Chet. The Vietnam War was full of the Mad Hatter's tea parties. Hanoi insisted, "Stop bombing or we won't talk"; you say we couldn't stop bombing on account of negotiations being so secret. Is that right? Doesn't it sound mad to you?

CHESTER COOPER: Hanoi also insisted on secrecy.

MARILYN YOUNG: Okay, sure. I'm just referring to the craziness of it.

CHESTER COOPER: The people in Hanoi, and the government in D.C., didn't want their publics to know that in fact negotiations were going on. If negotiations resulted in some sort of a peace, then they would both claim a great triumph.

MARILYN YOUNG: So you prayed for rain to halt the bombing.

CHESTER COOPER: Exactly. We prayed for rain.

Walt Rostow: "Dr. Pangloss" of the War in Vietnam

The conversation now moves deeper into the question of when, or whether, LBJ might have been prepared to try to negotiate an end to the conflict in Vietnam. LBJ certainly tried earnestly and repeatedly to give the public the impression that he was ready to go anywhere, meet with anyone, and put everything on the table if he thought via some such route peace might be achieved. His 1966 appointment of Averell Harriman to head a highly publicized effort to seek negotiations was part of this strategy (with Chet Cooper serving as Harriman's principal deputy).

Cooper then specifies exactly why he thinks his work with Harriman came to naught. It can be explained, as he often said, in two words: Walt Rostow. Rostow's objective, according to Cooper, was to ensure that the Hanoi government and their NLF allies in the South understood that the U.S. would stand firm in Southeast Asia until and unless the Vietnamese communists "came to their senses" and sued for peace. In so doing, they would in effect surrender, thereby guaranteeing that South Vietnam would remain perpetually "free and independent." Anything short of this achieved via the give and take of negotiation, was, in Rostow's view, an American surrender. This was Rostow's fantasy, according to Cooper, and it became LBJ's fantasy—whether because of Rostow or simply reinforced by Rostow, Cooper does not profess to know. This perspective, which was earnestly and continuously pressed on LBJ by Rostow, seemed (and still seems) delusional to most observers. But because of it, Cooper now believes he and Harriman were sent on a fool's errand, seeking a negotiated peace, when in fact Johnson and Rostow would be satisfied with nothing less than what turned out to be impossible: bringing the Vietnamese communists to their knees via continuously escalating the level of punishment they received from U.S. air and ground forces until the communists gave up.

In the midst of the following discussion on the personality and influence of Walt Rostow, Bill Moyers tells Chet Cooper that after early 1965, the Rostow view held sway with Johnson. Not for a minute, he tells Cooper, did LBJ believe a negotiated peace could be achieved. Here is an excerpt from that conversation.

> **Bill Moyers:** . . . After '65 there was no effort to massage the genie out of the bottle. There was simply an investment of faith—the other side would bleed so much, and hurt so much, that they would cry for peace—peace being an independent South Vietnam. It was in that period of time—and then of course in '66, when Bundy left—that I never saw any evidence of any favorable interest in the negotiations that you were mentioning.
>
> **Chester Cooper:** Any unfavorable?
>
> **Bill Moyers:** I never saw anything favorable. I mean, LBJ never believed after January '65 that there was a serious feather on the table, in terms of a dove.

This is a difficult and poignant moment in the conference. For Chet Cooper would never hear this from a more knowledgeable, less-biased source than Bill Moyers, who confirms to him what he already strongly suspected: that he and Harriman had been hung out to dry to give the public the false impression that Johnson really sought a negotiated peace.

What more effective way to involve Cooper in the scheme, as a pawn in the lie, than by leading him (and Harriman) to believe that LBJ was sincere when he told them, as he did repeatedly, that he would do almost anything to get to a peace settlement. The most effective liars are often those who believe they are telling the truth, whether they are pathological liars or, like Chet Cooper, have been duped by their superiors.

Walt Rostow's influence on LBJ and his role in the Johnson administration is debated in what follows. Walt Whitman Rostow was sui generis, a memorandum machine, first in the Kennedy administration, then in the Johnson White House. McGeorge Bundy, who brought him into the Kennedy White House in 1961, said on many occasions that Rostow could quickly survey 500 incoming cables, and if 499 of them seem to refute some point or other that he had made, he would almost instantly seize on the one that might be construed as providing confirmatory evidence for his thesis. He could then, according to Bundy, work it up into a dogmatic, take-no-prisoners memorandum in less time than it would take most people eventually to read it, and he could keep doing this until everyone else was exhausted.

In addition to his undoubted industriousness, his imperviousness to disconfirming data involved a theater-of-the-absurd quality. Rostow's briefings for Johnson became legendary—long-winded, dogged efforts to explain to LBJ that everything was going smoothly and why that was the case, while in fact the disaster in Vietnam was growing daily more obvious to many others around Johnson. Historian Barbara Tuchman, citing LBJ speechwriter Harry MacPherson, has written, "Rostow was a positivist, a Dr. Pangloss who . . . would advise the president on learning of a nuclear attack on Manhattan that the first phase of urban renewal had been accomplished at no cost to the treasury."[63] The comparison with Dr. Pangloss is apt. Voltaire's original, upon watching someone fall overboard and drown in the Bay of Lisbon, declared his pleasure at the sight. Why? Because, according to Dr. Pangloss, that very bay was obviously created for just this eventuality. The drowning was thus yet another reason, according to the good doctor, for celebrating this "best of all possible worlds." That such a man, Dr. Walt Rostow, would be LBJ's choice for national security adviser following McGeorge Bundy's departure, still mystifies many of the participants in the conversation that follows, especially those who actually worked with Rostow: Moyers, Cooper, and Hughes.

Dr. Pangloss/Dr. Rostow specialized in feeding his boss ever more baroque arguments meant to convince him that the U.S. was winning, that the enemy knew the U.S. was winning, and that if LBJ therefore just did not let himself suffer a failure of nerve, then the U.S. would prevail. Stay

the course. Don't cut and run. Stick by your guns. Do this, and you'll be a
great hero, Mr. President. This was Rostow's message to an increasingly
isolated, depressed, and needy LBJ.

But Bill Moyers cautions that we should be careful in demonizing Walt
Rostow, because he was only doing what he had always done. JFK tolerated
him in the White House for less than a year until November 1961, when
he happily exiled him to the Policy Planning Office in the State Depart-
ment, where he could, as JFK put it, write all the memos he wanted. And
he wrote them without noticeable impact by the hundreds and by the thou-
sands from late 1961 until early 1966, when Lyndon Johnson brought Ros-
tow back from his exile in the State Department into the White House as
his national security adviser.

jANET LANG: I'd like to bring Walt Rostow back into the discussion.
I'd like to hear from people with experience in the administration, and
scholars who have other angles into Rostow. But what I'm especially interested in—and perhaps, Tom, we can start with you—is whether it is
overstating the case to say that Walt Rostow was a huge obstacle to negotiations? If we imagine that in principle the majority of officials in the
State Department were not intrinsically opposed to negotiations, then
how and why did Rostow's views come to dominate LBJ's thinking—I
mean the adamance against negotiating with Hanoi.

The other thing is this: Bill, you were, I believe, a regular attendee at
LBJ's Tuesday lunches. What I remember from talking with a number of
people about those lunches, including Nick Katzenbach, is that the Tuesday lunches provided a convenient forum for Rostow to really put the
kabob on the possibility of moving forward with—

JAMES BLIGHT: Do you mean *the kybosh?*

jANET LANG: Kybosh, sure.

THOMAS BLANTON: Well Rostow skewered the whole process anyhow. Roasted it and set it on fire. *Kabob* was right. [Laughter.]

CHESTER COOPER: No, no he *screwed* it, not skewered it. [Uproari-
ous laughter.]

jANET LANG: That too. Was Rostow doing more or less what Johnson
wanted him to do?[64]

THOMAS HUGHES: Yes, Rostow is one of the most fascinating, curious stories of the whole period. The night of Rusk's appointment in December of 1960, he showed up at [Chester] Bowles's in Washington, and

the three of us had dinner.[65] Rusk said all the nice things about how he wouldn't have thought of taking the job unless Bowles was there to be his deputy, and so on. Bowles was busy casting ambassadors and making appointments at the State Department, so naturally he said to Rusk, "You probably have some ideas of your own about whom you like to have at the State Department." And Dean said, "No, not really." He said, "There is one person I insist on having, and that's U. Alexis Johnson, my old colleague from way back; and there is one person I refuse to have anything to do with.[66] I don't want him at the State Department." And that was Walt Rostow. Where this all came from, I don't know. They were both Rhodes Scholars, but not together. Anyway, there was more than a disinclination: there was a refusal. And it was a stand-up refusal, because he didn't seem to think negatively about anyone else, or positively about anyone else—just that Rostow was not to be in the State Department. So Rostow was appointed to the White House.

Then when the shuffle—the so-called "Thanksgiving Day massacre"— occurs in November '61, either Kennedy is sufficiently fed up with Rostow's memoranda to impose him on Rusk, or he's sufficiently fed up with Rusk to penalize him, so he sends Rostow over to the State Department.[67] Either way he ends up at the State Department after all, where he continues to write the same kind of memos that he wrote before directly to the president—this time not necessarily informing Rusk, let alone Bundy.

Walt Whitman Rostow and Eugene Victor Debs Rostow were the sons of a nice, pacifist, socialist Jewish immigrant family, and the only thing Rusk ever said to me about Rostow later was, "Isn't it strange that they think the way to get ahead is to have their CVs stamped by the JCS?"— which is, of course, what they did. I never really had a satisfactory explanation for this strange relationship, and of course the ultimate irony is that Rusk and Rostow end up as the twin hawks at the end of the Johnson administration.

BILL MOYERS: Do you have any idea how Rostow came to succeed Bundy?

THOMAS HUGHES: Well, you would have more of an idea there. You may remember Mac Bundy's memo to LBJ proposing you as his successor and me as an alternate. He did not recommend Rostow.[68]

BILL MOYERS: But I don't know who pushed for Rostow.

THOMAS HUGHES: Somebody said this morning that [Robert] Komer was another alternative; I mean, something shifty was going on.[69]

JOHN PRADOS: Komer acted as national security adviser for approximately a month after Mac left.

MARILYN YOUNG: Good God!

THOMAS HUGHES: But President Johnson must have had a favorable feeling about Rostow; he obviously didn't pick any others.

BILL MOYERS: But until Rostow's appointment, he didn't have enough exposure to Rostow to have a personal opinion.

THOMAS HUGHES: Somehow he must have. I don't know how good Vice President Johnson's staff was during the first Kennedy years, but I assume that they must have gotten wind of the Rostow recommendations. They certainly knew about the Rostow-Taylor mission. It wasn't as though Rostow was a secret around town; people knew pretty well what he thought.

FREDRIK LOGEVALL: Bill, I'm interested in hearing your response to janet's question about the Tuesday lunches; but on this issue, isn't part of the answer that Rostow is a hawk, and we have a beleaguered president by this point who is still certainly sounding very, very hawkish? Here's somebody who—even though he may not know him very well, as Bill said—is going to be like-minded on the war. That may be part of the explanation.

CHESTER COOPER: To some extent Rostow was a courtier. I can remember a letter or a memo he wrote—I think it was a letter—in which he compared the president to Abraham Lincoln, and Rostow pointed out that the problems that Johnson was having in Vietnam were very much akin to the problems that Lincoln had during the Civil War. Maybe he was right on that, but I have a feeling he was buttering him up.

BILL MOYERS: But what was his position to butter him up? He left the White House at the November [1961] massacre, right? He went to the State Department as assistant secretary of state for policy. He stayed there until Bundy left, right?

JOHN PRADOS: That's right.

BILL MOYERS: I never saw him, because I was not involved in foreign affairs, but I did not see any connection—or flow of information, or advice, or even exposure—between the president and Rostow in that period of time. I've always wished I could have asked Rusk about all this.

My impression—and this is totally subjective—is that Rusk becoming hawkish during the '65–'66 period caused him to recommend to LBJ that he take Rostow to succeed Bundy because he did not want me, and he did not want you [gesturing toward Tom Hughes]. We were both too dovish. And since Rusk had become a hawk, he had in Rostow an insider to support the hawkish position. That's my thesis; I do not have any evidence to back it up.

THOMAS HUGHES: Could well be. Of course, Rostow is writing a stream of memoranda, both personally and institutionally from the policy planning council all the time he's in the State Department. Incidentally, Rostow's staff there also gives him trouble. For example, Robert Johnson is busy with his own long study making recommendations on Vietnam quite contrary to what Rostow himself was recommending.

BILL MOYERS: Remember, I was only seeing this as a domestic policy LBJ confidant just listening to things. He never asked me for my advice on foreign policy. What I know, however, is that before '65 LBJ thought if he just kept rubbing the bottle harder and harder, the genie would appear—the genie being somebody, something, some process, some event that would offer a way out. A resolution. A satisfactory resolution: an independent South Vietnam and no war. After the "fork in the road" memo—which I didn't see at the time, but which I did feel the full reverberation of LBJ's response to—he grew suddenly morose, as it was clear to him what the two choices were [**Document 5-4**]. He stayed morose for months until he made the decision in that summer. But after '65, there was no effort to massage the genie out of the bottle. There was simply an investment of faith—the other side would bleed so much, and hurt so much, that they would cry for peace—peace being an independent South Vietnam. It was in that period of time—and then of course in '66, when Bundy left—that I never saw any evidence of any favorable interest in the negotiations that you were mentioning.

CHESTER COOPER: Any unfavorable?

BILL MOYERS: I never saw anything favorable. I mean, LBJ never believed after January '65 that there was a serious feather on the table, in terms of a dove.

CHESTER COOPER: Well, my experience was very personal. It was very hard after a while for me to ignore what I thought was an attempt to discourage, or even pull the rug out from under, some negotiations we got going. Here's an example of one I have in mind. Rostow and the president were very much displeased with [British Prime Minister] Harold Wilson when Wilson began to meet with [Soviet Prime Minister] Alexei Kosygin in 1967. They pointed out to Kosygin that Wilson was looking for a Nobel Prize, which I'm sure he was, but they didn't trust Wilson. The British didn't participate in the Vietnam War at all. In a sense, there wasn't a good relationship between Wilson and the president anyway, and Rostow didn't help. Mac, at least, would have tried to put a little oil into the machinery there, and Rostow didn't—I think he probably put some sand into the machine.

At the end of the Kosygin visit [in January 1967], we thought we had a deal, which I had cleared—McNamara in Hanoi remembered this.[70] They forgot what the deal was: phase A/phase B, and so on. They just forgot. And so the deal they were ready to make with the Russians was one that the Russians knew was the same one that Hanoi had turned down time and time again. When I tried to convince Walt that this wasn't going anywhere, and time was of the essence, with the Russians returning to Moscow, we got some very nasty replies.

BILL MOYERS: I think we should be very careful about making Rostow a demon, because he wasn't—any more than anyone else was. He was a true believer, and to marry a true believer to a president who felt inexperienced in the nuances of foreign policy is a dangerous thing in any circumstance.

THOMAS HUGHES: Rostow starts lecturing in public, of course, early in 1961. He's one of the first to talk about counterinsurgency.

CHESTER COOPER: Let me just say one thing about the difference between Rostow and Bundy. Bundy would suggest that the president see people who were very smart—

FREDRIK LOGEVALL: People like Walter Lippmann.

CHESTER COOPER: That's right.

FRANCES FITZGERALD: Once Rostow took over, of course, the intelligence suffered.

JAMES HERSHBERG: On Rostow: he had a kind of unremitting optimism that seemed impervious to reality. It just radiates out of his memos in a continuous way. He just seems to follow the same note continuously. But on the question on Rostow and intelligence—

JAMES BLIGHT: Remember that Walt Rostow reiterated shortly before he died that the U.S. actually won the war in Vietnam.[71]

THOMAS BLANTON: Because we put off the communists.

JAMES BLIGHT: Yes, because we prevented the communists from conquering Southeast Asia.

JAMES HERSHBERG: Just on Frankie's comment on Rostow and intelligence, there was a one-sentence memo I came across from Rostow to Johnson that was reminiscent of recent debates about intelligence and Iraq. It is about policy pressure on intelligence to find the intelligence to fit the policy. This was Rostow to [CIA director] Richard Helms, copied to the president. It said, "Go back and dig a little further to see if you can find some French secret aid to the VC [Vietcong]: find that the French were actually sabotaging us by sending arms in. We need that intelligence."[72]

LBJ and "the Sage of Gettysburg"

On the war in Vietnam, LBJ was especially solicitous of the views of Dwight D. Eisenhower, one of his predecessors as president, a stalwart Republican, and of course the great American military hero of World War II. In the brief excerpt that follows, both Tom Hughes and Gordon Goldstein comment on LBJ's slavish pursuit of the endorsement of Eisenhower, especially in the period just before LBJ's late July 1965 decision to Americanize the war. Goldstein recalls that his collaborator, McGeorge Bundy, used to refer to Eisenhower as "the Sage of Gettysburg," a reference to what Bundy felt was LBJ's groveling attitude toward Eisenhower (Gettysburg being the location of the Eisenhower farm in Pennsylvania, where he was spending his retirement).

In the following excerpt from a transcript of an LBJ phone tape on July 2, 1965, LBJ calls Eisenhower to talk about the recommendations to escalate the war that he is getting from McNamara; General William Westmoreland, the U.S. field commander in South Vietnam; and General Earle Wheeler, chairman of the Joint Chiefs of Staff.

> **LBJ:** I'm having a meeting this morning with my top people . . . McNamara recommends really what Westmoreland and Wheeler do— quite an expanded operation . . . an all-out operation. We don't know whether we can beat 'em with that or not . . . You don't think that we can just have a holding operation, from a military standpoint, do you?
>
> **Eisenhower:** . . . You've got to go along with your military advisers . . .

My advice is, do what you have to do . . . I would go ahead and do it as quickly as I could.

LBJ: . . . You're the best chief of staff I've got . . . I've got to rely on you on this one.[73]

The editor of the Johnson tapes, historian Michael Beschloss, adds a foot-note of considerable understatement to this passage, as follows: "LBJ is try-ing to implicate Eisenhower in escalating the war."[74] And so he has, apparently to his satisfaction. Having gotten the Sage of Gettysburg to en-dorse the program to escalate the war in Vietnam, LBJ can now turn to his other Republican problem—getting enough of them to sign off on his do-mestic agenda so that he can push through the Voting Rights Bill and the Medicare Bill in the month following his conversation with Eisenhower. Only then, and only partially, will he inform the American public that the country is embarking on a major (if undeclared) war in Vietnam.

THOMAS HUGHES: I think the Republican support for the war is one of the major elements of this whole picture, and has been neglected. Forget about Senator Aiken, who doesn't count.[75] I mean the mainstream Republicans. Eisenhower, who himself doesn't go into Indochina in 1954, is unremittingly full of dominoes all the way through. There are all these desperate visits to Eisenhower. [John] McCone is appointed direc-tor of Central Intelligence [in 1961] in part because of his Eisenhower connection, and Kennedy sends him up to talk to Eisenhower, and he always comes back saying, "You must stick, you must increase, you must send troops"—that is a regular, unremitting signal all the way through both administrations.

Johnson sends [General Andrew] Goodpaster up to talk to him and he gets the same message.[76] Eisenhower is hopelessly hawkish on Vietnam. And this is key for the rest of the so-called moderate Republicans on Capitol Hill. [Senator Everett] Dirksen—Johnson's old associate from the Hill—is no help on Vietnam in terms of any extrication.[77] So there is a big Republican story there.

GORDON GOLDSTEIN: I recall that Mac Bundy focused repeatedly on the role of Eisenhower and Johnson's fixation with Eisenhower. I think Mac referred to Ike as "the Sage of Gettysburg." He talked about how critical it was for Johnson to have the blessing of the Sage of Gettys-burg. He's got to bring him up to the White House and lobby him. The metaphor that Mac often used was, "Johnson is a Senate majority leader, and in addition to getting Senator Westmoreland"—which meant signing him on in the summer of '65 through the 44-battalion escalation—"he needs to get the vote of the Sage of Gettysburg."

Hubert Humphrey and the Dark Side of LBJ

*Obsessed with secrecy as to the scale of the escalation he was contemplating in Vietnam, Johnson slipped over the edge of suspicious eccentricity into full-blown paranoia during the early phases of the air war that would soon become widely known by its code name, ROLLING THUNDER. He refused to discuss publicly, or even privately with Democratic leaders in Congress, what was going on in Vietnam and what was coming. In mid-February 1965 Vice President Hubert Humphrey broke two of LBJ's unwritten but ironclad rules: (1) don't tell the president what he doesn't want to hear and (2) don't make any public statements that might constrain Johnson as he maneuvered in secret. With significant assistance from Tom Hughes, Humphrey drafted a February 15, 1965, memorandum for Johnson on "the politics of Vietnam," that is, as Fred Logevall says in the brief excerpt that follows, "just extraordinary" [**Document 5-6**].⁷⁸ It is all that and more. It is a lucid, temperate, well-organized, and highly persuasive document explaining to LBJ why he should begin immediately to move toward negotiations with the Vietnamese communists, thereby cutting his political losses in Vietnam by planning to withdraw. As Bill Moyers says in response to Logevall, Johnson's response was to ostracize Humphrey for many months and to completely exclude him from discussions of Vietnam policy until Humphrey proclaimed himself "more hawkish than the president." This, says Moyers, reveals a "dark side" of LBJ—a side that was unreceptive to inconvenient advice and vindictive to those who offered it. George Ball was only an apparent exception. LBJ had informally anointed Ball the "official" bearer of bad tidings, the devil's advocate, because Johnson knew that Ball would argue a good case against him and then vote with the others in a unanimous endorsement of whatever the president wanted to do.*

But Humphrey didn't just write LBJ a private memorandum. He also began at the same time to make speeches and other public statements suggesting that it might be time to move toward negotiations with the adversary in Vietnam. This infuriated LBJ and led him to urge his advisers to put Humphrey quite literally under surveillance and to muzzle him, if necessary, to prevent him from advocating a nonescalatory policy. The following excerpt is from a telephone conversation between LBJ and McGeorge Bundy on February 18, 1965, the day after Johnson had received the memorandum from Hubert Humphrey on the politics of Vietnam. It reveals not only LBJ's disgruntlement with Humphrey, but also his manner of dealing with an adviser, in Bundy, who clearly felt that Humphrey, at the very least, had done nothing wrong. LBJ does not overtly disagree with Bundy. He simply ignores Bundy's responses and essentially grinds him down until he capitulates—a telephone variant, without the intended humor, of the "Johnson treatment" of General Earle Wheeler described previously by Tom Hughes.

LBJ: Get old Hubert to clear very carefully what he said in New York with you.

Bundy: He did.

LBJ: I see he's got a good deal of negotiation in it . . . I don't want anybody, while I'm president, talking about it until we have some indication that some of them [Vietnamese communist leaders] might be willing to. That's the first essential of negotiation. [Reading from the *Baltimore Sun*]: "His remarks obviously have been cleared in advance with President Johnson. Thus it signals an American diplomatic offensive" . . . I would just as soon he stay out of the peacekeeping and negotiating field at this point. So let's just watch him very carefully.

Bundy: I will.

LBJ: I told him the other day . . . "You're really the last man to get into the atomic field"—because he's regarded as pretty liberal— "and if I were you, I would try to stay on some of these subjects that you're dealing with and not get into negotiating." Now I just really feel very deeply about that—God, I want to negotiate more than any man in the world! I'll guarantee you that.

Bundy: I'll bet.

LBJ: But I don't think my wanting to negotiate is necessarily the best way to win the girl.

Bundy: Exactly.[79]

McGeorge Bundy once taught international relations at Harvard and perhaps can be given credit for knowing something about the field, including having a few thoughts about when, and when not, to explore negotiations with an adversary. Moreover, Bundy obviously thought Hubert Humphrey's speech was just fine as delivered because the vice president had, as directed, cleared it with Bundy, the national security adviser. But note Bundy's multifaceted, preemptive capitulation in the face of the telephone variant of the "Johnson treatment." In the space of considerably less than five minutes, Bundy has implicitly agreed that the speech wasn't fine and that he shouldn't have cleared it for presentation, he has explicitly agreed to put the vice president of the U.S. under his personal surveillance, and he has noted the perfect aptness of the president's analogy between conducting international relations and obtaining a girl's favors. Approximately one year later, Bundy would resign, recommending Bill Moyers as his replacement because, as Bundy told friends and colleagues, he felt Moyers stood a better chance of actually communicating with LBJ.

FREDRIK LOGEVALL: I think you could make a very good argument that, for each of these three presidents—I would add Nixon to the list— Vietnam mattered in substantial measure because of what it could do to their domestic political position.

When we talk about domestic politics, we have to come back to Humphrey's memo, which I think is just extraordinary [**Document 5-6**]. If a book comes out of this conference, I think we should try to include the February 17th memo, because it talks about how the Republicans have never been weaker: "This is why you have such freedom, Mr. President." I'm paraphrasing, of course, but he says, "You've defeated Goldwater; they're as weak as they've ever been, and this is the year of minimal political risk for this administration." One interesting question we could explore, or think about, is whether Lyndon Johnson—who is thought of as being this master politician—actually has his finger on the political pulse of the nation, or whether it was Hubert Humphrey who did. He was no slouch when it came to understanding the nation's politics. Humphrey better understood the degree to which (a) LBJ had freedom to maneuver in terms of domestic politics and (b) was going to do something very dangerous if he pursued an escalatory policy in Vietnam.[80]

BILL MOYERS: Two points on that. One is that Humphrey often did the right thing when the polls didn't support him, all the way back to being mayor of Minneapolis. Remember how he won that race, and also his speech in 1948 to the Democratic convention. Truman had the only television set in Washington in 1948, and he watched Hubert Humphrey make that speech—this is recorded—he turned his head, "He's a kook; he's an outlaw." Humphrey would do that kind of thing. But look at what happened.[81]

This also shows the dark side of Lyndon Johnson, which is something that all of us who served him grappled with. After Humphrey wrote that memo, he got a session with him and he made the case eloquently that this was the year to take the big gamble and get out of Vietnam.[82] He was banned from all meetings thereafter for the next year, and he only came back into the good graces of the president when he became more hawkish than the president. Talk about the tragedy of continuing a course when you know it's leading to disaster! This was a tragedy.

Choosing War: LBJ's Fateful Decision

On April 30, 1975, the final American helicopter left the rooftop of the U.S. embassy in Saigon carrying the last of those who would escape before the takeover by communist forces. Almost from that moment down to the present, scholars, journalists, and memoirists of the war have been preoccupied by variants of two questions. First, how and why did the tragedy happen? Second, might the tragedy have been avoided? On the escalation to an American war under Lyndon Johnson, many have asked: might Johnson have made different choices, leading to a different (i.e., a better) outcome? That Johnson made the key choices to escalate the war is well established, and a great deal of information is now available from declassified documents that shed light on LBJ's motives and perceptions. Moreover, since the release of hundreds of hours of tape-recorded conversations made by LBJ while president, we can also observe his apparently genuine and profound anguish at feeling trapped by hopeless circumstances not of his making or choosing. Might Johnson have chosen differently? Might war have been avoided? Is it possible to examine these questions without indulging in the specious pseudowisdom of hindsight—the all-too-easy judgments of those of us who know how tragically things turned out but did not have to carry the burden of responsibility on our shoulders, as LBJ did?

Our understanding of these questions has been greatly enriched by Fred Logevall's 1999 masterpiece, Choosing War. *One of his most significant contributions has been to demonstrate the utility of splitting the inquiry into Johnson, his war, and his choices into two distinct questions. First, were other, realistic options available that, if chosen, would likely have led to a much less costly war, or even completely avoided an American war in Vietnam? Second, what about President Lyndon Johnson—the man himself, in all his singularity, as he emerges from the wealth of information now available on him? Can we imagine* him *choosing less disastrous options we have identified as realistic? To question one, Logevall answers yes, absolutely, there were other realistic choices available. But to question number two, Logevall answers absolutely not! It is unimaginable that Lyndon Johnson would under any realistic scenario have been able to make the choices necessary to avoid a catastrophic war.*

This is the stuff of tragedy. The essence of it is this: many others, back then and ever since, can see other possible courses of action, can imagine themselves and others actually choosing such courses of action, and can see

*clearly the advantages of doing do. But the figure at the center of the tragedy
cannot do what must be done to avoid the oncoming disaster, cannot bring
himself to believe it is within his power or in his interest to do so. Those with
a psychoanalytic orientation might be tempted to interpret the behavior of
someone like Johnson as self-destructive or irrational due to his proclivity
to choose a path that, as others predicted then, and as we understand with
even greater clarity now, was destined to lead to disaster. But labels like
these, while not necessarily inappropriate descriptions of Johnson's behavior, don't go very far toward explaining the enigma of LBJ. To address these
issues effectively, we need to identify specific features of LBJ that led him
to choose as he did—that, in short, shed some light on the logic of his
choices, the needs that were met by the choices he made. Here again, Logevall is helpful. He lists three principal factors that drove LBJ's choice to
escalate the war in Vietnam to the monumental disaster it became.*

1. *Personalization of the war.* LBJ was unable to imagine America losing in Vietnam in a way that would not also bring him a degree of personal humiliation
   he would find intolerable. His personal insecurity, which was legendary among
   those who worked for him, led him to choose escalation even though he
   doubted that victory was possible, and in fact thought it was highly unlikely.
   Any outcome, it seems, was for Johnson better than losing.
2. *Intolerance of dissent.* To Johnson, dissent from any consensus that he sought,
   or felt he had already achieved, was regarded as traitorous. In LBJ's view, this
   was the worst sin a subordinate could commit—not being wrong, not making a
   misjudgment, but deviating from a line LBJ himself had laid down. This was
   Hubert Humphrey's transgression with his February 15, 1965 memorandum
   recommending a negotiated settlement rather than escalation.
3. *Intimidation of opposition.* Consensus—zero dissent from LBJ's line—was
   achieved mainly via the threat of severe punishment, such as the banishment
   of Humphrey. LBJ's techniques were varied, and included rumor-mongering,
   vicious gossip, and outright lies.[83]

*According to Logevall's analysis, LBJ's choices begin to make sense only as
we are able to understand what he was, in some deeper psychological sense,
trying to accomplish. They include the following: protecting himself from
intolerable personal humiliation, protecting himself from the intolerable
threat posed by dissenters, and crushing all opposition by whatever means
were at his disposal. Logevall admits that, of course, LBJ would have much
preferred a different outcome in Vietnam. But the implications of Logevall's assessment are worth contemplating: LBJ was not willing to bear the
personal risk required to achieve that outcome. This is not necessarily the
same thing as being cowardly. But it does indicate that, at a minimum, the*

person of Johnson and the position of successor to JFK were a supremely bad fit in regard to the war in Vietnam.

The end point of countless discussions between Johnson and his national security team was always complete agreement on the course to be followed. Johnson demanded this, and in so doing was applying a formula he had used successively as Senate majority leader to executive decisions on matters of war and peace. The approach had these elements: don't bring the issue up for a vote until all the important people are on board; if they are, then fine, let the vote proceed; if not, then let's have however many more meetings it takes for the recalcitrant people to understand that it is going to be done the president's way—no ifs, ands, or buts.

*Thus it is, in retrospect, that we see that after more than six months of meetings that have the superficial appearance of serious discussions, we arrive at one of the eeriest sentences ever committed to print in a document recording deliberations on whether to Americanize the war in Vietnam. Johnson has worn all the opposition down. All the estimates from the military about the possibility of five to twenty additional years of war, the need for 500,000 American troops; all the intelligence estimates expressing doubt as to whether such an effort would yield a positive outcome; all the warnings from congressional leaders and foreign leaders—after all of this, we come to a vote that concludes a meeting of Johnson's cabinet on July 27, 1965. The question is how to respond to General William Westmoreland's request from Saigon to more than double the size of the U.S. combat troop strength in South Vietnam, which at that moment is about 85,000 [**Document 5-8**]. We who read this document decades after the fact know for certain what is about to happen. The U.S. will plunge itself and all of Southeast Asia into a catastrophic downward spiral of death and destruction from which all parties to the conflict are still recovering. Bromley Smith, secretary of the National Security Council, records in the minutes that when, at approximately 6:20 p.m. on July 27, 1965, LBJ asked for a vote, "There was no response when the president asked whether anyone in the room opposed the course of action decided upon" [**Document 5-8**].*

In the discussion that concludes this chapter, the scholars and former officials debate these issues: whether it is possible to judge Johnson's choices in a way that is not hostage to our retrospective angle on the events and even whether each of the participants at the table might, or might not, have made the choices LBJ made. In an illuminating intervention toward the end of the discussion, Bill Moyers says that in listening to the tapes and in reading the transcripts of the tapes in preparation for the conference, he realized now, as he had back during the events under scrutiny, that the people advising Johnson and debating all these courses of action in Vietnam did not really know what they were talking about. They were ignorant and they were arrogant. Robert McNamara, who listened to the LBJ tapes in the early 1990s when he was writing his 1995 Vietnam memoir, In Retrospect, *came to a similar conclusion. McGeorge Bundy had also come to this assessment shortly before he died in 1996.*

Yet McNamara and Bundy, along with many others who advised LBJ on the war, also had advised JFK. From the point of view of Bill Moyers's assessment, it seems unlikely that McNamara or Bundy or any of their fellow presidential advisers were any more ignorant or arrogant under LBJ than they were under JFK. But whereas Johnson chose war, a good deal of newly available documentation suggests that JFK had chosen to withdraw from Vietnam. (As noted throughout the discussions that make up the core of this book, even the strongest advocates of the view that JFK decided to withdraw—Jamie Galbraith and Gordon Goldstein—acknowledge that JFK, having decided to withdraw, might conceivably have reversed or somehow altered that decision later on.) JFK seems to have made this decision not later than October 1963, but he may have made it as early as November 1961. Even for those participants around the table who are not convinced that JFK had made a firm decision to withdraw, it is inescapable that, at a minimum, JFK seemed to be preparing to absorb whatever political heat a withdrawal might generate. He is known to have discussed the issue on many occasions with his advisers and with others in and out of government. In Logevall's terms, JFK was able to face the withdrawal issue far more directly than LBJ did because (1) he did not personalize the issue, (2) he was remarkably open to dissenting views, and (3), as we have learned from the recently available tapes of Kennedy's meetings with his advisers, he preferred to try, by a variety of means, to persuade his dissenting subordinates, rather than exploit the office of president to intimidate them. In the matter of war or peace in Vietnam, therefore, the identity and character of the U.S. president appears to have made a big difference.

JAMES GALBRAITH: I've listened to this part of the conversation very, very carefully. I wonder if we are a little bit in danger of judging these decisions in light of the subsequent events and the scale of the tragedy that unfolded. If you go back and put yourself in the position of Johnson in 1965, things are falling apart. It's very clear. [Senator Mike] Mansfield says: "Now, if we think they're winning, you can imagine what they think; they know they're winning," so the status quo is untenable and Johnson faces a choice. As he says, "To me it is shaping up to look like either you get out or you get in" [**Document 5-7**]. At that point, withdrawal—which was a viable option for Kennedy at a time when South Vietnam would not have collapsed—is no longer politically viable. Hubert Humphrey may think so, and Hubert Humphrey may have been right, but Johnson has confidence in his own political judgments, and Johnson clearly doesn't think so. Clearly not. Having analyzed the situation at that point, escalation—if not to resolve the issue, at least to forestall a calamity by military means—becomes his only logical option. That is clearly the way things played out in his mind.

My question for us is: how are we so sure that if we'd been in that position that we would have come to the contrary view? We could not have known what was going to happen from 1965 to 1974.

MARILYN YOUNG: Are you asking me that question?

JAMES GALBRAITH: Yes, I'm asking all of you.

MARILYN YOUNG: *Very* confident.

FREDRIK LOGEVALL: I think what is striking in that spring period, though, is Wallace Greene's and Harold Johnson's answer to the question, and one or two other senior military leaders'. They say, "We're looking at five years, 500,000 troops."[84] We've already referred to Humphrey; you're right, Jamie, I can't know how I would have reacted; none of us could know for sure. But it seems to me what is important to keep in mind is that the image we have had of a Johnson who is so penned in and doing the only thing that any reasonable person in his shoes would do is just not tenable.

The other point that is important to note is that, from at least the spring of 1965, this whole administration is not really interested in pursuing negotiations. That seems clear from this very interesting session, and particularly from the remarks of Tom, Chet, and Bill. I mean, Johnson's interested only if it involves a kind of surrender by the North Vietnamese.

JAMES GALBRAITH: From the North Vietnamese perspective, as in '63, negotiations were a way of saving face to cover an American withdrawal. So there is a large gap between them.

FREDRIK LOGEVALL: They have a very high—

JAMES GALBRAITH: Really my question is to Bill, I guess. Everything that Johnson wants to achieve in his elected term in office—at that point, it could have well have been two terms—is on the line here. It seems to me that what we are talking about puts his decision in a highly comprehensible context, at least from his point of view. Even your point, Fred, about five years and 500,000 men presumes that we would have success at that point.

FREDRIK LOGEVALL: But where does that put LBJ as the 1968 campaign is wrapping up? It puts him in the middle of a stalemated, bloody war, and, I think, from a domestic political perspective, that is terrible.

JAMES GALBRAITH: Not necessarily. After all, look at what happened to George W. Bush in 2004: he is in the middle of a stalemated, bloody war, but it is not necessarily politically costly.

JAMES BLIGHT: Marilyn, did you want to comment?

MARILYN YOUNG: On this, I think Fred's book is really totally convincing.[85] Johnson chose; he *chose*! And there were people who were choosing differently. If there was nobody around who had any other notion, then you might say, "Well, what would any of us have done, after all? There were no alternatives." But there were lots of alternatives, and people were writing about them, talking about them, and secretly negotiating.

JAMES GALBRAITH: Johnson is clear about that; I just read the section. He says [to Senator Mike Mansfield]: "It is shaping up like this either you get out or you get in" [**Document 5-7**].

MARILYN YOUNG: Right, get out!

JAMES GALBRAITH: He's posing the choice and making it. It is not to say that he is unaware of a choice; he is aware.

MARILYN YOUNG: So then what's the sense in a question like, "What would any of us have done?"

JAMES GALBRAITH: The sense of it, it seems to me, is that in the conversations we've had, there was a bit of presumption that in 1965 the right choice would have been as clear to us as it appears to us now. I don't think that's quite correct.

BILL MOYERS: Well, I think *we* wish for what *they* hoped for: an alternative to what actually happened.

Another reason I haven't written or talked much about it is that I don't want to be retrospectively omniscient. I was there, but I can't tell you that I suggested or did the right thing. I heard all these people for three and a half intense years, and, quite frankly, it struck me, listening to the tape this morning, that no one really knew what the hell was going on.

Those who were most often right were intuitive, and those that were most often wrong were assertive. Decisions were made with far too little knowledge of the real politics on the ground. It was only the facts on the ground that ever brought anyone reality. This was Tet, Pleiku, and that sort of thing. But very busy people who were very tentative about their judgments and thought they were making the right choice were making these decisions. Johnson thought he was making the right choice. He knew more than anyone in the room what it was going to cost him: everything, as he kept saying, was on the table. His agenda, and lives, and knowing more than anyone else, he still made the choice. It was his to make; no one made it for him.

"Virtual JFK . . . is really actual JFK rendered in considerable detail, but reimagined in circumstances he did not live to confront."

CHAPTER 6

Virtual JFK, *Not* Counterfactual JFK: Vietnam If Kennedy Had Lived

Historians on Counterfactuals: Beware of Cleopatra's Nose

Having examined in some detail what JFK did and what LBJ did with regard to the war in Vietnam, we now turn our attention to what might have been—to virtual JFK, Vietnam if Kennedy had lived. *In doing so we enter into what is traditionally, for historians, a methodological no-man's-land. The problem, typically, is not that historians find alternative pasts, also called "what ifs" and "counterfactuals," inherently uninteresting.*[1] *On the contrary, there is no reason to believe they find them any less intriguing than the rest of us, who tend to find questions of "what might have been, if only . . ." quite fascinating. But professional historians have developed an aversion to sanctioning this particular pursuit as real* history *because of their inability to rigorously distinguish between counterfactuals that are plausible from the presumably infinite number that are just fanciful. Believing it is impossible to distinguish the relative plausibility of counterfactuals, historians by and large have adopted a procrustean, take-no-prisoners approach: counterfactuals are off-limits.*[2]

A number of silly counterfactuals have been given almost canonical status by historians in an effort to suggest that there is something inherently unserious, even absurd, about the entire enterprise of examining alternative pasts. One favorite we encountered many years ago as beginning students of the history of U.S. foreign policy is, "Might Napoleon at Waterloo have done better if he had been able to call on air force attack planes (presuming the enemy had none, of course)?" Doubtless he would have, but alas the counterfactual violates what we believe we know about the history of aviation. Another one cherished by several generations of European historians is, "What if Hitler had been a better artist—might he have continued painting and selling his postcards and never entered politics, thus sparing the world the rise of Nazi Germany, the Holocaust, World War II, the Cold War, and so on?" Maybe, but only if one also assumes that the history of the twentieth century was completely devoid of significant causes of this tragic progression of events other than the decisions and actions of one Adolf Hitler.[3] These and similar counterfactual absurdities are, to one degree or another, variations on the most notorious of them all, "Cleopatra's nose," a popular version of which holds that if the nose of the lady in question had been longer or misshapen, and hence less attractive, Marc Antony would not have been attracted to her, hence the history of the Roman Empire would have been fundamentally different, as would the subsequent history of the world and, in fact, the history of the entire human race, given the seminal stature of the history of ancient Rome. Just about everything—the world as we know it today—can therefore be attributed to the shapeliness of but one solitary ancient Egyptian proboscis.[4] And so on.

For those who are not members of the fraternity of professional historians, the emotion associated with this issue within the club comes as a surprise, as does the categorical refusal by many to countenance any exceptions to the rule "no counterfactuals." For example, the eminent British philosopher and historian Michael Oakeshott is offended by what he takes to be the mistaken importation into history of the scientific method, the use of counterfactuals being a feeble effort, as he sees it, to pretend to manipulate "variables," to "experiment," with history. Rising to a fever of indignation and sneering condescension, historian E. H. Carr writes, "The view that examination results are a lottery will always be popular among those who have been placed in the third class." And the great historian of the working class, E. P. Thompson, once dismissed "counterfactual fictions" as "Geschichtswissenschlopff, historical shit."[5] While there have been exceptions among historians to the "no counterfactuals" rule—Yale's John Lewis Gaddis notable among them—disdain for considering alternate histories runs deep among historians.[6]

Why the methodological bias against counterfactuals? A one-word answer is: fear! The craft of writing history simply must, according to the great majority of historians, be limited to an account of what, insofar as can be determined, actually happened. To assume otherwise is to confuse history with historical fiction and is as illegitimate as failing to observe the fundamental difference between science and science fiction. Both scientists and historians endeavor to operate within the constraints of what they believe to be a preexisting objective reality (however complex, however unfathomable it may be), while practitioners of science fiction and histori-

cal fiction are free to launch into all sorts of fantastic "possibilities," constrained not by reality, but only by what the authors believe their readers will let them get away with. The use of counterfactuals, in this view, reduces the craft of history to show business and "showing off." It is a betrayal of the historians' responsibility and commitment to try to understand the past—the past that happened, not one or more of the infinite pasts that did not happen.

Virtual History: A Revolutionary Idea

We feel that something essential is missing from histories that lack all reference to paths not taken, decisions not made, histories that seem almost to have happened, but did not quite. Such histories seem sanitized, unreal, lacking in the contingency and uncertainty of historical moments as they pass by, one by one, full of anxiety and (often) regret for those involved. British historian H. R. Trevor-Roper has explained why historians are wrong to shun alternative histories as if they are inoculating themselves against a communicable disease: first, we all know intuitively that history does not seem to unfold in a counterfactual-free zone. (Otherwise, why should we feel anxious, confused, excited, or uncertain as we daily try to live out our own personal histories?) Second, if whatever happened could not have been other than it was, why should anyone care what happened? Historical determinism is devoid of the drama of real life with all its imponderables. Finally, how are historians supposed to draw lessons from a history that was inevitable, no matter what? If historical events could not have been other than they were, then the basis of drawing lessons from experience—comparing what happened with what might have happened—is rendered nonsensical.

According to Trevor-Roper,

> At any given moment in history there are real alternatives. . . . How can we "explain what happened and why" if we only look at what happened and never consider the alternatives. . . . It is only if we place ourselves before the alternatives of the past . . . only if we live for a moment, as the men of the time lived, in its still fluid context and among its still unresolved problems, if we see those problems coming upon us . . . that we can draw useful lessons from history.[7]

Only by empathizing with the figures whose decisions and actions created the history can we endeavor to understand, can we begin to appreciate the range of possibilities that confronted them, the choices they might have made but, for one reason or another, did not. In this way, history comes alive and we are able to come to judgments about the actions of historical figures that take the form, "They chose such and such, but should have chosen thus and so, which was a live option for them at the time." The use of what ifs permits us to identify options, to assess whether the choices made were (or were not) the best choices that one can plausibly imagine having been made, and draw more general conclusions—i.e., lessons—from the exercise. This, to use the telling metaphor favored by Trevor-Roper, is writing history as if we were trying to understand the decisions and actions of living human beings, rather than dissecting inert corpses on a pathologist's examining table.[8]

Among the current generation of historians, there is no stronger proponent than Niall Ferguson of the use of what ifs. Given the prejudice against counterfactual history, however, he has given this sort of exercise a new name: virtual history. But he has done far more than this. Borrowing freely from the cognitive sciences, he has staked out a middle ground in which scenarios can be evaluated in a relative sense based on their correspondence to the historical facts as they are known. According to Ferguson, "By narrowing down the historical alternatives we consider to those which are plausible . . . we solve the dilemma of choosing between a single deterministic past and an unmanageably infinite number of possible pasts. The counterfactual scenarios we therefore need to construct are not mere fantasy: they are simulations based on calculations about the relative probability of plausible outcomes in a chaotic world (hence 'virtual history')."[9]

According to Ferguson, "virtual history is a necessary antidote to determinism."[10] *Virtual history serves another purpose as well: it is also an antidote to the silliness of counterfactual history. It is hard-nosed history, a close examination of what happened, but with a virtual component. A very useful, though possibly annoying, screensaver would read as follows: "***Counterfactual History***: That's preposterous, that's entertainment!* ***Virtual History***: That's plausible, that's instructive!"*

A slightly longer version, suitable perhaps for framing and placement on the wall in the offices of historians at universities, is:

> **Counterfactual History**, or "tweaking history," is historical fiction of the Cleopatra's nose variety, and is driven by a fascination with paths leading away from what actually happened toward some fanciful alternative universe, world, nation, life, or whatever is the domain of interest. Its purpose is to amaze, confound, confuse, frighten, or otherwise entertain. It is fiction. We learn nothing about history from the exercise. Indeed, the result of tweaking history with absurd counterfactuals is unrelated to truth or falsehood. It is instead a performance art, and its quality should be judged by whatever standards exist, if any, in that art form.

Whereas:

Virtual History requires the historian to move in the opposite direction from that of the tweakers and their counterfactuals—more deeply *into* the experience of a historical character (or characters) and/or events of interest. It involves four steps. *First,* virtual historians embed their what if in a web of historical fact that is as thick and complex as the documentation will permit. *Second,* they build their "models" of people, processes, or whatever is under scrutiny in a way that is as consistent as possible with the historical record. *Third,* they simulate an alternative history by inserting their models into history and come to judgments about its plausibility. *Fourth* and finally, they draw any lessons that may follow from a comparison between the two histories—what happened and what did not happen. We can in principle learn a good deal about history from the exercise: why what happened did happen; why what didn't happen, didn't; and whether the difference between the two is relevant to issues that concern us now.[11]

Counterfactual JFK Versus Virtual JFK: Two Scenarios

Virtual history provides a way to engage the past in its inherent contingency and uncertainty, and thus to move closer to the psychological reality of the past, to the situations as they appeared to the historical actors themselves— their conditions of mind, feelings, objectives, anticipations, biases, fears, and other cognitive and emotional states that may have been very real, even decisive, to those who are the subjects of our historical investigations. In listening to the audiotapes of Lyndon Johnson which deal with the war in Vietnam, for example, one is struck by the anxiety of the president, by his twisting and turning in the face of decision after decision to incrementally escalate the war, and by his anguished search for alternatives to deeper U.S. involvement, only a limited portion of which are to be found in the official written documents of the period. Was the course of the war determined? Lyndon Johnson certainly didn't think so, as he struggled to decide what to do. Moreover, his memoirs are full of thinly veiled, very deep regret over decisions made and not made and a kind of cosmic melancholy and perplexity as to how things could have gone so wrong in Vietnam. But regret makes sense only if paths not taken were live options, as they seemed to LBJ in real time and retrospectively. We have no reason to doubt that LBJ might have decided differently and, if he had, that events might have unfolded differently. Likewise, a different kind of U.S. president, framing the issues, events, and his own priorities differently, might well have decided differently. Thus we arrive at the virtual history of the American war in Vietnam, and virtual JFK.

Niall Ferguson's most seminal contribution to the methodology of history is his distinction between counterfactual history and virtual history—a dis-

tinction that, while somewhat opaque in his analysis, is nevertheless both critically important and highly illuminating. It points the way to a history of decisions leading to the American war in Vietnam that is awash in the uncertainty and contingency of those successive moments in the 1960s when the escalation occurred, as it was lived forward, yet does not force the historian to retreat to the absurdity of so many of the standard-issue counterfactuals.

Just to give one example of this critical difference between counterfactual history and virtual history, suppose we ask, "What would JFK have decided, had he been president on February 7–8, 1965, when the insurgent attack on the Pleiku barracks occurred, killing several Americans and wounding more than a hundred others?"[12] The counterfactual is this: John F. Kennedy was president, not Lyndon B. Johnson. Consider the two possible scenarios: in one, LBJ has been president between JFK's assassination and the attack on Pleiku. JFK is metaphorically "parachuted" back into the Oval Office at the appropriate moment, having come from God-knows-where to resume his duties as president. And consider a second scenario, in which JFK escaped assassination, serves continuously as president after November 22, 1963, and, on February 7, 1965, he faces what LBJ faced. We know what LBJ did. What would JFK have done?

Here is scenario number one. Imagine you are reading along in your authoritative history of the war in Vietnam when, suddenly, you read that JFK is the president. Yes, that's right: John F. Kennedy, long thought assassinated, has returned from—from where? From, oh, let's say an extended bout of amnesia, which he spent at a Buddhist monastery in northern India. Yes, yes, it's a bit of a stretch, but it is precisely this stage of "stretching" that is usually among those features omitted by enthusiastic proponents of historical counterfactuals. (Another possibility appears in the 2003 feature film, Bubba Ho-Tep, the tale of two eccentric inhabitants of a "rest home" in east Texas, one of whom [played by Bruce Campbell] believes he is Elvis Presley, while his buddy [played by the African-American star Ossie Davis], believes he is JFK.)[13] If neither of these fantasies suit you, then you are free to imagine JFK's return to the White House after an absence of roughly a year and a half via any route you like. But somehow or other, JFK walks into the Oval Office and takes over, as LBJ understandably faints from the shock. What, in these circumstances, would Kennedy have done with regard to the attack on the Pleiku barracks? A facetious answer is: it is as easy, and as difficult, to reach a plausible answer to this question as it would be if the question were, "What would JFK's 'buddy,' Elvis Presley, have done?" Or Mickey Mouse? Or the family dog? This is an example of "tweaking" in counterfactual history, except the embarrassing and usually omitted *question—how in the world did this happen?—has been asked. It consists of the imaginary manipulation of a historical moment that for some reason we find fascinating.*

Now let's try the second, superficially more plausible, scenario, in which JFK never left office, and again address the question: what would JFK have done? We can ignore the "where in the world did JFK come from?" issue and consider the other alternative: that JFK has not disappeared between November 22, 1963, and February 7, 1965. The bullet missed him in Dallas, or he didn't go to Dallas, or in some other fashion he lived and was reelected. It is now February 7, 1965, and we ask: now in his second term, what does JFK do when he hears of the attack in Pleiku? Unfortunately for counterfactual enthusiasts, this variant of the alternate history is also ridiculous. With each successive moment after November 22–23, 1963, the war in Vietnam became progressively and irrevocably LBJ's war, a function of LBJ's decisions, not JFK's: the slow but steady escalation of the American presence, the Americanization of covert operations against North Vietnam, the air strikes on North Vietnam following the events in the Tonkin Gulf, the authorization of plans in all relevant U.S. agencies to prepare to take over the war in 1965, and so on. Every one of these events and trends were ordered by Lyndon Johnson, not John F. Kennedy. This is why we find Fred Logevall's argument persuasive. "During the [Vietnam] conflict itself," he has written, "and to some degree in the years after, much noise was made about Vietnam being 'McNamara's War,' but it was never the defense secretary's war. From 23 November 1963 it was 'Lyndon Johnson's War.'"[14]

The answer to what Kennedy would have done in February 1965 is almost fully determined by an unstated assumption underlying the question: that, with JFK as president from November 22, 1963, to February 8–9, 1965, events would have transpired under him exactly as they did under LBJ. If we believe that changing presidents would have made no difference during the more than fourteen months between JFK's death and the attack on Pleiku, there is no reason to believe that JFK's decisions and actions would have differed from LBJ's during the forty-eight hours in question in early February 1965. In other words, we must assume that, on all relevant dimensions, JFK was LBJ, an absurdity that is not only unlikely, it is unimaginable, and thus of dubious entertainment value even to fans of historical fiction. Even the hallucinatory JFK character played by Ossie Davis in Bubba Ho-Tep didn't believe he was JFK impersonating LBJ. No, that would not be credible, even in a work of wild historical fiction.

But as practitioners of virtual history, we are interested in the question of Vietnam if Kennedy had lived. How do we proceed? First, we don't begin the inquiry with what Lyndon Johnson did or did not do regarding the attack on Pleiku or regarding anything else. We begin with JFK: we try to understand him in his historical context, moving forward through time and events. To the degree possible, we try to determine what JFK did in circumstances that we believe are relevant to the question about him to which we seek an answer—a question about what he might have done with regard to Vietnam, had he not been assassinated. In this way, we build an informal model of JFK along the dimensions we believe are relevant to the issue of Vietnam if Kennedy had lived. We look for a pattern in his decisions and his behavior. We try to get a feel for this particular president. We try to take the measure of the man, to understand whatever it is we think we need to know about him that will help us address the question of what he would have done with regard to the conflict in Vietnam. When we feel we have built the most accurate model of JFK that the relevant historical documentation will allow, we will have taken the penultimate step in our virtual history. The final step is the "simulation," in which we, in effect, "spin" the model into history as we understand it. We ask of this particular (virtual) JFK, "What would he have done?" Based on everything we have been able to learn about his proclivities in decisions regarding war and peace, based on whatever we might imagine his advisers telling him about Vietnam, based on whatever we might imagine to be the range of situations in Vietnam itself that JFK might have faced, and based on whatever else we believe is relevant, we arrive at an answer: "Vietnam, if Kennedy had lived, would probably have unfolded as follows . . ." This history of the war in Vietnam is not a tweaked and fantasized edition of LBJ and Vietnam, it is history reimagined, consistent with the facts about JFK as we understand them.

This is, in fact, the kind of exercise with which we are concerned in this chapter. The conference participants, having for nearly two days reviewed and debated what Kennedy did and what Johnson did with regard to the war in Vietnam, have now earned the right to consider Vietnam if Kennedy had lived.

David Welch's Results: Would JFK Have Americanized the War? Yes—Oops, I Mean No

The opening provocation is provided by one of this book's coauthors, David Welch, who begins by discussing the results of a questionnaire the conference participants have completed and handed in to him overnight.[15] *The questionnaire consists of four broad questions. The first two*

*are straightforwardly "counterfactual" questions: (1) ". . . imagine Kennedy is making the decision in January–February 1965, not Johnson . . ."
and (2) what is your response to "Fredrik Logevall's argument [in material
the participants read in preparation for the conference] that, on balance,
Kennedy was likely not to have committed American troops to Vietnam"?[16]
These are counterfactual questions because the respondents are asked simply (in question 1), what do we think would have happened if history
had been tweaked in the way suggested ("Kennedy had lived and been
reelected"), while the second asks what we think about Fred Logevall's
conclusions regarding such tweaking. Of course, the respondents know a
great deal about the documentation bearing on this historical tweaking,
but that is implied, not explicit. (The same questions could have been put
to a random sample of people. The only prerequisite would in that case
have been some rudimentary knowledge of U.S. history in the 1960s: there
was a President Kennedy, followed by a President Johnson, there was a
Vietnam War, etc.) The results: based on responses to these two questions,
the respondents felt as a group that JFK would probably have embarked
on a course of what was called in the questionnaire "Americanization
Lite"—that is, JFK would have escalated a little bit, but not as much as
LBJ.*

*The plot thickens, however, when the results of the third and fourth
questions are revealed. Question 3 asks "for your estimate of how Kennedy
would have perceived pressures" to escalate the war, while question 4 asks
respondents to state "what considerations Kennedy cared about"—
international opinion, domestic political factors, personal proclivities, and
so on. These are the kinds of questions the practitioner of virtual history
asks. They require rumination on some aspects of JFK's character, his
strengths and weaknesses, and his priorities. In short, in their necessarily
abbreviated but still suggestive way, questions 3 and 4 ask the respondents
to take the measure of this man, JFK, and to reach some conclusions via
that route regarding what he might or might not have done regarding
Vietnam.*

*The results, as noted by Welch, are comparatively quite fascinating:
based only on an analysis of questions 3 and 4, the group as a whole felt
JFK would have withdrawn from Vietnam rather than undertake something
like "Americanization Lite." This means, as he says, that the group is "collectively inconsistent." But the inconsistency is only apparent. It reveals
more about the difference between counterfactual history and virtual history than about the historical judgments of the respondents. When asked to
tweak the history of the war in Vietnam by "deleting" LBJ and "inserting"
JFK, the respondents as a group felt JFK would have escalated the war,*

*though less than LBJ. When asked about JFK's proclivities regarding war
and peace, the group felt he would have withdrawn from Vietnam without
committing any combat troops. Of course, this questionnaire was used primarily for its value in provoking discussion. It is not, as Welch emphasized,
a scientifically valid instrument, or anything like it. Still, this group's ver-
dict is that virtual JFK would* not *have Americanized the war in South
Vietnam. Instead, the group felt he would have withdrawn, accepted the
political heat, and moved on.*

*When the group was asked implicitly to focus initially on LBJ—his dif-
ficulties, his anguish, his obvious dislike for all his alternatives on Vietnam
as he imagined them—it was more difficult for the group to imagine JFK
acting in a fundamentally different way, presumably because the difficulty
of the task—avoiding an American war—just seemed too great. But when
they were asked implicitly to begin their analysis with virtual JFK, and thus
to build their "model" of him event by event, decision by decision, it was
easier to imagine virtual JFK doing in Vietnam what he had consistently
done elsewhere, but which LBJ was unable to do: resist the pressure to take
the nation to war. Using the virtual history route, therefore, the group felt
JFK would have withdrawn. As more relevant historical data on JFK is
plugged into the model of his behavior, the more probable it seems to become that he would have withdrawn, thus avoiding the Americanization of
the war in Vietnam altogether. So as a group, in response to the question
of whether JFK would have Americanized the war in Vietnam, it is as if
they first said, "Yes, though not as massively as LBJ," and then, "Oops, I
mean no, not at all."*

*It is important to stress, however, that the history of the war after No-
vember 22, 1963, is not and cannot simply be ignored in any "simulation"
using a model of virtual JFK. That history is part of the context that must
be considered before arriving at a conclusion as to what virtual JFK would
have done regarding the war in Vietnam. The key to pursuing virtual history and avoiding counterfactual nonsense is this: Begin at the beginning;
begin with the phenomenon you wish to understand; begin with the question you want to answer. Then build your model. Finally, insert the model
into the historical context, that is, "simulate" or reimagine the alternative
history. All solutions will be, to a considerable degree, subjective, of course,
but they will not all be equally persuasive. The most persuasive will be
those whose scenarios contain believable matches between a model and the
historical context into which it is simulated. It will be, in other words,*
plausible. *Once the plausibility of an example of virtual history is established, a veritable cascade of questions which make little sense in the absence of this sort of enterprise can be asked, beginning with the most*

important question of all: why do the two histories, the actual and the virtual, differ? In the case we are concerned with here, why did the conflict in Vietnam escalate to a major American war under LBJ while it is likely that under JFK, America would have withdrawn and avoided further military involvement?

Welch concludes with some examples of the intensely personal way LBJ framed the issues of escalation and withdrawal in Vietnam and asks: would virtual JFK have framed these issues as Johnson framed them and, if not, what difference might that have made to the course of the conflict in Vietnam? Of particular interest is LBJ's tendency to personalize the war, to see it as a referendum on himself as a president and as a person, and thus to imagine a "loss" in Vietnam in terms of catastrophic personal humiliation. Welch asks: did JFK approach the conflict this way, and if not, why might this have led to a different outcome if Kennedy had returned alive from Dallas?

DAVID WELCH: I bet you're all dying to know what the answer is to the question, "Would Kennedy have gone into Vietnam or not?" I now have the answer for you. [Laughter.] The results of my survey were rather interesting. Let me just give them to you and say a few brief words about them to set up Fred's remarks. The punch line here is that there is obviously room for debate, and we are of mixed opinion. [Laughter.]

JAMES BLIGHT: We needed a questionnaire for that?

MARILYN YOUNG: It's social science; they do this all the time. [Laughter.]

DAVID WELCH: More interestingly, we are collectively inconsistent. I will explain why.

The first question asks, "Which of these four outcomes is most plausible, imagining that Kennedy is the one making the decision in January and February 1965, not Johnson?" The survey asked to hold everything else constant in your mind as much as you possibly can, and then rank the four outcomes in terms of plausibility. It turns out that the most plausible outcome, according to the group, was Americanization Lite. This was the most common response, followed by the status quo, then withdrawal, and the least plausible outcome, you collectively thought, was Americanization LBJ style. So, as a group—collectively—we tended to think on first blush that JFK would have gone into Vietnam, but not on the scale that Johnson did.

JAMES HERSHBERG: I'd like a clarification, because I thought there was a—

DAVID WELCH: No clarifications allowed yet. [Laughter.] I'll get through it, and then you can complicate it. Of course there are ambiguities.

Question 2 asked, "Was Fred right in thinking that, on balance— weighing the arguments for and against—Kennedy would not have gone into Vietnam the way Johnson did?" Fifty percent thought Fred made the case. Half the group agreed that the arguments Fred presented, taken at face value, suggested JFK was likely to withdraw. Thirty percent thought that the evidence Fred presented actually suggested that Kennedy would have made a commitment to Vietnam similar to LBJ's. The rest weren't sure; they thought it was too close to call.

Questions 3 and 4 tried to break the decision down, to take it to a finer level of detail, by asking what pressures Kennedy would have faced and how heavily he would have weighed them in his mind. These questions were trying to tap into your judgments of those factors, to re-create the predicament he faced as he would have experienced it. I took your answers and assigned them some numbers so that I could integrate the results.

The punch line here is that because you [as a group] tended to think he was so strongly inclined to withdraw from a personal perspective, and because as a group you thought he paid quite a lot of attention to his personal impulses, when you aggregate all of the numbers, it actually predicts that he would withdraw. Remember that the most common answer to question 1 was Americanization Lite. But when you try to gauge what he would have done by considering constraints and susceptibilities, it turns out that, as a group, you thought he would have withdrawn. That strikes me as a rather interesting inconsistency.

Before Fred takes over, I want to raise the question of key differences between Kennedy and LBJ. Of course, LBJ *did* face the situation that we are imagining Kennedy would have faced in '64 and '65. The question of whether the two would have framed their choices the same way is therefore very important.

The U.S. military talked about winning in Vietnam, but Johnson and his key advisers almost never talked about winning in Vietnam: they talked about *not losing*. What were the options that Johnson thought he had to choose from? He simplified things quite a bit. At the end of the day, he saw only three possible options, but he thought only two were even worth considering from a practical perspective. As he put it very pithily to John Knight, chairman of the board at the *Miami Herald*, on February 3rd, 1964—in one of the great taped phone conversations— Johnson said, "There's one of three things you can do. One is run and let the dominoes start falling over. And God Almighty, what they said about us leaving China would just be warming up compared to what they'd say now. . . . You can run, or you can fight, as we are doing, or you can sit down and agree to neutralize all of it. But nobody is going to neutralize North Vietnam, so that's totally impractical. And so it really boils down to one or two decisions—getting out or getting in."[17] It's very interesting to me how he wrote off the neutralization option.

FREDRIK LOGEVALL: That's early '64?

DAVID WELCH: That's right, yes.

Later, when he's out of office, he made a very interesting statement to Doris Kearns, which I think shows how acutely Johnson was paying attention to pressures and constraints. This is what he said to Doris.

> Everything I knew about history told me that if I got out of Vietnam and let Ho Chi Minh run through the streets of Saigon, then I'd be doing exactly what Chamberlain did in World War II. I'd be giving a big fat reward to aggression. And I knew that if we let Communist aggression succeed in taking over South Vietnam, there would follow in this country an endless national debate—a mean and destructive debate—that would shatter my Presidency, kill my administration, and damage our democracy. I knew that Harry Truman and Dean Acheson had lost their effectiveness from the day that the Communists took over in China. I believed that the loss of China had played a large role in the rise of Joe McCarthy. And I knew that all these problems, taken together, were chickenshit compared with what might happen if we lost Vietnam. . . . Losing the Great Society was a terrible thought, but not so terrible as the thought of being responsible for America's losing a war to the Communists. Nothing could possibly be worse than that.[18]

DAVID WELCH: What I would like to ask collectively is whether you all think Kennedy would have shared that perspective? How did he differ from Johnson as a thinker, as a person integrating all of these complex issues and deciding what trade-off could and could not be made? Was Kennedy susceptible to different kinds of pressures from Johnson? Would he have framed the choice in a similar way? I'll leave that with you and pass things over to Fred.

Fredrik Logevall's Virtual JFK: Would JFK Have Americanized the War? Maybe, but Probably Not

If Niall Ferguson can be credited with formulating an approach to virtual history that brings it "out of the closet" for professional historians, then Cornell historian Fred Logevall is the foremost practitioner and advocate of that approach on the subject of JFK and the war in Vietnam. In his 1999 book, Choosing War: The Lost Chance for Peace and the Escalation of War in Vietnam, *Logevall provided an exemplary case history of the practice of virtual history as an intellectually exhilarating historical enterprise. In so doing, he also reinvigorated the discussion of what would probably have happened in Vietnam if Kennedy had lived.*[19]

Before the appearance of Logevall's book, the use of what if history was, to historians of American foreign policy, a marginal activity at best. Of course, counterfactual approaches to this question have provided a good deal of popular entertainment ever since Kennedy's death. Many of those involved, however, have constituted a rogues' gallery of pseudo-history: conspiracy theorists, paranoid oddballs, Kennedy assassination freaks, and those claiming to have discovered the existence of a U.S. "shadow government," some portion of which they believe was responsible for killing Kennedy because he was going to withdraw from Vietnam.[20]

Two of Logevall's conclusions remain controversial. First, contrary to what is commonly believed, and contrary to what Logevall says he himself believed when he began his research, LBJ and his inner circle of advisers understood that their prospects in Vietnam were poor, that however it turned out, it would be costly, bloody, and politically debilitating, both domestically and internationally. Logevall admits to having been shocked to discover that, in effect, Johnson, McNamara, Rusk, Bundy, and many of the others believed the result of Americanizing the war in Vietnam might well be a quagmire—a disastrous quagmire—and yet they went ahead and Americanized the war anyway, preferring a bloody stalemate to "losing" Vietnam to communism. Second, Logevall concluded that virtual JFK probably would not have escalated the war in Vietnam, but would instead have found a way to withdraw.[21]

In the provocation that follows, Logevall demonstrates in outline what is required of those who practice virtual history. First, he admits what is obvious yet must always be kept in mind: virtual history is an inherently uncertain enterprise in which reasonable and informed scholars can come to different conclusions. He then sketches out elements of what he considers to be the best argument for believing that virtual JFK would have Americanized the war in Vietnam. He acknowledges that it is possible. Finally, he then gives eight reasons for believing that, on balance, it is more likely that JFK would not have escalated the war in Vietnam but, instead, would have withdrawn after the 1964 election. Note Logevall's trajectory: he begins with JFK, not LBJ, and proceeds to draw a portrait of JFK as a relatively objective, skeptical, open-minded realist.

FREDRIK LOGEVALL: I'll give you a number of propositions that may not seem quite as provocative as they might have been had I not just heard that as a group, as Dave said, you feel it likely that he would have opted for withdrawal. Nevertheless, here are a number of propositions to get us started. If you've had a chance to read either the essay in the briefing book, or the chapter from *Choosing War* included there, most of this will seem familiar, although I have a couple of new things to add.[22]

The first proposition is that a what if analysis can have great utility. I want to say that, provided you follow some ground rules—I talk about those in the essay—provided you do it carefully, it can help us better understand what did happen. In other words, for me this is not just a parlor game, although the game part of it can be enjoyable. I think it helps us better understand what Lyndon Johnson *did do* to think carefully about what Kennedy *might have done*. I think the Kennedy what if is particularly conducive to this kind of analysis. It meets the ground rules that I believe are essential. Historians and political scientists, whenever we deal with questions of causality, at least implicitly consider alternatives or unrealized possibilities. What I am getting at is that we should be explicit about this, rather than simply implicit.

My second proposition is that John F. Kennedy had not made a firm decision on what to do with the Vietnam problem when he left for Dallas in November 1963. In my mind, the evidence is strongest—by a considerable margin—that he remained committed to the war; that, like the good politician that he was, he was going to postpone the difficult decisions for as long as he could; and that he would have spoken differently in private and in public. It is very possible, however—here I don't want to be misunderstood—that he had decided in his mind that this would never become an American war; that he was never going to make this a large-scale combat commitment. In this respect, though Jamie and I disagree on this question, I do concur with Jamie that there is an important difference between a combat commitment and an advisory commitment, even if some of those advisers are leading ARVN troops into combat, or are themselves in combat. There is an important distinction to be made, and it is entirely possible that he had decided that this was going to remain limited. But I sense that he still wants an independent South Vietnam to survive. He wants to defeat the insurgency when he boards the plane for Dallas.

The third proposition is that his policies in 1961 to '63 were an important expansion of the war. Here we're talking about the escalation of U.S. presence; we're talking about his support for the coup. I find it very interesting how, in the tape that Marc and Tim played for us last night—when he speaks into the recorder on November 4th, 1963—he speaks of this being a three-month discussion about the coup.[23] This very much suggests that this is something the administration is debating: they are considering whether they should go through with it. That complicity is important, as a couple of people mentioned—Marilyn, I believe, mentioned it yesterday, and others as well. And his rejection of negotiations, which is something we haven't really discussed at this conference—his noninterest in any kind of diplomatic settlement in '61–'63—is also important. What this does is complicate the situation for himself and for his successor.

My fourth proposition is that a good argument can be made that he would have opted for some kind of major escalation had push come to shove. The moment of decision would have come at roughly the same time it came for LBJ. Both men wanted to keep the war on the back burner through the 1964 election. I think that in those months afterwards, you could make a good argument that he would have had to opt for some kind of Americanized war.

But the better argument is that he would *not* have done so. I think what's important about this argument is that the components that go into it are not persuasive standing alone. In order to make this case, they need to be considered systematically; they need to be considered in terms of their cumulative impact. Since you've had a chance to read the two pieces, I'll list them briefly for the sake of discussion.

- The first point here is, as we noted, that he was always ambivalent about the war and expressed a strong opposition to ground troops. Again, he saw an important difference between combat commitment and an advisory one—a distinction that I share.
- Second, he was far more interested in, and solicitous of, international opinion. I think it became a kind of prerequisite for him to have allied international backing. The United States was isolated on the Vietnam question by the end of 1964, with two or three rare exceptions. Allied governments were saying, "Do not do this." I think it matters. Kennedy—unlike his successor, who was downright irritated by the

efforts of allies to prevent the Americanization—would have felt the impact of this. I think it matters that Kennedy felt differently.

- Third, he was more seasoned—more battle-tested in foreign policy—than was his successor. He had a sizable fund of foreign-policy credibility in late 1963.

- Fourth, the timing of the assassination. As a couple of people have mentioned this weekend, this is important. John F. Kennedy would have come to this difficult decision—crunch time—in his second term. I think presidents who are never again going to run for reelection approach these questions differently from those who are, in effect—as was certainly the case for LBJ—in their first term.

- Fifth, he was not a Southeast Asia expert, by any means, but my sense is he had a more sophisticated understanding of the issues at stake. He was more conscious of the fact that you needed reforms in Saigon and you needed a more representative government if you are going to have any hope of defeating the insurgency. One of the first things LBJ did in November 1963 was to say, "We focus too much on reforms; let's get on with winning the war."[24]

- Sixth, there was a very complicated set of issues that have to do with personality differences. I just want to mention a couple of things here. Kennedy had a skeptical worldview in a way that Lyndon Johnson did not, and I think that matters. When Dean Rusk speaks of saving Christian civilization in Southeast Asia, this resonates with Lyndon Johnson in a way that it never would have done with JFK. He did not have LBJ's self-doubt when it came to foreign policy issues. To go to Dave's quote, it is impossible for me to imagine John F. Kennedy saying, "Well, we can either bomb the hell out of China, or we can retreat to San Francisco." Kennedy did not speak in such terms. I've mentioned the parochialism, the suspicion of foreign and allied opinion that LBJ had—these were not things JFK had.

- Seventh, there is something very important that we haven't talked about yet, and I'd be very interested to hear Bill, Tom, and Chet speak to this issue: Johnson's tendency to personalize the war. This is very evident in the later stages, but I think it's right there from the very beginning. In November 1963, he says, "I will not be the President who lost Vietnam." See and hear LBJ's 1966 phone conversation with Senator Eugene McCarthy.[25] That is something that I doubt Kennedy would have felt to the same extent.

- Eighth and final point on this, and then I have a couple brief concluding comments: Kennedy's tolerance for dissent—Kennedy's more open advisory system—stands in contrast to his successor's.

That matters, because that tolerance for dissent in an open advisory system, combined with interest in seeking allied opinion and a recently won reelection, make it much more likely that Kennedy is going to listen to the many, many voices in American society and abroad who are urging caution in these critical months. Here we're talking about most allied governments; we're talking about the Senate Democratic leadership; we're talking about key elements in the press, including the *New York Times*, Walter Lippmann, and others; and we're talking about the public. The public is often thought of as being hawkish on Vietnam; it is not. It becomes hawkish on Vietnam after the troops are committed. There is a rally 'round the flag effect. If you look at the few polls we have early in the year, there is deep ambivalence on the part of the public. And I mentioned yesterday that McNamara, from my view, is a pessimist in the early stages. I don't think he's a true believer on the war. I'm not convinced that Mac Bundy is a true believer on the war in the same way that say Dean Rusk is, either. And so I don't think he would have faced that bureaucratic pressure that the survey suggests he would have faced. We could also talk about a number of mid-level people—like John McNaughton and George Ball.[26]

Is there a price to be paid for getting out? Of course there is. There is a price to be paid by Lyndon Johnson for getting out; there is a price to be paid by John F. Kennedy for getting out—even a second-term Kennedy who's got a lot of advantages. There is a price to pay; this is a set of poor options that they face. But I don't think that the price is exorbitant. And I do think that price has to be compared to the price he could expect to pay if he took what by early 1965 is the only reasonable alternative, and that is major escalation. The status quo will no longer work. Many people warned LBJ about this. We talked about Humphrey [**Document 5-6**] and the uniformed military telling him, even as they are advocating escalation, "Five years; 500,000 troops; this is going to get worse before it gets better."[27] You have to compare the price to be paid for going in if you are going to talk about the price for not going in.

Could he have chosen what Dave calls "Americanization Lite"? It is possible. We've put it here in sort of binary terms; it's very possible that even LBJ could have opted for what Bill Bundy in the spring of 1965 talked about as a middle option—some kind of enclave strategy in which what you do is hold the major South Vietnamese centers and you commit far fewer troops.[28] There are various things we could speak of. But it has to mean, it seems to me, a major, major expansion of the war effort, involving bombing and certainly troops. I think, on balance, that a surviving John F. Kennedy chooses—and there is a choice here—very differently.

LBJ's Dilemmas in Succeeding JFK

Jamie Galbraith is the strongest advocate among the conference participants of the view that JFK had absolutely decided to withdraw from Vietnam at the time of his assassination, a view from which even Fred Logevall draws back. Unlike Jamie Galbraith, Fred Logevall believes it is likely that JFK would have made a firm and final decision to withdraw at some point fairly soon after his presumed reelection in November 1964. Galbraith considers Kennedy's decision to withdraw a matter of actual history, not virtual history. Logevall attempts to register his dissent from Galbraith's view in what follows, but is cut off.

Yet Jamie Galbraith does not want his view to be misunderstood as full of praise for JFK and condemnation for LBJ. JFK, in Galbraith's view, decided to withdraw because he was sophisticated in foreign affairs, because he was confident that his own understanding of the issues in Vietnam exceeded that of his senior advisers, because he was determined to prevail, and because he had a few forceful and equally determined advisers, led by Robert McNamara, on whom he could rely to ensure that his will prevailed—that withdrawal from Vietnam was carried out. LBJ, on the other hand, is, in Galbraith's opinion, thrice the victim of unfortunate circumstances regarding his options in Vietnam.

(1) *He had to navigate nearly a year as an unelected president and, even after his 1964 election, he lacked the freedom of maneuver Kennedy would have had in his second and final term.*

(2) *As the successor to the murdered president during the most dangerous days of the Cold War, LBJ had reason to fear that U.S. hawks, especially (but not only) in the military, might be willing to risk or even to force a nuclear confrontation with the USSR (whom some held responsible for Kennedy's murder, even in the absence of convincing evidence), and thus their endlessly repetitive recommendations to escalate in Vietnam could not simply be ignored by Johnson. And*

(3) *LBJ's priorities were domestic rather than international, and to a certain extent Johnson's willingness to escalate in Vietnam must be seen as an attempt to retain the votes in Congress of conservative Democrats for programs such as Medicare, Medicaid, and for voting*

rights, and similar measures. Anyone in these circumstances, according to Galbraith, would have confronted the same insurmountable difficulties in Vietnam that plagued LBJ, difficulties JFK never had to face.

In response, Bill Moyers wonders whether JFK would in a second term have been able to sustain what Moyers believes was Kennedy's "disdain or indifference toward Congress," or whether, in effect, Kennedy too would have had to make some of the hard trade-offs—domestic versus international—that Johnson found it impossible to avoid. Why? Because Kennedy, too, according to Moyers, believed in the Great Society. Could JFK have had it both ways? Bill Moyers is skeptical.

JAMES GALBRAITH: Yesterday nobody contested the facts that I presented. We don't need to guess whether Kennedy might have made a decision at some time in 1964 or 1965. There *was* a decision. That is the precise word that Robert McNamara uses. He uses it for good and sufficient reasons. So treating a point of fact as though it were a what if is intrinsically misleading.

FREDRIK LOGEVALL: But it is not a point of fact—

JAMES GALBRAITH: Now, let me finish. The fact of the decision is a fact that—as I said yesterday—was quite independent of what reservations may have accompanied that fact. A correctly framed what if would have been, "Would Kennedy have reversed his previous decision to begin the withdrawal of U.S. forces in Vietnam?" That decision was a fact in October 1963. We can talk about whether circumstances might have forced him to reconsider that decision; that's an interesting question. Fred has already raised one very important point of distinction, which is to say (and I agree with him) that Kennedy could never have faced the precise circumstances that LBJ faced. One reason is that Kennedy would have been in his second term, whereas Johnson was in his first term.

There are two other reasons that seem to me very important here. One of them is the fact that when Kennedy died in Dallas, it was not because of a heart attack or a stroke. He was murdered in Dallas. The circumstances of that murder, which we now tend to treat as accepted, were certainly not established in the early weeks and months of Johnson's presidency. It is quite unreasonable to suppose that Johnson was operating under the same beliefs that most people today operate under. We know that when Johnson established the Warren Commission, he said in a taped conversation with Richard Russell that the purpose of the Warren

Commission was to make sure no one got the impression that Khrushchev or Castro was responsible for Kennedy's murder.[29] He had very good reasons for wanting to make sure that that did not become part of American political discourse, because there was a distinct possibility that such a thing would lead to an actual pretext for war. One tends in retrospect to discount Johnson's comments, but when I listen to those tapes, my tendency is to believe that he meant exactly what he said. Knowing what one knows now about the nuclear balance and about the attitudes of the senior strategists on that question, and indeed about the nuclear-war-fighting plan that the United States had as of 1961—it was essentially a plan to use an overwhelming force in a preventive war—Johnson had every reason to be extremely worried about that problem.[30] That indeed, it seems to me, changes circumstances in a way that Kennedy could never have faced.

The third reason is that the two administrations had fundamentally different overwhelming priorities. We talked about this a bit yesterday. By the middle of 1963, Kennedy was certainly moving in the direction of defusing the Cold War. That is the message of the American University speech; his energy was in things like the test ban.[31] There is a reason why he asked my father in early 1963 to consider taking an assignment as U.S. ambassador to Moscow. Johnson's priority was something else altogether. Johnson wanted the Great Society. At the same time, Kennedy was not as committed and certainly did not have his energies devoted to those objectives in the same way that Johnson did. So there again it seems to me that as Johnson moved down the road, he was weighing the costs of not going into Vietnam in a very different way than how Kennedy would have weighed them. For Kennedy, there would have been less to lose on the domestic front. He wasn't as ambitious as Johnson was domestically.

It seems to me from that point of view that there are many reasons to think that speculating on how Kennedy would have acted had he arrived in 1965 is at least a little bit misleading unless one takes account of what, I think, are inescapable differences in the situations between the two presidents.

JAMES BLIGHT: Bill, would you like to comment?

BILL MOYERS: Well, I hadn't intended to respond, although I appreciate very much both presentations. I find it fascinating. I'm not a very speculative person, but it is interesting to allow yourself to do that. I would like to make a number of very quick comments.

Johnson was older than Kennedy.[32] Johnson had a deeper imprint from what the Republicans, in particular Nixon and McCarthy, did as a consequence of China and Korea.[33] I don't think Kennedy was as concerned about all that; intellectually, yes, but not emotionally, personally, or politically. It did not get at him that way. Maybe it would have if he'd been in the Senate for the six years from '52 on, but he had not been in the Senate; he'd been out campaigning for the vice presidency and presidency.[34] He just wasn't etched as sharply as Johnson was by the Republicans. Nixon and McCarthy and the right wing poisoned American politics in the postwar period.

But LBJ did actually consult more than Kennedy, I think. Kennedy probably consulted more with establishment figures than Lyndon Johnson did, but Johnson was constantly on the phone asking people about this and that. The phone conversations that I've looked at are just a minor portion (although a fascinating and revealing portion) of the total conversations he carried on throughout the course of his presidency.

One of the things that puzzles me is how Kennedy would have handled Congress if the war had gone badly after his reelection—or even in '64, because Kennedy did not have a sure hand with Congress. Civil rights, the war on poverty, and tax cuts all got bogged down. Kennedy was not a creature of Congress; he had a kind of disdain or indifference toward Congress. It was there to be suffered, but not to be wooed and won and challenged. In '64, as Nixon and Goldwater escalated their rhetoric and their call for standing firm against communism, I wonder what Kennedy would have done with an increasingly conservative Congress, particularly if after his reelection he had failed to rise to the challenge of civil rights and had failed to get a civil rights bill in '64 or '65. I think that would have aroused the opposition in Congress, and would have actually increased his concern for domestic political issues over international issues. I do think that if there had been a withdrawal—and there was an opportunity for one after the '64 election—Kennedy would have been better at explaining it publicly than Johnson. LBJ was not an effective public speaker, except on rare occasions, such as the "we shall overcome" speech, or the State of the Union in 1965.[35] However, if we had to put a cover over withdrawal from a deteriorating situation in Indochina, Kennedy would have been better at that than Johnson. Remember that Johnson was deeply imprinted with the mythology of the Alamo: you draw a line in the sand and you stake a stand; you don't negotiate with the Mexicans to get them to get out. These are just a few factors that I wonder about.

Kennedy did want the Great Society, Jamie, but the Great Society was really Dick Goodwin's mantra applied to John F. Kennedy's program, which Lyndon Johnson fulfilled and enlarged.[36] I wish we had never put the name Great Society on that, by the way, because Johnson disliked those words; but they caught on, so he adopted them.

When Paradigms Collide, Part I: Was "Americanization Lite" a Viable Option for JFK?

The historian of science Thomas S. Kuhn famously argued that the theories and evidence produced by scholars in any discipline must be understood within the context of the paradigms in which their intellectual traditions are embedded.[37] Although Kuhn gave paradigm several definitions, it has been taken by scholars in the humanities and social sciences to refer to the absolutely core set of assumptions that constitute the foundations of a discipline. When what Kuhn called a paradigm shift occurs among some of the practitioners in a discipline, it becomes increasingly difficult and eventually impossible for practitioners working within the older and the newer paradigms even to understand one another, let alone appreciate or agree with one another's points of view. Kuhn's own favorite illustration of his thesis was the Copernican Revolution. Copernican and Ptolemaic astronomers—those who believed the Earth orbited the sun, and those who believed the reverse—had according to Kuhn ultimately little choice but to reject one another's views entirely as utter nonsense, because at some point in the emergence of Copernican cosmology, there was no common intellectual ground left on which adherents of each view could figuratively stand and address one another.[38] Kuhn and others have provided many other examples of paradigm shifts in the sciences and their disorienting consequences. Once a new paradigm has replaced the old one, Kuhn believed, we are justified in saying that an intellectual revolution has occurred—an event, extended in time, comparable in many ways to profound political revolutions such as the French or Russian revolutions.

We believe the following portion of the argument at the Musgrove conference reveals just such a case of a collision between two incompatible points of view regarding Vietnam if Kennedy had lived. One group sees their mission in traditional terms as protecting their specialty—the history of the war in Vietnam—from the silliness, arbitrariness, irrationality, and downright embarrassment of counterfactual history. These are our Musgrove skeptics, acting as anti-counterfactual vigilantes. They argue, in one way or another, that it is highly unlikely that Vietnam if Kennedy had lived would have differed in any essential respects from the "Vietnam" that evolved under LBJ in the wake of JFK's assassination. They are led by John Prados, who is clearly frustrated, even a little aggravated, by some of the claims of others at the table that Kennedy had made a firm decision before he was killed to withdraw from Vietnam, or even that he was about to make such a decision. Irate, in fact, is probably not too strong a description of Prados's state of mind when he peers directly across the conference table and, tongue-in-cheek, offers his "gratitude" to Jamie Galbraith for mentioning NSAM 273 in a previous discussion [Document 4-7].[39] *Prados believes the content of NSAM 273, drafted by McGeorge Bundy for JFK but never seen by Kennedy and ultimately signed by Johnson, proves his own point, not Galbraith's. And Prados's point is this: if one looks in detail and with understanding at the decisions LBJ made in the long 1964, it is clear that no good alternatives were available to him, and thus none would have been available to JFK (or anybody else) either.*

The particular issue that ignites this discussion is David Welch's use of the term Americanization Lite *in his questionnaire [Appendix B]. Prados sees this term as more or less equivalent to what was called in the mid-1960s the "enclave" strategy, according to which the U.S. would secure a limited number of areas, chiefly U.S. bases, Saigon, and a few other areas deemed to be strategically significant.*[40] *Their purpose would thus be defensive, and would require, so the theory went, far fewer U.S. combat troops (and would thus result in far fewer U.S. casualties) than an offensive strategy, whose purpose would be to "win the war" against the NLF insurgency and their allies in Hanoi. Prados says this strategy had no chance of succeeding politically, even though militarily the option was, in theory, a possible alternative to the massive escalation ultimately undertaken by LBJ. Prados is what we call a skeptic. Frankie FitzGerald is, too. Once the fighting units had been committed, she says, the military leadership would have been relentless in pursuit of whatever they felt they needed to take the fight to the enemy rather than just sit tight and wait to be attacked. And as usual, she says, the military brass would have gotten their way.*

Thus, Prados and FitzGerald agree on two broad points: first, LBJ was correct in his many assertions that his choice was either to get in big or to get out; and second, his only viable choice, given the way the war was going, was to "get in big." Neither sees any reason to believe, given the enormous pressure on LBJ throughout the long 1964, that JFK could have avoided the same set of alternatives, or that JFK's ultimate decision would have differed significantly from LBJ's ultimate decision to get in big. The conditions would not have allowed it. JFK's desires, hopes, and proclivities to limit U.S. engagement—however strong they may or may not have been— would thus have been irrelevant to the final outcome. In this counterfactual, in other words, you can delete "LBJ" and insert "JFK" if you wish, and

IT MAKES A DIFFERENCE WHO IS PRESIDENT

JFK's bottom line was, "It's too dangerous, therefore no war!"
LBJ's bottom line was, "It's too important, therefore no defeat."

Kennedy said no to his advisers' recommendation that he Americanize the conflict in Vietnam.

"the politics of Vietnam"

"We have never stood for military solutions alone"

"The public is worried and confused."

"Always hard to cut losses. But...1965 is the year of minimal political risk"

Johnson said no to Vice President Hubert Humphrey's (above left) recommendation that he not Americanize the conflict in Vietnam.

It makes a difference who is president in matters of war and peace.

the "*JFK*" *you insert can be personally opposed to Americanizing the war to whatever degree you like, but it won't matter a bit.*

Gordon Goldstein then comments, ostensibly in response to Prados and FitzGerald, but his comment cannot really be called a response in the strict sense. Goldstein's remarks come from a different paradigm, that of virtual history. The incommensurability of their basic assumptions does not permit Goldstein a direct line of critique with regard to the views of Prados and FitzGerald. Instead, he provides a brief recital of what we call in this book the radical approach, the main assumptions of which are also shared by fellow radicals Jamie Galbraith and Fred Logevall, which turns the Prados-FitzGerald argument inside out or, if you like, upside down. This inside out/upside down transformation of "figure" and "ground" is a common feature of a paradigm shift. This is a classic case of a collision of perspectives deriving from a disagreement in which the argument occurs across a great divide separating two incommensurable paradigms. As they see it, Prados and FitzGerald are defending the barricades against the onslaught of counterfactual, sentimental nonsense about Kennedy. Goldstein is describing the model of virtual JFK deriving from his work with McGeorge Bundy and simulating, or reimagining, the history of the war in Vietnam if Kennedy had lived.

The paradigm shift is profound and disorienting to those involved in the conversation. Prados and FitzGerald are particularly concerned that LBJ's situation, with all its terrible options, be fully grasped. Contra Prados and FitzGerald, Goldstein's remarks are not about Johnson, not about the Joint Chiefs, not about the pressure brought to bear on the White House in the first six months of 1965 by the situation on the ground in South Vietnam, nor about anything else experienced by Lyndon Johnson. In fact, Goldstein never even mentions Johnson's name! His remarks are all and only about JFK. He outlines his model of Kennedy, and his reasons for believing that any reasonable simulation of this model of JFK just does not result in an Americanized war in Vietnam. According to his analysis, and that of his collaborator Mac Bundy, JFK understood perfectly well that his choice was to send in the army en masse or not at all, which is why, according to the Goldstein-Bundy viewpoint, there is virtually no chance that JFK would have taken the nation to war in Vietnam. The Goldstein-Bundy model of Kennedy, which Goldstein believes provides the best fit with the facts of Kennedy's decisions on matters of war and peace as president, will not permit it.

Under the Goldstein-Bundy virtual JFK hypothesis, there would have been no American war in Vietnam. To Prados and FitzGerald, this claim seems indistinguishable from the blatant absurdity of Cleopatra's nose–type *history. In their view, Goldstein's insertion of JFK into the history of LBJ's escalation of the war in Vietnam merely replaces Cleopatra's fictional nose with an equally fictional U.S. president. To them, LBJ's escalation has to be multiply determined, which means that retrospectively exchanging LBJ for JFK won't be sufficient to avoid the war. To Goldstein, as to Logevall and Galbraith, the discussion should not be focused on LBJ at all, but on JFK's commitment to withdraw from Vietnam and to avoid an American war.*

Join us now for the continuing collision between the paradigms of counterfactual history and virtual history.

JOHN PRADOS: I want to start by saying I'm really tired of being told what we've decided authoritatively here. The only conclusion we came to was that Kennedy had decided to withdraw 1,000 men from South Vietnam. What I just heard this morning was a conflation of what we talked about yesterday—intent versus desire—into a hardened decision to do this thing.

I'm very glad that yesterday afternoon Jamie put on the record NSAM 273 [**Document 4-7**], because NSAM 273 embodies the authoritative policy as it existed on the day of Kennedy's death. That policy provides for the unilateral assumption on the part of the United States of the covert operation against North Vietnam. This policy was based on the notion that the operations thus far had been ineffective and would be more effective with unilateral control. Once again, this is a piece of evidence that the United States was moving forward, not backward, in Vietnam. I think this whole question of what was decided in 1963 should now be taken off the table. I think we should move ahead to talk about what we are supposed to be talking about.

In that context, I want to move to the whole question of the strategy in early 1965—whether there was a premature or a very rapid move from that original enclave strategy, which Fred mentioned, to a much larger scale offensive use of American combat troops. The move from the eighteen-battalion strategy to the forty-four-battalion strategy takes place between January/February and July 1965, and is really the key strategic decision throughout this whole process. It makes it impossible to follow a strategy of Americanization Lite, which we're theorizing might have been the outcome of a second Kennedy term. I think we really need to pay more attention to this question. Why did they move from the enclaves to the offensive strategy? Why did this occur so quickly? Westmoreland had barely dealt with the forces for the provisional thousand program when he was already pushing for the forty-four-battalion program. Why didn't someone call Westmoreland on that? These are key paradoxes and dilemmas in this situation, and they are additional things we should be considering.

JAMES BLIGHT: On this point of whether Americanization Lite was a real or fantastic notion—

JOHN PRADOS: No, no, I think there was an enclave option that might have worked; it's not a fantastic idea.

GORDON GOLDSTEIN: It's just that it's superseded.

JOHN PRADOS: Yes, it's superseded.

JAMES HERSHBERG: Would it have worked indefinitely, or just put off the inevitable?

FRANCES FITZGERALD: It's not a fantastic option in terms of the military situation on the ground. I think it is a fantastic option if you consider that once you put the Marines in Da Nang, you have the Chiefs in the water.[41] Johnson and McNamara are not going to stop them; at that point it is too late. The Chiefs have always wanted this large escalation, and even in 1967 they practically resigned because they weren't getting enough.[42] Kennedy was not really able to neutralize the Chiefs. He temporized with them, perhaps, with this business in November 1961 and October 1963, but frankly those were really no-brainers.[43] It was out of the question to go in with a large force in 1961 or 1963. Once you've decided to bomb the North, once you have Marines protecting Da Nang and the Vietcong are right next door, you have to have a robust enclave strategy in order to make it militarily tenable on the ground. After that, they rule: the Chiefs are in charge. You cannot say to them, "No, you cannot have X amount more." I don't see how any politician could put a ceiling right then and there. No one in Congress would permit that.

JOHN PRADOS: So if it is a fantastical strategy, then the thing we have been theorizing as the more likely outcome was not possible.

JAMES BLIGHT: Would either of the two original presenters care to take a shot at that?

DAVID WELCH: Well, Johnson did resist the Chiefs. He didn't let them take the war more aggressively to the North, for example. He wasn't allergic to ceilings. And after the Tonkin Gulf Resolution, he didn't have to worry about Congress micromanaging the war.

When Johnson Americanized the war effort, he instructed his entire team to represent it as a continuation of existing policy. He did that by trying to get people to focus on the fact that the goal had not changed (the goal of maintaining an independent South Vietnam). The means had changed dramatically, but he tried to get people not to notice that. To some extent, that kept the operational details under the radar and gave him the opportunity to rein in the Chiefs if he wanted to.

The withdrawal option was something you couldn't pretend to be a continuation of existing policy. If you withdraw, South Vietnam collapses and the NLF takes over.

FREDRIK LOGEVALL: Except there are fig leaves here that are, I think, possible, as far as decent intervals and coalition governments and so on are concerned—but I think ultimately, yes, complete withdrawal means the loss of Saigon.

DAVID WELCH: I'd like to hear some discussion of the price to be paid by letting all of that happen. Johnson is clearly not willing to let it happen.

FREDRIK LOGEVALL: That is something we should talk about, but I'd like to continue for a moment with Frankie's thought—and John's question is also a good one; he raises an intriguing option that I've been wondering about. But to get back to what Frankie brought up, I would only note that there was a military argument put forth against the enclave strategy. That means it was at least considered. The military—or, at least, major elements of the military—decided that things had progressed too far. They felt the enclave strategy did not give us a reasonable chance of achieving success, and argued that we therefore had to opt for some version of what followed.

GORDON GOLDSTEIN: There seem to be two questions that should be parsed, and Fred notes both of them in his presentation. The first question is: was there in fact a decision in 1963? When Kennedy goes to Dallas, has he decided precisely what he will and will not do in Vietnam? I think there's a serious debate to be had on that question, and over the course of the weekend here we have heard very persuasive arguments on both sides. So in no way is it a settled issue in my mind.

The second question is, I think, easier to answer. Did Kennedy go to Dallas with at least an upper limit in mind with respect to an American commitment of combat troops? As I argued yesterday, I think the evidence of Kennedy's thinking on the issue, if you look at the totality of it, shows consistently that he is highly skeptical about the viability of sending in combat troops. He feels passionately about it. That evidence seems to me to be very consistent. For that reason, I think the Americanization Lite scenario is an implausible one. To postulate that Kennedy would have tried to hold on through '65 via the Americanization Lite strategy is to postulate that Kennedy would have been able to contain his apprehension about a limited use of combat troops remaining limited. As John [Prados] points out, the case as it actually plays out seems to suggest that it is extraordinarily difficult to keep a combat troop deployment limited to a specific geographical area. It's difficult to say they're going to be contained in numbers and to be unresponsive to proposals and lobbying by the Chiefs to expand their numbers and their area of operations. I think Kennedy would have had great doubt about the viability of all of that. I think, for Kennedy, it was going to be an either/or proposition: send in combat troops, or not at all. Given Kennedy's skepticism, it seems to me clear that he is just not interested in an American war in Vietnam.

JFK's Priorities: The USSR and China

Kennedy's overwhelming ambition for his (presumed) second term as president was to begin to end the Cold War. This would involve at least these three steps: (1) begin to reduce East-West political tension; (2) reduce the risk of a nuclear confrontation between the U.S. and the Soviet Union, especially in Europe; and (3) begin the process that subsequent generations would call arms control, a concept that was still in its infancy in the early 1960s. As Gordon Goldstein points out in his comment below, JFK's priorities were those of a classic "realist." America's interests, according to this view, must be understood in a hardheaded fashion, befitting the approach required of a responsible superpower. If Goldstein is right, Kennedy's top priorities were unrelated to whether South Vietnam, or even the rest of Southeast Asia, "went communist," in the shorthand lingo of JFK's era. JFK's realist perspective would have reinforced his deep-seated skepticism regarding efforts to solve political problems via the application of military force, according to Goldstein. In fact, JFK told Goldstein's collaborator, McGeorge Bundy, that he also had a fourth step in mind for his second term: normalizing relations with communist China (roughly a decade and a half before it occurred historically, during the Carter administration). Moreover, according to Tom Hughes, even his boss, Dean Rusk, who greatly distrusted the Chinese communists, admitted that JFK was determined to do this. This would have been yet one more reason, Goldstein implies, for JFK to have believed that a U.S. war in Vietnam would not have been in America's interest, that it would have been a distraction from the pursuit of America's most important international priorities and objectives.

GORDON GOLDSTEIN: May I make a comment about Kennedy's priorities? Bill [Moyers] points out something important when we think about Kennedy's perspective on this. In addition to all the documentary evidence that we've examined, there is what we know about how the president perceived the stakes. On the question of whether he has the "religion," so to speak, this Cold War theology, the way that Johnson does—it seems there is a consensus that he did not: Kennedy is far more skeptical, discerning, and nuanced in his thinking. It seems that he did not want to allow Vietnam to be perceived and defined as a primary struggle in the Cold War. He thought of it as a secondary struggle, and other issues would have had greater prominence in his agenda in his second term. Managing the U.S.-Soviet relationship after the missile crisis obviously would have been a central priority. Another priority that Mac Bundy noted was that Kennedy once mentioned to him that he wanted to explore the possibility of normalizing the relationship with China in his second term. It wasn't a clear plan, but it was something he noted to Bundy as an issue to be addressed in a second term. For all of these reasons, I think the evidence should lead us to conclude that Kennedy would not want to stake his presidency on a major combat troop commitment in South Vietnam in a second term. To the extent that he would avail himself of any of these fig leaves, or covering mechanisms, to get out, he would try to diminish the perceived importance of South Vietnam, rather than to raise it.

JAMES GALBRAITH: A brief coda on the question: there was a Galbraith cable on that subject early in my father's ambassadorship that provoked a response from Rusk that we cherished in family history. It read, in its entirety: "Your views on this subject insofar as they have any merit have already been considered and rejected." [Laughter.]

THOMAS HUGHES: I have a comment on that. Rusk used to tell me that he was not the village idiot. China would be considered at some point. He said that he and Kennedy had discussed this, and that it would happen in the second term.

When Paradigms Collide, Part II: Would JFK Have Tolerated a Third-World Loss in the Long 1964?

One of the most interesting features of paradigmatic incommensurability— such as that which seems to us to divide virtual history from counterfactual history—is the radically different way those on either side of the great divide frame an issue.[44] *They are in many ways the inverse of one another. The sun revolves around the earth, or it is the other way around. If what if history is understood to mean counterfactual entertainment or performance art, then Vietnam if Kennedy had lived is all, and almost only, about the situation faced by LBJ in the fourteen months leading up to his decision to Americanize the war. When put forward as a kind of straw man to be blown down, leaving the historical endeavor untainted with the irrational and the ridiculous, the result can be a kind of closet determinism. LBJ didn't want the war; LBJ did the best he could to avoid war, but could not; thus JFK, who would have been subject to the same dilemmas, would have done no better than Johnson at avoiding the American war. But when Vietnam if Kennedy had lived is approached within the framework of virtual history, the emphasis is reversed, with the focus on Kennedy. For example, in his model of JFK's decision making, Fred Logevall identifies eight features that distinguished Kennedy from Johnson with regard to Vietnam, which, considered together, point toward the opposite conclusion: JFK was a fundamentally different kind of presidential decisionmaker than LBJ, and probably would have avoided an American war.*

If you suspect that all versions of the what if are counterfactuals more or less as irrational as that of Cleopatra's nose, then you are not much concerned with a detailed examination of JFK's history. Why bother, if the entire enterprise is silly and demeaning to historians who take the history of the war in Vietnam seriously? But if you approach it as virtual history, you will want to know everything you can discover about JFK's approach to deciding in matters of war and peace; you will want to organize your findings into a model, whether you call it that or not; you will be assiduous in your concomitant study of the situation faced by LBJ; you will reimagine the history under scrutiny with JFK as president; and you will conclude in as data-driven a manner as possible. One group—our skeptics—looks hard at LBJ, seeing, in this context, a bit of JFK, but Kennedy is largely occluded by the ghostly image of Cleopatra's nose and the grave dangers that kind of pseudo-history pose for practitioners of serious history. The other group— our radicals—builds its model of JFK, seeks to determine why LBJ was unable to stem the march toward Americanizing the war in Vietnam, and asks if the JFK represented in the model might have decided differently.

A revealing example of just how incommensurable these two what if paradigms are may be found in the following conversation involving two Musgrove skeptics, Tim Naftali and Jim Hershberg. Naftali outlines what might be thought of as the hypothetical long 1964 of JFK, if he had lived, with special attention to the Third World. Naftali sets out to describe the Third World scene that confronted Johnson and would also, as he sees it, have confronted Kennedy. The situation described by Naftali is grim: Sai-

gon is in a perpetual state of near-collapse. The Dominican Republic is a mess and potentially susceptible to Fidel Castro's influence. (It would erupt in a coup in April 1965, in response to which LBJ sent in thousands of U.S. Marines.) Americans are being held hostage in the Congo (pointed out by John Prados). Vietnam's neighbor, Laos, is chaotic and dangerous. And America's principal nemesis in the Western Hemisphere, Fidel Castro, will throughout the long 1964 be looking for ways to spread his militant communism, thus presenting a difficult challenge to any U.S. president. According to Tim Naftali, "Kennedy doesn't like to lose, and he is about to lose"—somewhere, sometime in JFK's long 1964, a U.S. Third World ally will by overthrown or otherwise defeated by communist forces. The interesting question raised by Tim Naftali is: when this happens, how will JFK react?

Both Tim Naftali and Jim Hershberg believe that JFK would very probably have responded by sending combat troops into South Vietnam and possibly elsewhere. He would have done so, they believe, either in an effort to prevent the collapse of the Saigon government or to compensate for an analogous "loss" to communism elsewhere in the Third World, or both. The counterfactual—JFK's hypothetical response to one or more developments in the Third World in the long 1964—is implicitly framed this way: LBJ couldn't avoid sending in the Marines to the Dominican Republic, LBJ couldn't avoid Americanizing the war in Vietnam, and so on—so why should we believe JFK could have done what LBJ could not do? Their implied answer: we should not believe it.

One of the striking features of the counterfactual put forward by Tim Naftali is this: it is advanced as if little or nothing is known about JFK that would bear on the answer to the question, "How would JFK have reacted if one or more Third World allies, South Vietnam included, had collapsed during the long 1964?" This is striking because we believe that JFK's handling of the Bay of Pigs fiasco of April 1961, three months after he took office, sheds considerable light on Kennedy's hypothetical reaction to the kind of long 1964 Third World loss postulated by Naftali. He briefly mentions the episode, saying only that JFK authorized "a half-assed air strike." While it is true that Kennedy personally scaled back U.S. air support for the CIA-trained Cuban exile brigade, the magnitude of the air support authorized by JFK sheds little or no light on key issues such as what Kennedy's understanding of the events was, what he learned from them, and how what he learned might affect his response in the face of another imminent Third World loss like the Bay of Pigs fiasco. To Naftali, the point of the failed Bay of Pigs invasion seems to be that JFK does this sort of thing—limited military interventions too big for the world not to notice, but not big enough to *succeed. It is strongly implied that no learning occurred based on what happened at the Bay of Pigs or any other events.*

This view is, in our opinion, at odds with the relevant historical facts. So we ask: What purpose is being served by posing the problem as Naftali poses it and by his own answer? Is this really about how JFK would have reacted to a Third World loss? We think not. We think he has long ago answered this question for himself: his answer is, "No, JFK would not have tolerated a Third World loss." Why? Because the Cold War environment of the time would not have permitted it. "Losing" a Third World hot spot was simply unacceptable for any American president. LBJ knew this and acted in ways consistent with this belief. JFK would have done the same. We think the deeper purpose of the counterfactual is to defend the historiography of the Kennedy and Johnson administrations from the machinations of those who would seek to transform the entire person and career of JFK into another Cleopatra's nose exercise.

But let us consider the Bay of Pigs invasion.[45] *There is very little mystery about JFK's performance in that crisis, what motivated it, or what he learned from it. JFK was urged on by increasingly hysterical advisers on April 19–20, 1961, to send the Marines into Cuba to rescue the invading, but overmatched, Cuban exile brigade. Kennedy firmly refused to oblige them. He resigned himself to the defeat of the CIA-backed exile force rather than invade Cuba and engage in what he believed would be a disastrous jungle war ninety miles from Florida. Moreover, JFK accepted personal responsibility for the disaster in a press conference on April 21, 1961, the day following the collapse of resistance of the exile brigade. In a statement that has been quoted often in recent years as Bush administration officials have refused to admit mistakes and responsibility for mistakes regarding the war in Iraq, JFK told the press, "Victory has a hundred fathers, but defeat is an orphan . . . I am the responsible officer of government."*[46] *In a remarkable public performance, given the humiliating circumstances, JFK appeared calm in accepting the defeat and in taking responsibility with equanimity. As a politician, JFK showed that he could tolerate the heat that comes with a public failure.*

But his private response revealed the resilience of a boxer who, knocked to the floor, is able to learn from his mistake on the fly and come back swinging, thereby turning an episodic defeat into, if not exactly a victory, then at least a resolve and a concrete plan never to allow anything like it to happen again. Chester Bowles, the principal deputy to Secretary of State Dean Rusk, participated in a top-level meeting on April 20, 1961, just hours after the totality of the defeat in Cuba became known. According to Bowles's journal entry describing that meeting, the president was "really quite shattered . . . he had been suffering acute shock" [**Document 6-1**]. According to Bowles, after forty-five minutes of pointless, high-volume, mutually accusatory rhetoric from his advisers, Kennedy simply got up and, without saying anything, walked out of the room, without either adjourning the meeting or returning to it. The degree of humiliation—both personal and political—that Kennedy felt over this debacle, barely three months into his presidency, was extraordinary. It shook him to the core. It is not difficult to imagine that, for a few moments, he may even have felt he would have to resign, such was the apparent emotional impact on him. But rather than let it ruin, perhaps even prematurely terminate, his presidency, JFK used the experience to strengthen it.

JFK's paralysis lasted hours, not days or weeks, and his actions in the wake of the Bay of Pigs invasion are as important for understanding the protean nature of this experience as the immediate emotional impact it had on him. He swung quickly into action. Three days after his press conference, on April 24, he received a memorandum he had requested from National Security Adviser McGeorge Bundy detailing the principal failures in the decision-making process leading up to the invasion [**Document 6-2**]. (Bundy listed ten, and JFK himself was personally implicated in all of them.) Kennedy then sent his White House aide, the historian Arthur Schlesinger, Jr., to Europe to ask U.S. allies for their honest—"absolutely candid"—appraisal of Kennedy, his administration, and U.S. foreign policy generally. Two weeks later Schlesinger, relaying what he had been told, let JFK have it with both barrels. "The first reactions to Cuba," he wrote to the president, "were of course shock and disillusion. . . . After Cuba, the American government seemed as self-righteous, trigger-happy and incompetent as it had ever been. 'Kennedy has lost his magic,' one person said to me. . . . Friends of America warned me not to underestimate the gravity of the damage" [**Document 6-3**]. This must have been hard to take for a president who deeply valued the opinions of America's most important European allies. But the more important point is that the criticism was solicited by JFK himself.

Moreover, as is well known but still insufficiently appreciated, JFK vowed never to be bamboozled or intimidated again by his military or intelligence advisers. And he wasn't. He brought retired Army General Maxwell D. Taylor back into the government to head a commission whose task was to interview the principal architects of the Bay of Pigs invasion, identify what went wrong, draw the appropriate lessons for the future, and make recommendations to Kennedy that would lower the odds that anything like it would happen again.[47] By the end of the year, Taylor would become JFK's personal military adviser; the following year, 1962, JFK appointed Taylor *chairman of the Joint Chiefs of Staff. Also by the end of 1961, the two top officials at the CIA, director Allen Dulles and Richard Bissell, deputy director for plans (i.e., covert operations) and mastermind of the Bay of Pigs operation, had left the government, never to return. Publicly, they both left voluntarily. In reality, JFK fired and replaced both of his top intelligence officials. Moreover, by recruiting his own chairman of the Joint Chiefs in Taylor, he effectively neutralized the hotheads among the Chiefs who were keen on Americanizing the conflict in Vietnam, invading Cuba, and challenging the Russians to a nuclear showdown over the status of Berlin.*

In a way, JFK was the most fortunate of presidents. At the outset of his tenure as president, he suffered a supreme humiliation, but it was one that carried minimal strategic significance. This allowed him to treat the Bay of Pigs episode as a kind of presidential learning experience. Nothing in the history of JFK's subsequent foreign policy decision making can be understood without an appreciation of the central significance of Kennedy's trial by fire in this supremely sobering episode.

The evidence, to us, is unequivocal: if one focuses on the available evidence from these seminal events of April 1961, it is difficult to imagine a scenario of Third World "defeat" in the long 1964 or any other comparable period that could have elicited from JFK a large-scale military intervention in the Third World. At potentially great political cost, Kennedy was willing to pull the plug on an invasion plan he inherited from his predecessor, President Dwight D. Eisenhower, occurring a little more than a hundred miles from U.S. shores, an invasion that would have been mounted against the regime of Cuban leader Fidel Castro, who was, at that moment, America's most prominent and vilified Third World opponent. After the Bay of Pigs, it is fair to ask: under what circumstances was JFK likely to have invaded a Third World country? The evidence is overwhelming that JFK not just decided to say "no" to an invasion of Cuba, but also set his bureaucracy the task of never letting anything like it happen again on his watch.

This is not to claim that Kennedy necessarily had the degree of tight control over his administration sufficient to absolutely ensure the prevention of a crisis like "another Bay of Pigs." Moreover, no matter how tight his control may have been, U.S. adversaries around the world would obviously have something to say about whether crises would erupt or not. But as a result of the Bay of Pigs episode, JFK's instinctual skepticism about using military force to address political problems was reinforced by the brutal experience of utter failure. Thus Kennedy decided—that is the most appropriate term—Kennedy decided that under no circumstances he could foresee would he be dragged into a major military conflict in the Third World.

This history—every bit of it—is well known to Naftali and Hershberg, who are two of their generation's very best historians of American foreign policy. They are intimately familiar with the scholarship on the Kennedy administration's foreign and defense policy. In fact, each has made important and highly original contributions over the past two decades to our understanding of JFK's foreign policy. So it is necessary to ask: knowing the history just summarized about JFK's experience and decisions deriving from the Bay of Pigs fiasco, why even pose the question, "How would Kennedy have responded to a Third World loss in the long 1964?" Or having posed it, why do they not address it by turning immediately to the available evidence on the Bay of Pigs, thence to a conclusion? The answer is both obvious and disorienting. It must be because they do not think the evidence yielded by the Bay of Pigs is relevant to the question, or at least not as relevant as other factors, beginning with the precarious state of U.S. interests throughout the Third World in the long 1964 as summarized by Naftali below.

Their approach seems to us indistinguishable from that of their fellow skeptics John Prados and Frankie FitzGerald in dealing with the earlier question of the feasibility of Americanization Lite. It is designed to prevent any interpretation of Vietnam if Kennedy had lived from descending into idiotic, irrational counterfactuals such as those symbolized by Cleopatra and her infamous nose. To ward off creeping "Cleopatra's Nose-ism," they would have us focus the analysis on what happened to LBJ or what LBJ confronted and then try to imagine how these factors would have constrained JFK, forced JFK's hand, and finally determined the decisions of any president, including JFK. As Jim Hershberg said several times during the Musgrove conference, the time was bound to arrive when JFK would have been forced to decide whether to allow the Saigon government to collapse and thus accept a communist takeover of all of Vietnam, or to send in U.S. combat troops in large numbers in an effort to stave off the defeat. When that happened, according to skeptics such as Naftali and Hershberg, the smart money would bet that JFK would commit America to a war in Vietnam.

We find ourselves smack in the middle, once again, of an instance of what Thomas Kuhn called the incommensurability of the way questions are framed on either side of a great intellectual divide created by a paradigm shift. To skeptics who approach the issue this way—if LBJ couldn't absorb a Third World loss in the long 1964, then neither could JFK—it's a no-brainer. Look at all that mess that LBJ had to face. JFK would have had to face it if he had survived Dallas. Take a good look at it. And while you're at it, look at all the pressure that would have been applied to him to prevent such a loss—from the military, from conservative Democrats in Congress, even from civilian hawks in his own administration, such as McGeorge Bundy, Walt Rostow, and Dean Rusk. The forces pushing even a skeptic like Kennedy on the benefits of military intervention would have been huge, much too great to resist, and they would all have pointed in the direction of intervention—in Vietnam, obviously, but also in the Congo, Laos, Cuba, or one or more other "hot spots" where Soviet-backed communists were about to hand Kennedy a "loss." Or so it seems to the skeptics.

Tim Naftali poses the question in an interesting way that causes radicals and skeptics to squarely face their differences. The hypothetical question is a no-brainer to those on the radical side of the paradigm shift. What makes this so interesting to us is that, figuratively speaking, "the sign is reversed" if we frame the answer to the question as an exercise in virtual history. Build the model: JFK absorbed a Third World "loss" three months into his presidency, he vowed on the basis of that humiliation never again to be pushed into a Third World military intervention, and he stuck to this resolve throughout his thousand or so days in office. Simulate the alternative history: insert the historical Kennedy into whatever Third World crisis you wish, and he finds a way to avoid a major U.S. military intervention because he is absolutely determined to do so. His commitment was as absolute on this issue as is possible to imagine in an elected politician. Therefore, of course, Kennedy would have been able to absorb a Third World loss in the long 1964 or any other period of time. Virtual JFK does not send the U.S. Marines in the long 1964 into South Vietnam or anywhere else. The probability of him doing so, based on what we now know, is close to zero. Or so it appears to the radicals.

Skeptics, who see their task as fighting the good and necessary fight against what they regard the silliness of all alternate histories, are pointing their slings and arrows at what we call "counterfactual JFK." They believe the odds of JFK Americanizing the war in Vietnam just as LBJ did are close to 1.0, whereas radicals are arguing that virtual JFK, whose approach to matters of war and peace was decisively molded in the crucible of the Bay of Pigs fiasco, the Cuban missile crisis, and other crises in addition to Vietnam, believe the odds of JFK escalating to an American war in Vietnam are close to zero. Either way, it's a no-brainer. Either way, the arguments being fired across the divide separating adherents of the competing paradigms are incommensurable, and are entirely (and mutually) incomprehensible. To the skeptics such as Naftali, Hershberg, FitzGerald, and Prados, those on the radical side of the argument have lost their minds. To radicals such as

Logevall, Goldstein, and Galbraith, the skeptics have unfortunately lost their data.

TIMOTHY NAFTALI: This is a lot of fun. [Laughter.]

I want to take a wide-angle lens and think about the world in the long 1964 that Kennedy would have faced, and also about things we can predict would have happened. China would have exploded its nuclear bomb anyway. The Soviets would have gotten rid of Khrushchev; they did that for domestic reasons, not international reasons, but Khrushchev was Kennedy's interlocutor, so Kennedy's going to be very worried about losing his interlocutor on international peace; that is going to happen in October [1964] or thereabouts. The situation is worsening in the Dominican Republic; this is going to raise Kennedy's concerns about the Third World. Of course, you all know about the crisis in Saigon that obviously is going to happen.

JOHN PRADOS: There is also the Congo. There are Americans held captive in Stanleyville.

TIMOTHY NAFTALI: Yes, the Congo was important. What we know about Kennedy, and what's consistent throughout this very brief presidency, is that he underestimated U.S. power in the Third World because, I think, he underestimated the power of American ideas in the Third World. He is pessimistic about the ability of democracies to compete with certain ideas in the Third World. And he overestimates Soviet power and the ability of people like Castro to recruit allies in the Third World. Even though he will become optimistic about America's brute force and strategic power, which he came to see as a useful form of persuasion after the Cuban missile crisis, I don't think his insecurities about the Third World disappear after the Cuban missile crisis.

The question I have for us is whether this will be a push-comes-to-shove moment for Kennedy. If we look at his decisions on the big issues in his thousand days, we notice he always chooses the least-worst alternative. Look at the Bay of Pigs: a half-assed air strike. Look at Berlin: tough rhetorical policy, but in the back channels an effort to move the issue— never moving as far as Khrushchev wants to go, but trying to renegotiate and redefine Berlin. Laos: nothing in '61, but in '62, when Laos looks like it's going to collapse and the U.S. is going to have to act, they discussed dividing Laos. Kennedy becomes very serious about putting troops in. Ultimately he doesn't go through with it, but he does put troops in Thailand. The Cuban missile crisis: we all know very well that his first reaction was hawkish.[48] Ultimately, he keeps that option alive, then seeks diplomacy and pushes very hard among his group and privately for diplomacy. In the Third World, if you look at the way in which he handles crises of American allies, it's always by responding, if possible, with covert action. He is absolutely committed to not losing allies.

Those are things we can debate, but I think I've generally hit the principles of how he deals with the world. He has very hawkish instincts, but if possible, dovish tactics. My question is: in this long 1964, the same period within which Fred Logevall has analyzed Johnson's march toward war in Vietnam, would JFK have been able to handle the loss of a Third World regime, given his insecurities about the United States and the Third World? China is becoming much more powerful. Even if he accepts that the Soviets are going to continue to play nice—which I don't think is an inevitable assumption, because Khrushchev is gone—is he going to let China have a victory in Saigon and in the South? I don't have the answer, but I think if we're going to talk about Americanization Lite and so forth, you've got to put into context the fact that, for all of his willingness to avoid the use of combat troops, Kennedy doesn't like to lose, and he's about to lose.

BILL MOYERS: You've left off one of the things he most didn't want to lose, which was the election. As Judith and I felt at the time, his reelection was probable, but not inevitable. That's a question for another discussion. [Bill Moyers refers to his wife, Judith Davidson Moyers.] Would he have been reelected? Johnson wasn't sure it was going to happen.[49] Johnson was opposed to Kennedy going to Texas a year before the election, and the Kennedy people told me one reason they wanted to go down a year before is because they thought it was up for grabs.

JAMES HERSHBERG: Tim is absolutely right, I think, that Kennedy would have put it off as long as possible, and that his ultimate decision would have reflected the broader context. But it also mattered very much, since presidents deal with life on a day-to-day basis, how Saigon collapsed. What was the manner? How did it play politically? Was there a hard-core group that was desperately counting on support, willing to fight? Was there a face-saving deal possible? How it was happening would very much affect the response. In other words, would there have been a small Americanization that could lead to incremental commitment? Or would Kennedy have said, "Hmm, I can take this hit, because something good just happened somewhere else"? I think it's utterly impossible to predict how he would react without knowing further details of various events as they play out.

Virtual JFK, After November 1964

In a coda to the discussion of Vietnam if Kennedy had lived, several of the participants agree that for a JFK who seemed instinctually opposed to Americanizing the conflict in Vietnam, 1965 would have been the key year, presuming of course that Kennedy had been reelected in November 1964. Unexpectedly, there is convergence on a single, central point among those who had previously found themselves on opposite sides of the divide separating skeptics and radicals. Fred Logevall, who is the conference's most proficient "model builder," mentions that he thinks JFK had a better sense than LBJ ever did of the price to be paid by a full-scale U.S. military intervention in Vietnam. Frankie FitzGerald, who had just minutes before expressed her skepticism as to whether JFK could have done any better than LBJ in saying "no" to the military brass, now says that we must not forget that Kennedy knew war firsthand. He had fought in the South Pacific, and he had a visceral sense of the terrible human cost of any military operation anywhere, but especially a guerrilla war in the jungles of Southeast Asia. She thinks JFK would have known, therefore, that the U.S. could scarcely be expected to "win," when measured against the cost. Bill Moyers, who at various times during the Musgrove conference has been openly skeptical about JFK's ability to avoid a war in Vietnam, agrees on this point with Frankie FitzGerald. Both feel that JFK's war experience must have contributed to his skeptical worldview and his skepticism about the utility of military interventions.

This is less than a full endorsement of Logevall's larger claim: that JFK would probably have withdrawn from Vietnam in 1965, at roughly the same time that LBJ chose to escalate the war massively. But it is clearly an attempt by two skeptics to acknowledge a key point made by the radicals at the table: JFK was very different from LBJ. Would this difference between the experience and characters of the two presidents have made the difference between war and peace in Vietnam?

DAVID WELCH: I don't mind admitting that I find my view on the question of what Kennedy would have done has changed as a result of the discussion we've had here. It is a question lacking a final answer, of course. It's a tragic question too, because with the benefit of hindsight we now know that a lot of the concerns that were driving U.S. foreign policy were just plain wrong. We didn't understand the North Vietnamese regime; we didn't understand its relationship with China or Moscow; we didn't understand that the domino theory was a far less serious problem than people thought, even though some were beginning to reconsider it at this time. This is a story full of misdiagnoses for a lot of things that either were not serious problems, or were not quite the problems people thought they were.

In retrospect, we can look back and say that withdrawal not only would have been the best option, it wouldn't have been a particularly costly option. But we can't deal with a magic counterfactual. We cannot wave our wand and have everyone in '64 and '65 suddenly be aware of things as we understand them today. Back then, of course, a lot of people believed withdrawal would be catastrophic. I would really like to know if Kennedy felt that way. I'm just not sure. Would he have been willing to pay whatever price he thought he'd have to pay by cutting and running? In early '65, that was the other option. You either send in U.S. troops, or you watch Saigon collapse. Kennedy would have faced the same dilemma Johnson faced. He might have been more creative in responding, but that's the point it would have come to.

GORDON GOLDSTEIN: But isn't Jim [Hershberg's] question very important? Doesn't it depend on how you fuzz it up and position it?

JAMES GALBRAITH: My father's got a very clear recollection on just this issue—whether Kennedy could take a loss in Vietnam. Kennedy's answer to that was, "Not this year." He could only take one at a time. Laos, Cuba, and Vietnam would wait. But if he had to take a loss in Vietnam, he was capable of taking it.

FREDRIK LOGEVALL: I would just say in response to Dave that I would be careful about asserting that American officials did not understand. What struck me as powerfully illuminating when I started to do research on this is what a good grasp they had of the stakes. It has become so common to speak of the Best and the Brightest not understanding the first thing about Vietnam history or policies, but what in fact strikes me when I look at '64 and '65 was what they grasped. They grasped the degree to which the Saigon government lacked popular support; they grasped the degree to which the North Vietnamese and the Vietcong were committed to this; they grasped the degree to which the North Vietnamese were directing the insurgency in the South, to a large extent; they understood that in fact the Vietnamese and the Chinese had been at each other's throats for a thousand years; they grasped that there was an emerging Sino-Soviet friction. It seems to me that a surviving Kennedy—who, I would argue, would have had at least a somewhat more nuanced grasp of the situation—would have perceived that as well.

There are all sorts of things I could say, but I'll simply leave it with Dave's earlier question, which is the right question: what is the price to be paid? If you have a menu of bad options, what is the price to be paid? I think, as I've argued before, that Johnson, by a considerable margin, exaggerated the price and failed to listen to those who said he would pay an even bigger price if he made this an American war. For the reasons I've suggested, I think that Kennedy, if he came back from Dallas alive, would have felt that the price that he had to pay by withdrawing in the early part of '65 would have been the lesser.

One final point: Bill talked about the election, and the election is critical. It is critical for both men. Vietnam matters most in how it affects their domestic political position, but I think crunch time comes for Kennedy after the election. I think he is able to keep it all on the back burner through 1964. That was Johnson's strategy; this we know. I think it would have been Kennedy's strategy as well. You are quite right, Bill, but I do think that it is after that point that we really have to think about what happens.

BILL MOYERS: I'd agree with that.

FRANCES FITZGERALD: Just on the point on the price to be paid: Kennedy knew better than Johnson. He had been to war. I think that is really important.

FREDRIK LOGEVALL: And in a couple different ways, maybe. I don't know if you'd agree, Frankie—people who knew Johnson better can talk about this—but I think there was a chip on Johnson's shoulder because he had not, in fact, been a military hero, as Kennedy had. I don't know if this in fact somehow contributed to his determination not to cut and run.

FRANCES FITZGERALD: Just being in battle and knowing what the price is has an effect.

BILL MOYERS: I think the experience of combat did contribute to Kennedy's skeptical view of the world.

Our "Radical" Verdict: No War in Vietnam, if Kennedy Had Lived

That is how the conference ended, on a note of convergence between the skeptics and the radicals, between the virtual historians and the anti-counterfactual historians. The virtual historians, our radicals, have looked hard at the historical data on JFK as a prerequisite to taking their figurative leaps into the world of virtual history: they have built their models of JFK's decision making, simulated the results, and concluded that it is very likely there would have been no American war in Vietnam if Kennedy had lived.

Our skeptics, fighting the good fight against ridiculous counterfactuals throughout the argument at Musgrove, disagreed only occasionally with their radical counterparts about the historical facts. Instead, they have more often questioned, often implicitly but sometimes explicitly, the rationality of any sort of enterprise dealing with what ifs. That is the key to their skepticism, it seems to us. Play it safe. Don't get involved with trying to figure out what would have happened if JFK had happened to survive Dallas. There are dangers in veering from the path of actual history and actual JFK: inaccuracy, irrelevance, confusion, and downright silliness.

Virtual history, like all history, is unavoidably subjective to a degree, and thus incapable of yielding absolutely final answers to important questions. But the evidence on virtual JFK, much of it available to scholars only in recent years, is in our view overwhelming. JFK was not going to Americanize the war in Vietnam. We believe virtual JFK easily survived the exacting scrutiny of our first-class group of skeptics. They raked our radicals and their ideas over the coals. They made them defend themselves. But in our view, virtual JFK passed with flying colors, both as to approach and as to conclusion. On the approach: we believe virtual history is a far cry from counterfactual history, and is in important respects its inverse. On the conclusion: we believe there would have been no American war in Vietnam if Kennedy had lived because this view is far more consistent with the relevant evidence than the alternative.

You may or may not believe this. Still skeptical? That's fine. We are pretty sure that some of those who arrived as skeptics at the Musgrove conference are still skeptical (although we have not asked the participants for public confessions one way or the other). But before you make up your mind, we recommend to you the following section in which we try to get a little deeper into the mindset of the skeptics, both to enrich your own understanding of what they were (and no doubt still are) worried about and also to shine a bright light on counterfactual history, as it is usually practiced, and virtual history, as it should be practiced.

The Deep Wisdom of the Musgrove Skeptics: "Bullshit Is a Greater Enemy of the Truth Than Lies Are"

The interventions of the skeptics at Musgrove do not, it seems to us, refute the arguments of the radicals. Instead, the skeptics, coming from deep inside another paradigm, had a different mission entirely. They meant to prevent Camelot sentimentality and other forms of Kennedy worship, and to try to ensure that the radicals were not given a free pass to ignore aspects of the historical record that might be inconvenient for anyone who believes there would have been no war in Vietnam if Kennedy had lived.

In standing firm against creeping irrationality and silliness in the retelling of the history of the war in Vietnam, the skeptics made an enormous contribution to the Musgrove argument. Their commitment to doing good history on so important and serious a question is laudable. They are against silly counterfactual history, and thus against the trivialization of the subject of our inquiry. They stand firm against turning the search for truth and wisdom from America's worst foreign policy disaster into kitsch. So do we. We think you should be wary of it as well.

To better appreciate the role and contribution of the skeptics, we invite you to think hard about where their skepticism comes from—about what lay behind their preemptive bias against dealing at Musgrove with the question of "what might have been" in Vietnam if Kennedy had lived? Ask yourself, "Why were they leery about crossing the divide between the virtual history paradigm and a paradigm that seeks to identify counterfactual bogeymen?" Were they afraid of being lumped together with the Camelot faction? Were they afraid of starting down a slippery slope by conjuring up non-events, stuff that didn't happen? Did they believe that if they had taken that first step, they may very well have slid over the precipice and down the kind of rabbit hole that swallowed up Lewis Carroll's Alice, leaving them, like poor confused Alice, awash in a wonderland of absurdities? The answer, we believe, is "yes," to all of the above. They were mortified by these possibilities.

Moreover, we strongly believe they are certifiably not paranoid. The threat identified by the skeptics is a clear and present danger to those committed to responsible history, whether of the actual or virtual variety. For evidence that the skeptics' fears are reality-based, you need look no further than the following case study of a prominent what if concerning Vietnam if Kennedy had lived. It is provided by Niall Ferguson himself, the Harvard historian who has emerged as the most trenchant and thoughtful theoretician of virtual history and one of its most enthusiastic proponents. He has taken a stab at our question, What would have happened in Vietnam if Kennedy had lived?—this time, not as a theoretician, but as a . . . as a what? This is the fundamental question that we ask you to address after coming to grips with Ferguson's what if.

The case study is excerpted from a chapter called "Afterword: A Virtual History, 1646–1996," which concludes Niall Ferguson's landmark 1997 book, Virtual History. [50] *The book opens with Ferguson's ninety-page theoretical tour de force, in which he argues brilliantly for a paradigm shift from counterfactual silliness to "virtual history," a term he coined, which we have adopted in this book. As to Ferguson's rendition of the JFK Vietnam what if, it is impossible (at least to us) to summarize the evolution of world history in Ferguson's account that leads up to the point at which he takes up Kennedy and the conflict in Vietnam. In the run-up to our subject, he attempts to splice together 300 years of political history, which are covered by various authors in the nine previous chapters, beginning with "England Without Cromwell" and concluding with "1989 Without Gorbachev." The more you know about modern history, the more difficulty you are likely to have. Why, in this case, is knowledge a handicap? Because you must imagine everything you think you know about world history since the English Revolution to be either irrelevant or roughly "inverted," utterly different from the facts that you know or believe to be true. We confess, Ferguson's account varies from what we thought we knew about modern political history far more than we can imagine. Anyway, fasten your seat belt, hold on tight, and be assured that the following two paragraphs appear unaltered exactly as they appear in Ferguson's book. Alas, we are not kidding. According to Niall Ferguson,*

No American Prime Minister did more to deepen American-Japanese confrontation than John F. Kennedy, the son of Roosevelt's Anglophobe consul in London, Joseph Kennedy. By a huge margin—mainly owing to the Catholic vote in the North's crowded cities—Kennedy won the 1960 election. The following year, he scored a minor triumph when a successful invasion reclaimed Cuba from the last remaining Nazi forces in Latin America. Emboldened, he began to examine the possibility of another military intervention, this time in support of Ho Chi Minh's Vietnamese revolt against the Japanese-backed regime of Ngo Dinh Diem.

In many ways, JFK was a lucky Prime Minister. He was spared the difficulties of the black suffrage movement which plagued the political career of his Southern counterpart, Lyndon Johnson. He survived an assassination attempt while visiting Johnson in Dallas in November 1963. His Centralist party smashed the states' righters led by Barry Goldwater in the elections of 1964. But Kennedy's good luck deserted him in Vietnam. True, the war was popular; but Kennedy could not win it. When he was forced to resign in 1967, following revelations that his brother, the Attorney-General Robert Kennedy, had authorised phone-tapping of political opponents, no fewer than half a million troops were fighting alongside the North Vietnamese forces. But the Japanese-backed regime was better equipped than had been expected, not least because of the rapid development of Japanese electrical engineering. When Richard Nixon swept to victory in the 1968 election, it was with a mandate to end the war. In a television debate with Nixon before his impeachment, a haggard Kennedy made his bitterness clear. "If I had been shot dead back in 1963," he exclaimed, "I would be a saint today." Although . . . Kennedy had a point, his remark was universally derided at the time.

And you thought Alice was confused in Wonderland? There are at least seven significant counterfactuals in the first paragraph, and at least twelve in the second. Of course, whether or not you agree with this estimate of nineteen "significant" what ifs depends on what one understands as significant. There are at least two to three times this number of events embedded in Ferguson's two paragraphs that never occurred, or are misattributed, misnamed, or in some other way at variance from the facts as we understand them. But who's counting? Serious historians are counting, that's who— like the skeptics involved in the argument at the Musgrove conference.

The more we know about JFK, the history of the 1960s, and the war in Vietnam, the more we become, reading Niall Ferguson's account, "strangers in a strange land," to borrow a phrase made famous by science fiction writer Robert Heinlein. There is no attempt to build a model of JFK (nor anyone nor anything else). Obviously, therefore, it is impossible to simulate the (nonexistent) model into the actual history as we understand it. Moreover, there is nothing historical to be learned from this immersion in Ferguson's hallucinatory wonderland, nor (obviously) are any lessons forthcoming that we might think about applying to our world now. To say that he has not practiced what he has preached about virtual history is like saying that New Orleans after Hurricane Katrina was a little damp. Confronted with this cute, irrelevant nonsense, anyone might be tempted to circle the wagons and write off all attempts to integrate what ifs into the craft of history.

Is all counterfactual history as bizarre as this? No, yet some is even worse. For example, Oliver Stone's extraordinarily successful 1991 movie JFK not only assumes Kennedy was going to withdraw from Vietnam, but that his intention to withdraw was the reason for his murder. According to Stone, the assassination was carried out by a nefarious combination of the Mafia, Cuban exiles, and disgruntled CIA operatives, and he strongly suggests that LBJ may have been involved in the conspiracy. Stone is a filmmaker who demands to be taken seriously. His approach and demeanor suggest someone who is not kidding. Yet the "history" on which his far-flung conspiracy theory depends is fantasy. He made it up from a few shards of hearsay and selective attention to the historical facts. Stone endeavors to convince us that Vietnam if Kennedy had lived would have been different—that the war would not have taken place. He does so by inventing an idiosyncratic pseudo-history responsible for the event that prevented the counterfactual history from actually occurring. One gets the impression that he feels fully justified in this because his subject is so weighty, so important. Once again, however, the analogy that comes to mind is Alice in Wonderland. Sure, the war in Vietnam is a serious matter. But being dishonest about history is also a serious matter.

Whereas Stone's counterfactual nonsense is in service of a persona of seriousness, sometimes counterfactuals are employed more or less to punctuate otherwise serious history with a taste of the absurd—the historian's equivalent of Tourette's syndrome. For example, the eminent historian of the Cold War, John Lewis Gaddis, has for decades urged historians of the Cold War to make use of counterfactuals in their work in order to justify the many causal inferences they can and must make if they expect to be taken seriously. Yet Gaddis inserts (without prior warning) into his otherwise fairly sober 2005 book, The Cold War: A New History, *a couple of paragraphs describing what happened when U.S. nuclear weapons were used during the Korean War—a war which spread to Europe, destroying Frankfurt and Hamburg. It might have happened, writes Gaddis. "But it didn't."*⁵¹

His message seems to be similar to that of Ferguson: "Just kidding." If you happen to think stunts like these are funny or profound for some reason, then you may choose to forgive authors like Ferguson and Gaddis for wandering off the historical reservation and into the counterfactual swamp. Lest we forget, however, Ferguson and Gaddis are icons in their respective fields—Ferguson in economic history, Gaddis in diplomatic history—holding prestigious chairs, respectively, at Harvard and Yale. Is it any wonder that life can be difficult for anyone endeavoring to provide a serious, data-based inquiry into Vietnam if Kennedy had lived? In response to counterfactual stunts such as those of Ferguson and Gaddis, we find it impossible to muster any response beyond, "Excuse me?"

Yet Niall Ferguson seems actually to believe his fantasy is an example of "virtual history." The term is in the subtitle: "A Virtual History, 1646–1996." Unfortunately, his effort bears no resemblance to virtual history as he himself describes the requirements in the introductory essay, several hundred pages earlier. (It is possible, of course, that calling it virtual history *is also part of some joke being played on his readers, though if this is the case, perhaps Ferguson might have done us the favor of putting the punch line, say, upside down at the bottom of the first page of his essay, so the slow-witted among us would not be left confused and offended.) But if it isn't virtual history, what is this kind of exercise in which the author seems to mimic a lunatic with an AK-47, with wacky counterfactuals as his bullets? There is one supremely appropriate English-language term for this kind of what if extremism. The term has recently been imported into serious philosophical discussion, possibly for the first time, in an influential 2005 essay by the Princeton philosopher Harry G. Frankfurt. The term is* bullshit, *and the propagators of it are* bullshitters. *According to Frankfurt:*

The fact about himself that the bullshitter hides . . . is that the truth values of his statements are of no central interest to him . . . [T]he bullshitter is neither on the side of the true nor on the side of the false. His eye is not on the facts at all, as the eyes of the honest man and the liar are, except insofar as they may be pertinent to his interest in getting away with what he says. He does not care whether the things he says describe reality correctly. He just picks them out, or makes them up, to suit his purpose . . . He does not reject the authority of the truth, as the liar does, and oppose himself to it. He pays no attention to it at all. By virtue of this, bullshit is a greater enemy of the truth than lies are.[52]

This strikes us as a concise summation of what must have been in the backs of the minds of our Musgrove skeptics. Their narrative, as we imagine it, goes like this: scholars, even eminent scholars, should not be permitted to prattle on like people with severe thought disorders about what never was—not without meeting resistance from responsible scholars. Why? Because the truth matters. At least, it should matter. After all, the American war in Vietnam would have been much less likely if American leaders of the time had been more interested in, and more familiar with, the truth about Vietnam and the Vietnamese.

The skeptics' fundamental problem, in our understanding, is not that questions were posed at Musgrove about events that did not occur, as in, "Whither Vietnam if Kennedy had lived?" What is offensive and threatening about counterfactual "bullshit" is the complete indifference among counterfactual enthusiasts to the historical record, from which they feel liberated to depart as they wish according to some scheme or fantasy or plot that is indecipherable to all but the "bullshitter." The liars, the plagiarists, and the lazy among historians will, ultimately, be unmasked for what they are because they will not have gotten it quite right and will at some point be caught in their deception. Something will be amiss, and it will eventually be discovered at some point, by someone. But in performance art masked as serious historical inquiry, such as that provided in the example from Niall Ferguson, almost everything is amiss, to such an extent that the word amiss is clearly amiss. Everything is amiss in the sense that something about the city of Dresden seemed "amiss" to the young Kurt Vonnegut as he emerged after the firebombing from Slaughterhouse Five.[53] In Dresden, as in Ferguson's 1960s (and Gaddis's Korean War and Stone's Vietnam narrative), things are not merely amiss. They are annihilated.

Radicals: A Case of Mistaken Identity?

To us it is quite unremarkable that concern about the implications of counterfactual history should lead scholars who are in earnest about their historical inquiries, like our Musgrove skeptics, to lean much of the time toward an attitude of take-no-prisoners repudiation of what ifs—not a case-by-case rejection according to individual circumstances, but repudiation of the entire enterprise of counterfactual "bullshit," in precisely the way the term is used by Frankfurt. Their credo is: bullshitters must be banned. They are dangerous. They trivialize even historical questions of momentous importance. Abstinence should be the rule with regard to what ifs.

In a 2006 essay, "On Truth," Frankfurt has specifically addressed himself to our subject, historical what ifs, in a way that suggests what is at stake. His subject is the effort to "get it right," to approach the craft of history as if, with luck and effort, one might get a little closer to the historical truth of the matter, while having no illusions about anyone ever settling matters once and for all.

No one in his right mind would rely on a builder, or submit to the care of a physician, who does not care about the truth. Even writers, artists, and musicians must—in their own ways—know how to get things right. They must at least be able to avoid getting them too far wrong. . . .

It is frequently claimed, to be sure, that the situation is different when it comes to historical analyses and to social commentaries, and especially when it comes to the evaluations of people and of policies that these analyses and commentaries generally include. The argument ordinarily offered in support of this claim is that such evaluations are always heavily influenced by the personal circumstances and attitudes of the people who make them, and for this reason we cannot expect works of history or of social commentary to be rigorously impartial or objective.

Admittedly, the element of subjectivity in such matters is inescapable. There are important limits, however, to what this admission implies concerning the range of variation in interpreting the facts that serious historians, for instance, may be expected to display. There is a dimension of reality into which even the boldest—or the laziest—indulgence of subjectivity cannot dare to intrude. This is the spirit of Georges Clemenceau's famous response, when he was asked to speculate as to what future historians would say about the First World War: "They will not say that Belgium invaded Germany."[54]

But this is precisely what Ferguson does in his what if regarding Vietnam if Kennedy had lived. How else are we to understand his dual fantasy that JFK, who resisted tremendous pressure on multiple occasions to invade both Cuba and Vietnam, decides to invade both countries? Should we call it science fiction? Maybe, if the fiction involves—as science fiction usually does—aspects of a morality play or a warning to the present generation to shape up or else. Should we call it historical fiction? Perhaps, if the plot involving the fictional characters with the names of actual historical figures involves drama, romance, and enough sentimentality to interest those who buy such items after perusing them in drugstore checkout lines. But Ferguson's account, with zero respect for the historical truth and with no decipherable plot, moral perspective, warning, or romance, but presumably with pretensions to some sort of legitimate what if history, isn't bad what if history at all. It is just "bullshit." And treating historical tragedy as bullshit should be identified and resisted.

Is it any wonder why most historians agree wholeheartedly with Frankfurt's assertion that "bullshit is a greater enemy of the truth than lies are"? And is it any wonder that the virtual history of Vietnam if Kennedy had lived was met with such skepticism? We think this involved a case of mistaken identity, as virtual history practiced with the knowledge and skill of Fred Logevall, Jamie Galbraith, and Gordon Goldstein is the furthest thing from the "bullshit" counterfactuals of a Niall Ferguson or a John Gaddis. Alas, we think the skeptics' bullshit detectors were just turned up too high—understandably, responsibly, even laudably high—for them to notice that the virtual history being proposed by the radicals around the table has nothing to do with the bullshit they abhor.

Coda: The Truth Matters to Skeptics and Radicals

The incommensurable approaches on either side of the Vietnam if Kennedy had lived argument might be characterized in something like the following manner. Those like Logevall, Galbraith, and Goldstein/Bundy, whose approach is consistent with the requirements of virtual history—build the model, simulate the model, analyze the result, and draw the lessons—do not relinquish their commitment to getting a little closer to the truth of the matter. Virtual JFK, as he emerges in the discussion, is really actual JFK rendered in considerable detail, but reimagined in circumstances he did not live to confront. Furthermore, virtual JFK has an important purpose: to provide a point of comparison for answering the questions, "How and why did it all go wrong under LBJ? And how can similar failures be prevented in the future?"

That the skeptics and radicals never quite made contact—these two groups deep inside two different what if paradigms—is not surprising. Virtual history is new and, we think, revolutionary, because it is the anti-counterfactual what if history. How were the skeptics to know or discern this at their first encounter? What is noteworthy, even inspiring, is the common commitment of both groups to the pursuit of historical truth, with one side pushing the boundaries of the new paradigm into the un-

*known, the other defending against an enemy they have resisted through-
out their professional lives: counterfactual "bullshit." This being so, it
should only be a matter of time and more good virtual history before they
realize they are on the same side of the most important issue of all: commitment to the truth.*

"It makes a difference who is president in matters of war and peace."
Top to bottom: Presidents John F. Kennedy,
Lyndon B. Johnson, and George W. Bush

Does It Matter Who Is President in Matters of War and Peace? A Tale of Three Choices

We return to where we began, with the big questions about *Virtual JFK* and Vietnam if Kennedy had lived. Does it matter who is president in matters of war and peace? If it does matter, how and why does it matter? Did it matter sufficiently for us to say, not with complete certainty but with considerable confidence, that the U.S. war in Vietnam would not have occurred if JFK had survived Dallas and been reelected in November 1964? We think the answer to this question is, "Yes, there would have been no war if Kennedy had lived."

Why do we believe this? What are the salient dimensions of JFK's approach to Vietnam and to war and peace generally, when contrasted with LBJ's, that permit us to reach such a conclusion? Moving beyond the history of the 1960s to the ongoing war in Iraq, does the analysis of Kennedy, Johnson, and Vietnam help us understand what went wrong when President George W. Bush decided to commit the U.S. to the war in Iraq? Finally, as citizens of Western democracies, can we derive from our analysis insights that inform our own deliberations when we, as an electorate, decide who should lead us in matters of war and peace?

We focus here on three documents, one each for Kennedy, Johnson, and George W. Bush, that we believe exemplify each president's approach to decisions about war and peace. They are: (1) the minutes of JFK's November 15, 1961, showdown with his top advisers over whether to Americanize the war in Vietnam [**Document 3-4**]; (2) Hubert Humphrey's memorandum to LBJ, dated February 15, 1965, recommending against Americanizing the war in Vietnam [**Document 5-6**]; and (3) the so-called Downing Street Memo of July 23, 2002, in which the head of British intelligence, having just arrived from meetings in Washington, divulges the thinking inside the Bush administration's planning for the upcoming war in Iraq [**Document E-1**]. These documents reveal Kennedy at his turning point away from war, Johnson about to slip past the point of no return toward war, and Bush far beyond the point of no return toward war, even though the Downing Street Memo was written more than six months before the invasion of Iraq would begin. Documents 1 and 2 were discussed extensively by the Musgrove conference participants. Document 3 is encountered here in the epilogue for the first time. After the discussion of the significance of these three documents, we offer comments on the analogy between the wars in Vietnam and Iraq before sketching out our own answers to the questions posed in the previous two paragraphs.

JFK's Turning Point: Deciding Against War in Vietnam, November 15–16, 1961

JFK's showdown with his advisers, on November 15, 1961, was the turning point in Kennedy's thinking about what to do regarding the declining fortunes of the U.S. government ally in Saigon, President Ngo Dinh Diem [**Document 3-4**]. At the end of an excruciating year, full of crises, humiliation, and much residual uncertainty about the ultimate outcome of any of his actions during 1961, Kennedy was consciously and deliberately put under as much pressure as his military and civilian advisers could muster to send American troops, ultimately in very large numbers, to prevent the triumph of communism in South Vietnam. Kennedy faced a near-unanimous phalanx of his top-level advisers who pushed for him to authorize combat troops for Vietnam. Kennedy refused. His *rationale* for not sending combat troops is as important for us as his *decision* to withhold them was at the time, because it points the way toward understanding his approach to the most important decision any president can face: whether to take the country to war or to keep the country out of war.

The minutes of the meeting on November 15, 1961, show Kennedy squaring off with everyone in his top national security team: McNamara, Rusk, Bundy, General Lyman Lemnitzer, and others. Kennedy's objections to Americanizing the war in Vietnam are many and varied. They fall into the following rough categories.

- **Allies:** Kennedy insisted on taking into account the views of the allies.
- **Guerrillas:** Kennedy was skeptical about whether American military power could prevail in a guerrilla struggle in the jungles of Southeast Asia against a highly motivated foe.

- **Interests:** Kennedy felt that the U.S. had other interests—especially the confrontation with the Soviets in Europe—that far outweighed any possible gain the U.S. might achieve even if it prevailed in a long, costly, protracted conflict half a world away in Vietnam.
- **Escalation:** Kennedy was fearful that in the nuclear age, any conflict had the potential to escalate for unpredicted reasons and to unpredictable levels of risk, perhaps even to the total destruction of American and other societies.

This meeting on November 15, 1961, was, we believe, the turning point for Kennedy's relationship to the war in Vietnam. It is remarkable, in retrospect, that the convictions of the advisers were so strongly held—so convinced were they that a U.S. takeover was inevitable that the majority of the advisers seem to have missed the significance of it: the president was not going to war in Vietnam. In its way, this seems to have been as incomprehensible to them as JFK's decision the previous April not to send U.S. Marines into Cuba to support the Cuban exiles at the Bay of Pigs. There was one exception, an all-important exception, and that was Robert McNamara. He "got it." Henceforth, he would be JFK's point man for finding a way out of the Vietnam conundrum without a U.S. war.

But a president isn't only a decisionmaker, dealing with advisers. The president is also an elected politician. In other words, the chief executive must be a salesman. The difficulty of making the sale to the public is increased as the politician finds it necessary to tell the public what it may not want to hear. The *public* phase of the turning point began with a widely publicized speech Kennedy gave in Seattle roughly twenty-four hours after the November 15 showdown with his advisers [**Document 3-6**]. This speech shows in microcosm how, when push came to shove, Kennedy endeavored to lead the American people to endorse his position on Vietnam in the face of the objections of anti-communist, Cold War ideologues in both parties. The tone and content of this November 16, 1961, speech are deeply at odds with what we have become used to in many of the public statements of Kennedy's successors.

Recall that 1961 was, for Kennedy, the presidential year from hell, with the Bay of Pigs disaster, a crisis in Laos, and a potential nuclear crisis in Berlin leading the double-digit list of foreign and domestic crises that occurred that year. One strategy he might have chosen to shore up his image would have been to play on the fears of voters. He could have encouraged his constituents to divide the world into good and evil, friend and foe, free and communist, declare war on some putatively beatable foe far away, let the band play "God Bless America," wave the flag, and send the troops in—to Vietnam, to Cuba, or both (as General Lemnitzer recommends to Kennedy at the November 15 meeting). Kennedy refused to do that. Instead, he chose a strategy that is something like the inverse of the easy way out. JFK asked Americans to open their eyes, take a good look at the new world just coming into being in the early 1960s, and make their peace with it. He asked them to be realistic. Here is Kennedy, speaking in Seattle on November 16, 1961.

> In short, we must face problems which do not lend themselves to easy or quick or permanent solutions. And we must face the fact that the United States is neither omniscient nor omnipotent—that we are only six percent of the world's population—that we cannot impose our will on the other ninety-four percent of mankind—that we cannot right every wrong or reverse every adversity—and that therefore there cannot be an American solution to every world problem [**Document 3-6**].

Already in November 1961, JFK is beginning to prepare the political groundwork for raising the odds that his inclination to avoid an American war in Vietnam can be rendered politically feasible. Underlying the message is another one just below the surface that some have attributed to Kennedy's reading of Reinhold Niebuhr, the most eminent American theologian and philosopher of Kennedy's time: that America must face its own shortcomings, its own guilt, its own imperfections, if it hopes to understand the rest of the world and to have a positive impact on it.[1]

Skeptics will of course rightly say that it is not that simple. They will point out, correctly, that Kennedy made many different kinds of public statements regarding foreign policy generally and the war in Vietnam in particular. He said on occasion, for instance, that he believed in the domino theory, and on other occasions that he was skeptical of it, and so on. But we learn little or nothing, in our view, about our subject, *Virtual JFK* and Vietnam if Kennedy had lived, by counting the number of times Kennedy seemed hawkish or dovish in public on Vietnam. We learn far more if we pay attention to what Kennedy *did*. We believe that what Kennedy did on November 15–16, 1961, was to decide against war in Vietnam and to begin to build his public case for that decision.

That most of his advisers, including his vice president, did not "get it" then, or even later, speaks more to the Cold War ideological prism though which they viewed the conflict in Vietnam than it does to JFK's failure to properly inform them of his motives and intentions [**Document 3-3**]. Their lack of comprehension was due more to their failure of imagination than to his failure in communication. With the significant exception of McNamara, Kennedy's advisers could not imagine withdrawing from

Vietnam under any condition short of a guarantee that South Vietnam would survive intact. Kennedy not only could imagine it, by November 1961 he began to understand that it was probably inevitable, and he and McNamara began to plan accordingly.

LBJ's Point of No Return: Deciding to Go to War by February 17, 1965

Lyndon Johnson was elected in November 1964 by a huge margin over his Republican challenger, Barry Goldwater. Moreover, the Democratic majority in both houses of Congress increased substantially. The Republican Party was devastated. LBJ was in a position few presidents are ever in: LBJ and his party were in overwhelming, unambiguous control of the legislative and executive branches of government. The voters had given him and his party a virtual blank check, at least in the immediate aftermath of the election, to enact the liberal reforms LBJ held dear: voting rights, civil rights, education, health care, and rights for the poor—all of which, taken together, would soon be called the Great Society program.

But almost immediately, the Vietnam problem reared its ugly head and forced Johnson to make the hardest choice a president has to make: whether to take the country to war [**Document 5-4**]. Johnson sent his national security adviser, McGeorge Bundy, to Vietnam in early February for an assessment of what was clearly a deteriorating situation. While Bundy was there, an attack occurred at Pleiku in the Central Highlands, killing eight Americans, wounding more than a hundred, and destroying a lot of equipment, including U.S. helicopters given to the South Vietnamese Army.

In response to the attack at Pleiku, Johnson orders, at Bundy's recommendation and with the concurrence of all his senior advisers, large-scale retaliatory air strikes on targets in North Vietnam [**Document 5-5**]. His stated purpose is to show Hanoi that there will be a huge price to pay for their attacks on Americans. Plans are drawn up for the introduction into South Vietnam of more aircraft that can attack the North and for the introduction of large numbers of U.S. combat troops—more than 180,000 by the end of 1965.

But Johnson repeatedly holds off making a final decision. He feels the war is inevitable. His national security team is unified, as they were when they served JFK, in their belief that there is really no alternative to Americanizing the war in Vietnam. Feeling trapped, LBJ develops various psychosomatic problems and he becomes oddly reclusive. This usually most gregarious of politicians becomes highly secretive about his deliberations with advisers and obsessed with leaks to the press. In fact, in early February 1965, the vast majority of Americans have no idea that an American war of great magnitude is in the works.

On February 17, in the midst of his fretful, reluctant engagement with the Vietnam issue, Johnson receives an unsolicited memorandum from Vice President Hubert Humphrey, dated two days earlier [**Document 5-6**]. Humphrey tells Johnson he has reviewed the latest classified intelligence, along with various escalatory actions Johnson had already authorized. He tells the president that he is deeply worried. Humphrey knows the hour of decision is near—that Johnson is nearing the point of no return in Americanizing the war in Vietnam. Yet Humphrey also knows—it is obvious from the deferential, almost obsequious, tone of the introduction to his memorandum—that Johnson hates criticism. He knows, furthermore, that LBJ can be extremely vindictive toward those he regards as disloyal: to Johnson, disloyalty is an unpardonable sin. So Humphrey introduces his memorandum with three paragraphs excusing himself, in effect, for intruding into the President's valuable time. Then he gives LBJ twelve reasons for not Americanizing the war in Vietnam. Humphrey gives Johnson a lesson in what he calls "the politics of Vietnam." The gist of that lesson is: the Americanization of the war in Vietnam is unwise, unnecessary, and unbecoming a president whose popularity and room for political maneuver will never be greater than at that moment, after his landslide victory just three months before. That is Humphrey's message: do not, Mr. President, send combat troops to Vietnam. If you do, says Humphrey, a disaster is likely: for LBJ, for his entire administration, for the country, and for the world.

Have another look at Humphrey's prescient, almost clairvoyant message to his boss [**Document 5-6**], as well as the discussion of it by the Musgrove conference participants in chapter 5. Then compare Humphrey's message to LBJ with JFK's message to his advisers of November 15, 1961 [**Document 3-4**]. Note the emphases. Like Kennedy, Humphrey urges that the views of U.S. *allies* be taken into account because the U.S. cannot go it alone in the world on the fundamental issue of war versus peace. Like Kennedy, Humphrey asks that consideration be given to the nature of the foe, who is fighting a *guerrilla* war that U.S. forces are unprepared to fight and unlikely to win at acceptable cost and risk. Also like Kennedy, Humphrey asks that a full accounting be given to U.S. *interests* worldwide and Vietnam's position in the hierarchy of interests. According to Humphrey, as well as Kennedy, Vietnam is nowhere near as important as the Cold War standoff in Europe, arms control negotiations with the Soviets, and related interests. Finally, note Humphrey's foreboding about the risks of a conflict in Southeast Asia *escalating* into a wider war involving the Chinese, the Soviets, or both. That risk, according to both Kennedy and Humphrey, is not worth taking in any foreseeable circumstance, let alone a civil conflict in a Southeast Asian country that most Americans, at this point, can scarcely locate on a map.

Humphrey's list of reasons for not taking the country to war in Vietnam in February 1965 is, we believe, fully compatible with Kennedy's reasoning in November 1961. In fact, the resemblance is remarkable, almost uncanny. (Of course, time and events have moved on between November 1963 and February 1965, leading Humphrey to add some items specific to February 1965 to his list of reasons. For example, he argues that LBJ should not do what he criticized his opponent for advocating in the recent election, that is, "going north" and invading North Vietnam.) For all the buttering up of Johnson that Humphrey does at the outset, he still has the courage to tell Johnson why it would be wrong, and why Johnson will be headed for disaster if he makes the decision to take the country to war in Vietnam.

President Johnson refused to follow, to consider, or even to discuss the advice of his vice president. Instead, seized by a vindictive rage, he punished Humphrey cruelly, excluding him from all high-level discussions of Vietnam policy in the administration. LBJ let Humphrey know that until he became a cheerleader, privately and publicly, for Johnson's escalation of American involvement in Vietnam, he would continue to be excluded. Humphrey, who longed to succeed LBJ as president and felt he could not become president without LBJ's endorsement, eventually caved in. Some months later, after becoming a vocal public supporter of the escalation, Humphrey was once again permitted to attend meetings devoted to the war in Vietnam.

After LBJ withdrew from the presidential race on March 31, 1968, Humphrey would gain the coveted Democratic nomination for president. But his capitulation to LBJ over Vietnam came back to haunt him as he lost a close election to Richard Nixon, chiefly because of the stigma of having publicly embraced the U.S. war in Vietnam. It is unfortunate, but perhaps also not altogether unfitting, that these two liberal Democrats, Johnson and Humphrey, who on many issues showed considerable courage and leadership throughout their careers, should now be remembered primarily for their lack of these attributes with regard to Vietnam. The escalation of the war during the Johnson administration, in fact, permanently blackened the reputation and legacy of each politician—the president for having taken the country to war, the vice president for having publicly embraced it.

George W. Bush Beyond the Point of No Return: Deciding to Go to War Long Before July 23, 2002

We believe that by November 15, 1961, JFK had chosen not to take the country to war in Vietnam. The choice was not irrevocable, as many of the Musgrove conference participants point out. Yet on reflection, we can imagine no plausible circumstances that would have caused Kennedy to violate his own logic as stated to his advisers on November 15, 1961—that is, to reject his own advice and to Americanize the conflict in Vietnam. Lyndon Johnson made the opposite choice, it seems to us, not later than February 17, 1965, the day he received his unsolicited and unwanted memorandum from Hubert Humphrey. Johnson chose to commit the U.S. to a ground and air war in Vietnam. His genuine anguish and obvious ambivalence in the face of the decision strongly suggest to us that LBJ knew the choice was his, and that he might have chosen differently.

The ongoing U.S. war in Iraq was also initiated as a war of choice. It is unclear exactly when the choice was made, but it may have been within hours or days of the terrorist attacks of September 11, 2001.[2] In any case, by the time the so-called Downing Street Memo [**Document E-1**] was drafted on July 23, 2002, the decision in Washington to take the country to war in Iraq had long since passed the point of no return. The head of British intelligence, Sir Richard Dearlove (referred to in the memo by his code designation, "C") has returned to London and briefs his senior colleagues, including Prime Minister Tony Blair, on where things stand. According to the memo:

> C reported on his recent talks in Washington. There was a perceptible shift in attitude. Military action was now seen as inevitable. Bush wanted to remove Saddam, through military action, justified by the conjunction of terrorism and WMD [weapons of mass destruction]. But the intelligence and facts were being fixed around the policy. The NSC had no patience with the UN route, and no enthusiasm for publishing material on the Iraqi regime's record. There was little discussion in Washington of the aftermath after military action.

By July 23, 2002, the Bush administration's proclivity toward forcible "regime change" in Iraq, as the British intelligence chief sees it, is no longer merely desirable to the U.S. government, it is inevitable. There is even a timetable in place for preparing to attack, according to Defense Secretary Geoffrey Hoon. The attack, he says, will take place early in 2003, possibly as early as January. Prime Minister Tony Blair, however, notices that the question of how to justify the attack (which he knows is needed to ensure British participation) is still not completely worked out.

Blair tells his colleagues that the "political context" needs work if the plan to overthrow Saddam Hussein by force is to gain political traction among his British constituents and with allies in Europe. His preferred solution, as stated in the Downing Street Memo, is the one ultimately undertaken by the U.S. and the British: an entrapment scheme by which Saddam will be made to appear to renege on promises to allow weapons inspectors to search in Iraq for evidence of a program to develop weapons of mass destruction (WMD), especially nuclear weapons.

In the immediate aftermath of the 9/11 attacks, the public justification for launching the war had been twofold. Leaders in Washington and London strongly implied, though evidence was scant at best, that the terrorist attacks of 9/11 were in some fashion authorized, or at least aided and abetted, by Saddam's Iraqi government. However, skepticism regarding the alleged connection between the Iraqis and the Saudi-based Al-Qaeda terrorists who carried out the attacks steadily increased as the months following the 9/11 attacks passed and no convincing evidence of the connection came to light. By the early spring of 2003, it seemed clear that Baghdad had nothing to do with the 9/11 attacks. The Bush and Blair governments needed another pretext if they were to sell a war against Iraq to their constituents.

Leaders in Washington and London, determined to overthrow the regime of Saddam Hussein by force, therefore chose to emphasize the second alleged justification for regime change in Baghdad: the claim that the Iraqis were actively pursuing WMD, with particular emphasis on Iraq's alleged pursuit of nuclear weapons. Toward this end, U.S. and British officials undertook a vigorous propaganda campaign, spearheaded by Vice President Dick Cheney. Leaders in both Washington and London maintained that the risk of a nuclear-armed Iraq under Saddam grew with each passing day. Cheney first referred publicly to Saddam's alleged nuclear ambitions on March 24, 2002, on CNN's *Late Edition*. "This is a man of great evil, as the President said," Cheney told his interviewer, "and he is actively pursuing nuclear weapons at this time."[3]

In the months that followed Cheney's first salvo connecting the regime in Baghdad with a nuclear threat, brinkmanship followed between Baghdad, on the one hand, and, on the other, Washington and London. Sometimes the threats and counterthreats were mediated via the United Nations, sometimes not. The Iraqis were formally accused of pursuing WMD in a pivotal February 5, 2003, speech to the UN by Secretary of State Colin Powell.[4] The Iraqis continued to deny the charges. Fundamentally, it didn't matter. The Bush and Blair administrations had for more than a year been planning to attack Iraq. The chief UN weapons inspector, Hans Blix, demanded more time to search for evidence of Iraqi WMD capabilities and intentions. But the invasion was to be driven by military readiness, not the findings of Blix's inspectors. On February 22, 2003, Bush informed Spanish Prime Minister José María Aznar during a conversation at Bush's ranch in Crawford, Texas, "In two weeks we'll be militarily ready. . . . We'll be in Baghdad by the end of March." When Aznar urged Bush to "have a little patience," Bush replied, "My patience has run out. I won't go beyond mid-March."[5]

We now know the Iraqis had no WMD capability, nor were they actively pursuing it. The UN sanctions put in place following the 1991 Gulf War were actually working quite effectively to thwart Saddam's desire to acquire nuclear weapons. But in a series of mysterious and self-destructive moves, the Iraqis played into the hands of Washington and London. They did so by refusing at key moments to cooperate with UN inspectors searching for evidence that they were pursuing WMD, even though the inspection teams, as we now know, would have come up empty-handed. Had Blix's inspectors been permitted unimpeded access inside Iraq, war might possibly have been delayed long enough for diplomats to make one final effort to find an acceptable option short of war.

The U.S.- and British-led attack began, as scheduled, on March 19, 2003. The invasion forces quickly overthrew the regime of Saddam Hussein. On May 1, 2003, President Bush landed on the deck of the aircraft carrier *Abraham Lincoln*, declared "mission accomplished," and announced that "major combat operations have ended."

But the war had barely begun. Civil war ensued and is ongoing, held partially in check principally by the continuing presence in Iraq of more than 100,000 U.S. combat troops. As we write, in April 2008, well over 650,000 Iraqis may have died in the conflict. (Tens of thousands more have died since the estimate of 650,000 was made in the summer of 2006.) More than 4,000 Americans have died in Iraq. There is, as yet, no end in sight to the tragedy still evolving in Iraq and throughout the Middle East region.[6]

The War in Iraq: "George Bush's Vietnam"

On April 10, 2003, less than a month after the invasion of Iraq commenced, the U.S. Defense Secretary Donald Rumsfeld received a top-secret memorandum from his old friend Pentagon consultant Stephen Herbits. It was titled, "Getting Post-Iraq Right." Herbits told Rumsfeld that postwar success in Iraq was the key to transforming the entire Middle East. If the U.S. were to establish a viable democratic government in Baghdad, according to Herbits, the democratic "dominoes" would begin to topple, providing not only "a model for the creation of a Palestinian state," but even an "Iranian overthrow." That was the good news, which perfectly reflected the neoconservative ideology that provided the intellectual justification for attacking Iraq. Herbits could be certain that Rumsfeld shared his enthusiasm for democratizing the Middle East. But then Herbits, already concerned about nascent chaos on the ground in Iraq, issued this warning, "In the months after the shooting stops," Herbits wrote to Rumsfeld, "it is essential that there be no civil war in Iraq. Civil wars hearken back to Vietnam. The president's strategy," he warned, "will die in the embrace of such a comparison."[7]

The warning went unheeded. By the time Herbits warned Rumsfeld, in fact, it was probably already too late to avert the civil war that ensued and that, more than five years later, still rages, and which did in fact smother with brute facts the Bush administration's flowery fantasies about "growing democracy" in the Middle East. In reality, the conditions for a desert apocalypse, not "democracy," were stimulated by the decision to invade Iraq. Alas, no one in the upper levels of the Bush administration had given serious and sustained thought to what should happen during the U.S. occupation.

This was becoming obvious even as Herbits drafted his memo to Rumsfeld. By early April, the U.S. and British occupation in Iraq was already unraveling into civil war, inviting just the kind of comparisons to the U.S. debacle in Vietnam that Stephen Herbits feared. On Wednesday, April 9, President Bush watched approvingly on television as a huge statue of Saddam Hussein was pulled down in Firdos Square in central Baghdad. Yet on the same day, the *New York Times* reported an interview with an unidentified Iraqi man, who said, "We hate Saddam but we hate the war." Of the Americans, he said, "We want them to finish Saddam Hussein" and "We want them to leave." The next day, April 10, the day Herbits sent his top-secret memorandum to Rumsfeld, the *New York Times* reported a story that appears ominous in retrospect. "There is absolutely no security on the street," said a UN official named Veronica Taveau. Asked by the *Times* reporter why the members of his unit had done nothing to bring the spreading chaos in Baghdad under control, a U.S. Marine officer at a checkpoint replied, "I tell them the truth," the officer said, "that we just don't have enough troops."[8] The invasion was over. The civil war had begun.

Less than a year after Bush's appearance on the deck of the *Abraham Lincoln* in which he declared victory in Iraq and the end of the war, the civil war in Iraq was already being compared to the disaster in Vietnam. On April 6, 2004, for example, Massachusetts Senator Edward Kennedy said in a speech, "Iraq is George Bush's Vietnam."[9] Perhaps such a remark from a liberal Democrat like Kennedy did not, in itself, unduly concern the administration. But the charge stuck. People on all sides of the Iraq issue began framing their views with respect to the debacle in Vietnam, an exercise that is still ongoing. The warning of Rumsfeld's aide Stephen Herbits now has the aura of prophecy. The administration's invasion and occupation of Iraq has in fact, in the minds of many, "die[d] in the embrace of such a comparison" between the wars in Vietnam and Iraq.

It is doubtful that even Herbits, however, could have anticipated the eventual avalanche of invidious comparisons between the two wars. A Google search on "Vietnam and Iraq," for example, returns more than 7,000,000 links.[10] The first link, in fact, is to a long 2005 article by the former U.S. Defense Secretary Melvin Laird.[11] In effect, Laird defends the invasion of Iraq by denying the salience of the analogy, thus inadvertently providing an example of what Lyndon Johnson used to call the no-win political nightmare (which he was particularly adept at inflicting on his political adversaries).[12] The nightmare involves its victim in something like the plot of the movie *Groundhog Day*, if it were a horror film made by Alfred Hitchcock rather than a comedy: you spend every day just as you spent the previous day, defending yourself by denying, over and over again, something alleged by your political adversaries.

Of course, as many have pointed out, there are significant differences between the U.S. war in Vietnam and the U.S. war in Iraq. In Vietnam, U.S. forces confronted triple-canopied jungles and jagged mountains. Iraq, on the other hand, is mostly desert. At its peak in the late 1960s, the U.S. presence in Vietnam reached more than a half million combat troops. The number of U.S. forces in Iraq is only a fraction of that total—approximately 130,000 or so. The war in Vietnam grew out of the global Cold War, but the Cold War ended more than a decade before the invasion and occupation of Iraq. And so on. Granted: Vietnam is not exactly Iraq.

For many, these differences don't matter very much. Musgrove conference participant Marilyn Young explains why.

> Iraq is not Vietnam. It was not Vietnam in 1991 [during the Gulf War] and it is not now. The history of Iraq, its demography, topography, resources, culture, and the nature of its resistance and insurgency are radically different from Vietnam. [But] Vietnam haunts the war in Iraq in part because it has begun to smell like defeat but more significantly, I think, because the task the U.S. has taken upon itself is similar: to bend a country about which it knows little, whose language and history are unknown to its soldiers, to its will. It is a haunting, rather than a serious engagement with the history of the Vietnam war or the direct application of lessons learned there. . . .[13]

The haunting feeling described by Marilyn Young might be summarized this way: "Oh my God, it is happening again—we have undertaken a huge military intervention without knowing what we're doing."

Any analogy can be overdrawn. Events, decisions, and experiences can be like and unlike one another in virtually limitless ways. Drawn with discretion and with the facts of each case firmly in mind, however, analogies can be illuminating. The analogy between Vietnam and Iraq—specifically, LBJ's decision to take the country to war in Vietnam and G. W. Bush's decision to invade and occupy Iraq—can help us understand some commonalities in what went wrong that led to both disasters. Three dimensions of the analogy seem especially compelling to us: delusional thinking, an obsession with falling "dominoes," and denial and dishonesty at the highest levels when the delusions about the dominoes proved false.

DELUSIONS

In both cases, Vietnam and Iraq, the thinking of key leaders seems to have been genuinely delusional, divorced from the local realities of the countries and regions they wished to influence via their military interventions. Because most leaders saw only various versions of "dominoes" when they debated how to achieve their objectives in Vietnam or Iraq, they were blissfully untroubled by, and fundamentally uninterested in, the vastness of their ignorance of the region and the history of the country and people against whom they had decided to wage war. Being ignorant didn't matter to them because, in their view, a domino is a domino. Willful obliviousness to the facts on the ground had disastrous consequences in each case. LBJ seems to have believed, without a shred of supporting evidence, that the U.S. could, to use the expression popular at the time, "bomb Ho Chi Minh to the conference table" and strike a deal by which the Hanoi government would give up its intention to unify the entire country under its leadership. Similarly, with regard to Iraq, U.S. President George W. Bush and British Prime Minister Tony Blair seem actually to have believed that following a regime change in Baghdad achieved by military force, a Western-style democracy would quickly emerge in Iraq. What did it matter that no such government had ever existed there before, or that regime change would be achieved via a bloody upheaval, or that religious and ethnic factionalism in Iraq had been kept in check only by the brutal, even sadistic, repression of Saddam Hussein's Baathist regime? The implicit answer of Bush and Blair to all such questions: it didn't matter at all. But Bush and Blair were wrong. It did matter.

DOMINOES

The delusions about Vietnam and Iraq were powered by self-justifying, abstract ideas originating mainly in think tanks and universities. These abstractions are often called "theories," which inappropriately glorifies them by implying that they are scientifically based and have been empirically tested. All emphasize one variant or another of the concept of falling "dominoes," and none of the variants is anything like a scientific theory. The U.S. intervention in Vietnam was, in the minds of its advocates, meant to prevent the South Vietnamese domino from falling—to prevent it from "going communist." By preventing the South Vietnamese domino from falling to communism, advocates of the U.S. war hoped to prevent a "domino effect"—a cascading collapse of the row of dominoes consisting of non-communist governments all over East Asia. But following the U.S. retreat from Vietnam, not a single country in the region fell to communism. The countries of Southeast Asia were not dominoes. The U.S. and British attack and occupation of Iraq was, according to its advocates, meant to initiate a "reverse domino effect" in the Middle East. In the delusions of leaders in Washington and London, the postwar government in Baghdad would become the first Arab democracy, thus stimulating first one, then another, Middle Eastern domino to "fall," that is, to "go democratic," ultimately resulting in the political transformation of the entire region. Instead, the entire Middle East runs the risk of becoming destabilized by the war in Iraq.

DISHONESTY

Finally, advocates of the interventions in Vietnam in 1965 and in Iraq in 2003, when told repeatedly by their own intelligence communities that reality did not conform to their delusions and theories, chose simply to fabricate, dissemble, misrepresent, and/or outright lie about the prospects or results of the interventions they championed. The burden of cognitive dissonance they felt between their aspirations and the reporting of their intelligence agencies seems to have been relieved by denial of some facts and the invention of others. During the initial buildup in Vietnam, Lyndon Johnson, supported by his advisers, made every effort to suppress negative, sometimes even dire, intelligence estimates indicating a probable U.S. disaster in Vietnam. LBJ also worked mightily to prevent the American public from learning even the basic facts about the massive initial escalation in the spring and summer of 1965. Later, when the Americanization of the war could no longer be hidden from public view, he professed endlessly to see "light at the end of the tunnel," even as the U.S. prospects in Vietnam became ever bleaker, even desperate, and in the face of intelligence estimates indicating that the war was unwinnable and that the U.S. could withdraw at manageable cost to its image and interests.[14] In Iraq, George W. Bush and Tony Blair oversaw the manufacture and sale to the public of false intelligence regarding Iraq's nonexistent nuclear program, and also falsehoods about alleged links between Saddam's regime and Al-Qaeda. Bush, Blair, and their subordinates operated like salesmen hawking merchandise they knew to be defective, treating their citizens like gullible children who would swallow any story, no matter how implausible, as long as they kept them frightened in the wake of the 9/11 and subsequent terrorist attacks in Europe and elsewhere.[15]

Grand delusions, implausible abstractions, and deceptive leaders—in Vietnam and Iraq—these were, we believe, among the most important common factors that combined to lead to disaster in each instance. By any standard, therefore, the decisions to intervene in Vietnam in 1965 and in Iraq in 2003 were plainly *irrational*. That is, the decisions and actions were not in conformity with the requirements of reality. Yet, though fully culpable, the leaders who made those irrational decisions governed modern Western democracies. In order to undertake their disastrous enterprises, Lyndon Johnson, George W. Bush, and Tony Blair needed to secure at least the tacit approval of a broad sector of their constituents. In that sense, the U.S. and British societies themselves, and the citizens who comprise them, also share in their leaders' culpability. In active or passive acquiescence to their leaders' delusions, abstractions, and falsehoods, ordinary citizens created what Musgrove conference participant Fred Logevall calls a "permissive context." This is an atmosphere in which public dissent or even public interest regarding a war of choice is minimal.[16] As Logevall points out, the propaganda campaign of the Johnson administration was as unrelenting as it was deceptively upbeat. "But," he adds, "John Q. Citizen was also ignorant because he preferred it that way."[17] This was true in spades regarding the free pass given Bush, Cheney, and others after 9/11. In the run-up to the invasion of Iraq, heads of state were far from the only individuals with their heads in the sand.

Three Presidents, Three Presidential Decisions

To return to our original question: does it matter who is president in matters of war and peace? It matters a great deal. One president, JFK, faced with a phalanx of hawkish advisers, defied them and chose not to lead his nation into a disastrous war. Two other presidents, LBJ and George W. Bush, faced with similarly hawkish unanimity among their advisers, chose differently, leading the U.S. into disaster in each case. But supposing it does matter who is president in matters of war and peace, what can we say about the *kind* of president who resists the path to war, and the kind of president who chooses war when he might have chosen otherwise?

These questions are central to any policy-relevant inquiry into the history of the wars in Vietnam and Iraq. By *policy-relevant*, we refer to the kind of historical investigation focused on the identification of misperceptions and misjudgments, an approach to history that is meant to yield insights applicable, to some degree, to the future. This is by no means a mechanical exercise in which point-to-point correspondences are drawn between the past and the future, like highways on a road map leading travelers from point A to point B.

We need to get the facts regarding our historical cases straight, of course. But decision making, our subject, is a difficult thing to nail down, often mysterious even to those who decide, let alone those who seek to observe it and understand it. Among the relevant facts must also be *psychological* facts—that is, some understanding of the way the situation looked and felt to the individual decisionmakers under scrutiny. In this category of facts fall the items listed in the previous section under delusions, dominoes, and deception. The two overriding questions for this sort of inquiry are these: what kind of president—what kind of individual—appears to be vulnerable to the distortions that led the U.S. into unnecessary wars, monumental unforced foreign policy errors, mistaken wars of choice (call them what you will)? The obverse question is equally interesting and important: what kind of individual is likely to resist the path toward catastrophic and unnecessary wars?

Neither of these questions can be addressed apart from an understanding of the specific personalities, experience, and proclivities of each president. That is, in effect, our database. We need to take the measure of the three presidents in question. We need to know something of their *biographies*. This book is manifestly not a biography of JFK or anything close to it, let alone a triple biography of the three presidents in question. But to suggest how, in principle, we might begin to address these two critical questions biographically—why Kennedy decided against a war of choice and why Johnson and Bush made the opposite choice—we offer three very brief sketches and a summary chart indicating in shorthand some ways we might compare and contrast the three presidents. There are other possible matrices, obviously. The sketches and matrix that follow are the result of a host of subjective judgments on our part about the decisions leading to the Vietnam and Iraq wars.

JOHN F. KENNEDY

Kennedy had an excellent grasp of foreign affairs, including both its diplomatic and military aspects. Confident in his own judgment, he sought advice from a wide range of advisers, many of whom he knew would disagree with each other, and with him, on many issues. He was confident, but not dogmatic. He felt the situation in Vietnam did not lend itself to simple solutions, especially simple military solutions involving the deployment of U.S. combat troops. Especially after the Bay of Pigs fiasco of April 1961, he was a minimalist in foreign and defense policy on the issue of the application of military force. The basic task was not to provoke a war that might escalate into a conflagration that could destroy everything. Kennedy, aided by McNamara, was firmly in charge of basic military doctrine and policy. For many reasons, including his own poor health, his World War II experience, and the Bay of Pigs (again!), Kennedy's view of history was tragic—one disaster after another. (His favorite book while he was president was *The Guns of August* by Barbara Tuchman, the story of the mistakes and misjudgments that led European leaders into the senseless slaughter that became World War I.) Finally, Kennedy made it a point to try never to underestimate an adversary, even an ostensibly poor and weak adversary, because he understood the advantages (for example) the Vietnamese communists would have fighting a guerrilla war in their own territory.

LYNDON B. JOHNSON

Johnson had almost no experience in foreign and defense policy when he assumed office on November 22, 1963. He had rarely been outside the U.S. before he assumed the vice presidency in January 1961. Among his advisers, he valued loyalty above all else. His basic understanding of the situation in Vietnam was that it was a potentially difficult situation for the U.S., but that the struggle to subdue the communists on behalf of the government in Saigon ultimately might be doable. He hoped so. He believed that the U.S. military, with all its power and sophistication, might eventually bring the Vietnamese communists to the conference table where the peace would be settled on terms acceptable to the U.S. To accomplish this, Johnson was a gradualist, seeking "no wider war," as he often said, and applying just as much pressure as he believed was needed to get Hanoi to cease and desist from supplying their NLF allies in the southern insurgency, but without tempting either the Chinese or the Soviets to intervene on Hanoi's and the NLF's behalf. One of Johnson's most salient traits as president was his fear of the U.S. military— fear of his own ignorance of military affairs and fear that if he did not unleash the military to dramatically escalate the war in Vietnam (as many wanted to do), the military leadership would provide ample political fuel to right-wingers in Congress who wanted to block his domestic social legislation and who might even seek to derail his chances of running for reelection in 1968. Johnson's view of history was basically hopeful, often rendered in homespun stories of his own hardscrabble youth—for example, when electricity was first brought to the Texas Hill Country in the 1930s, changing his life and the lives of those around him for the better in fundamental ways. Johnson did not think that the Vietnamese communist adversaries were weak, but he did not see any compelling reason for believing they weren't beatable. He believed that they would ultimately give up, because the U.S. was just too strong. Mere commitment to the communist cause could never compensate for U.S. power and its can-do approach to problems, including the Vietnamese "problem."

GEORGE W. BUSH

Despite his Ivy League background, Bush fashioned himself into an anti-intellectual, a person who boasted of his willful ignorance, as when he described making decisions based on gut feelings or "looking into the soul" of another leader, rather than relying on an analysis of the facts. He certainly did this with regard to Iraq. Bush believed the rosy predictions of what would happen in Iraq given to him by some (though by no means all) of his senior military and civilian advisers. Perhaps in part liberated by the absence of another military superpower that might forcibly resist U.S. policies (like his so-called doctrine of preemption) and actions (like the invasion of Iraq), Bush was a risk-taker who liked to go for maximum gain and effect. Although a few in the military did try to resist Bush's proclivity to take the country to war in Iraq, he either demoted, fired, or ignored the naysayers and made it clear that no deviation from the party line would be tolerated, not even in private. If we take Bush's religious pronouncements literally, then we must conclude that he regarded himself as a heroic Christian warrior. Finally, his portrayal of the enemy essentially rendered them as cartoons—crazy, evil, weird, and supremely primitive in their resistance to American efforts to promote their "freedom." The Bush universe was composed of two groups: those who agree with his crusade to Americanize the world, and those who unaccountably "hate our freedom."

Table 1 offers a matrix of comparative adjectives relevant to the decisions of these three presidents to resist or to initiate a war of choice.

Obviously, a matrix such as this will take us only so far toward an understanding of the war- and peace-related decisions of these three individuals. It is hard to know what lessons such an analysis might imply, because the matrix contains no extrapolations beyond the individual historical cases. To go beyond the data is always a risky business, of course, but to avoid the exercise renders opaque at best any effort to connect the past with the future—to say something that is policy-relevant. Connecting the past with the future requires, moreover, that we try to identify some of the underlying processes of decision making. It means building a rough model of the kind of president we believe JFK was with regard to matters of war and peace and contrasting it with a description of the kinds of presidents Johnson and Bush were on the same issues. We turn briefly to this enterprise in the next section.

Resisting the Biases Toward War: A Little Social Science

One of our teachers, Graham Allison, warned us years ago against succumbing to what he called "terminal social science."[18] By this he meant that we should be careful about importing assumptions, frameworks, and findings from the social sciences—political science, psychology and sociology, and related disciplines—into any analysis that is intended to be policy-relevant. The problem, as he saw it, is twofold. First, social science is larded with jargon that is virtually incomprehensible to busy, practically oriented policymakers one hopes to influence. Overreliance on the jargon will alienate and confuse policymakers, who typically are not members of the fraternity/sorority in which the jargon originates. A second, deeper problem is that social "science" isn't really a science at all, in the sense that physics or chemistry or even biology is a science, nor is

Table 1

	Grasp?	Criticism?	Difficult?	Strategy?	Military?	History?	Enemy?
JFK	excellent	curious	very	minimalist	in charge	tragic	strong
LBJ	weak	intolerant	doable	gradualist	in fear	hopeful	beatable
GWB	poor	intolerant	easy	maximalist	in cahoots	heroic	evil

it a collection of sciences. It is, instead, a group of disciplines forever fruitlessly aspiring to the status of science. Thus the findings derived from most social science research are often not replicable, and are just as often trivial, because of the misplaced emphasis in many branches of social science on statistical "significance." For all these reasons, we acknowledge the need to be careful when relying on the findings of social science to confirm some of our intuitions or conclusions.

That said, there are exceptions to the "Graham Allison rule." Every so often an example of social science research comes along that is greatly clarifying, and which can also claim an outstanding pedigree of empirically sound research to back it up. Instead of making things murkier, it actually makes things clearer. An instance of this exception is, for us, a recent contribution by Daniel Kahneman, a Nobel laureate in economics who is nevertheless a psychologist by training, inclination, and academic appointment, and Jonathan Renshon, from the Department of Government at Harvard.[19] Kahneman and Renshon reviewed some forty-odd years of research in behavioral decision theory, a field pioneered by Kahneman and the late Amos Tversky. This approach has provided valuable corrections to the assumptions of many economists, who for the sake of theoretical elegance and simplicity oddly but persistently assume that human behavior is rational. What Kahneman, Tversky, and their colleagues have been able to show is that biases, or what they sometimes call *heuristics*, often short-circuit whatever proclivities toward rationality we may have. Just to take one example given by Kahneman and Renshon, "about 80 percent of us believe that our driving skills are better than average."[20] Obviously, this has worrisome implications for the safety of drivers and their passengers on our streets and highways. In their new analysis, they wanted to know whether there may be systematic biases regarding the urge among leaders and their advisers to take their country to war, or the converse, whether systematic biases exist toward avoiding war. For shorthand, the authors call these the hawkish and the dovish biases.

According to Kahneman and Renshon, ". . . We were startled by what we found: all the biases in our list favor hawks. These psychological impulses—only a few of which we discuss here—incline national leaders to exaggerate the evil intentions of adversaries, to misjudge how adversaries perceive them, to be overly sanguine when hostilities start, and overly reluctant to make necessary concessions in negotiations. In short, these biases have the effect of making wars more likely to begin and more difficult to end."[21]

The authors are quick to point out that "none of this means that hawks are always wrong. . . . The biases we have examined, however, operate over and beyond . . . rules of prudence and are not the product of thoughtful consideration."[22] That is, they are *biases*—ways we bypass whatever rational faculties we may have. They are relatively independent, therefore, of the empirical world. They yield points of view and decisions that, while not entirely independent of the empirical world, nonetheless yield perceptions that are filtered, shaped, and warped. If these biases are not identified and counteracted, they can lead to very suboptimal decision making.

In matters of war and peace, failure to acknowledge and counteract certain biases can mean disaster. Kahneman and Renshon identify five biases they regard as particularly salient regarding whether "hawks" or "doves" win the arguments about whether or not to go to war. They are:

- **The Fundamental Attribution Error:** The powerful tendency to attribute the behavior of adversaries to their intrinsically sinister (even evil) nature, character, or motives, rather than to anything we might have done, or are doing, to provoke it. (*Your hostility toward us is unprovoked. Our hostility toward you is only a necessary reaction to your hostility.*)
- **The Illusion of Control:** People consistently exaggerate the amount of control they have over outcomes that are important to them, even when the outcomes are largely random or determined by other forces. (*Entering into a war of choice makes sense because we will make sure we are in control of each successive situation. We can withdraw at any time if it seems like the thing to do.*)
- **Excessive Optimism:** A large majority of people believe themselves to be smarter and more talented than average, and they thus reliably overestimate their future success. This tendency appears to be particularly prevalent in leaders, whose successful careers have led them to positions in which decisions about war and peace rest on their shoulders. (*Our side is smarter, better prepared, better equipped, and more highly motivated than the adversary, and thus destined to be victorious.*)
- **Reactive Devaluation:** A strong tendency exists to reject arguments by doves seeking negotiated solutions because of the feeling that the proposals of adversaries should not be taken seriously because they cannot be trusted. (*Yes, we know the adversary has sued for peace, but we know we cannot trust them to abide by the terms of any negotiated agreement, which means we should force them, if possible, to accept an unconditional surrender.*)
- **Aversion to Cutting Losses:** When things are going badly in a conflict,

the aversion to cutting losses, compounded by an infusion of wishful thinking, tends to dominate the calculus of the losing side. (*We cannot give up now, even though we seem to be losing, because we are just about to turn the corner and go on the offensive; in addition, to end hostilities now, in a losing situation, would dishonor those who have sacrificed for our cause.*)

Just to be clear: Kahneman and Renshon are arguing that certain key aspects of decision making on matters of war and peace are not just products of individual situations and individual personalities, even though these factors are obviously important. They contend, in addition, that certain dominant biases in human decision making are, in a sense, hardwired into human nature. There is no other way, in their view, to account for the replicability of results in behavioral decision research over forty years across many different cultures and situations. Leaders not only often seem irrational, they often *are* irrational, but they are irrational in ways that reliably favor hawkishness—the tendency to take a country to war and, once in a war, to fight on rather than seek a way out that will require compromise and negotiation.

If they are correct, Kahneman and Renshon have helped explain what, in retrospect, seems like inexplicably irrational behavior in two of our cases: Lyndon Johnson's decisions in February 1965, which set in train the Americanization of the war in Vietnam, and George Bush's decisions in late 2001 to go to war in Iraq. As an exercise, take the foregoing five biases listed as most salient by Kahneman and Renshon and plug in the LBJ who emerges in the course of this book. It all makes sense. Not *rational* sense, because taking the country to war in Vietnam wasn't rational in any ordinary sense of rational. Rather, the biases begin to help us grasp the dimensions of Johnson's irrationality in taking the country to war in Vietnam in 1965. They help us to understand it: why, initially, he chose war; why, when things began to go badly, he chose massive escalation; why, when the prospect of a negotiated settlement was raised by McNamara and others, he refused to consider the option. Likewise with Bush and the war in Iraq: why he assumed at the outset it would be easy; why he thought it would lead to a democratic revolution across the entire Middle East; and why, despite much evidence to the contrary, he continued to believe that by persevering, the U.S. would yet prevail.

But what about Kennedy, who chose *not* to take the country to war in Vietnam (or anywhere else, for that matter)? JFK does not fit the pattern. He understood that U.S. actions, past and present, had a great deal to do with the hostility of Vietnamese communists; he worried constantly about situations of crisis or conflict in which he might lose control; he was fundamentally pessimistic about what could be accomplished in foreign policy, whose purpose, he believed, should be mainly to reduce the risk of disaster; he was open to negotiated solutions and, in fact, welcomed them as the only realistic alternative to war or surrender; and as a student of diplomatic history, and also as a veteran of the war in the Pacific, he appreciated how difficult it can be for civilian and military leaders to cut losses, once the blood begins to flow.

*   *   *

Toward the conclusion of the Errol Morris documentary *The Fog of War*, the film's subject, Robert McNamara, addresses the question of whether the twenty-first century need be as violent and bloody as the twentieth. He says, pessimistically, "You're not going to change human nature any time soon," a statement the filmmaker identifies as one of the eleven lessons he derives from McNamara's life and analysis. In his analysis, McNamara echoes the conclusion of the American psychiatrist Karl Menninger, made many years earlier, also in reaction to the unprecedented bloodiness of the twentieth century. "The voice of intelligence," he wrote despairingly, "is soft and weak. It is drowned out by the roar of fear. It is ignored by the voice of desire. It is contradicted by the voice of shame. It is hissed away by hate and extinguished by anger. Most of all, it is silenced by ignorance."[23]

McNamara and Menninger are undeniably correct to describe the twentieth century, their century, as darkly as they do. But must their description of the twentieth century also be our prediction for the twenty-first century? We're not so sure. Maybe we can't change human nature in ways that make disastrous wars of choice, fueled by hawkish biases, less likely. But the findings of Kahneman and Renshon suggest that if we are aware of some of the biases that contribute to our human nature—as leaders or as ordinary citizens—we may be less likely to short-circuit our rational faculties and more likely to resist our hardwired biases toward war. Can we identify, elect, and encourage leaders, especially presidents, who are also aware of these biases and who are able to act on their awareness? A close look at "virtual JFK," we believe, shows us that this is not a utopian dream. It actually happened, not in some fantastic Camelot, but in the White House occupied by John F. Kennedy. Might it again be possible? If it is, how do we proceed? These seem to us to be among the most pressing problems we face in trying to prevent this twenty-first century from becoming even bloodier than the twentieth.

Secret

SUBJECT: South Vietnam

MEMORANDUM FOR THE PRESIDENT
TOP SECRET

TOP SECRET/SENSITIVE
FOR THE PRESIDENT ONLY

National Security Action Memorandum

TOP SECRET-EYES ONLY

"Only in the last decade or two have some of the most revealing documents and audiotapes been declassified, deciphered, and analyzed, allowing outsiders like us to form independent judgments."

Excerpts From Declassified Documents and Secret Audiotapes

[Document 3-1: Robert S. McNamara, Memorandum for the President, November 8, 1961][1]

In the fall of 1961, President Kennedy responds to the pleas of his advisers to become militarily involved in an effort to thwart communism, this time in South Vietnam. A team led by General Maxwell Taylor has just returned from Saigon on November 2 and their report—the "Taylor Report"— recommends that the president authorize the immediate deployment of between 8,000 and 10,000 American combat troops to Vietnam, with more to follow. Kennedy is not enthusiastic, and he delays a decision. To impress upon his commander in chief the gravity of the situation, including the need for immediate action, Secretary of Defense Robert McNamara, writing on behalf of himself, his deputy Roswell Gilpatric, and the Joint Chiefs of Staff, sends the president a memorandum on November 8 laying out what is at stake and recommending that Kennedy begin thinking in terms of an ultimate commitment of up to 205,000 U.S. combat troops.

Still, Kennedy defers a decision and asks for other opinions. JFK appears not to have appreciated the memorandum, and he conveys this to McNamara, though we do not know precisely what passed between the two men. Kennedy's reaction was sufficiently negative, however, to convince McNamara that JFK, at least at this point in November 1961, was simply not willing to make the kind of commitment to preserving the Saigon government that McNamara and others state is necessary to accomplish this objective. In fact, this memorandum represents perhaps the last time while JFK is president that McNamara will agree with the Joint Chiefs on what is to be done in Vietnam. Convinced that his boss is opposed to escalation in

Vietnam, McNamara will henceforth become Kennedy's bulwark against the Chiefs' proclivities toward a big war in Vietnam. In so doing, McNamara becomes the principal instrument of JFK's inclination to begin withdrawing U.S. advisers at the end of 1963. That McNamara, who took charge of the details of JFK's planned withdrawal from Vietnam, would become a principal architect of the escalation of the war in Vietnam under LBJ and the war's most prominent public defender, is one of history's tragic ironies.

MEMORANDUM FOR THE PRESIDENT

Top Secret
November 8, 1961

The basic issue framed by the Taylor Report is whether the U.S. shall:

a. Commit itself to the clear objective of preventing the fall of South Vietnam to Communism, and

b. Support this commitment by necessary immediate military actions and preparations for possible later actions.

The Joint Chiefs, Mr. [Roswell] Gilpatric [Deputy Secretary of Defense] and I have reached the following conclusions:

1. The fall of South Vietnam to Communism would lead to the fairly rapid extension of Communist control, or complete accommodation to Communism, in the rest of mainland Southeast Asia and in Indonesia. The strategic implications worldwide, particularly in the Orient, would be extremely serious.

2. The chances are against, probably sharply against, preventing that fall by any measures short of the introduction of U.S. forces on a substantial scale. We accept General Taylor's judgment that the various measures proposed by him short of this are useful but will not in themselves do the job of restoring confidence and setting [South Vietnamese President Ngo Dinh] Diem on the way to winning his fight.

3. The introduction of a U.S. force of the magnitude of an initial 8,000 men in a flood relief context will be of great help to Diem. However, it will not convince the other side (whether the shots are called from Moscow, Peiping [Beijing], or Hanoi) that we mean business. Moreover, it probably will not tip the scales decisively. We would be almost certain to get mired down in an inconclusive struggle.

4. The other side can be convinced we mean business only if we accompany the initial force introduction by a clear commitment to the full objective stated above, accompanied by a warning through some channel

to Hanoi that continued support of the Viet Cong will lead to punitive retaliation against North Vietnam.

5. If we act in this way, the ultimate possible extent of our military commitment must be faced. The struggle may be prolonged and Hanoi and Peiping may intervene overtly. In view of the logistic difficulties faced by the other side, I believe we can assume that the maximum U.S. forces required on the ground in Southeast Asia will not exceed six divisions, or about 205,000 men. . . . Our military posture is, or with the addition of more National Guard or regular Army divisions can be made, adequate to furnish these forces without serious interference with our present Berlin plans. . . .

[Document 3-2: Walt W. Rostow, Memorandum to the President, November 11, 1961][2]

Deputy National Security Adviser Walt W. Rostow has just returned from South Vietnam, where he and General Maxwell Taylor headed a fact-finding group sent by President Kennedy to assess South Vietnam's viability and to suggest ways of improving Saigon's ability to fight the growing communist insurgency. Rostow is alarmed not only by what he believes is the precarious state of South Vietnam but also by the U.S. State Department's timidity in the face of the communist threat. As Rostow sees it, the State Department prefers that the Kennedy administration back down rather than confront the threat head-on with a show of military force. But according to Rostow, backing down in order to avoid an escalating conflict will actually increase the likelihood of such a conflict by encouraging the communists to be more aggressive. Ironically, JFK will "exile" Rostow to the State Department within days of his receipt of this memorandum, thus ridding himself of the incessant, alarmist memoranda from Rostow, the gist of which might be summarized as follows: fight the Vietnamese communists now, when they are relatively weak, or fight them later, when they are much stronger. If the Soviet Union and/or China come to their aid, so be it, because that inevitable eventuality should be faced sooner rather than later. Do not be defensive, go on the offensive, not excluding a full-scale invasion of North Vietnam and possibly the use of tactical nuclear weapons if North Vietnam continues its infiltration of the South. In short, according to Rostow, prepare now, in November 1961, for a possible World War III arising out of the Vietnam conflict. In preparing now, he believes, with warnings given along the proper channels, there is a good chance that the communists will back down, assuring victory in Vietnam and an even greater victory over the Soviets and Chinese in America's Cold War struggle with them all across the globe.

JFK probably does not know whether to laugh or cry when he receives Rostow's avalanche of memoranda, such as the one that follows. In any event, shortly after receiving this one and several others like it, Rostow will be given over to Secretary of State Dean Rusk, whether as punishment for Rostow, or Rusk, or both, it is difficult to say.

MEMORANDUM TO THE PRESIDENT

Top Secret
Copy to Gen. Taylor only—no further distribution
November 11, 1961

Mr. Rusk will table this morning a proposal for action in Vietnam that stops short of installing U.S. forces now, but commits us—in our minds—to a full scale U.S. effort to save that country.

I appreciate, of course, the difficulty of the decision and the reasons for reserving the move; but I should like to set out as clearly as I can the reasons for placing some minimal U.S. ground force in Vietnam as part of the initial package.

This problem has been bedeviled by confusion about the various things a U.S. force could initially accomplish: from fighting in the paddies and jungles (which no one proposes), to guarding engineer units. To simplify the matter, I shall make the case for placing immediately a U.S. (Or SEATO) force of (say) 5,000 men on the 17th parallel. . . .

There is a general attitude in the State Department which I regard as dangerous. It would inhibit U.S. action on our side of the truce lines of the Cold War for fear of enemy escalation. The lesson of the post-war, it seems to me, is that we must be prepared on our side of the line to do whatever we believe necessary to protect our own and the Free World's interest. No one is proposing that we liberate North Vietnam. No one is proposing at this stage—although the issue may have to be faced— selective action in North Vietnam if Communist infiltration does not stop. General Taylor's proposals are, in my view, conservative proposals for action on our side of the Cold War truce lines, to buy time and permit negotiation to take over for an interval, under reasonably favorable circumstances. I think it unwise to inhibit ourselves in these regions for fear of what the enemy may do by way of reaction.

The steps proposed—including those which are now agreed—should, of course, not be taken unless we are deeply prepared for all the possible consequences. But, if the enemy goes to war—in Laos, South Vietnam, or both—because of our actions on our side of the line, it means he has already decided to take Southeast Asia by whatever means are necessary; and that his actions up to this point simply meant that he was prepared to take South Vietnam by cheap means and Laos by slow means, if possible. If he goes to war because of what we do on our side of the line, it does not mean he went to war because of what we did. It means he had already determined to face war rather than forego victory in South Vietnam, and that only our surrender in South Vietnam could prevent war. . . .

If we move without ambiguity—without the sickly pallor of our positions on Cuba and Laos—I believe we can unite the country and the Free World; and there is a better than even chance that the Communists will back down and bide their time. This we should cheerfully accept; because the underlying forces in Asia are with us, if we do not surrender and vigorously exploit them.

[Document 3-3: McGeorge Bundy, "Memorandum for the President," November 15, 1961][3]

A showdown between JFK and his senior national security advisers on Vietnam has been looming ever since the Taylor-Rostow team returned from South Vietnam in early November. The advisers, all of whom favor committing U.S. combat troops to Vietnam, have postponed the meeting with Kennedy, until they feel the president understands the gravity of the situation, which they feel can be addressed successfully only by transforming the conflict in Vietnam, in large part, into an American war. The meeting cannot be postponed any longer, however, and is set for 10:00 a.m. on November 15, the day before JFK must deliver a speech in Seattle, at the University of Washington. National Security Adviser McGeorge Bundy gives JFK a memorandum that he and the president discuss just prior to the meeting with the entire group of advisers.

This missive from Bundy to Kennedy is notable in several respects. First, it is written in a breezy, casual style, which is perhaps more appropriate in a note asking JFK if he wants to play squash rather than recommending the sending of U.S. combat troops to fight and die against insurgents in the jungles of Vietnam. Late in life, Bundy rediscovered this memorandum and was appalled retrospectively by the apparent lack of seriousness in it given the eventual escalation of the war under LBJ, in which Bundy played a major role. Second, it is supremely condescending toward the Vietnamese, both North and South. If the North Vietnamese invade, then, according to Bundy, the U.S. will just have to send enough troops to shove them back up north where they belong. And America's South Vietnamese allies don't fight very well, in Bundy's view, but they still "are usable." Finally, note Bundy's cavalier proposition: "South Vietnam," he asserts, "is and wants to be" ours. There is no record of what happened in Bundy's discussion of this memorandum with JFK, but the minutes of the meeting with all the advisers immediately following their meeting [Document 3-4] make it clear that Kennedy disagreed with virtually everything in it. It is clear that Bundy, who had known his old friend JFK since they attended grammar school together in Brookline, Massachusetts, did not, on the issue of Vietnam, know the mind of his friend, now his boss, the president of the U.S.

MEMORANDUM FOR THE PRESIDENT

Top Secret
November 15, 1961

So many people have offered their opinions on South Vietnam that more may not be helpful. But the other day at the swimming pool you asked me what I thought and here it is.

A. *We should now agree to send about one division when needed for military action inside South Vietnam.*

I believe we should commit *limited* U.S. combat units, if necessary for *military* purposes (not for morale), to help save South Vietnam. A victory here would produce great effects all over the world. A defeat would hurt, but not much more than a loss of South Vietnam with the levels of U.S. help now committed or planned.

I believe our willingness to make this commitment, *if necessary*, should be clearly understood, by us and by Diem, before we begin the actions now planned. I think without this decision the whole program will be half-hearted. *With* this decision, I believe the odds are almost even that the commitment will not have to be carried out. This conclusion is, I believe, the inner conviction of your Vice President, your Secretaries of State and Defense, and the two heads of your special mission, and that is why I am troubled by your most natural desire to act on other items now, without taking the troop decision. Whatever the reason, this has become a sort of touchstone of our will. . . .

The use of force up to a total of 20–25,000, *inside* Vietnam, is not on the same footing as the larger forces that might become necessary if the Vietminh move to direct invasion. I would *not* make the larger decision on a war against North Vietnam today.

B. *We can manage the political consequences of this line of action.*

I believe South Vietnam stands, internally and externally, on a footing wholly different from Laos. Laos was never really ours after 1954. South Vietnam is and wants to be. Laotians have fought very little. South Vietnam troops are not U.S. Marines, but they are usable. This makes the opinion problem different at home and abroad. . . .

[Document 3-4: Colonel Howard L. Burris, Notes on National Security Council Meeting, November 15, 1961][4]

The showdown in the Kennedy administration arrives at last at 10:00 a.m. on November 15, 1961. The minutes of the November 15 meeting were taken by LBJ's military attaché, Colonel Howard L. Burris. Johnson was away from Washington and unable to attend the meeting. All of JFK's senior advisers are in favor of committing combat troops to Vietnam. In response to their various arguments for the urgency of sending U.S. combat troops, Kennedy argues along the following lines: clarity is lacking regarding the rationale for a military intervention—it is not as clear, for example, as Korea in 1950 or Berlin in 1961; the most important U.S. allies do not support an intervention; many millions of dollars have already been spent, with little or no effect; you cannot bluff (or deter) guerrillas, you have to fight them, and no invading army is likely to win such a fight; and U.S. forces would be vulnerable, leading to attacks on them, followed by U.S. retaliation, which would carry with it a significant risk of escalation to a wider war. For all these reasons, Kennedy's answer to the request to Americanize the war in Vietnam is "no." Despite the unanimous request of his advisers that the U.S. begin to take over the war in Vietnam from its South Vietnamese allies, Kennedy says no. JFK somewhat assuages his hawkish cabinet by authorizing the dispatch of more U.S. advisers and equipment to be put at the disposal of the South Vietnamese army— advisers, yes, but no combat troops, a decision formalized on November 22 [Document 3-5].

It seems likely that this confrontation with his advisers galvanizes and stiffens Kennedy's resistance to sending U.S. combat troops to Vietnam. Yet though JFK's reasoning seems remarkably clear from the minutes of the meeting, many of the advisers still don't get it. They carry on as if JFK's decision is only a stopgap measure. They assume he will eventually have no choice but to Americanize the war. Among his senior advisers, only Defense Secretary Robert McNamara and (possibly) General Maxwell Taylor sense that a pivotal turning point has just been reached. JFK, for whatever reasons, is probably not going to authorize combat troops for Vietnam, not now—not ever. Period. Or so it seems, on the basis of the conversation reported in this document. But years later, even McNamara and Taylor will

*be perplexed as to exactly how and why Kennedy had reached his decision
and just how "final" his decision really was.*

Top Secret
November 15, 1961, 10:00 AM.

Mr. Rusk explained the Draft of Memorandum on South Vietnam. He
added the hope that, in spite of the magnitude of the proposal, any U.S.
actions would not be hampered by lack of funds nor failure to pursue the
program vigorously.

The President expressed the fear of becoming involved simultaneously
on two fronts on opposite sides of the world. He questioned the wisdom
of involvement in Vietnam since the basis thereof is not completely clear.
By comparison he noted that Korea was a case of clear aggression which
was opposed by the United States and other members of the UN. The
conflict in Vietnam is more obscure and less flagrant. The President then
expressed his strong feeling that in such a situation the United States
needs even more the support of its allies in such an endeavor as Vietnam
in order to avoid sharp domestic partisan criticism as well as strong objections from other nations of the world. The President said that he could
even make a rather strong case against intervening in an area 10,000
miles away against 16,000 guerrillas with a native army of 200,000,
where millions have been spent for years with no success. The President
repeated his apprehension concerning support, adding that none could
be expected from the French. (Mr. Rusk interrupted to say that the British were tending more and more to take the French point of view.) The
President compared the obscurity of the issues in Vietnam to the clarity
of the positions in Berlin, in contrast of which could even make leading
Democrats wary of proposed activities in the Far East.

Mr. Rusk suggested that firmness in Vietnam in the manner and form
of that in Berlin might achieve desired results in Vietnam without resort
to combat. The President disagreed with the suggestion on the basis that
the issue was clearly defined in Berlin and opposing forces identified,
whereas in Vietnam the issue is vague and action is by guerrillas, sometimes in a phantom-like fashion. Mr. McNamara expressed an opinion
that action would become clear if U.S. forces were involved since this
power would be applied against sources of Vietcong power including
those in North Vietnam. The President observed that it was not clear to
him just where these U.S. forces would base their operations other than
from aircraft carriers which seemed to him to be quite vulnerable. General Lemnitzer confirmed that carriers would be involved to a consider-

able degree and stated that Taiwan and the Philippines would also become principal bases of action.

With regard to sources of power in North Vietnam, Mr. Rusk cited Hanoi as the most important center in North Vietnam and it would be hit. However, he considered it more a political target than a military one and under these circumstances such an attack would "raise serious question[s]." He expressed the hope that any plan of action in North Vietnam would strike first of all any Vietcong airlift into South Vietnam in order to avoid the establishment of a procedure of supply similar to that which the Soviets have conducted for so long with impunity in Laos.

Mr. [McGeorge] Bundy raised the question as to whether or not U.S. action in Vietnam would not render the Laotian settlement more difficult. Mr. Rusk said that it would to a certain degree but qualified his statement with the caveat that the difficulties could be controlled somewhat by the manner in which actions in Vietnam are initiated.

The President returned the discussion to the point of what will be done next in Vietnam rather than whether or not the U.S. would become involved.

[Document 3-5: National Security Action Memorandum No. 111][5]

Each major presidential decision regarding U.S. national security is formalized in an official, often opaque, statement called a National Security Action Memorandum. Such a memorandum is universally referred to within the government by its acronym, NSAM, which is pronounced "NIS'm." NSAM 111 is one of the fundamental documents associated with America's war in Vietnam and is included here in full. Written by McGeorge Bundy and signed by JFK on November 22, 1961, the memorandum is directed to Secretary of State Dean Rusk. His instructions are to convey it to U.S. Ambassador in Saigon, Frederick Nolting, who is subsequently to bring it to the attention of South Vietnamese President Ngo Dinh Diem for the purpose of obtaining Diem's consent to the provisions in it. Most of NSAM 111 is concerned with what the U.S. is willing to do to preserve the South Vietnamese government (GVN, or Government of Vietnam, in the memorandum) and with the degree of assistance it is willing to provide to Saigon for its counterinsurgency struggle against the communists.

But the key to understanding the significance of NSAM 111, we believe, lies in the last three propositions, which briefly allude to what Diem's government must agree to. These three propositions also reveal why Diem's reaction to NSAM 111 was profoundly ambivalent, as was his reaction to *nearly every request made of him by his American patrons during the roughly eight years he was in power. On the one hand, Diem is helpless against the growing insurgency without U.S. assistance of the kind, and at the level, described in the first ten points. The U.S. government describes itself in those points as a sort of Santa Claus for the counterinsurgency. You want it, you've got it. But the three "requests" of Diem and his government at the end of the document are written as if sent from a scolding parent to a disobedient child. This greatly aggravates Diem. In the first proposition, Diem is asked/told to give up some of his power. He will not do that. He believes he rules, as he often said, "with the mandate of heaven." The second proposition accuses Diem indirectly of prosecuting the war incompetently, which he deeply resents, since he feels the Americans have little or no understanding of the threat he faces and the constraints within which he must operate. The third proposition requires Diem to permit the Americans to try to create an American-style South Vietnamese army, closely overseen by the Americans and commanded by South Vietnamese officers chosen by the Americans, not Diem. Diem, in the end, will do none of these things and for his recalcitrance, the Kennedy administration authorizes a coup by South Vietnamese military officers, during which Diem and his brother, Ngo Dinh Nhu, Diem's internal security chief, will both be killed [**Document 4-2**]. It will be Kennedy's biggest foreign policy blunder as president, because the chaos that followed proved far more difficult to manage then Diem's recalcitrance. LBJ, who took over three weeks after the coup in the midst of this chaos, will prove unable, perhaps because he is unwilling, to resist the Americanization of the war. This will lead to the disaster referred to in shorthand in the U.S. simply as "Vietnam."*

Washington, November 22, 1961
Secret
To: The Secretary of State
Subject: First Phase of Vietnam Program

The President has authorized the Secretary of State to instruct our Ambassador to Vietnam to inform President Diem as follows:

1. The U.S. Government is prepared to join the Vietnam Government in a sharply increased joint effort to avoid a further deterioration in the situation in South Vietnam.

2. The joint effort requires undertakings by both Governments as outlined below:

a. On its part the U.S. would immediately undertake the following actions in support of the GVN:

(1) Provide increased air lift to the GVN forces, including helicop-

ters, light aviation, and transport aircraft, manned to the extent necessary by United States uniformed personnel and under United States operational control.

(2) Provide such additional equipment and United States uniformed personnel as may be necessary for air reconnaissance, photography, instruction in and execution of air-ground support techniques, and for special intelligence.

(3) Provide the GVN with small craft, including such United States uniformed advisers and operating personnel as may be necessary for operations in effecting surveillance and control over coastal waters and inland waterways.

(4) Provide expedited training and equipping of the civil guard and the self-defense corps with the objective of relieving the regular Army of static missions and freeing it for mobile offensive operations.

(5) Provide such personnel and equipment as may be necessary to improve the military-political intelligence system beginning at the provincial level and extending upward through the Government and the armed forces to the Central Intelligence Organization.

(6) Provide such new terms of reference, reorganization and additional personnel for United States military forces as are required for increased United States military assistance in the operational collaboration with the GVN and operational direction of U.S. forces to carry out the other increased responsibilities which accrue to the U.S. military authorities under these recommendations.

(7) Provide such increased economic aid as may be required to permit the GVN to pursue a vigorous flood relief and rehabilitation program, to supply material in support of the security efforts, and to give priority to projects in support of this expanded counter-insurgency program. (This could include increases in military pay, a full supply of a wide range of materials such as food, medical supplies, transportation equipment, communications equipment, and any other items where material help could assist the GVN in winning the war against the Vietcong.)

(8) Encourage and support (including financial support) a request by the GVN to the FAO or any other appropriate international organization for multilateral assistance in the relief and rehabilitation of the flood area.

(9) Provide individual administrators and advisers for the Governmental machinery of South Vietnam in types and numbers to be agreed upon by the two Governments.

(10) Provide personnel for a joint survey with the GVN of condi-

tions in each of the provinces to assess the social, political, intelligence, and military factors bearing on the prosecution of the counter-insurgency program in order to reach a common estimate of these factors and a common determination of how to deal with them.

b. On its part, the GVN would initiate the following actions:

(1) Prompt and appropriate legislative and administrative action to put the nation on a wartime footing to mobilize its entire resources. (This would include a decentralization and broadening of the Government so as to realize the full potential of all non-communist elements in the country willing to contribute to the common struggle.)

(2) The vitalization of appropriate Governmental wartime agencies with adequate authority to perform their functions effectively.

(3) Overhaul of the military establishment and command structure so as to create an effective military organization for the prosecution of the war and assure a mobile offensive capability for the Army.

McGeorge Bundy

[Document 3-6: President John F. Kennedy's Address in Seattle at the University of Washington's 100th Anniversary Program, November 16, 1961][6]

Every one of JFK's 1,036 days as president was the 100th anniversary of an event in the American Civil War. As a one-time history major at Harvard and lifelong history buff, Kennedy seems to have reflected fairly often on the similarities and differences between the early 1860s and the early 1960s. His special counsel, Theodore Sorensen, wrote that to Kennedy, the October 1962 Cuban missile crisis was "the Gettysburg of the Cold War." At Gettysburg, the Union came closest to defeat, as the Confederate army pushed north into Pennsylvania. It is essential to remember that during the Cuban missile crisis, neither Kennedy nor anyone involved in it knew that it would end as it did, peacefully, after striking fear of Armageddon into politicians and citizens alike. Was this the moment the world, or a significant part of it, would be destroyed in a nuclear holocaust? In the midst of the crisis, many felt the answer was "yes."

The following document differs from the previous documents in that it is an excerpt from a public utterance (rather than a formerly classified memorandum or secret audiotape). It is taken from an address at the University of Washington in Seattle on the 100th anniversary of its founding. In the speech, JFK digs deeply into his trove of historical knowledge in an effort to explain to his audience in Seattle and to the American people just how difficult and dangerous is the nuclear age. Kennedy's soaring rhetoric is vividly on display. It is political rhetoric of a sort with which we are no longer familiar. It is not designed to move the masses to shout patriotic slogans or to march off to war—as political rhetoric, in Kennedy's time (and in ours) so often is. Instead it is, paradoxically, rhetoric in the service of caution and moderation, of reduced expectations, of a calm and accepting spirit of grim warning of what he called on many occasions "the long twilight struggle"—a struggle not only to meet the communist threat, but also a struggle to survive without a war between the superpowers that might destroy everything the Cold War was being waged to protect and preserve.

JFK begins with a reference to the Civil War and moves subsequently through the similarities and differences between 1861 and 1961. But he returns repeatedly to a single theme: the world has become so complex, so dangerous, so multipolar (to use a phrase from our time), that America must now be both careful in its behavior and respectful of the views and capabilities of other nations, and it must do so consistently. It must therefore work toward reasonable compromise, not just in exceptional and obviously dangerous cases (for example, in the Berlin Wall crisis, which was far from over at the moment Kennedy delivered his speech in Seattle, and later in the Cuban missile crisis in October 1962). America must be cautious, according to JFK, because any crisis, anywhere, at any moment, might escalate via miscalculation and misperception into a catastrophic nuclear war.

. . . This university was founded when the Civil War was already on, and no one could be sure in 1861 whether this country would survive. But the picture which the student of 1961 has of the world, and indeed the picture which our citizens have of the world, is infinitely more complicated and infinitely more dangerous.

In 1961 the world relations of this country have become tangled and complex. One of our former allies has become our adversary—and he has his own adversaries who are not our allies. Heroes are removed from their tombs—history rewritten—the names of cities changed overnight. . . .

We cannot, as a free nation, compete with our adversaries in tactics of terror, assassination, false promises, counterfeit mobs and crises.

We cannot, under the scrutiny of a free press and public, tell different stories to different audiences, foreign and domestic, friendly and hostile.

We cannot abandon the slow processes of consulting with our allies to match the swift expediencies of those who merely dictate to their satellites.

We can neither abandon nor control the international organization in which we now cast less than 1 percent of the vote in the General Assembly.

We possess weapons of tremendous power—but they are least effective in combating the weapons most often used by freedom's foes: subversion, infiltration, guerrilla warfare, civil disorder.

We send arms to other peoples—just as we send them the ideals of democracy in which we believe—but we cannot send them the will to use those arms or to abide by those ideals.

And while we believe not only in the force of arms but the light of right and reason, we have learned that reason does not always appeal to unreasonable men—that it is not always true that "a soft answer turneth away wrath"—and that might does not always make right.

In short, we must face problems which do not lend themselves to easy or quick or permanent solutions. And we must face the fact that the United States is neither omnipotent or omniscient—that we are only 6 percent of the world's population—that we cannot impose our will upon the other 94 percent of mankind—that we cannot right every wrong or reverse each adversity—and that therefore there cannot be an American solution to every problem.

These burdens and frustrations are accepted by most Americans with maturity and understanding. They may long for the days when war meant charging up San Juan Hill—or when our isolation was guarded by two oceans—or when the atomic bomb was ours alone—or when much of the industrialized world depended upon our resources and our aid. But they now know that those days are gone—and that gone with them are the old policies and the old complacencies. And they know, too, that we must make the best of our new problems and our new opportunities, whatever the risk and cost.

[Document 4-1: Memorandum for the Record of the Secretary of Defense Conference, Honolulu, May 6, 1963][7]

In important respects, this memorandum reads like a surreal fantasy—it could almost be a piece of historical fiction. This is because we know what happened in Vietnam subsequent to the meeting whose minutes are recorded in the document. From the U.S. perspective, events in South Vietnam will begin to head downhill fast in the fall of 1963. After JFK's assassination, LBJ will order an enormous military buildup, beginning in earnest in early 1965. The U.S. gradually will all but abandon Kennedy's emphasis on counterinsurgency—often summarized as the U.S. attempt to "win the hearts and minds" of the South Vietnamese people. These are key elements of the multidimensional tragedy that will begin after Kennedy's death, proceed incrementally through 1964, and then explode into public view from early 1965 onward, following which it will remain the most contentious U.S. foreign policy issue until the conclusion of the war in Vietnam, which will end with a communist victory on April 30, 1975. That is what will happen. Looking back, we know the extent of the tragedy that is unfolding.

But you would never guess from this memorandum that disaster is just around the corner. Here are a couple of the more surreal highlights: General Paul Harkins, the U.S. field commander in South Vietnam, predicts that the back of the insurgency will be broken soon, possibly by the end of 1965, although he says it might take a little longer than that. Perhaps even more surprising is that Defense Secretary Robert McNamara, who under Johnson became the most important public defender of the war's escalation, is in these minutes unequivocal in his view that the U.S. forces must begin to withdraw and that the withdrawal must occur faster than some of the military's plans require. McNamara orders his subordinates to speed things up so that the first 1,000 U.S. advisers can be withdrawn by the end of 1963, or about seven months hence, and he also wants the longer-term planning to speed up so that the bulk of the U.S. forces in South Vietnam can be withdrawn by the end of 1965. The mood on the military side is optimistic. In two and a half years, they clearly intend to have removed Vietnam from its position on the list of top-tier U.S. national security issues.

Frederick Nolting, the U.S. ambassador in Saigon, sounds the only cautionary note. There are emerging political problems between Washington and Saigon, he says, regarding who is actually in charge of the counterinsurgency (CI) efforts in the provinces. Out in the South Vietnamese countryside, Nolting implies, U.S. advisers are not winning the hearts and minds of the people. Particularly objectionable, according to Nolting, are counterinsurgency policies such as herding people into so-called "strategic hamlets," in order to "protect" them from communist insurgents. In fact, this will prove to be the Achilles' heel of the entire counterinsurgency effort: in order to combat the insurgents, the U.S. will be forced to undermine the ancient, village-centered social systems of the Vietnamese people, which will in turn make the peasants in the countryside all the more receptive to the insurgents' call to expel the Americans and the people running the South Vietnamese government in Saigon, whom they refer to as the American "puppets."

SUBJECT:

Notes and Necessary Actions Resulting From SecDef Honolulu Conference on Vietnam, 6 May 1963

Item 1. Evaluation of the Situation in RVN

  a. General Harkins discussed the over-all progress that had been made since the last meeting [convened October 2, 1962] and conveyed the feeling of optimism that all elements of the Country Team now have. General Harkins did not attempt to predict a date when the insurgency would be broken, but did feel that we are certainly on the right track and that we are winning the war in Vietnam, although the struggle will still be a protracted one. . . .

Item 2. Comprehensive Plan South Vietnam

a. CINCPAC presented the proposed '64–'69 RVNAF force structure and the proposed phasing in of equipment to the RVNAF. The Secretary questioned some of the figures, in that they showed larger forces in '68 than in '64, whereas we are operating on the assumption that the back of the insurgency would be broken by FY '65. . . .

(9) *Action:* The Secretary also stated that the phase out of US personnel is too slow and that we should try to get US numbers down to a minimum level earlier than FY '66. . . .

Item 4. US-GVN Relations.

a. Ambassador Nolting stated that the atmosphere of US-GVN relations is somewhat less cordial than it was six months ago. There remains a sense of touchiness in the GVN resulting from the CI fund discussions. He also attributed this situation to an increasing sense of nationalism and from misgivings on US policy in SEA. . . .

In regard to advisors, he states that he feels no specific measures are called for to remove any blocks of advisors. The GVN concern re: US advisors is not with any advisors who are in the strictly military field, but rather with the group of advisors, civilian and military, now in each province and concerned with advising and assisting the Province Chiefs. While these advisors are the ones that cause the GVN concern, at the same time it is these advisors who are most valuable in the over-all CI effort.

(15) *Action:* The Secretary stated that we should have a plan for phasing out US personnel; as the situation improves we should phase down our effort. This will be required if we are to get continued US support for our effort in Vietnam. The Secretary also stated that the last category he would take out would be advisors. He still desires that we lay down a plan to have the RVNAF take over some functions this year so that we can take out 1,000 or so personnel late this year if the situation allows. The Secretary repeated that we should lay down a plan to expedite training to get VN personnel to take over tasks being performed by US personnel. . . .

L.C. Heinz
Rear Admiral, USN
Director, Far East Region

[Document 4-2: Telegram From the Department of State to the Embassy in Vietnam, August 24, 1963][8]

Part of the lore of the U.S. State Department is the "August surprise." Some of the most unexpected developments affecting U.S. foreign policy seem to occur in the month of August, when many of the top decisionmakers are out of Washington and difficult to reach and when the city virtually shuts down for the month. Some famous examples are the "guns of August" fired in Europe that signaled the beginning of World War I and caught much of the entire world by surprise. More recently, the August 1990 invasion of Kuwait by Iraq caused jaws to drop in Washington, as did the August 18, 1991, coup in the Soviet Union against Mikhail Gorbachev. Sometimes, however, this "August fever" hits closer to home, smack in the middle of official Washington. A prime example is an August 24, 1963, cable from Undersecretary of State George Ball to the new U.S. ambassador in Saigon, Henry Cabot Lodge. The document will become known variously as the "coup telegram" or the "green light telegram," because it gives official authorization to Lodge to begin serious explorations in Saigon of an alternative to the leadership of President Ngo Dinh Diem and his brother, Ngo Dinh Nhu, head of the secret police and the regime's chief enforcer.

It is Ball who eventually signs off on the cable and authorizes its transmission to Lodge. President Kennedy and all his top advisers are out of town enjoying a late summer holiday, leaving Ball the highest-ranking foreign policy official in town. It was August, as Ball reports in his memoir, and nothing much was going on this particular Saturday, August 24, 1963, so he and his deputy, U. Alexis Johnson, decide to indulge in a rare game of golf. Here is the scene, according to Ball.

> We had time for only nine holes, and as we came up on the ninth green (where I made my only good approach shot of the day), I found Averell Harriman (then Undersecretary of State for Political Affairs) and Roger Hilsman (then the Assistant Secretary for Far Eastern Affairs) waiting for me to finish my game. The four of us drove back to my house.
>
> Averell brought me up to the minute on the Vietnam cable traffic and showed me a proposed telegram he and Hilsman wished to send to Cabot Lodge, our new ambassador in Saigon. It was drafted in response to a telegram from Lodge reporting coup feelers from certain of Diem's top generals and was obviously explosive . . . I did not object to the telegram except to improve the drafting. . . . The decision, however, was not mine but the President's, so I telephoned him in Hyannis Port to bring him up to date and read him the relevant passages. . . . Finally he said, "George . . . go ahead."[9]

And so it begins, in this quickly drafted, barely scrutinized set of instructions from Washington to Saigon signaling the end of America's investment in Diem and Nhu and the beginning of the end of even a modicum of credible, indigenous leadership in South Vietnam. Although the communists, North and South, refer to Diem as a "puppet" of the Americans, he is in fact defiant and it is for his defiance that the Kennedy administration ultimately feels it must get rid of him. The incompetent gang that followed Diem would be puppets in a more profound sense, happy to let the Americans take over the war, thus transforming what has been a bitter but still fairly circumscribed civil conflict, with Diem as president, into the national and regional catastrophe that the American war in Vietnam eventually became.

(Note: the cable appears in its original syntax, sometimes called "State Departmentese," according to which many articles and other connecting words are omitted. The practice originated back in the days when it was important to save all available space in telegrams sent in Morse code via telegrapher's key.)

Washington, August 24, 1963—9:36 PM
Eyes only Ambassador Lodge.
No further distribution

It is now clear that whether military proposed martial law or whether Nhu tricked them into it, Nhu took advantage of its imposition to smash pagodas with police and Tung's Special Forces loyal to him, thus placing onus on military in eyes of world and Vietnamese people. Also clear that Nhu has maneuvered himself into commanding position.

US Government cannot tolerate situation in which power lies in Nhu's hands. Diem must be given chance to rid himself of Nhu and his coterie and replace them with best military and political personalities available.

If, in spite of all your efforts, Diem remains obdurate and refuses, then we must face the possibility that Diem himself cannot be preserved. . . .

. . . Ambassador and country team should urgently examine all possible alternative leadership and make detailed plans as to how we might bring about Diem's replacement if this should become necessary.

Assume you will consult with General Harkins re: any precautions necessary protect American personnel during crisis period.

You will understand that we cannot from Washington give you detailed instructions as to how this operation should proceed, but you will also know we will back you to the hilt on actions you take to achieve our objectives.

Needless to say we have held knowledge of this telegram to minimum essential people and assume you will take similar precautions to prevent premature leaks.

[George] Ball

[Document 4-3: Robert S. McNamara and General Maxwell D. Taylor, "Report to the President on the Situation in South Vietnam," October 2, 1963][10]

President Kennedy has sent Defense Secretary Robert McNamara and General Maxwell Taylor, chairman of the Joint Chiefs of Staff, to South Vietnam in late September 1963 to gather information on what appears to many to be a rapidly deteriorating situation. The regime, led by President Ngo Dinh Diem and his brother, Ngo Dinh Nhu, has over the past year become increasingly brutal and incompetent in its efforts to suppress the communist insurgency. In addition, Diem and Nhu have undertaken to repress all public expressions of disagreement with their conduct. Thousands have been arrested, jailed, and/or executed. The most dramatic challenge yet to Diem and Nhu has come during the late spring and summer of 1963 during an uprising of Buddhist monks, whom the militantly Roman Catholic Ngo brothers have crushed with so much wanton brutality that Buddhist monks began to set fire to themselves in public places in protest— events that shocked the world.

The report delivered to Kennedy on October 2, 1963, by McNamara and Taylor has somehow to address this conundrum: the situation in Saigon and in the countryside is deteriorating, which would seem to increase the need for U.S. troops if South Vietnam is to be saved from a communist takeover, on the one hand, while on the other hand, McNamara and Taylor know that Kennedy manifestly opposes turning the struggle into a U.S. war, which it would become if American combat troops were sent to Vietnam in substantial numbers. They believe this for good reason: Kennedy has already, in the spring of 1963, ordered McNamara and the Joint Chiefs to set the bureaucratic wheels in motion to withdraw most, if not all, U.S. advisers by the end of 1965 [Document 4-1].

What to do? This time, there will be no showdown between a president and at least these two advisers—McNamara and Taylor—as there was in November 1961. By the fall of 1963, these two leaders of the fact-finding mission to Saigon have locked onto the wavelength of the president. They split the issue into two parts: Militarily, they say that the anti-communist effort is succeeding and will continue to succeed. Thus the withdrawal of U.S. advisers can begin by pulling out 1,000 by the end of the calendar year (1963). The political situation, however, is worse than ever and, while Diem and Nhu are the worst kind of authoritarians—both brutal and in-

competent at the same time—McNamara and Taylor do not recommend, at least for the time being, throwing U.S. support behind a group of South Vietnamese military officials seeking to overthrow the Diem government via a coup d'etat.

*In the excerpt from the McNamara-Taylor Report, note that there is nothing remotely resembling the recommendation to JFK that he eventually be prepared to deploy 205,000 combat troops in South Vietnam, as there was in McNamara's memorandum of two years before [**Document 3-1**]. Instead, the emphasis is on the mechanics of taking people out. Also absent from the McNamara-Taylor Report are any illusions about prospects for the success of the Diem government or any conceivable government that might replace it. McNamara and Taylor seem to be of one mind with President Kennedy, who, they believe, has decided to get out of Vietnam—as quietly as possible, gradually, and with no dramatic moves, at least until after the 1964 presidential election. In any case, this report to JFK is focused on how the U.S. should get out of Vietnam, not why the U.S. needs to get more deeply in.*

2 October 1963
Memorandum for the President
Subject: Report of McNamara-Taylor Mission to South Vietnam

Conclusions

- The military campaign has made great progress and continues to progress.
- There are serious political tensions in Saigon (and perhaps elsewhere in South Vietnam) where the Diem-Nhu government is becoming increasingly unpopular.
- Further repressive actions by Diem and Nhu could change the present favorable military trends. On the other hand, a return to more moderate methods of control and administration, unlikely though it may be, would substantially mitigate the political crisis.
- It is not clear that pressures exerted by the U.S. will move Diem and Nhu toward moderation. Indeed, pressures may increase their obduracy. But unless such pressures are exerted, they are almost certain to continue their past patterns of behavior.
- The prospects that a replacement regime would be an improvement appear to be about 50-50. Initially, only a strong authoritarian regime would be able to pull the government together and maintain order. In view of the preeminent role of the military in Vietnam today, it is prob-

able that this role would be filled by a military officer, perhaps taking power after the selective process of a junta dispute. Such an authoritarian military regime, perhaps after an initial period of euphoria at the departure of Diem and Nhu, would be apt to entail a resumption of the repression at least of Diem, the corruption of the Vietnamese Establishment before Diem, and an emphasis on conventional military rather than social, economic and political considerations, with at least an equivalent degree of xenophobic nationalism.

Recommendations

We recommend that:

- General [Paul] Harkins review with Diem the military changes necessary to complete the military campaign in the Northern and Central areas by the end of 1964, and in the [Mekong] Delta by the end of 1965.
- A program be established to train Vietnamese so that essential functions now performed by U.S. military personnel can be carried out by Vietnamese by the end of 1965. It should be possible to withdraw the bulk of U.S. personnel by that time.
- In accordance with the program to train progressively Vietnamese to take over military functions, the Defense Department should announce in the very near future presently prepared plans to withdraw 1000 U.S. military personnel by the end of 1963.

To impress upon Diem our disapproval of his political program we:

- Withhold important financial support of his development programs.
- Maintain the present purely "correct" relations with the top of the South Vietnamese government.
- Monitor the situation closely to see what steps Diem takes to reduce repressive practices and to improve the effectiveness of the military effort. We should recognize we may have to decide in two to four months to move to more drastic action.
- We not take any initiative to encourage actively a change in government.

[Document 4-4: Transcript of Audiotape Recordings of White House Meetings Regarding Vietnam, October 2, 1963, 6:05 p.m.–6:30 p.m.][11]

Inside the Kennedy administration, the McNamara-Taylor Report provokes an intense debate that is carried on over several days. The most con-

tentious issues are related to one of the report's key recommendations: that a phased withdrawal from South Vietnam of U.S. military personnel begin immediately, with (a) the first 1,000 (of the total of 16,000 then in Vietnam) to return to the U.S. by December 31, 1963 (approximately three months hence), and (b) the bulk of the remaining U.S. personnel to be withdrawn by the end of 1965 or as soon thereafter as feasible.

Many of JFK's advisers evidently do not want to get tied publicly to specific dates for the withdrawal due to the uncertainty of the situation in South Vietnam. At bottom, the issue is a potential domestic political issue: if the communist insurgency should strengthen its hold in the country, a simultaneous U.S. withdrawal will be portrayed by most Republicans and even some conservative Democrats as acceptance of a U.S. defeat in South Vietnam. We have lately learned much more than we knew before about the way this debate played out inside the administration. This is because secret audiotapes made by JFK of some of the pivotal meetings on the withdrawal plan have now been deciphered and made available to scholars. In the following excerpt from a meeting in the White House on October 2, 1963, at 6:05 p.m., we see the case against stating a policy of withdrawal argued by National Security Adviser McGeorge Bundy, while Defense Secretary Robert McNamara forcefully argues for the 1,000-man withdrawal immediately, with all but approximately 3,500 of the remaining forces to be withdrawn by the end of 1965. Ultimately, McNamara requests approval from Kennedy twice during this conversation and twice JFK responds, "all right." So the U.S. withdrawal from South Vietnam may be said to begin then and there.

*One of the most significant revelations to be derived from these secret audiotapes concerns the position of an individual who is present, but who does not speak: Vice President Lyndon Johnson. The president's daily diary lists LBJ as present during this discussion, although he remains silent throughout the meeting. Later, in February 1964, President Johnson will tell McNamara that he totally disagreed with McNamara's argument for withdrawal and with JFK's decision to begin the phased withdrawal [**Document 5-2**]. As president, LBJ will not even consider a withdrawal until the U.S. and its South Vietnamese allies are unambiguously "winning" the war—a situation that will never materialize. (Note: We come in on the discussion of a draft of a public statement on the results of the McNamara-Taylor mission, which when finished is to be read at a press briefing by Kennedy's press secretary, Pierre Salinger.)*

McGeorge Bundy: Then the next sentence, after "to do so," [unclear] say "These actions have not yet significantly affected the military effort but could do so in the future."

The president is himself . . . wants to be sure that the document as a whole reflects the notion that the object here is to win the war and he thinks putting the sentences in those order—

Robert McNamara: [Unclear] that order?

Bundy:—strengthens that proposition—

McNamara: Why did you say the president wanted to make clear, Mac, that the primary objective was to win the war?

Bundy: He wanted the—he thought the . . . didn't want to have it said that we were just Pollyannas who couldn't stand a little authoritarian government, or that we were—to making these noises out of a sort of a . . . we're making them because they're really seriously related to this central purpose . . .

Bundy: Then on page one of the draft statement itself, the president is concerned about this sentence about "the major part of the U.S. military task can be completed by the end of 1965," and asks whether it wouldn't be better to say that it is the judgment reported by Secretary McNamara and General Taylor.

McNamara: I would like that.

Bundy: So that what we might say is "Secretary McNamara and General Taylor reported their judgment *that* the major part of the U.S. military task can be completed by . . ."

McNamara: Yeah. That's fine . . .

President Kennedy enters the Cabinet Room.

Bundy: The other question—I think that's a good—Mr. President, there is some difference of opinion in paragraph three, the last sentence, "By the end of this year . . ." Again, I think the State Department's feeling is that there may be—that this signal may be ambiguously read and we're not quite sure what people will think it means. Bob [McNamara] has a strong reason for stating it . . .

President Kennedy: My only reservation about it is that it commits us to a kind of a . . . if the war doesn't continue to go well, it'll look like we were overly optimistic, and I don't—I'm not sure we—I'd like to know what benefit we get out [of it] at this time, announcing a thousand.

McNamara: Mr. President, we have the thousand split by units, so that if the war doesn't go well, we can say these thousand would not have influenced the course of action.

President Kennedy: And the advantage of taking them out—

McNamara: And the advantage of taking them out is that we can say to the Congress and the people that we *do* have a plan for reducing the exposure of U.S. combat personnel to the guerrilla actions in

South Vietnam—actions that the people of South Vietnam should gradually develop a capability to suppress themselves. And I think this will be of great value to us in meeting the very strong views of [Sen. J. William] Fulbright and others that we're bogged down in Asia and will be there for decades.

President Kennedy: All right. [Unclear] . . .

Maxwell Taylor: [Unclear: I think if it's vigorously pursued might . . .] completing it by the end of 1965.

President Kennedy: That's what I meant. I meant—I was talking about this '65 date.

Bundy: [Unclear] about this before, yeah.

President Kennedy: Not the thousand.

McNamara: Whether it's vigorously pursued or not, we'll have a training program such that we can take them out, and we ought to be charged with the responsibility of doing that.

[Pause.]

President Kennedy: All right. . . .

[Document 4-5: Transcript of Audiotape Recordings of White House Meetings Regarding Vietnam, October 5, 1963, 9:30 a.m.][12]

Three days after the meeting recorded in the previous document, JFK and his advisers meet one more time to finalize their position on the McNamara-Taylor recommendations. Once again, Kennedy points out that a withdrawal of U.S. forces in the face of advances by the communists in South Vietnam will seem "illogical," as he puts it. Undeterred, McNamara presses on until JFK gives his approval. He tells McNamara to go ahead, but without making a formal announcement about it, by which he means without commenting on the exact formula for which units are to be withdrawn. This opacity with regard to the mechanics of the withdrawal will also, for the time being, permit the U.S. ambassador in Saigon, Henry Cabot Lodge, to avoid formally confronting President Diem about the withdrawal, which would be perceived by Diem as a threat to withdraw U.S. support from his government, thus adding more fuel to the fire in his dispute with the Americans, particularly the combative Lodge. The U.S. has already informed Diem that Washington's support for him is at risk unless he agrees to the U.S. demand that he fire his brother, Ngo Dinh Nhu, the chief of internal security, and his wife, Madame Nhu, both of whom have lately taken to issuing blatantly anti-American statements. Nhu has even been rumored to have gone around the Americans to cut a secret deal with the insurgents and their allies in Hanoi, a deal said to be directed at an "all-Vietnamese solution"—that is, an agreement between Vietnamese communists and anti-communists that will exclude the Americans, in which both Vietnamese factions will require the U.S. to withdraw. With that caveat, however—there is to be no formal statement about its implementation—Kennedy orders McNamara to begin the withdrawal. This time it is McNamara who responds, "All right."

Present at the meeting, in addition to JFK, were Vice President Lyndon Johnson, Budget Director David Bell, National Security Adviser McGeorge Bundy, National Security Council Vietnam specialist Michael Forrestal, Assistant Secretary of State Averell Harriman, CIA Director John McCone, Defense Secretary Robert McNamara, Secretary of State Dean Rusk, and Chairman of the Joint Chiefs of Staff General Maxwell D. Taylor. It is quite likely that all of Kennedy's advisers in the room, except for McNamara (and possibly Taylor), disagreed with his decision to begin the withdrawal of U.S. advisers from South Vietnam. One may wonder: did McNamara convince Kennedy that the withdrawal should begin, or was McNamara convinced that JFK had already made up his mind to withdraw and therefore that his task was merely to put the argument to the president one more time, in front of the key advisers, so they all understood where he—the president—stood on the issue? Less than two months later, JFK would be dead. One of the officials present in these meetings about the withdrawal would become the new president. The new president, moreover, would retain as his inner core of foreign policy advisers all the others who were present. It is hardly surprising, therefore, that after November 22, 1963, there will be no more talk of withdrawal and the agonizing but inexorable march toward escalation to an American war in Vietnam will begin in earnest.

> **Robert McNamara:** Mr. President, we would like to have formal approval of items one, two, and three. One, I think you've already [unclear].
>
> **President Kennedy:** [Unclear]
>
> [Pause.]
>
> **President Kennedy:** Yeah, the question with this would be part [unclear] of the . . . next month bringing us militarily [unclear].
>
> **McNamara:** Well, but not really, because what—the thousand people are just not needed out there. We're training the [South] Vietnamese to carry on certain functions. There's no reason to keep them in there.

President Kennedy: Well, I think the only thing is if it's going horribly, just from the public point of view, a withdrawal would seem illogical. It's going to have to be formally announced rather than just do it by [unclear], if you really are doing it. I think if we're doing it—it may have—for some impact, then I think you can't do it unless [unclear: the war is . . . seems to be proceeding]. Otherwise we ought to just do it by rotation of [unclear: sounds like "lodgement"].

McNamara: That's the way we've authorized—

President Kennedy: Without any formal [unclear: with an] announcement in the near future. I think . . . I think [unclear: we might go with this/we can't deal with this].

McNamara: Or we do it just through normal attrition . . . [unclear: normal rotation].

President Kennedy: Yeah.

McNamara: Normal rotation.

[Mixed voices.]

President Kennedy: But then we made the point now about [unclear: shortly]. Let's just go ahead and do it without making a formal statement about it.

McNamara: All right.

[Document 4-6: National Security Action Memorandum No. 263, October 11, 1963][13]

The military recommendations of McNamara and Taylor are formally approved by JFK on October 11, 1963, when he signs National Security Action Memorandum No. 263, a portion of which is included below. It retains the 1,000-man withdrawal by the end of 1963, and also the ambiguity as to how it will be achieved.

Earlier, on October 2, 1963, the White House Press Secretary Pierre Salinger had issued a statement summarizing the McNamara-Taylor Report on South Vietnam. By all accounts, the statement was regarded by the press as fairly uncontroversial. Like many such statements, it had contained a good deal of "on the one hand," and "on the other hand" assessments. On the one hand, according to the press release, "the military program in South Vietnam has made progress and is sound in principle," but on the other hand, "improvements are being energetically sought." On the one hand, "the major part of the U.S. military task can be completed by the end of 1965" and 1,000 U.S. military personnel can be withdrawn by the end of 1963. But on the other hand, "the political situation remains deeply serious" and "repressive actions" by the Saigon government might eventually imperil the military effort to suppress the insurgency.[14] So, according to the press release: Things are going pretty well, but they could be better, in fact a lot better. And things may or may not continue to go as well as they have, depending mainly on the performance of Washington's consistently underperforming political allies in Saigon.

At a press conference a week after this statement is issued, a reporter asks JFK about a recently published interview with former CIA Director Allen Dulles, who has accused the Kennedy administration "of a lack of a clear-cut operational policy" in Vietnam. According to Dulles, this lack of a clear direction has led to strong disagreements about Vietnam within the administration. The reporter asks JFK to comment. Here is Kennedy's response.

. . . [Since] General Taylor and Secretary McNamara came back [from South Vietnam], I know of no disagreement between the State Department at the top, CIA at the top, Defense at the top, the White House and Ambassador Lodge, on what our basic policies will be and what steps we will take to implement it. Now if down below there is disagreement, I think in part it will be because they are not wholly informed of what actions we are taking.[15]

We now know from the secret Kennedy tapes, from the Johnson telephone tapes, and from testimony from Robert McNamara in his memoir and in the film The Fog of War *that JFK's response was far from candid. Disagreement with his withdrawal policy began at the top and permeated deeply into the ranks, precisely because of actions he had ordered—especially the steps toward withdrawing U.S. forces from Vietnam, the chief overseer of which would have been McNamara, the same McNamara who was Kennedy's chief instrument of de-escalation during the climactic conclusion to the October 1962 Cuban missile crisis.[16]*

As Jamie Galbraith argued at the Musgrove conference, it appears that only McNamara, among JFK's advisers "at the top," was enthusiastic about the withdrawal whether or not the Saigon government was winning its fight against the insurgency. This policy, which was mandated at the very top—that is, with JFK—was proving to be a tough sell within his own administration. He knew it would be a tough sell to the press, the Congress, and the American people. Kennedy wanted to try to "sell" the unconditional withdrawal policy (whether or not the U.S. ally was winning or losing) if and when he won reelection in November 1964. He never got that chance.

The White House
Washington

TOP SECRET—EYES ONLY
TO: Secretary of State
        Secretary of Defense
        Chairman of the Joint Chiefs of Staff

SUBJECT: South Vietnam
At a meeting on October 5, 1963, the President considered the recommendations contained in the report of Secretary McNamara and General Taylor on their mission to South Vietnam.
The President approved the military recommendations contained . . . in the report, but directed that no formal announcement be made of the implementation of plans to withdraw 1,000 U.S. military personnel by the end of 1963. . . .

McGeorge Bundy

[Document 4-7: National Security Action Memorandum No. 273, November 26, 1963][17]

On November 20–21, 1963, a meeting is held in Honolulu to discuss U.S. policy in South Vietnam, particularly the implications of the November 1 coup and murder of Diem and Nhu and their replacement by a military junta. U.S. military and civilian officials from both Saigon and Washington take part. National Security Adviser McGeorge Bundy participates as President Kennedy's personal representative. Bundy is also charged by JFK to draft the sense of the meeting and to work it up into a new National Security Action Memorandum, which can update NSAM 263 [Document 4-6], of October 11, 1963, in light of the changed conditions in South Vietnam.

Immediately following the Honolulu meeting, Bundy prepares a draft intended for JFK's consideration. The draft acknowledges that all is not going well in South Vietnam, especially in the three weeks since the coup that overthrew Diem. Plans are drawn up to intensify the struggle against the ascendant communist insurgency. But Bundy also drafts a paragraph that emphasizes—or rather reemphasizes—the central role of the South Vietnamese forces, as follows.

7. With respect to action against North Vietnam, there should be a detailed plan for the development of additional Government of [South] Vietnam resources, es-

pecially for sea-going activity, and such planning should indicate the time and investment necessary to achieve a wholly new level of effectiveness in this field of action.[18]

James K. Galbraith believes that, led by General Maxwell Taylor, U.S. military officials were already sabotaging Kennedy's withdrawal plan by sending various groupings of individual soldiers to Vietnam to compensate for the loss of units being rotated out of the country under the JFK-McNamara withdrawal plan.[19] Galbraith believes that these and other planned escalatory actions would never have been approved by McNamara once he had been shown the document. (McNamara did not attend the Honolulu meeting.)

By the early afternoon of November 22, 1963, President Kennedy is dead and Lyndon Johnson is president. Sometime between the time LBJ was sworn in as president aboard Air Force One and his signing of National Security Action Memorandum 273 on November 26, paragraph 7 just quoted, emphasizing the South Vietnamese role in the struggle against the insurgency, is deleted and replaced by the passage indicated in the excerpt below under 7. None of the participants at the Musgrove conference professed to know anything about the process regarding how or by whom this change in NSAM 273 was made. It is obviously an important change. Does it originate with LBJ, or with one or more of his senior advisers? If the latter, who proposes such a change to the new president, whose knowledge of the relevant issues is thin at best? And did LBJ and the advisers believe they were reversing JFK's policy?

Washington, November 26, 1963
TO: The Secretary of State
        The Secretary of Defense
        The Director of Central Intelligence
        The Director, USIA

The President has reviewed the discussions of South Vietnam which occurred in Honolulu, and has discussed the matter further with Ambassador Lodge. He directs that the following guidance be issued to all concerned:

1. It remains the central object of the United States in South Vietnam to assist the people and Government of that country to win their contest against the externally directed and supported Communist conspiracy. The test of all U.S. decisions and actions in this area should be the effectiveness of their contribution to this purpose.

2. The objectives of the United States with respect to the withdrawal

of U.S. military personnel remain as stated in the White House statement of October 2, 1963. . . .

7. Planning should include different levels of possible increased activity, and in each instance there should be estimates of such factors as:

A. Resulting damage to North Vietnam;

B. The plausibility of denial;

C. Possible North Vietnamese retaliation;

D. Other international reaction.

Plans should be submitted promptly for approval by higher authority. (Action: State, DOD, and CIA.)

8. With respect to Laos, a plan should be developed and submitted for approval by higher authority for military operations up to a line up to 50 kilometers inside Laos, together with political plans for minimizing the international hazards of such an enterprise. Since it is agreed that operational responsibility for such undertakings should pass from CAS to MACV, this plan should include a redefined method of political guidance for such operations, since their timing and characteristics can have an intimate relation to the fluctuating situation in Laos. . . .[20]

10. . . . [I]t is desired that we should develop as strong and persuasive a case as possible to demonstrate to the world the degree to which the Vietcong is controlled, sustained and supplied from Hanoi, through Laos, and other channels. . . .

(Action: Department of State with other agencies, as necessary.)

McGeorge Bundy

[Document 5-1: Transcript of a Telephone Conversation Between President Lyndon Johnson and Secretary of Defense Robert McNamara, January 13, 1965, 3:07 p.m.][21]

The following transcript of a telephone conversation between LBJ and Robert McNamara occurs in mid-January 1965. Thus, chronologically, it comes after several of the documents that follow it in this section. It is included here as the first document in the group associated with chapter 5 because it demonstrates exquisitely a key element in LBJ's approach to Vietnam that is present from Johnson's first hours as president. This is Johnson's supreme insecurity about being a rough-hewn, drawling, poorly educated president from rural Texas who has had the misfortune to follow in the footsteps of the suave, Harvard-educated, eloquent John F. Kennedy—a man, moreover, whose assassination has instantly elevated him to heroic status among his supporters and even many of his former adversaries.

Against the advice of some of his longtime advisers, such as Musgrove conference participant Bill Moyers, Johnson decides to retain nearly all of JFK's senior advisers so as not to appear disloyal to the fallen leader. But Johnson will demand a degree of personal loyalty to himself that is at least equal to that which he seems to have felt he had shown to the legacy of JFK in the aftermath of his death. Those who were closest to Kennedy, like McNamara, learned to expect an unending barrage of informal loyalty tests from LBJ so that Johnson can reassure himself, over and over again, that these "Harvards," as he called them, are really serving his interests—that they are not trying in one way or another to embellish the posthumous reputation of JFK at LBJ's expense.

During 1965, the focus of Johnson's hypervigilance regarding loyalty to him (versus loyalty to the legacy of JFK) will become the war in Vietnam. LBJ will go to great lengths throughout the escalation of the war to persuade the American public that he is carrying on in the tradition of Kennedy—that the war is, in effect, Kennedy's war, which he has merely inherited and of which he is only the humble custodian. What he fears from November 22, 1963, onward is that he will somehow be betrayed by one or more of the high-ranking Kennedy loyalists he has retained in his administration, among whom McNamara is by far the most eminent. Robert Kennedy and LBJ and their respective backers will begin their vicious trench warfare almost from the day LBJ succeeds JFK as president. Their struggle will cover many issues, but the most important of these is what Robert Kennedy's older brother would or would not have done with regard to Vietnam if he had lived. By January 1965, Vietnam is, in fact, beginning to become a contentious issue. There are as yet no "official" U.S. combat troops in South Vietnam. (The first contingent of U.S. Marines will arrive in March, followed by tens of thousands of soldiers by the end of 1965.) But pressure is building among many of LBJ's civilian and military advisers for LBJ to prepare to commit U.S. combat troops to Vietnam. If LBJ is to do this, he wants above all to make sure that he is understood to be doing more or less exactly what Kennedy would have done.

LBJ has heard a rumor about a conversation at a party in Georgetown during which he (LBJ) was accused by someone in the "Kennedy crowd" of trying "to put the war on Kennedy's tomb." One aspect of McNamara's response is strikingly ambivalent. It is unclear whether Johnson catches the secretary's unease when McNamara says, "President Kennedy's decisions to engage in this war, if you want to call it that." Did McNamara believe what he was saying? Did it slip his mind that he was Kennedy's bulwark against the widespread opposition (including LBJ's opposition) in his administration to the October 1963 plans for withdrawal? Was revising his own history of his service under Kennedy part of the price he thought he had to pay to

*appear loyal to Johnson when speaking to him? Did Johnson believe that
Kennedy had decided to go to war in South Vietnam? Did McNamara really
feel as jovial as he seems to be in this conversation about "being tagged with
the war"—a war that, under Kennedy, he had been charged to prevent?
And did LBJ believe McNamara's somewhat florid commendation of Johnson for his loyalty in extremis to the departed Kennedy?*

> **President Johnson:** . . . They have these little parties out at George-
> town, and they discuss. Bill Moyers tells me—I just wanna be sure
> there's no basis for *this*—that they had a party last night, and Joe
> Alsop called up very excited today and said that he and Kraft and
> [Rowland] Evans—
>
> **Robert McNamara:** Was this at Evans' house?
>
> **President Johnson:** Yeah.
>
> **McNamara:** I know I was invited to one [party], and I couldn't remem-
> ber what night it was.
>
> **President Johnson:** Well, it was [at] Evans' house. And the Kennedy
> crowd *decided* that I had framed up to get [the] Armed Services
> [Committee] in the Senate to call McCone to put the Vietnam War
> on Kennedy's tomb. And that I had a conspiracy going on to show
> that it was Kennedy's immaturity and poor judgment that originally
> led us *into* this thing, that got us involved. And that his execution
> of it had brought havoc to the country [Vietnam]. And that McCone
> had gone up [to the Senate] and done it. And that this was my
> game: to lay Vietnam off onto Kennedy's inexperience and immatu-
> rity, and so forth. [There was] a good deal more, but that was the
> guts of it.
>
> I explained by sayin' [to Moyers] that I knew nothin' about his
> [McCone] being called, that was Russell's doing. That McCone told
> me he was going. McCone told me he was distressed about some
> [strategic] weapons, but I told Bill not to tell 'em that. That's all he
> [McCone] talked to me about; he didn't *mention* Vietnam. But I
> subsequently checked with McNamara, and he thought things were
> alright, so I assumed, since McNamara was a part of the adminis-
> tration, that—
>
> **Robert McNamara:** [amused] And he was going to be tagged with the
> war in any case!
>
> **President Johnson:** What?
>
> **Robert McNamara:** And [he] is going to be tagged with the war in
> any case! [laughing]
>
> **President Johnson:** [chuckles] That since he was a part of the admin-

istration, I had assumed that he [McNamara] didn't resent very much what was said or he would have said to me that it didn't go well, or it wasn't true or somethin'. But he told me that the hearing went off all right, and I guess he'd be a good authority to tell 'em that. [I told Moyers] that I considered myself responsible for every decision made by Kennedy, beginning with the nomination of the vice president and the adoption of the platform, through the Bay of Pigs, through the Dominican Republic and Diem problems, and right down to that day in Dallas.

. . . Whatever he did, I supported. And if they can find a more loyal man in this town to him or to his memory, I'd like for 'em to *produce* him . . .

Robert McNamara: I think that Alsop *strongly* supported President Kennedy's decisions to engage in this war, if you want to call it that. So I can't imagine now he'd be going back and trying to accuse him of making some serious errors in getting mixed up with it.

President Johnson: Well, no *Alsop's* not. Alsop is sayin' that *I'm* doing it. Alsop's charging that I'm gettin' McCone to go up and lay the blame for Vietnam on Kennedy. Have you ever heard me blame Kennedy for anything?

Robert McNamara: None. None. Absolutely not.

President Johnson: Even when you knew that I did not share opinions?

Robert McNamara: That's right. Now I've mentioned this to Jackie several times. I've been very impressed by your attitude on that [as well as when] the president was alive, as a matter of fact.

President Johnson: I may not have anything *else* in my life, but I got loyalty. Well, anyway, I want you to know it, and I want you to straighten it out.

[Document 5-2: Transcripts of Two Telephone Conversations Between President Lyndon Johnson and Secretary of Defense Robert McNamara, February 20, 1964, and March 2, 1964][22]

*In the transcripts of the Kennedy audiotapes of October 2 and 5, 1963, it is clear that, among all of JFK's advisers, Robert McNamara is the only one pushing hard for the withdrawal plan [**Documents 4-4 and 4-5**]. It remains an open question as to why McNamara is so insistent on the withdrawal, but the most plausible reason for his enthusiasm for the withdrawal plan is that Kennedy had instructed him to argue precisely as he did and to do it in meetings with Kennedy and his advisers. This would have permitted*

Kennedy the ruse of "thinking over" what McNamara had to say and then agreeing with him. This seems to have been a favorite tactic of Kennedy, who much preferred to bring around his advisers via indirection—which sometimes involved a certain amount of deception—rather than by outright coercion. For example, JFK did just this during the climactic weekend of the Cuban missile crisis by instructing Secretary of State Dean Rusk to contact Andrew Cordier, a former United Nations official, to stand ready to call Acting UN Secretary General U Thant and to give him this message: U Thant should immediately call a news conference to announce his offer to broker a trade of Soviet missiles in Cuba for NATO missiles in Turkey as part of a deal to end the standoff in the Caribbean. Most of JFK's advisers believed such a public "trade" of Cuban for Turkish missiles would cause the Turks to withdraw from NATO, leading in all probability to the collapse of the entire NATO alliance. Yet Kennedy, virtually alone in the room with his Cabinet, questioned his advisers as to whether the Turks really understood that the alternative to trading their precious missiles might be nuclear devastation. It is Kennedy who pushes his advisers gently but relentlessly toward acceptance of the trade as an alternative to an air strike and invasion of Cuba. In the end, the public trade proved unnecessary because Soviet leader Nikita Khrushchev agreed to a private trade of missiles in addition to the public bargain struck by the U.S. and Soviet Union: the Soviets agreed to withdraw their missiles, while the U.S. pledged not to invade Cuba.[23]

In the following excerpts from two telephone conversations with LBJ in early 1964, we may observe McNamara still in the process of acclimating himself to his new boss. McNamara was accustomed to interrupting JFK in mid-sentence. JFK expected McNamara and his other advisers to state their views regardless of whether they were consistent with the president's. McNamara is learning that this will not be tolerated by Johnson, who grinds his defense secretary down without even inquiring about McNamara's obvious doubts regarding U.S. policy in Vietnam. On Vietnam, McNamara appears to be at something of a choice point in his transition from being Kennedy's man in the Pentagon to Johnson's top adviser on national security affairs. McNamara's dilemma was roughly as follows: in these and other conversations in late 1963 and early 1964, he can continue to try to press on the new president his reservations about escalating the war in Vietnam, as he had pressed them on Kennedy, but if he chooses to confront LBJ, he will appear to Johnson disloyal, and he will incur his wrath.

In the excerpt below from February 20, 1964, McNamara appears to register his misgivings about Vietnam to the president. But it is obvious from this encounter with LBJ that every time McNamara wishes to ques-

tion, qualify, or amend something Johnson believes about Vietnam, LBJ forces his defense secretary into silence. It is also obvious that Johnson knows exactly what he is doing. He is angry with McNamara and LBJ's tone lets him know that this new president is not pleased with all these complications and thorny issues that McNamara has been accustomed to discussing with Kennedy. Ultimately, McNamara decides to back off his previous advocacy of withdrawing from South Vietnam. He becomes the principal public spokesman and advocate for a conflict Johnson is determined to win, but which McNamara believes (as Kennedy believed) is not "winnable" in any meaningful sense. Many, including us, regret that McNamara chose the path of less resistance. McNamara himself also seems full of regret that he was unable to mount a successful challenge to LBJ's dual proclivities: paranoia about personal loyalty to him by Kennedy's appointees like McNamara combined with his persistent denial of just the sort of unpleasant realities regarding Vietnam about which McNamara (and not only McNamara) tried to inform the president. The depth of McNamara's own personal regret may be imagined based on the dissonance between two comments from his Vietnam memoir. "I think it highly probable," he wrote, "that, had President Kennedy lived, he would have pulled us out of Vietnam." Yet he also wrote that, because Johnson was afraid of public and Congressional reaction, LBJ chose to embark on the war by "subterfuge. . . . We were," he realized, "sinking into quicksand."[24]

February 20, 1964:

President Lyndon Johnson: Hello, Bob?

Robert McNamara: Yes, Mr. President.

President Johnson: I hate to modify your speech any because it's been a good one, but I just wonder if we should find two minutes in there for Vietnam.

Robert McNamara: Yeah, the problem is what to say about it.

President Johnson: I'll tell you what I would say about it. I would say that we have a commitment to Vietnamese freedom. We could pull out of there, the dominoes would fall, and that part of the world would go to the Communists. We could send our Marines in there, and we could get tied down in a Third World War or another Korean action. Nobody really understands what it is out there. They're asking questions and saying why don't we do more. Well, I think this: you can have more war or more appeasement. But we don't want more of either. Our purpose is to train these people [the South Vietnamese] and our trainin's goin' good.

Robert McNamara: Alright, sir, I'll—

President Johnson: I always thought it was foolish for you to make any statements about withdrawing. I thought it was bad psychologically. But you and the president thought otherwise, and I just sat silent.

Robert McNamara: The problem is—

President Johnson: Then come the questions: how in the hell does McNamara think, when he's losing a war, he can pull men out of there?

March 2, 1964:

President Johnson: [speaking to Robert McNamara] I want you to dictate to me a memorandum of a couple of pages. Four letter words and short sentences on the situation in Vietnam, the "Vietnam picture." I've got to have some kind of summarized, logical, factual analysis. Something in my own words I can say, "Well, here are the alternatives."

Now, why'd you say you'd send a thousand home [in October 1963]? I'd put a sentence in that "because they'd completed their mission." "Why did McNamara say they were coming back [home] in '65?" Because when you say you're going to give a man a high school education and he's in the 10th grade and you've got two years to do it, you can train him in two years. That doesn't mean everybody comes back, but that means your training ought to be in pretty good shape by that time. That's what's said, not anything inconsistent.

[Document 5-3: Transcripts of Telephone Conversations Between President Lyndon Johnson and Secretary of Defense Robert McNamara, August 3, 4, and 8, 1964][25]

For approximately the first six months of 1964, a CIA program called OPLAN 34-A has been underway in Vietnam. CIA pilots, flying CIA aircraft, have been secretly airlifting South Vietnamese commandos into North Vietnam. The objective is for the South Vietnamese forces to engage in various forms of covert sabotage, blowing up bridges and roads and so on. The 34-A operations do little harm to the North Vietnamese cause; most of the commandos are captured or killed and are never heard from again. The program is continued not because of its negligible military effectiveness, but because it gives the South Vietnamese forces a mission that keeps the U.S. hand well hidden. (Officially, the U.S. military has only advisers in South Vietnam, not combat troops. These advisers include the pilots of the planes dropping South Vietnamese covert operations specialists into North Vietnam.) In addition, the U.S. Navy regularly enters North Vietnamese waters in the Tonkin Gulf as part of its "DeSoto" operations, which are designed to detect the location and type of North Vietnamese radar. These installations will be among the first targets to be bombed if the war of proxies between Hanoi and Washington escalates to a shooting war between American and North Vietnamese forces. In that case, the U.S. (as planned) would launch an air attack on the North. Hanoi has complained about these operations, but does not at first seek to challenge the U.S. ships and planes supporting the 34-A guerrilla operations and the DeSoto surveillance program.

Then on August 2, North Vietnamese patrol boats attack the U.S. destroyer Maddox. LBJ chooses not to retaliate, but issues a stern warning. On August 4, word comes from the Pacific through McNamara to Johnson that the North Vietnamese have again attacked the Maddox and another ship, the Turner Joy. This time, despite highly equivocal information regarding whether a second attack had actually occurred (we now know it had not occurred), LBJ orders an air strike on installations along the North Vietnamese coast believed to be supporting the patrol boat attacks. In a televised address just before midnight Washington time on August 4, Johnson announces that a U.S. air attack is underway over North Vietnam.

The immediate aftermath of these August 1964 events in the Tonkin Gulf have put President Lyndon Johnson in an uncomfortable situation. He doesn't want to appear "soft" in response to North Vietnamese actions, fearing attacks from the right wing of his own Democratic party and from his Republican challenger in the upcoming November 1964 election, Senator Barry Goldwater of Arizona. But neither does he want to appear overly eager to get into a war in Asia, as Goldwater seems intent on doing. So on August 3, the day after the attack on the Maddox, Johnson tells McNamara to present the administration's case to the congressional leadership as "firm as hell," but not "dangerous." The following day, August 4, is a case study of "the fog of war" as leaders in Washington attempt to determine what, if anything, actually happened in the Tonkin Gulf earlier in the day. Johnson orders McNamara to prepare for a retaliatory strike, but only if they are sure one or more U.S. ships were actually attacked. Johnson is obviously concerned to be seen as retaliating, rather than initiating combat operations, because the U.S. is not officially at war in Southeast Asia. But on August 8, a newspaper story will appear that emphasizes Hanoi's claim that their actions were in retaliation for U.S.-backed attacks on North Vietnam (via the OPLAN 34-A covert action program). Johnson asks McNamara for guidance on how to respond to questions about the story without appearing either to confirm or to deny it. This is, as McNamara tells Johnson, a "very delicate subject." McNamara's recommendation is one with which LBJ is familiar and comfortable. He urges the president simply to deny U.S. involvement with the covert operations.

Monday, August 3, 1964, 10:20 a.m.:

> **President Johnson:** I wonder if you don't think it'd be wise for you and Rusk to get the Speaker [of the House Carl Albert] and [Senate Majority Leader Mike] Mansfield to call a group of fifteen or twenty people together from the Armed Services, Foreign Relations [Committees]. Tell 'em what happened.
>
> **Robert McNamara:** Right. I've been thinking about this myself.
>
> **President Johnson:** They're gonna start an investigation if you don't . . . You say, "They fired at us; we responded immediately and we took out one of their boats and put the other two running and we're putting out boats right there and we're not running 'em in."
>
> **Robert McNamara:** . . . We should also at that time, Mr. President, explain this OPLAN 34A, these covert operations. There's no question that that had bearing on it. On Friday night, as you probably know, we had four PT boats from [South] Vietnam manned by Vietnamese or other nationals attack two islands . . . following twenty-four hours after that, with this destroyer [the *Maddox*] in that same area—undoubtedly led them to connect the two events.
>
> **President Johnson:** Say that to [Senate Minority Leader Everett] Dirksen. You notice Dirksen says this morning that "we got to reassess our situation—do something about it." I'd tell him that we're doing what he's talking about.
>
> **Robert McNamara:** You want us to do it at the White House or would you rather do it at State or Defense?
>
> **President Johnson:** I believe it'd be better to do it up on the Hill . . . I'd tell 'em awfully quiet though so they won't go in and be making a bunch of speeches . . .
>
> Now I wish you'd give me some guidance on what we ought to say. I want to leave an impression on background . . . that we're gonna be firm as hell without saying something that's dangerous . . . The people that're calling me up . . . all feel that the Navy responded wonderfully. And that's good. But they want to be damn sure I don't pull 'em out and run . . . That's what all the country wants because [Senator Barry] Goldwater is raising so much hell about how he's gonna blow 'em off the moon. And they say that we

oughtn't to do anything that the national interest doesn't require, but we sure ought to always leave the impression that if you shoot at us, you're gonna get hit.

Robert McNamara: I think you would want to instruct [Presidential Press Secretary] George Reedy this morning . . . to say that you personally have ordered the Navy to carry on the routine patrols off the coast of North Vietnam, to add an additional destroyer to the one that has been carrying on the patrols, to provide an air cap, and to issue instructions to the commanders to destroy any force that attacks our force in international waters. . . .

Tuesday, August 4, 1964, 11:06 a.m.:

Robert McNamara: Mr. President, we just had word by telephone from Admiral [U. S. G.] Sharp that the destroyer is under torpedo attack.

President Johnson: [Almost inaudible sound.]

Robert McNamara: I think I might get Dean Rusk and Mac Bundy and have them come over here and we'll go over these retaliatory actions and then we ought to—

President Johnson: I sure think you ought to agree to that. Yeah . . . now where are these torpedoes coming from?

Robert McNamara: We don't know. Presumably from these unidentified [craft] that I mentioned to you a moment ago. We thought that the unidentified craft might include one PT boat, which has torpedo capability, and two Swatow boats, which we don't credit with torpedo capability, although they may have it.

President Johnson: What are these planes of ours doing around while they're being attacked?

Robert McNamara: Presumably the planes are attacking the ships. We don't have any word from Sharp on that. The planes would be in the area at the present time. All eight of them.

President Johnson: Okay, you get them over there and then you come over here.

Saturday, August 8, 1964, 8:24 a.m.:

Robert McNamara: I do think that if you have a press conference today you're going to get questions on the claim of the North Vietnamese that their strike on the second against the *Maddox* was retaliation for U.S. participation in the strike of July thirtieth and thirty-first against those islands . . . this is a very delicate subject.

President Johnson: What's the net of it?

Robert McNamara: The net of it is that you state categorically that U.S. forces did not participate in, were not associated with, any alleged incident of that kind . . .

President Johnson: Is this the outgrowth of [CIA Director] John [McCone's] briefing?

Robert McNamara: It's the outgrowth of a lot of conversation . . . in the press . . . and I think it's one you have to disassociate yourself from and certainly not admit that any such incident took place. But neither should you get in a position of denying it. Because the North Vietnamese have asked the ICC [International Control Commission] to come in there and examine the site and it would be very unfortunate if they developed proof that you in effect had misstated the case.

President Johnson: Did the South Vietnamese launch an attack that period?

Robert McNamara: On the night of the thirtieth and continuing into the morning of the thirty-first, the South Vietnamese ran one of these patrol boat raids against these two North Vietnamese islands. Part of that covert operational plan [OPLAN 34-A]. It was what John [McCone] was alluding to when he talked to the [congressional] leaders . . . The *Washington Post* has quite an article on it today. . . . "*Maddox* Incident Reexamined—Miscalculation Theory Weighed in Viet Crisis." This is by Murray Marder. He goes on to say that it's now thought it was probably a reprisal action by North Vietnam.

[Document 5-4: Memorandum for the President From McGeorge Bundy, January 27, 1965][26]

It is one week after Lyndon Johnson's inauguration as president (on January 20, 1965). He has been elected by a landslide over his Republican opponent, Arizona Senator Barry Goldwater. Democratic majorities in both the House and the Senate have been increased substantially on the coattails of LBJ's electoral victory. With the campaign behind him, Johnson is no longer an unelected president who has inherited the office under tragic circumstances. Johnson is now poised to dive back into the domestic reforms that have come to be known collectively as the Great Society program: voting rights, civil rights, Medicare, Medicaid—the most ambitious expansion of social programs in the U.S. since the days of President Franklin Roosevelt and the New Deal.

Yet just below the public's radar, big trouble is brewing in Vietnam. Johnson knows this, but he makes a strenuous effort to avoid a public debate over Vietnam policy. The Saigon leadership, to the extent that it exists at all, has careened from one incompetent group of pretenders to another for more than a year. The situation has become so chaotic that Secretary of State Dean Rusk has, on December 23, 1964, threatened to cut off all U.S. aid to South Vietnam. But Rusk is bluffing. The response from Saigon is essentially: So what? Who needs your money, anyway? Equally troubling, the military situation is deteriorating rapidly. On Christmas Eve, December 24, 1964, the communist insurgents have bombed the Brinks Hotel in central Saigon, killing two Americans and wounding fifty-two. After considerable soul-searching, LBJ decides not to retaliate in response to the Brinks bombing. The following week, South Vietnamese military units are humiliated by insurgents in pitched battles not far from Saigon.[27]

This is the immediate background for the January 27, 1965, memorandum from McGeorge Bundy and Robert McNamara to LBJ, which is excerpted below. It has become known as the "fork in the road" memorandum, because Bundy and McNamara believe the U.S. has arrived at a critical juncture at which a fundamental choice must be made with regard to Vietnam, a choice only a president can make. That choice is get in militarily all the way with massive numbers of combat forces, effectively transforming the war into an American war, or get out, but because the U.S. is leaving an essentially hopeless cause, try to find a face-saving way to enter into negotiations with the communists to disguise the fact that Washington is, in fact, abandoning the South Vietnamese cause and heading home. It is evident that Johnson does not want to hear this news during the very first week of his postinaugural administration, but McNamara and Bundy do not believe the matter can be postponed. Like it or not, as McNamara later wrote in his memoir, "After months of uncertainty and indecision, we had reached the fork in the road."[28]

White House
Washington

SECRET
MEMORANDUM FOR THE PRESIDENT:
RE: *Basic Policy in Vietnam*

1. Bob McNamara and I have asked for a meeting with you at 11:30 in order to have a very private discussion of the basic situation in Vietnam. . . .

2. What we have to say to you is that both of us are now pretty well convinced that our current policy can lead only to disastrous defeat. . . .

3. The underlying difficulties in Saigon arise from the spreading conviction there that the future is without hope for anti-Communists. More and more the good men are covering their flanks and avoiding executive responsibility for firm anti-Communist policy. Our best friends have been somewhat discouraged by our own inactivity in the face of major attacks on our own installations. The Vietnamese know just as well as we do that the Viet Cong are gaining in the countryside. Meanwhile, they see the enormous power of the United States withheld, and they get little sense of firm and active U.S. policy. They feel that we are unwilling to take serious risks. In one sense, all of this is outrageous, in the light of all that we have done and all that we are ready to do if they will only pull up their socks. But it is a fact—or at least so McNamara and I now think.

4. The uncertainty and lack of direction which pervades the Vietnamese authorities are also increasingly visible among our own people, even the most loyal and determined. . . .

5. Bob and I believe that the worst course of action is to continue in this essentially passive role which can only lead to eventual defeat and an invitation to get out in humiliating circumstances. . . .

6. *We see two alternatives.* The *first* is to use our military power in the Far East and to force a change of Communist policy. The *second* is to deploy all our resources along a track of negotiation, aimed at salvaging what little can be preserved with no major addition to our present military risks. Bob and I tend to favor the first course, but we believe that both should be studied and that alternative programs should be argued out before you.

7. Both of us understand the very grave questions presented by any decision of this sort. We both recognize that the ultimate responsibility is not ours. . . .

8. You should know that Dean Rusk does not agree with us. He does not quarrel with our assertion that things are going very badly and that the situation is unraveling. He does not assert that this deterioration can be stopped. What he does say is that the consequences of both escalation and withdrawal are so bad that we simply must find a way of making our present policy work. This would be good if was possible. Bob and I do not think it is.

9. A topic of this magnitude can only be opened for initial discussion this morning, but McNamara and I have reached the point where our obligations to you simply do not permit us to administer our present directives in silence and let you think we see real hope in them.

McG. B.
[McGeorge Bundy]

[Document 5-5: Memorandum for the President From McGeorge Bundy, February 7, 1965][29]

*The "fork in the road" memorandum [**Document 5-4**] is briefly discussed with LBJ late on the morning of January 27, 1965. But there is no serious consideration of the core dilemma named in point 6 of the memorandum—whether "to use our military power in the Far East and to force a change of Communist policy," or "to deploy all our resources along a track of negotiation." Instead, LBJ temporizes by deciding to send McGeorge Bundy to South Vietnam for yet another fact-finding visit of the sort that McNamara had been making on a regular basis since before LBJ came to office. This will be Bundy's first trip to South Vietnam. His task is to act as LBJ's personal representative, to gather as much information as possible in a few days, and to return to Washington with a recommendation for Johnson to take one "fork" or the other—to get fully into the conflict in Vietnam militarily or to get out as gracefully as possible.*

Upon his arrival, Bundy, in shirtsleeves due to the heat and humidity of Saigon, is greeted by the U.S. field commander, General William Westmoreland. Bundy has a full program of meetings organized by his special assistant for Vietnam, longtime East Asia hand (and Musgrove conference participant) Chester L. Cooper. The itinerary includes discussions not only with U.S. military officers and Saigon government officials but also with groups on the fringes of power, such as the Buddhist monks, who have been attempting to carve out a middle ground between the communists and the anti-communists.

It is difficult to say what Bundy's group might have recommended to Johnson had the visit gone according to the plan laid out by Cooper. But all the planning, all the discussions and strategizing, all the weighing of pluses and minuses of each fork in the road for U.S. policy in Vietnam—all of it—is made irrelevant by an unexpected event on February 7, the last day of Bundy's visit. At 2:00 a.m. on the seventh, communist insurgents attack a U.S. airfield at Pleiku, in northern South Vietnam, and also the U.S. helicopter base at Camp Holloway four miles away. Of the 137 Americans wounded, nine died and seventy-six had to be evacuated for medical reasons. Upon hearing the news, the Bundy group flies immediately to Pleiku, where Bundy, Westmoreland, Cooper, and the others review the damage. Bundy is appalled. At the Musgrove conference, Bill Moyers mentions that Bundy also appears to have been uncharacteristically emotional and upset by all the death and destruction he witnessed in Pleiku. Moyers was in the room with LBJ and the National Security Council when they took the call from Bundy on a speakerphone, during which he described the carnage at Pleiku.

The memorandum excerpted below was drafted initially by Chet Cooper on the long plane ride back to Washington from Saigon before being amended and authorized by Bundy. (A key assumption underlying the drastic U.S. military response to the events in Pleiku is that the Hanoi government authorized the attack to embarrass the Bundy delegation during their visit. More than thirty years later, however, in June 1997, a Vietnamese general who had been present in the attack zone told a conference in Hanoi that he and his men had no idea Bundy was even in the country. And in February 1998, a Vietnamese colonel revealed that the insurgent group responsible for the attack at Pleiku did not even know any Americans were present.)[30] Cooper recalled several years after the events that "on our return trip to Washington, we heard the White House statement over the plane's radio" describing the "sustained reprisals" that had begun against North Vietnam and which, as Operation ROLLING THUNDER, would become one of the most devastating bombing programs in history. There was no further discussion of the "fork in the road" memorandum. Looking back, Cooper believed that this was the moment when the American war began, when "the war . . . changed in kind rather than degree."[31]

The White House
Washington

TOP SECRET
MEMORANDUM FOR THE PRESIDENT
RE: *The Situation in Vietnam*

This memorandum attempts to describe the situation, the stakes and the measures which I think should now be taken.

I. *Summary Conclusions*

The situation in Vietnam is deteriorating, and without new U.S. action defeat appears inevitable—probably not in a matter of weeks or perhaps even months, but within the next year or so. There is still time to turn it around, but not much.

The stakes in Vietnam are extremely high. The American investment is very large, and American responsibility is a fact of life which is palpable in the atmosphere of Asia, and even elsewhere. The international prestige of the United States, and a substantial part of our influence, are directly at risk in Vietnam. There is no way of unloading the burden on the Vietnamese themselves, and there is no way of negotiating ourselves out of

Vietnam which offers any serious promise at present. It is possible that at some future time a neutral non-Communist force may emerge, perhaps under Buddhist leadership, but no such force currently exists, and any negotiated U.S. withdrawal today would mean surrender on the installment plan.

The policy of graduated and sustained reprisal . . . is the most promising course available, in my judgment. That judgment is shared by all who accompanied me from Washington [to South Vietnam], and I think by all members of the country team.

The events of the last twenty-four hours have produced a practicable point of departure for this policy of reprisal, and for the removal of U.S. dependents. They may also have catalyzed the formation of a new Vietnamese government. If so, the situation may be at a turning point. . . .

VI. *The Basic U.S. Commitment.*

The prospect in Vietnam is grim. The energy and persistence of the Viet Cong are astonishing. They can appear anywhere—and at almost any time. They have accepted extraordinary losses and they come back for more. They show skill in their sneak attacks and ferocity when cornered. Yet the weary country does not want them to win.

There are a host of things the Vietnamese need to do better and areas in which we need to help them. The place where we can help most is in the clarity and firmness of our own commitment to what is in fact as well as in rhetoric a common cause. There is one grave weakness in our posture in Vietnam which is within our own power to fix—and that is a widespread belief that we do not have the will and force and patience and determination to take the necessary action and stay the course.

This is the overriding reason for our present recommendation of a policy of sustained reprisal. Once such a policy is put in force, we shall be able to speak in Vietnam on many topics and in many ways, with growing force and effectiveness.

One final word. At its very best the struggle in Vietnam will be long. It seems to us important that this fundamental fact be made clear and our understanding of it be made clear to our own people and to the people of Vietnam. Too often in the past we have conveyed the impression that we expect an early solution when those who live with this war know that no early solution is possible. It is our own belief that the people of the United States have the necessary will to accept and to execute a policy that rests upon the reality that there is no short cut to success in South Vietnam.

McG. B
[McGeorge Bundy]

[Document 5-6: Memorandum to Lyndon Johnson From Hubert Humphrey, February 15, 1965][32]

*LBJ has acted immediately on McGeorge Bundy's recommendations of February 7, 1965, above [**Document 5-5**]. The so-called "sustained reprisals"—which will soon become a massive air war against North Vietnam— have begun from U.S. aircraft based on carriers near Vietnam. Preparations are being made to send the first contingent of U.S. Marines to South Vietnam, initially to protect Americans building an airstrip near Da Nang in the east-central part of the country. (The Marines will arrive in late March.) All of LBJ's principal national security officials have endorsed these actions, by which the U.S. has, in effect, begun the final approach to transforming the conflict in Vietnam into an American war. The hawks include, at this point, Defense Secretary Robert McNamara, Secretary of State Dean Rusk, National Security Adviser McGeorge Bundy, and CIA Director John McCone, in addition to all the Joint Chiefs of Staff.*

Technically, the U.S. has not yet deployed combat troops to Vietnam; its personnel are still officially listed as advisers to the South Vietnamese forces. Opponents of escalation within the administration know they have little time to try to stave off a massive American war in Vietnam—perhaps a few days, a few weeks at most, before the line will be crossed, combat troops will arrive in South Vietnam, and there will be no turning back from a massive U.S. war effort in Vietnam. The leading doves in the administration, at this point, are Undersecretary of State George Ball and the newly elected vice president, Hubert Humphrey, the liberal former mayor of Minneapolis and senator from Minnesota. The previous October, Ball had argued strenuously in classified memoranda and in oral discussions with Johnson and his other advisers that if the U.S. goes to war in Vietnam, it will very likely enter a monumental quagmire from which it will ultimately be forced to extricate itself in defeat and humiliation. Ball had gotten nowhere with Johnson; or with his immediate boss, Dean Rusk; or with anyone else inside the administration. At the upper levels of government, Ball became a lonely (and, as we now know, prophetic) voice.

Johnson and Humphrey have just been inaugurated on January 20, 1965. Almost immediately after taking office, Vice President Humphrey begins organizing his thoughts about Vietnam with the intention of writing the president a personal, top-secret memorandum, "politician-to-politician." Within days of the initiation of the bombing of North Vietnam, Humphrey decides to spend a weekend in Georgia, ostensibly quail-hunting with Minnesota businessman Ford Bell. But the vice president is also joined at the Georgia retreat by fellow Minnesotan and former aide Thomas L.

Hughes, director of the Bureau of Intelligence and Research (INR) at the State Department (and a Musgrove conference participant). Together, Humphrey and Hughes collaborate on the real purpose of the weekend retreat. Hughes briefs Humphrey at length on the latest intelligence estimates coming out of Vietnam. They are grim. Politically and militarily, the Saigon government is losing ground rapidly to the communist insurgents. By the end of the weekend in Georgia, Hughes provides the vice president with a handwritten first draft of Humphrey's main points, which Humphrey edits by hand on the plane ride back up to Washington, D.C. Hughes has it typed up when he returns, dated February 15, 1965, and he hand-delivers it to Humphrey personally at his office in the Executive Office Building.[33]

The Humphrey memorandum is, as Fred Logevall said at the Musgrove conference, simply "extraordinary." It is, first of all, modest. The vice president does not claim to be an expert on Southeast Asia or on military affairs. He is giving his boss and fellow politician, LBJ, some advice on "the politics of Vietnam." It is also concise, yet it contains a comprehensive survey of the political reasons for avoiding a war in Vietnam and does so powerfully, with a clear-eyed assessment of the deteriorating situation in Vietnam. It is also eerily prophetic in its portrayal of the tragedy that will ensue for Johnson personally, for his administration, for America, and for Vietnam. Humphrey, having had the memorandum retyped on his own stationery, hand-delivered his message to the White House on February 17, 1965.

Instead of gratitude from Johnson, or in any case a discussion of the issues, Humphrey is punished: he is ostracized from all meetings on Vietnam and McGeorge Bundy is told by Johnson to keep the vice president under surveillance, lest his heretical views on Vietnam become public knowledge. Only many months later, after agreeing to become an exuberant supporter of the war in Vietnam, is Humphrey allowed back into LBJ's inner circle. The change in Humphrey was widely noted: from an independent and cautious critic of the war to a cheerleader for LBJ. The American satirical songwriter Tom Lehrer spoke for many Americans in his "Whatever Became of Hubert?" (1965).[34]

It is clear that Humphrey will fall in line with Johnson's escalation of the war because he wants desperately to succeed LBJ as president. Yet his decision to stifle himself, to ignore his own prescient advice given in the February 15, 1965, memorandum, will prove to be his undoing as a candidate for president in 1968 following Johnson's March 31, 1968, announcement that he would not seek reelection. Humphrey's public support of the war angered and alienated many in his core constituency of liberal Democrats. Had he come out strongly against the war in the campaign of 1968, *he would very likely have beaten Richard Nixon. Even so, the courage and prescience of his February 15, 1965, memorandum to LBJ remains admirable. Likewise, Johnson's denial of its hard truths remains tragic and irresponsible, but also emblematic of what would become LBJ's somewhat reluctant but ultimately emphatic embrace of the arguments for escalation in Vietnam. The decline and fall of Lyndon Johnson began in earnest when he decided in mid-February 1965 to ignore and ostracize his vice president. It may have been his last important opportunity to avoid an American war in Vietnam.*

February 15, 1965
MEMORANDUM FOR THE PRESIDENT
RE: The Politics of Vietnam

I have been in Georgia over the weekend, and for the first time since inauguration, have had time to read and think about the fateful decisions which you have just been required to make, and will continue to be making, on Vietnam. I have been reading the Vietnam cables and intelligence estimates of the last two weeks. Because these may be the most fateful decisions of your administration, I wanted to give you my personal views. You know that I have nothing but sympathy for you and complete understanding for the burden and the anguish which surrounds such decisions. There is obviously no quick or easy solution, and no clear course of right or wrong. Whatever you decide, we will be taking big historical gambles, and we won't know for sure whether they were right until months or perhaps years afterwards. The moral dilemmas are inescapable.

I want to put my comments in the most useful framework. In asking me to be your vice president, you made it clear that you expected my loyalty, help, and support. I am determined to give it. I don't intend to second-guess your decisions, or kibitz after the fact. You do not need me to analyze or interpret our information from Vietnam. You have a whole intelligence community for that purpose. You do not need me for foreign policy advice. You have a wise secretary of state and whole staffs and departments to do that. I am not a military expert. Plenty of others are.

But because I have been privileged to share with you many years of political life in the Senate, because we have recently come through a successful national election together, because I think your respect for me and my value to you significantly consists of my ability to relate politics and policies, and because I believe strongly that the sustainability of the Vietnam policies now being decided are likely to profoundly affect the success of your administration, I want to summarize my views on what I call the politics of Vietnam.

1. In the recent campaign, Goldwater and Nixon stressed the Vietnam issue, advocated escalation, and stood for a military "solution." The country was frightened by the trigger-happy bomber image which came through from the Goldwater campaign. By contrast we stressed steadiness, staying the course, not enlarging the war, taking on the longer and more difficult task of finding political-military solutions in the South where the war will be won or lost. Already, because of recent decisions on retaliatory bombing, both Goldwater and the Kremlin are now alleging that we have bought the Goldwater position of "going North."

2. In the public mind the Republicans have traditionally been associated with extreme accusations against Democratic administrations, whether for "losing China," or for failing to win the Korean War, or for failing to invade Cuba during the missile crisis. By contrast we have had to live with responsibility. Some things are beyond our power to prevent. Always we have sought the best possible settlements short of World War III, combinations of firmness and restraint, leaving opponents some options for credit and face-saving, as in Cuba. We have never stood for military solutions alone, or for victory through air power. We have always stressed the political, economic and social dimensions.

3. This administration has a heavy investment in policies which can be jeopardized by an escalation in Vietnam: the President's image and the American image, the development of the Sino-Soviet rift, progress on detente and arms control, summit meetings with Kosygin, reordering relations with our European allies, progress at the United Nations, stabilizing defense expenditures, drafting reservists.

4. American wars have to be politically understandable by the American public. There has to be a cogent, convincing case if we are to enjoy sustained public support. In World Wars I and II we had this. In Korea we were moving under United Nations auspices to defend South Korea against dramatic, across-the-border, conventional aggression. Yet even with these advantages, we could not sustain American political support for fighting Chinese in Korea in 1952.

   Today in Vietnam we lack the very advantages we had in Korea. The public is worried and confused. Our rationale for action has shifted away now even from the notion that we are there as advisers on request of a free government, to the simple and politically barren argument of our "national interest." We have not succeeded in making this national interest interesting enough at home or abroad to generate support. The arguments in fact are probably too complicated (or too weak) to be politically useful or effective.

5. If we go north, people will find it increasingly hard to understand why we risk World War III by enlarging a war under terms we found unacceptable 12 years ago in Korea. Politically people think of North Vietnam and North Korea as similar. They recall all the "lessons" of 1950–53: the limitations of air power, the Chinese intervention, the "Never Again Club" against GIs fighting a land war against Asians in Asia, the frank recognition of all these factors in the Eisenhower Administration's compromise of 1953.

   If a war with China was ruled out by the Truman and Eisenhower administrations alike in 1952–53, at a time when we alone had nuclear weapons, people will find it hard to contemplate such a war with China now. No one really believes the Soviet Union would allow us to destroy Communist China with nuclear weapons.

6. People can't understand why we would run grave risks to support a country which is totally unable to put its own house in order. The chronic instability in Saigon directly undermines American political support for our policy.

7. It is hard to justify dramatic 150-plane U.S. air bombardments across a border as a response to camouflaged, often nonsensational, elusive, small-scale terror which has been going on for ten years in what looks largely like a civil war in the South.

8. Politically in Washington, beneath the surface, the opposition is more Democratic than Republican. This may be even more true at the grassroots across the country.

9. It is always hard to cut losses. But the Johnson Administration is in a stronger position to do so now than any administration in this century. 1965 is the year of minimum political risk for the Johnson Administration. Indeed it is the first year when we can face the Vietnam problem without being occupied by political repercussions from the Republican right. As indicated earlier, our political problems are likely to come from new and different sources (Democratic liberals, independents, labor) if we pursue an enlarged military very long.

10. We now risk creating the impression that we are the prisoner of events in Vietnam. This blurs the Administration's leadership role

and has spill-over effects across the board. It also helps erode confidence and credibility in our policies.

11. President Johnson is personally identified with, and greatly admired for, political ingenuity. He will be expected to pull all this great political sense to work now for international political solutions. People will be counting upon him to use on the world scene his unrivaled talents as a politician. They will be watching to see how he makes this transition from the domestic to the world stage.

    The best possible outcome a year from now would be a Vietnam settlement which turns out to be better than was in the cards because LBJ's political talents for the first time came to grips with a fateful world crisis and did so successfully. It goes without saying that the subsequent domestic political benefits of such an outcome, and such a new dimension for the President, would be enormous.

12. If, on the other hand, we find ourselves leading from frustration to escalation and end up short of a war with China but embroiled deeper in fighting in Vietnam over the next few months, political opposition will steadily mount. It will underwrite all the negativism and disillusionment which we already have about foreign involvement generally—with serious and direct effects for all the Democratic internationalist programs to which the Johnson Administration remains committed: AID, United Nations, arms control, and socially humane and constructive policies generally.

For all these reasons, the decisions now being made on Vietnam will affect the future of this Administration fundamentally. I intend to support the Administration whatever the President's decisions. But these are my views.

[Document 5-7: Transcript of a Telephone Conversation Between Lyndon Johnson and Mike Mansfield, June 8, 1965][35]

By early June 1965, LBJ is faced with epochal decisions about the scale of the escalation in Vietnam. He has already authorized the deployment of approximately 85,000 combat troops requested by the American field commander in Saigon, General William Westmoreland. But even before all these troops arrive, Westmoreland has sent another request to Johnson via McNamara for an additional 85,000 troops. The situation on the ground in South Vietnam is deteriorating rapidly, the general has reported.

The expected offensive by the communist insurgents has begun and the South Vietnamese Army is wholly incapable of containing it. According to Westmoreland, only a massive U.S. intervention can prevent the entire country from being overrun by the communist insurgents and their allies in Hanoi.

As happened in early February when LBJ faced the decision as to whether to begin sustained bombing of North Vietnam, the president has again in June taken to his bed. (This is a persistent Johnson trait: when difficult decisions are approaching about the war, he often develops an uns- pecified "illness," goes to bed, and prefers to talk with his advisers on the phone from his bed rather than confront them face-to-face.) By June 1965, the dilemma LBJ faces is so acute, so devoid of acceptable options, that it might have tempted anyone to lapse into denial and seclusion in an effort to wish away the mess. Here is the gist of it: Johnson has become absolutely convinced that he must yield to Westmoreland's request to further escalate the war. He seems to believe that this is the only way to avoid defeat in South Vietnam. He fears, with an intensity approaching paranoia, that if he were to accept defeat in Vietnam, he would be personally humiliated and he would also lose support in the Congress for the program of social reforms he is pushing, which collectively will come to be known as the Great Society program. Of course, he expects trouble from some Republi- cans and conservative Democrats for prosecuting the war in Vietnam with insufficient enthusiasm. What he has not counted on is the forthright oppo- sition to escalation from members of the Democratic leadership in Con- gress, especially in the Senate. Some of his most powerful allies, in fact, seem to be defecting from his cause.

In an effort to prevent further deterioration in congressional support, Johnson, from his sickbed, calls Senate Majority Leader Mike Mansfield, a Democrat of Montana and a liberal former ally of Johnson's in the Senate. LBJ tells Mansfield he wants his advice, but what Johnson really wants is Mansfield's support, and congressional support generally, for escalating the war. Toward that end, Johnson tells Mansfield he is considering making a speech to Congress explaining that escalation of the war is in the tradition of Eisenhower and JFK, his immediate predecessors, when they intervened militarily to prevent communist takeovers in various locales. Mansfield will have none of it. He tells the president that J. William Fulbright, the power- ful chairman of the Senate Foreign Relations Committee, is "tremendously disturbed" by the situation in Vietnam, and implies that Fulbright is impla- cably opposed to escalation. Mansfield himself believes escalation will be a terrible mistake and he tells Johnson why. Johnson does not appear to dis- agree with Mansfield about the probable outcome of escalation: the U.S.

*will likely lose the war and alienate most of the world. Remarkably, Johnson
will still press ahead with the escalation.*

Tuesday, June 8, 1965, 5:05 p.m.

President Johnson: I don't see exactly the medium for pulling out [of
Vietnam] . . . [But] I want to talk to you . . . Rusk doesn't know that
I'm thinking this. McNamara doesn't know I'm thinking this. Bundy
doesn't. I haven't talked to a human. I'm over here in bed. I just
tried to take a nap and get going with my second day, and I couldn't.
I just decided I'd call you. But I think I'll say to the Congress that
General Eisenhower thought we ought to go in there and do here
what we . . . did in Greece and Turkey, and . . . President Kennedy
thought we ought to do this . . . But all of my military people tell
me . . . that we cannot do this [with] the commitment [of American
forces] we have now. It's got to be materially increased. And the
outcome is not really predictable at the moment. . . . I would say
. . . that our seventy-five thousand men are going to be in great
danger unless they have seventy-five thousand more. . . . I'm no
military man at all. But . . . if they get a hundred and fifty [thousand
Americans], they'll have to have *another* hundred and fifty. So, the
big question then is: What does the Congress want to do about
it? . . . I know what the military wants to do. I really know what
Rusk and McNamara want to do . . . and I think I know what the
country wants to do *now*. But I'm not sure that they want to do that
six months from now. I want you to give me your best thinking on
it. See how we ought to handle it, if we handle it at all. . . . We have
. . . some very bad news on the government [in Saigon] . . . Westmoreland says that the offensive that he has anticipated, that he's
been fearful of, is now on. And he wants people as quickly as he
can get them.

Mike Mansfield: [Fulbright] is tremendously disturbed about the situation in Vietnam.

President Johnson: Well, we *all* are.

Mike Mansfield: I know, but I mean, *really* . . . He just feels it's too
little and too late. . . .

President Johnson: . . . Unless you can guard what you're doing, you
can't do anything. We can't build an *airport*, by God . . . it takes
more people to *guard* us in building an airport than it does to *build*
the airport. . . .

Mike Mansfield: Yeah, but some people seem to think that we're just building it for the Vietcong to take over.

President Johnson: It could very well be. But I have the feeling from the way Bill Fulbright talked . . . that the feeling on the Hill was that we ought to be doing more of that, that it might be a better answer than bombs.

Mike Mansfield: There's a feeling of apprehension and suspense up here that's pretty hard to define.

President Johnson: Well, we have it *here* . . . Do you have any thoughts about the approach we ought to make to the Congress—whether one is wise, and if so, how?

Mike Mansfield: If you make another approach to the Congress, I really think the roof will blow off this time, because people who have remained quiet will no longer remain silent . . . I think you'd be in for some trouble. The debate would spread right out.

President Johnson: I think you might near got to have the debate, though, hadn't you?

Mike Mansfield: Yes, sir.

President Johnson: Do you think that we ought to send all these troops without a debate?

Mike Mansfield: No, sir. I think we've got too many in there now. And we've been bombing the North without any appreciable results. . . .

President Johnson: What do we do about [Westmoreland's] request for more men? . . . If it assumes the proportions that I can see it assuming, shouldn't we say to the Congress, "What do you want to do about it?"

Mike Mansfield: I would hate to be the one to say it because, as you said earlier, it's seventy-five thousand, then it's a hundred and fifty thousand, then it's three hundred thousand. Where do you stop?

President Johnson: You don't . . . to me, it's shaping up like this, Mike—you either get out or you get *in* . . . we've tried all the neutral things. And we think they are winning. Now, if *we* think they're winning, you can imagine what *they* think.

Mike Mansfield: They *know* they're winning.

President Johnson: And if they know that, you can see that they're not anxious to find any answer to it . . . we seem to have tried everything that we know how to do. I stayed here for over a year when they were urging us to bomb before I'd go beyond the line. I have stayed away from [bombing] their industrial targets and their civilian population, although they [the Joint Chiefs] urge you to do it.

Mike Mansfield: Yeah, but Hanoi and Haiphong are spit clean, and have been for months. You bomb them, you get nothing. You just build up more hatred. You get these people tied more closely together because they are tied by blood, whether from the North or the South.

President Johnson: I think that's true. I think that you've done nearly everything that you can do, except make it a complete white man's war.

Mike Mansfield: If you do that, then you might as well say goodbye to all of Asia and to most of the world.

President Johnson: That's probably right. . . .

[Document 5-8: National Security Council Meeting, July 27, 1965][36]

Musgrove conference participant Fred Logevall recalls that as he was researching and writing his landmark 1999 book, Choosing War, *he discovered a puzzle that, to this day, leaves him mystified.[37] He concluded that nearly all of the major players in the U.S. decisions to escalate the conflict in Vietnam to an American war actually did not believe the Americanization of the war, with all its cost in blood and treasure, would be successful. Of course, no one could be certain that the U.S. was destined to lose the war that, by mid-1965, was about to become an American war in Vietnam. But almost no one expected the U.S. to win it outright. Logevall was astounded by this finding. How, he wondered, did the U.S. leadership— including LBJ, McNamara, Rusk, McGeorge Bundy, and the Joint Chiefs of Staff—justify entering into a protracted and massive war they doubted they could win in any meaningful sense? And why, in light of the considerable evidence in the declassified documents supporting Logevall's thesis, did LBJ and his inner circle try to publicly minimize the significance of the massive escalation as it occurred? Did they really think they could hide the depth of American involvement from the American public? How does their private skepticism on the war square, if at all, with the Johnson administration's repeated statements to the U.S. public, the Congress, and the world of some version of Saigon field commander General William Westmoreland's often-used delusion—that there was "light at the end of the tunnel?"[38]*

The default answer given by many over the more than four decades since the escalation began in earnest in 1965 is the one Johnson himself favored. It is this: LBJ and his associates had little or no choice. The Cold War ethos, which required any U.S. president to hold the line against the communists all over the world, left Johnson and the others with no option other than to try to hold out in Vietnam, to frustrate the communists until they abandoned their insurgency, and to do so without appearing so aggressive that the Soviets and/or Chinese became involved, which would have carried the risk of World War III. According to this view, we may well be anguished in retrospect by that brutal war, as Johnson clearly was anguished as the escalation unfolded. We may regret, moreover, that the U.S. ever got involved militarily in Vietnam, as many who served in the Johnson administration eventually did. We may even hold LBJ responsible for misdemeanors such as failing to come clean with the American public on the escalation and the resulting "credibility gap," which was in part responsible for Johnson's decision in March 1968 not to seek reelection. But the scholarly consensus that has prevailed since the 1960s holds that we should not blame LBJ and his advisers for the high crimes for which they are held responsible by many of the most radical opponents of Americanizing the war. Why? Because they were trapped by forces and events. Another president with other advisers would have done the same, more or less.[39] It is this view that Fred Logevall rejects. Johnson, according to Logevall, chose war. He could have chosen otherwise. But he elected not to do so.

The issue of whether or not LBJ chose war unnecessarily will not be decided with finality by any document or cluster of documents because the question is in some respects deeply philosophical. The issue of whether our choices are determined by forces beyond ourselves—whether our apparent choices are real or illusory—has engaged thinkers since the beginning of recorded history. But with the declassification of a vast number of documents related to the decision to escalate the war during the first half of 1965, we are now in a position to anchor our assessment of LBJ's choice to take the nation to war in Vietnam—was the choice real or illusory?—in a richly empirical context.

The following minutes of a meeting on July 27, 1965, is just such a document. LBJ and his advisers have been meeting all day in an effort, as Johnson says, to "formalize" their decisions. Rusk, giving the opening remarks, explains to his colleagues that they must, in effect, square the circle—by appearing determined and tough to the Vietnamese communists, but reasonable and "low-key" to Hanoi's allies in Moscow and Beijing. McNamara then describes the military situation in almost apocalyptic terms. Nothing, he reports, has worked so far to stem the tide of the communist insurgency. McNamara reminds his colleagues that General Westmoreland needs roughly double the number of troops he said he needed just a few weeks before, and he recommends giving the general what he has requested. General Earle Wheeler, the chairman of the Joint Chiefs of Staff, passes along the delusionary assessment of Westmoreland, who will become infamous for his mantra that there is always "light at the end of the tunnel." The newly requested troops and equipment, according to Westmoreland and Wheeler, will turn the tide.

It is unclear whether anyone in the room really believes Westmoreland's prediction. Why should they? The general had said virtually the same thing only weeks before when he requested the initial installment, which he now says is only half of what he needs. The grim mood is broken only by a surreal pause for a photo opportunity, during which LBJ and the other participants in the discussion doubtless smiled for the cameras just as they reached the conclusion of their discussion of what degree of death and destruction would meet their dual objectives: bringing the Vietnamese communists to their knees without causing the Russians and/or the Chinese to enter the war on behalf of Hanoi and its southern allies. Following the photo op, they resume their meeting. It concludes when, as the note-taker reports, there was "no response" after Johnson asked whether anyone in the room objected to giving Westmoreland what he has asked for: more than 175,000 combat troops, all the helicopters and other equipment commensurate with an all-out effort to subdue the insurgency, and an escalation of the already ferocious bombing campaign against North Vietnam. These are key aspects of Johnson's proposal for dealing with Vietnam to which no one in the room registers any objection or qualification.

*Return to the original question: Did LBJ have a real choice in this matter? Were there no viable options? Before answering, read Vice President Hubert Humphrey's memorandum to Johnson again [**Document 5-6**], keeping in mind that when Humphrey delivered his memorandum, the U.S. still had not yet technically committed any combat troops to South Vietnam. Was Humphrey wrong to believe LBJ was at a choice point, and that the choice was real? Could Johnson have chosen otherwise? What about the advisers? Could they have chosen to object when LBJ asked if anyone disagreed with his decision? Why was there "no response"? What factors conspired to force everyone in that room into silence when LBJ asked whether anyone objected to Americanizing the war?*

TOP SECRET/SENSITIVE
FOR THE PRESIDENT ONLY
July 27, 1965—5:40 PM–6:20 PM
SUBJECT: Deployment of Additional Troops to Vietnam
The President: Before formalizing decisions on the deployment of additional U.S. forces to Vietnam, he wished to review the present situation with Council members present. . . .

Secretary Rusk:

. . . The U.S. actions we are taking should be presented publicly in a low key but in such a way as to convey accurately that we are determined to prevent South Vietnam from being taken over by Hanoi. At the same time, we seek to avoid a confrontation with either the Chinese Communists or the Soviet Union.

Secretary McNamara: Summarized the military situation in Vietnam:

a. The number of Viet Cong forces has increased and the percentage of these forces committed to battle has increased.

b. The geographic area of South Vietnam controlled by the Viet Cong has increased.

c. The Viet Cong have isolated the cities and disrupted the economy of South Vietnam. The cities are separated from the countryside.

d. Increased desertions from the South Vietnamese Army have prevented an increase in the total number of South Vietnamese troops available for combat.

e. About half of all U.S. Army helicopters are now in South Vietnam, in addition to over 500 U.S. planes.

The military requirements are:

a. More combat battalions from the U.S. are necessary. A total of 13 additional battalions need to be sent now. On June 15, we announced a total of 75,000 men, or 15 battalions.

b. A total of 28 battalions is now necessary.

c. Over the next 15 months, 350,000 men would be added to regular U.S. forces.

d. In January, we go to Congress for a supplementary appropriation to pay the costs of the Vietnam war. We would ask now for a billion, in addition to the existing 1966 budget. . . .

The attack on SAM sites in North Vietnam was necessary to protect our planes. Attacks on other priority targets in North Vietnam are required. . . .

General Wheeler: . . . With the additional forces to be sent to South Vietnam, General Westmoreland believes we can hold our present position and possibly move back into areas now contested. . . .

[The meeting was interrupted briefly to permit the photographers to take some pictures.]

The President: The situation in Vietnam is deteriorating. Even though we have 80 to 90,000 men there, the situation is not very safe. We have these choices:

a. Use our massive firepower, including SAC, to bring the enemy to his knees. Less than 10% of our people urge this course of action.

b. We could get out, on the grounds that we don't belong there. Not very many people feel this way about Vietnam. Most feel that our national honor is at stake and that we must keep our commitments there.

c. We could keep our forces at the present level, approximately 80,000 men, but suffer the consequences of losing additional territory and of accepting increased casualties. We could "hunker up." No one is recommending this course.

d. We could ask for everything we might desire from Congress— money, authority to call up reserves, acceptance of the deployment of more combat battalions. This dramatic course of action would involve declaring a state of emergency and a request for several billion dollars. Many favor this course. However, if we go all out in this fashion, Hanoi would be able to ask the Chinese Communists and the Soviets to increase aid and add to their existing commitments.

e. We have chosen to do what is necessary to meet the present situation, but not to be unnecessarily provocative to either the Russians or the Communist Chinese. We will give the commanders the men they say they need and, out of existing materiel in the U.S., we will give them the materiel they say they need. We will get the necessary money in the new budget and will use our transfer authority until January. We will neither brag about what we are doing or thunder at the Chinese Communists and the Russians.

This course of action will keep us there during the critical monsoon season and possibly result in some gains. Meanwhile, we will push on the diplomatic side. This means that we will use up our manpower reserves. We will not deplete them, but there will be a substantial reduction. Quietly, we will push up the level of our reserve force. We will let Congress push us but, if necessary, we will call the legislators back.

We will hold until January. The alternatives are to put in our big stack now or hold back until Ambassadors [Henry Cabot] Lodge and [Arthur] Goldberg and the diplomats can work.

Secretary [Henry] Fowler: Do we ask for standby authority now to call the reserves, but not actually call them?

The President: Under the approved plan, we would not ask for such authority now.

There was no response when the President asked whether anyone in the room opposed the course of action decided upon.

[Documents 6-1, 6-2, and 6-3: Memoranda by John F. Kennedy's Advisers on the Bay of Pigs Fiasco, April 20, April 24, and May 3, 1961]

Shortly after midnight on April 17, 1961, approximately 1,200 commandos began to arrive at the Bay of Pigs on the south coast of Cuba. Trained by the CIA, their goal was to establish a beachhead and hold it against counterattack by the army and militia of Cuban government forces led by Fidel Castro, whose movement had come to power in Cuba in January 1959. The invaders, like their U.S. sponsors, believed the Cuban people would rally to their side. They did not. The invaders were defeated in fierce fighting within seventy-two hours by Cuban government forces. U.S. forces did not intervene. The new administration of President John F. Kennedy was humiliated. The invaders who survived were imprisoned and subjected to a public "show-trial" in Havana, which represented the beginning of a virulent anti-Americanism on the part of the Cuban government. The regime of Fidel Castro was consolidated and became instantly pro-Soviet. The Kennedy administration was left in disarray and confusion.

The Bay of Pigs debacle remains arguably the single most humiliating event in the recent history of U.S. foreign policy. It was not the biggest disaster or the most costly, but it may well have been the most ridiculous or absurd, the most psychologically incomprehensible to most Americans as well as the rest of the world. It was the "perfect failure," as one journalist wrote at the time.[40] As the world saw it, the greatest power on earth was defeated in three days by one of the poorest and weakest of nations. Upon hearing the news of the disaster, the new president said to his aide, Theodore Sorensen, "How could I have been so far off base . . . How could I have been so stupid to let them go ahead?"[41] Kennedy would not make that mistake again.

We have included three excerpts from documents that were not written for public consumption, documents that contain a brutal honesty seldom seen in public pronouncements or published memoirs of government officials. Note especially the eyewitness account in the diary entry of Chester Bowles of the Kennedy State Department of how shattered Kennedy appears to have been by the events. But note, too, in the excerpts from McGeorge Bundy and Arthur Schlesinger, Jr., that Kennedy has pointedly asked each of these aides to be as critical as possible of those responsible, beginning with Kennedy himself. They are to pull no punches. Bundy gives it to him straight: never delegate to the military decisions of any magnitude; never underestimate the enemy. And Schlesinger reports to Kennedy with brutal honesty that, in effect, the NATO allies worry that, contrary to what they thought prior to the Bay of Pigs fiasco, Kennedy may well be an incompetent fool with a penchant for military adventures. It is an unusually curious and confident president who asks for and receives that kind of blunt feedback.

All of Kennedy's decisions on Vietnam would be deeply affected by this chastening experience. Other events of course also played a role in Kennedy's ongoing evolution as president. But none compared in psychological impact to the Bay of Pigs debacle.

[Document 6-1: Chester Bowles, Notes on Cuban Crisis, April 20, 1961][42]

Cabinet meeting on Thursday, April 20th, the first day immediately after the collapse of the Cuban expedition became known.

I attended the Cabinet meeting in Rusk's absence and it was about as grim as any meeting I can remember in all my experience in government, which is saying a good deal.

The President was really quite shattered, and understandably so. Almost without exception, his public career had been a long series of successes, without any noteworthy setbacks. Those disappointments which did come his way, such as his failure to get the nomination for Vice President in 1956, were clearly attributable to religion.

Here for the first time he faced a situation where his judgment had been mistaken, in spite of the fact that week after week of conferences had taken place before he gave the green light. . . .

The discussion simply rambled in circles with no real coherent thought. Finally after three-quarters of an hour the President got up and walked toward his office. . . .

When a newcomer enters the field and finds himself confronted by the nuances of international questions, he becomes an easy target for the military-CIA-paramilitary type answers which are often in specific logistical terms which can be added, subtracted, multiplied or divided.

This kind of thinking was almost dominant in the conference and I found it most alarming. The President appeared the most calm, yet it was clear . . . that he had been suffering an acute shock and it was an open question in my mind as to what his reaction would be.

[Document 6-2: McGeorge Bundy, Some Preliminary Lessons of the Cuban Expedition, April 24, 1961][43]

First, the President's advisers must speak up in council. Second, secrecy must never take precedence over careful thought and study. Third, the President and his advisers must second-guess even military plans. Fourth, we must estimate the enemy without hope or fear. Fifth, those who are to offer serious advice on major issues must themselves do the necessary work. Sixth, the President's desires must be fully acted on, and he must know the full state of mind of friends whose lives his decisions affect. Seventh, forced choices are seldom as necessary as they seem, and the fire can be much hotter than the frying pan. Eighth, what is and is not implied in any specific partial decision must always be thought through. Ninth: What is large in scale must always be open, with all the consequences of openness. Tenth: Success is what succeeds.

[Document 6-3: Arthur Schlesinger, Jr., Memorandum for the President: Reactions to Cuba in Western Europe, May 3, 1961][44]

The first reactions to Cuba were, of course, acute shock and disillusion. . . . After Cuba, the American government seemed as self-righteous, trigger happy and incompetent as it had ever been. . . . "Kennedy has lost his magic," one person said to me. "It will take years before we can accept the leadership of the Kennedy Administration again," said another. Friends of America warned me not to underestimate the gravity of the damage: "Make sure that our people in Washington understand how much ground we have lost" (Drew Middleton); "It was a terrible blow, and it will take a long, long time for us to recover from it" (Lord Boothby).

I should add that nearly all the reactions I encountered expressed sorrow over the decision to invade rather than the failure of the invasion. "Why was Cuba such a threat to you? Why couldn't you live with Cuba, as the USSR lives with Turkey and Finland?" . . .

A number of people seriously believe, on the basis of newspaper stories from Washington, that an American invasion of Cuba is a distinct and imminent possibility. A [London] *Observer* editor said to me, "If Cuba were just an accident, alright. But everything since Cuba suggests that the Kennedy who launched that invasion was the *real* Kennedy—that all his talk about "new methods" of warfare and countering guerrillas represents his *real* approach to the problems of the Cold War—that he thinks the West will beat communism by adopting communist methods and transforming itself into a regimented paramilitary society on the model of the Soviet Union." Several people said, "It's not Cuba that worries me; it's the aftermath."

[Document E-1: Matthew Rycroft, Iraq: Prime Minister's Meeting, July 23, 2002][45]

The salient similarities between the decisions to go to war in Vietnam and Iraq—such as self-delusion, attachment to abstract ideas, and the willingness to deceive the public—are vividly on display in a remarkable document known as "The Downing Street Memo." The document consists of the minutes of a meeting on July 23, 2002—nearly eight months before the invasion of Iraq—between British Prime Minister Tony Blair and his top national security advisers. The head of British intelligence has just returned from meetings in the U.S. with top U.S. officials. He reports that the Bush administration has decided irrevocably to go to war in Iraq, probably in early 2003, and that, especially with regard to alleged "evidence" of Iraqi pursuit of nuclear weapons, "intelligence and facts were being fixed around the policy." Translation: the allegation of an Iraqi nuclear program is a pretext. Furthermore, in an eerie foreshadowing of Stephen Herbits's warning to Donald Rumsfeld, the British intelligence chief found that "there was little discussion in Washington of the aftermath after military action." Thus one sees in this document the U.S. delusions and deceptions about Middle East "dominoes" refracted through a Blair government that is especially keen to be a partner in the delusionary and deceptive enterprise in Iraq. Blair, in particular, will become a kind of one-man cheerleading team for the U.S.-led war and occupation in Iraq, and he will continue to justify the war until his departure from the government in 2007 and beyond, even after many initial supporters of the war had abandoned the cause.

In the following excerpt from the Downing Street Memo, these British officials appear:

> Tony Blair, *prime minister*
> Sir Richard Dearlove, *called "C" in the Memo, head of MI6 (the "British CIA")*
> Lord Goldsmith, *attorney general*
> Geoffrey Hoon, *defense secretary*
> John Scarlett, *head of the Joint Intelligence Committee (an intelligence oversight board)*
> Jack Straw, *foreign secretary*

The Downing Street Memo was prepared for Sir David Manning, foreign policy adviser to the Prime Minister (roughly equivalent to the U.S.

national security adviser), by his aide, Matthew Rycroft. The memo recounts the meeting of July 23, 2002. The public first learned of the existence of the memo when it appeared in the London Times *on May 1, 2005.*

SECRET AND STRICTLY PERSONAL—UK EYES ONLY
DAVID MANNING
From: Matthew Rycroft
Date: 23 July 2002
IRAQ: PRIME MINISTER'S MEETING, 23 JULY
[Y]ou met the Prime Minister on 23 July to discuss Iraq.

This record is extremely sensitive. No further copies should be made. It should be shown only to those with a genuine need to know its contents.

John Scarlett summarised the intelligence and latest JCS [U.S. Joint Chiefs of Staff] assessment. Saddam's regime was tough and based on extreme fear. The only way to overthrow it was likely to be by massive military action. Saddam was worried and expected an attack, probably by air and land, but he was not convinced that it would be immediate or overwhelming. His regime expected their neighbors to line up with the US. Saddam knew that regular army morale was poor. Real support for Saddam among the public was probably narrowly based.

C reported on his recent talks in Washington. There was a perceptible shift in attitude. Military action was now seen as inevitable. Bush wanted to remove Saddam, through military action, justified by the conjunction of terrorism and WMD [weapons of mass destruction]. But the intelligence and facts were being fixed around the policy. The NSC had no patience with the UN route, and no enthusiasm for publishing material on the Iraqi regime's record. There was little discussion in Washington of the aftermath after military action. . . .

The *Defence Secretary* said that the US had already begun "spikes of activity" to put pressure on the regime. No decisions had been taken, but he thought the most likely timing in US minds for military action to begin was January, with the timeline beginning 30 days before the US Congressional elections.

The *Foreign Secretary* said he would discuss this with Colin Powell next week. It seemed clear that Bush had made up his mind to take military action, even if the timing was not yet decided. But the case was thin. Saddam was not threatening his neighbors, and his WMD capability was less than that of Libya, North Korea or Iran. We should work up a plan for an ultimatum to Saddam to allow back in the UN weapons inspectors. This would also help with the legal justification for the use of force.

The *Attorney General* said that the desire for regime change was not a legal base for military action. There were three possible legal bases: self-defence, humanitarian intervention, or UNSC [United Nations Security Council] authorisation. The first and second could not be the base in this case. Relying on UNSCR [UN Security Council Resolution] 1205 of three years ago would be difficult.[46] The situation might of course change.

The *Prime Minister* said that it would make a big difference politically and legally if Saddam refused to allow in the UN inspectors. Regime change and WMD were linked in the sense that it was the regime that was producing the WMD. There were different strategies for dealing with Libya and Iran. If the political context were right, people would support regime change. The two key issues were whether the military plan worked and whether we had the political strategy to give the military plan the space to work.

"The questionnaire was used primarily for its value in provoking discussion. It is not, as its creator emphasized, a scientifically validated instrument or anything like it."
Top: James Hershberg. Bottom: Thomas Blanton

JFK What If Questionnaire for Musgrove Participants

This questionnaire has two purposes: first, to kick-start thinking and discussion for session 5; second, if the results prove to be interesting, to serve as grist for a paper I am writing on how to think through a counterfactual.[1] Your participation is entirely optional, but the greater the number of participants, the better the results.

You may respond by name, or pseudonymously, but please put some name here that you can remember, for reasons I will later explain (whether you use your name or not, I will not identify respondents in any respect—the only merit to using your real name is that it would enable me to ask you questions later about your reasoning on particular points, so as to help me understand your thinking better. But please do not feel obliged to use your real name).

Name or pseudonym: _____

QUESTION 1. Consider the following four statements:

1. If Kennedy had lived and been reelected, he would have withdrawn all, or virtually all, American troops from Vietnam ("Withdrawal" option).
2. If Kennedy had lived and been reelected, he would have continued to attempt to support the South Vietnamese with a significant number of military "advisers" ("Status Quo" option).
3. If Kennedy had lived and been reelected, he would have committed American military forces to Vietnam in combat roles, though in much lower numbers than LBJ authorized ("Americanization Lite").

4. If Kennedy had lived and been reelected, he would have committed American military forces to Vietnam more or less as LBJ did ("Americanization LBJ Style").

Based on what you know and strongly believe, how would you rank the following outcomes, from most plausible (1) to least plausible (4)? For equally plausible outcomes, use the same number and skip the next (e.g., 1, 2, 2, 4). When thinking about your ranking, imagine political and military events in Vietnam transpiring precisely as they actually did through 1964.

_____ Withdrawal
_____ Status Quo
_____ Americanization Lite
_____ Americanization LBJ Style

QUESTION 2. In his essay in Mark White's volume, Fred Logevall argued that, on balance, Kennedy was likely not to have committed American troops to Vietnam.[2] Which of the following statements best characterizes your reaction to Logevall's essay? Please try to consider Logevall's argument on its merits, bracketing any preconceptions of your own.

_____ I agreed with Logevall that the considerations suggesting Kennedy would not have Americanized the war were on balance weightier than the considerations suggesting that he would have.

_____ I thought the considerations Logevall advanced suggesting Kennedy would have Americanized the war were actually weightier.

_____ I thought the considerations Logevall advanced on both sides of the issue were more or less equally weighty.

_____ I did not read Logevall's essay.

The remaining questions are specifically about the four outcomes I listed on the previous page. When attempting to decide what to do had he lived and been reelected, Kennedy may have felt various things were at stake, he may have felt pressures from various quarters, but it is likely that he would not have cared equally about every stake, nor felt equally susceptible to different kinds of pressures.

For the sake of simplicity, let us reduce the stakes and pressures to five sets of considerations.

(a) **INTERNATIONAL**: "hard" military geopolitical considerations, global or regional, affecting the balance of military power with the communist world, as well as "soft" geopolitical considerations, including alliance politics, American reputation and prestige at the UN or in the Third World. Count "Domino" considerations and other countries' positive or negative attitude toward U.S. foreign policy here.

(b) **DOMESTIC**: Party politics, electoral politics, U.S. public opinion, any implicated domestic program, JFK's personal popularity with the American people.

(c) **BUREAUCRATIC**: The preferences and general happiness of important units of government, such as the Pentagon, the State Department, etc.

(d) **PERSONAL**: Kennedy's own beliefs, desires, fears, needs, etc. Count here anything having to do with Kennedy's own world view, conscious or subconscious drives, etc. (for example, Logevall's argument that LBJ was strongly driven by a need to preserve his sense of manhood would count as a personal pressure; if JFK had a similar need, in your view, count it here).

(e) **SUNK COSTS**: Some people are unwilling to write off sunk costs; others are more willing. Count here any pressure you think Kennedy would have felt to try to recoup costs already paid trying to bolster South Vietnam.

QUESTION 3. Please tick the appropriate box for your estimate of how Kennedy would have *perceived* pressures. This is quite a different consideration from whether he *cared* about a particular pressure. For example, he may have perceived that domestic political considerations favored Americanization Lite, but he may not have given domestic political considerations much weight in his own thinking. This question is *only* about how he perceived the pressures. The next question will be about what pressures were influential in his thinking.

If you believe, for example, that Kennedy would have seen important bureaucratic players as on balance inclined toward Americanization Lite, though with some doubts and uncertainties, tick "Weakly for" Americanization Lite in the **BUREAUCRATIC** category. If you believe that Kennedy strongly desired to withdraw, and would have done so in the absence of any other kinds of constraints, tick "Strongly for" Withdrawal in the **PERSONAL** category.

		Strongly against	Weakly against	Neithe for nor against	Weakly for	Strongly for
INTERNATIONAL	Withdrawal					
	Status Quo					
	Americanization Lite					
	Americanization LBJ Style					
DOMESTIC	Withdrawal					
	Status Quo					
	Americanization Lite					
	Americanization LBJ Style					
BUREAUCRATIC	Withdrawal					
	Status Quo					
	Americanization Lite					
	Americanization LBJ Style					
PERSONAL	Withdrawal					
	Status Quo					
	Americanization Lite					
	Americanization LBJ Style					
SUNK COSTS	Withdrawal					
	Status Quo					
	Americanization Lite					
	Americanization LBJ Style					

QUESTION 4. This question is about what considerations Kennedy cared about, regardless of what direction he thought any particular consideration was pushing him toward.

Please tick the appropriate box for your estimate of how susceptible Kennedy was to a particular kind of pressure. For example, if you believe he did not care in the least about what the Pentagon or State Department or CIA thought, tick the "Immune" box in the **BUREAUCRATIC** column. If you believe he was highly sensitive to domestic political considerations, tick the "Highly susceptible" box in the **DOMESTIC** column. If you believe he felt some pressure to try to recoup the sunk costs of earlier policy, tick the "Somewhat susceptible" box in the **SUNK COSTS** column.

	International	Domestic	Bureaucratic	Personal	Sunk Costs
Immune					
Virtually immune					
Slightly susceptible					
Somewhat susceptible					
Moderately susceptible					
Quite susceptible					
Very susceptible					
Strongly susceptible					
Highly susceptible					
Extremely susceptible					

Cover

White House, WHCA Sound Studio. President Kennedy telephones birthday greetings to former President Harry Truman. Photograph by Cecil Stoughton in the John F. Kennedy Presidential Library and Museum, Boston, MA.

Chapter-Opening Photos

Prologue:
    (top) USIA, May 1968.
    http://www.defenseimagery.mil/imageDownload.action
    ?guid = 384935be6f23e0687c9a171e851860a6b481ee4d.
    (bottom) http://commons.wikimedia.org/wiki/Image:Long_khanh
    _fallen.jpg

Chapter 1:
    (top) http://commons.wikimedia.org/wiki/Image:Hueyassaultviet
    namese1970.jpg
    (bottom) http://www.defenselink.mil/photos/newsphoto.aspx?new
    sphotoid = 9731
    Country outlines added by the authors.

Chapter 2:
    Photos from the Musgrove conference, April 2005, by Nick Toth
    (darkroom@adelphia.net).

Chapter 3:
    (top) Quotes from Document 3-3, in Appendix A.
    (bottom) Quote from Document 3-4, in Appendix A.

Chapter 4:
    (top) Quote from Document 4-1, in Appendix A.
    (bottom) Quote from Document 4-3, in Appendix A.

Chapter 5:
    (top) http://commons.wikimedia.org/wiki/Image:BombVietnam
    1967VC.jpg

(bottom) http://commons.wikimedia.org/wiki/Image:Operation Georgia1966.jpg

Chapter 6:

John F. Kennedy tours Strategic Air Command underground command post at Offutt Air Force base, Omaha, Nebraska, ca. 1955(?). The John F. Kennedy Presidential Library and Museum, Boston, MA.

Epilogue:

(top) The John F. Kennedy Presidential Library and Museum, Boston, MA.

(middle) Image taken from reel #MP865 from the Lyndon Baines Johnson Library and Museum.

(bottom) Getty Images, #57502826

Appendix B: Photos from the Musgrove conference, April 2005, by Nick Toth (darkroom@adelphia.net).

First Photo Essay: The Foreign Policy Education of John F. Kennedy

Page 1:

(top) From the *New York Times*, April 21, 1961.

(bottom) Getty Images, #50563845.

Page 2: Screen captures from *Virtual JFK: Vietnam If Kennedy Had Lived*, a film directed by Koji Masutani; originally from The John F. Kennedy Library Foundation, Boston, MA.

Page 3: Photos from the National Archives and Records Administration (NARA).

Page 4:

(top) Quotes from Document 3-2, in Appendix A.

(bottom) Quote from Document 3-4, in Appendix A.

Page 5: Stills from The John F. Kennedy Presidential Library and Museum, Boston, MA.

Page 6: Screen captures from *Virtual JFK*; originally from The John F. Kennedy Library Foundation, Boston, MA.

Second Photo Essay: Critical Oral History in Action

Page 1: Project logo, designed by Murphy and Murphy.

Page 3 (bottom): Photo from the Musgrove conference, April 2005, by Barbara Elias.

All other photos from the Musgrove conference, April 2005, by Nick Toth (darkroom@adelphia.net).

Third Photo Essay: It Makes a Difference Who Is President

Page 1:

(top) Screen captures from *Virtual JFK*; originally from The John F. Kennedy Library Foundation, Boston, MA.

(bottom) Still from the Lyndon Baines Johnson Library and Museum.

Page 2: From Document 3-1, in Appendix A.

Page 3:

(left) Cropped from a still from The John F. Kennedy Presidential Library and Museum, Boston, MA.

(right) Quotes from Document 5-6, in Appendix A.

Page 4: U.S. Department of Defense photo, http://commons.wikimedia .org/wiki/Image:WhSouthLawn.jpg

Epigraph

1. Kurt Vonnegut, *A Man Without a Country* (New York: Seven Stories Press, 2005), p. 3.

Prologue

1. For a recent, comprehensive U.S.-Vietnamese examination of missed opportunities to avoid escalation to an American war in Vietnam, see Robert S. McNamara, James G. Blight, and Robert K. Brigham, with Thomas J. Biersteker and Col. Herbert Y. Schandler, *Argument Without End: In Search of Answers to the Vietnam Tragedy* (New York: PublicAffairs, 1999). The book addresses a host of what ifs regarding the war, such as the considerable degree to which mutual misperception fueled escalation on both sides from the late 1950s through the mid-1960s, and whether negotiations might have begun much earlier than mid-1968, when talks opened in Paris. The book deals only obliquely, however, with the question of Vietnam if Kennedy had lived, because of the focus throughout on mutual misjudgments by leaders in both Hanoi and Washington. It is clear, however, that the Vietnamese communists did not believe the identity of the American president made much difference regarding the escalation, which they believed at the time was derived from a strong imperialist urge in the U.S. to subdue or even to destroy communism in Southeast Asia, irrespective of who was the U.S. president.

Chapter 1

1. Tim O'Brien, *The Things They Carried* (New York: Penguin, 1990), p. 208.
2. For example, see the following four works, which together largely shaped public opinion throughout the 1960s with regard to JFK's role in the October 1962 Cuban missile crisis: Arthur M. Schlesinger, Jr., *A Thousand Days: John F. Kennedy in the White House* (New York: Ballantine, 1965); Theodore C. Sorensen, *Kennedy* (New York: Harper & Row, 1965); Elie Abel, *The Missile Crisis* (Philadelphia: Lippincott, 1966); and Robert F. Kennedy, *Thirteen Days: A Memoir of the Cuban Missile Crisis* (New York: Norton, 1969). Schlesinger and Soren-

sen served in the Kennedy White House. Abel, an NBC News White House correspondent, was given extraordinary access to JFK and his associates. And of course *Thirteen Days*, written by the president's brother, the attorney general, was phenomenally successful, and has been made into two successful movies, *The Missiles of October* (1971) and *Thirteen Days* (2000). To put the matter in quantitative terms, these four books, which come to just over 2,000 pages of laudatory, sometimes awestruck admiration for their subject, the assassinated president, contain a combined total of *zero* endnotes. They are based entirely on privileged information, which for many years was impossible to verify or refute with reference to any available paper trail. One had to accept what was said or reject it based on little more than intuition, fed by whatever preexisting biases one might have, be they pro-Kennedy or anti-Kennedy.

3. Ronald Reagan (speech, Washington DC, November 11, 1988), American Rhetoric Online Speech Bank, www.americanrhetoric.com/speeches/ronald reaganvietnammemorial.html.

4. Gloria Emerson, *Winners and Losers: Battles, Retreats, Gains, Losses and Ruins from the Vietnam War* (New York: Penguin, 1985), p. vii.

5. Joseph Lelyveld, quoted in Arnold R. Isaacs, *Vietnam Shadows: The War, Its Ghosts, and Its Legacy* (Baltimore: Johns Hopkins University Press, 1997), p. 137.

6. Marilyn B. Young, "The Vietnam Laugh Track," in *Vietnam in Iraq: Tactics, Lessons, Legacies and Ghosts*, ed. John Dumbrell and David Ryan (New York: Routledge, 2007), pp. 31–47, p. 43.

7. Kennedy made the charge on April 6, 2004, in a speech at the Brookings Institution in Washington, DC. For the text and commentary see www.cnn.com/2004/ALLPOLITICS/04/05/kennedy.speech/index.html.

8. The question of civilian casualties in Iraq is controversial. The U.S. government has an incentive to underreport them, and in addition, Iraq is so chaotic on the ground that accuracy is difficult to assess. This is why Les Roberts, a Columbia University epidemiologist, and Gilbert Burnham, codirector of the Center for Refugee and Disaster Response at Johns Hopkins University, have twice gathered a team of investigators (in 2004 and 2006) to estimate how many civilians have died due to the Iraq War. The design of these studies involved a standard cluster approach, used all over the world by the United Nations and other organizations, to estimate civilian mortality. See Les Roberts, Riyadh Lafta, Richard Garfield, Jamal Khudhairi, and Gilbert Burnham, "Mortality before and after the 2003 Invasion of Iraq: Cluster Sample Survey," *The Lancet* 364 (2004): pp. 1857–64 and Gilbert Burnham, Shannon Doocy, Elizabeth Dzeng, Riyadh Lafta, and Les Roberts, "Mortality after the 2003 Invasion of Iraq: A Cross-sectional Cluster Sample Survey," *The Lancet* 368 (2006): pp. 1421–28. The estimate from the first study, covering the period of March 2003 through August

2004, was 98,000 excess Iraqi deaths. The second study looked at the period from March 2003 to July 2006 and estimated more than 650,000 excess Iraqi deaths. As of this writing, April 2008, there had been twenty additional months of war in Iraq after the estimate of 650,000 excess Iraqi deaths.

There are many organizations, both governmental and private, monitoring U.S. military casualties in Iraq. As of April 1, 2008, the death toll is 4,012. For details, see http://icasualties.org/oif/. The site also reports 309 deaths among other coalition forces.

9. See William E. Odom, "Iraq Through the Prism of Vietnam," posted on the March 2006 edition of Nieman Watchdog: www.niemanwatchdog.org/index .cfm?fuseaction = background.view&backgroundid = 0078. See also Robert K. Brigham, *Is Iraq Another Vietnam?* (New York: PublicAffairs, 2006), and Dumbrell and Ryan, eds., *Vietnam in Iraq*. Brigham is an outstanding historian of the Vietnamese perspective on the war, and the strength of his fine book is its careful analysis of the way U.S. blindness toward Vietnam, and toward Iraq, has led to disaster. The Dumbrell and Ryan volume contains essays by many first-rate historians and political scientists. Especially trenchant is the essay by Marilyn Young, "The Vietnam Laugh Track," pp. 31–47.

10. Quoted in John Patrick Diggins, *John Adams* (New York: Times Books, 2003), p. 147.

11. The record and interpretation of that conference is in James G. Blight, Bruce J. Allyn, and David A. Welch, *Cuba on the Brink: Castro, the Missile Crisis and the Soviet Collapse*, 2nd ed. (Lanham, MD: Rowman & Littlefield, 2002), first edition published in 1993.

12. We began in the mid-1980s by reexamining the Cuban missile crisis, the most dangerous moment of the Cold War, by assembling Americans, Russians, and Cubans over a period of years and asking them to cross-question one another about the origins, conduct, danger, and meaning of that epochal confrontation we call the Cuban missile crisis. See for example James G. Blight, *The Shattered Crystal Ball: Fear and Learning in the Cuban Missile Crisis* (Lanham, MD: Rowman & Littlefield, 1989); James G. Blight and David A. Welch, *On the Brink: Americans and Soviets Reexamine the Cuban Missile Crisis* (New York: Hill and Wang, 1990); Blight, Allyn, and Welch, *Cuba on the Brink*; James G. Blight and David A. Welch, eds., *Intelligence and the Cuban Missile Crisis* (London: Cass, 1998); and James G. Blight and Philip Brenner, *Sad and Luminous Days: Cuba's Struggle with the Superpowers After the Missile Crisis* (Lanham, MD: Rowman & Littlefield, 2002). In 1988–1989, we turned our attention to the Berlin Wall crisis of the summer and fall of 1961 in an effort to explore, in a comparative way, the nuclear danger posed by the missile crisis and the Berlin crisis. We ran a faculty seminar at Harvard's Kennedy School of Government, to which we invited many significant players in the events of 1961, including American, Soviet,

and German military and civilian officials. In the early 1990s, we moved our focus even further backward in time from the missile crisis to the failed Bay of Pigs invasion of April 1961. See James G. Blight and Peter Kornbluh, *Politics of Illusion: The Bay of Pigs Invasion Reexamined* (Boulder, CO: Lynne Rienner, 1998). Our inquiries into the missile crisis and the Bay of Pigs invasion continued all through the 1990s and into the twenty-first century, culminating in two conferences in Havana, Cuba, in March 2001 (on the Bay of Pigs) and in October 2002 (on the missile crisis). Finally, between 1995 and 1999 we tackled the most disastrous and controversial episode in the history of U.S. foreign policy, the war in Vietnam. See McNamara et al., *Argument Without End*. The research on the war in Vietnam, however, was not concerned primarily with JFK's decision making, but rather was focused on the perception of the war by the government in Hanoi.

13. Our work has been carried out within a large international network of like-minded researchers. There are two principal intellectual "clearinghouses" for information of every sort, to which we are hugely indebted: the National Security Archive at George Washington University and the Cold War International History Project at the Woodrow Wilson Center for Scholars. To gain access to their vast, well-organized collections of declassified documents, visit their helpful websites at www.gwu.edu/~nsarchiv/ and www.wilsoncenter.org/index.cfm?fuseaction= topics.home&topic_id=1409.

14. This is the title of Jonathan Schell's 1982 book, which synthesized in one small volume the fears and hopes of those concerned with nuclear danger during the first Reagan administration. The book was reissued in 2000 by Stanford University Press in a single volume along with Schell's 1984 book, *The Abolition*, in which the author presents his plan for implementing the elimination of the nuclear threat.

15. Many recently published works in addition to our own might profitably be consulted for background on Kennedy and what he learned from his foreign policy crises. Among the best recent volumes are these: David Talbot, *Brothers: The Hidden History of the Kennedy Years* (New York: Free Press, 2007), pp. 1–234; Robert Dallek, *An Unfinished Life: John F. Kennedy 1917–1963* (Boston: Little, Brown, 2003); and especially Lawrence Freedman, *Kennedy's Wars: Berlin, Cuba, Laos, and Vietnam* (New York: Oxford University Press, 2000). The title of Freedman's book is ironical, whether intended or not, because of course each of "Kennedy's wars" dealt with by the author was in fact a war avoided, not a war fought—at least by Kennedy. The title notwithstanding, Freedman's account is succinct, well argued, and highly illuminating.

16. See Schlesinger, *A Thousand Days*, p. 104. Schlesinger notes that among Kennedy's favorite books was Duff Cooper's biography of Talleyrand.

17. Gordon Wood, "History Lessons," *New York Review of Books*, March 29, 1984, p. 8.

18. Transcript of a secret tape recording of a meeting of JFK's Executive Committee of the National Security Council, 4:00 p.m. Saturday, October 27, 1962. In Ernest R. May and Philip D. Zelikow, eds., *The Kennedy Tapes: Inside the White House during the Cuban Missile Crisis* (Cambridge, MA: Harvard University Press, 1997), p. 602.

19. Ibid., pp. 602–3.

20. Dean Rusk, the one adviser who was privy to JFK's fallback plan to end the missile crisis with a public trade of missiles, told us in a May 1987 interview that he did not believe JFK had even informed his brother, Attorney General Robert Kennedy, of the fallback plan, though Rusk admitted he couldn't be sure that the attorney general was, like all the others, in the dark. See James G. Blight, Joseph S. Nye, Jr., and David A. Welch, "The Cuban Missile Crisis Revisited." *Foreign Affairs* 66, no. 1 (Fall 1987), pp. 170–88; and Blight and Welch, *On the Brink*, pp. 83–84 and 173–74.

21. Bundy's transcription of the tapes of the meetings of October 27, 1962, was the vehicle by which those discussions were first made available to the public. See McGeorge Bundy and James G. Blight, "October 27, 1962: Transcripts of the Meetings of the ExComm," *International Security* 12, no. 3 (Winter 1987–1988), pp. 30–92; and David A. Welch and James G. Blight, "The Eleventh Hour of the Cuban Missile Crisis: An Introduction to the ExComm Transcripts," *International Security* 12, no. 3 (Winter 1987–1988), pp. 5–29.

22. The phrase "America's longest war" comes from the pioneering U.S. historian of the war in Vietnam, George C. Herring, *America's Longest War: The United States and Vietnam, 1950–1975*, 4th ed. (New York: McGraw-Hill, 2001), first published 1979.

23. The closest we have come to such an effort ourselves may be found in McNamara et al., *Argument Without End*. This book presents and interprets our findings regarding the forces—from the points of view of both Washington and Hanoi—driving the escalation of the war from a relatively small and isolated civil conflict during JFK's presidency to the catastrophic war it became. Especially relevant is chapter 5, "Escalation," pp. 151–217, and the endnotes to the chapter.

24. Scholars tend to formulate the debate about Kennedy, Johnson, and Vietnam this way, especially since the publication of a 1997 book that is devoted to this issue (the continuity thesis versus the discontinuity thesis). That is, did LBJ continue JFK's policy in Vietnam, or did his decisions mark a decisive break with JFK's approach? See Lloyd C. Gardner and Ted Gittinger, eds., *Vietnam: The Early Decisions* (Austin: University of Texas Press, 1997). Especially relevant and thought-provoking are the essays by William Conrad Gibbons, a strong proponent of the view that LBJ did what JFK would have done (gone to war in Vietnam); John M. Newman, who argues with equal forcefulness that LBJ reversed JFK's basic policy of not escalating the conflict in Vietnam to an American war; and Larry Berman, who takes a position somewhere in between those of Gibbons and

Newman, but in the end seems to endorse Gibbons's position. These issues are taken up in greater detail in chapter 6 of this book.

25. On the method of critical oral history, the best general source is James G. Blight and janet M. Lang, *The Fog of War: Lessons From the Life of Robert S. McNamara* (Lanham, MD: Rowman & Littlefield, 2005), especially the prologue, pp. 1–25. The endnotes to the prologue contain dozens of references to books and articles deriving from the authors' experience with critical oral history over more than two decades.

26. Quoted in Blight, *The Shattered Crystal Ball*, p. 55.

27. Pieter Geyl, *Debates With Historians* (Cleveland: Meridian, 1958). See also McNamara et al., *Argument Without End*.

28. Jack Beatty, "JFK and the Might-Have-Beens," *Boston Globe*, November 1, 1987, p. A27.

29. Diane Kunz, "Camelot Continued: What if John F. Kennedy Had Lived?" in *Virtual History: Alternatives and Counterfactuals*, ed. Niall Ferguson (New York: Basic Books, 1997), pp. 368–91, quote from pp. 368–69. A large, polemical literature exists dedicated to defending one side or the other of the "Camelot" and "anti-Camelot" views of Vietnam if Kennedy had lived. The controversy began immediately following Kennedy's assassination when Johnson assumed office. But it was given a huge burst of new energy by the appearance of Oliver Stone's 1991 feature film, *JFK*, which alleges that JFK was assassinated by some nefarious combination of interests who were fed up with his "appeasement" of the communists in Cuba, but especially in Vietnam. Stone even indulges somewhat obliquely in the paranoid fantasy that LBJ himself may have been in cahoots with the dark elements who killed JFK: CIA operatives, Cuban exiles, and members of organized crime syndicates. Shortly thereafter, the linguist and political commentator Noam Chomsky published *Rethinking Camelot: JFK, the Vietnam War, and U.S. Political Culture* (Boston: South End Press, 1993), a small book with large ambitions and Olympian disdain for Stone and his ilk. Chomsky dismisses Kennedy, far from being the victim of a nefarious conspiracy impatient to go to war in Vietnam, as "the man who escalated the war [in Vietnam] from terror to aggression" (36). See chapters 5 and 6 of this book, where this controversy is taken up in more detail, and the relevant references to sources in the endnotes.

30. Ferguson, ed., *Virtual History*, pp. 1–90.

Chapter 2

1. Lady Bird Johnson quoted in Peter S. Cannellos, "Unlike LBJ, Bush Seems Free of War Doubts," *Boston Globe*, August 28, 2007, p. A2.

2. Ibid. Italics in original.

3. Bill Moyers, "Bill Moyers Essay: Listening to History," The Moyers Blog,

June 1, 2007, www.pbs.org/moyers/journal/blog/2007/06/bill_moyers_essay_
listening_to_1.html.

4. Ibid.

5. See his website for further details: www.utexas.edu/lbj/faculty/galbraith
.html.

6. Robert S. McNamara, quoted in James K. Galbraith, "McNamara's War
In Retrospect," *Texas Observer*, June 30, 1995. Reprinted in an appendix to the
paperback edition of Robert S. McNamara, *In Retrospect: The Tragedy and Lessons of Vietnam* (New York: Vintage, 1996), pp. 443–47.

7. See chapter 4 for references and details.

8. The line is from Act III. See www.sff.net/people/mberry/rosen.htp.

Chapter 3

1. McNamara, *In Retrospect*.

2. See *Foreign Relations of the United States, 1961–1963 (Vietnam)* (Washington, DC: U.S. Government Printing Office), 1:477–522. See also the illuminating discussion of the Taylor mission and Taylor-Rostow Report in Mike Gravel,
*The Pentagon Papers: The Defense Department History of United States Decision-
making on Vietnam* (Boston: Beacon Press, 1971), 2:73–120.

3. For a detailed analysis of the lead-up to the November 15 National Security Council meeting, and an insightful reading of the record of what happened,
see David Kaiser, *American Tragedy: Kennedy, Johnson, and the Origins of the
Vietnam War* (Cambridge, MA: Harvard University Press, 2000), pp.113–21.

4. General Maxwell D. Taylor, quoted in Richard Parker, *John Kenneth Galbraith: His Life, His Politics, His Economics* (New York: Farrar, Straus & Giroux,
2005), p. 369. Taylor's remark was made in a memorandum for the record on
November 6, 1961. Parker reports that when JFK received the Taylor-Rostow
Report, he became fed up with "near-uniform pressure from his national security
advisers, who were arguing that anything less than a major engagement in Vietnam would risk disastrous consequences" (p. 369). Kennedy's tactic in dealing
with this pressure, according to Parker, was to begin leaking to the press his
opposition to sending troops to South Vietnam. The information was attributed
to the usual "senior White House officials," though this time the leaker was the
president himself. See, as an example of the stories derived from Kennedy's leak
to the press, E. W. Kenworthy, "President Is Cool on Asia Troop Aid," *New York
Times*, November 4, 1961, p. 1.

5. On September 25, 1963, for example, Kennedy told newsman Walter
Cronkite of CBS: "In the final analysis it is the people and government [of South
Vietnam] itself who have to win or lose this struggle. All we can do is help . . ."
Yet Kennedy still concluded by saying: "But I don't agree with those who say we
should withdraw. That would be a great mistake." See John F. Kennedy, interview

with Walter Cronkite of CBS Television News, September 25, 1963. Quoted in Gravel, *Pentagon Papers*, 2:827.

6. The Rostow memorandum, excerpted in **Document 3-2**, contains many of Rostow's trademark assertions, such as: communists respond only to toughness, never to conciliation; the U.S. can and should do as it wishes, more or less regardless of the communist response, dealing with U.S. decisions being their problem, not an American problem; and the communists mean to take over Vietnam and all of Southeast Asia, and only American military force can prevent this from happening. For an extended discussion of the role of Walt Rostow in the Johnson administration, see chapter 5.

7. Hughes refers to the minutes of the November 15, 1961 meeting of Kennedy's National Security Council, recorded by Colonel Howard Burris, Johnson's military attaché. It is also possible to interpret Rusk's position not as a call to combat in South Vietnam, but as a call to a show of force (such as the U.S. mounted in Berlin), which, if sufficiently threatening to the communists, might actually inhibit them from taking on the Americans altogether. This is how JFK seems to interpret Rusk, as given in the minutes, when he responds that the Berlin situation is clear-cut, whereas Vietnam is a murky mess, with the adversary not amenable to deterrence by a massive show of force.

8. Roger Hilsman, assistant secretary of state for Intelligence and Research, to Secretary of State Dean Rusk, marked "Top Secret," November 16, 1961. Vietnam Documentation Project, National Security Archive. In addition to the U.S. combat troops, Hilsman gives a long laundry list of political and military requirements in South Vietnam.

9. To Rostow, the U.S. problem in Vietnam could be summarized in one word: *infiltration*. Time and again, Rostow emphasizes that those who oppose deploying U.S. combat troops in Vietnam mistakenly believe the problem is an insurgency. No, says Rostow. The problem is that the North Vietnamese communists are invading the South and are committing aggression against the South, and the U.S. is treaty-bound to come to the aid of the Saigon government. JFK never bought this argument, in 1961 or later. LBJ, on the other hand, was much impressed by it. After he named Rostow his national security adviser in early 1966, Johnson's own public statements became infused with Rostow's emphasis on cross-border aggression.

10. General Lyman Lemnitzer, chairman of the Joint Chiefs of Staff, to Secretary of Defense Robert McNamara, January 13, 1962, in Gravel, *Pentagon Papers*, 2:663–64. In a cover memo for Kennedy dated January 27, McNamara gives evidence that he understands his boss's views better than Lemnitzer does. McNamara writes that he is "not prepared to endorse" the recommendations of the Chiefs. See McNamara, "Memorandum for the President," January 27, 1962, in ibid., 2:662.

11. Forrestal was an assistant for Southeast Asia to National Security Adviser

McGeorge Bundy. See chapter 4 of this book for a discussion of the coup against Diem and Nhu.

12. See James K. Galbraith, "Exit Strategy: In 1963, JFK Ordered a Complete Withdrawal from Vietnam," *Boston Review*, November 24, 2003. Thomas Hughes is paraphrasing Galbraith's endnote 6, which reads: "My father has said many times that Kennedy sent him to Vietnam 'because he knew I did not have an open mind.'" See also Parker, *John Kenneth Galbraith*, pp. 372–77, for an account of Kennedy's use of Galbraith to counter "insubordination" in the State Department and elsewhere.

13. See John M. Newman, *JFK and Vietnam: Deception, Intrigue, and the Struggle for Power* (New York: Warner Books, 1992). For example, in October–November 1961, Newman argues, General Maxwell Taylor (who favored the introduction of U.S. combat troops into South Vietnam) attempted to deceive Kennedy by "sneaking" a few thousand into the country for "flood relief," while Kennedy, in effect, deceived his hawkish advisers by refusing to absolutely rule out the introduction of troops even though, Newman believes, Kennedy had already decided against it (pp. 130–47). See also Newman, "The Kennedy-Johnson Transition: The Case for Policy Reversal," in *Vietnam: The Early Decisions*, Gardner and Gittinger, pp. 158–76.

14. This may have been the understatement of the entire Musgrove conference. The Chiefs hated McNamara, and were even suspicious of Taylor, who had been imposed on them by JFK following the Bay of Pigs fiasco. For LeMay's view, see Blight and Lang, *Fog of War*. According to LeMay, "We started off trying to talk to him [McNamara]. It was just like talking to a brick wall. We got nowhere. Finally, it was just a waste of time and effort. We would state opinions when we had a chance. That was all . . . We in the military felt we were not in the decision-making process" (p. 83). During the Kennedy administration, it was in fact JFK's objective to keep LeMay and his colleagues, as far as possible, out of the loop. McNamara was his chief instrument of implementation for keeping the generals and admirals under control.

15. See Herbert Y. Schandler, *The Unmaking of a President: Lyndon Johnson and Vietnam* (Princeton, NJ: Princeton University Press, 1977); see also Schandler, "U.S. Military Victory in Vietnam: A Dangerous Illusion?" in McNamara et al., *Argument Without End*, pp. 313–71.

16. During World War II, Chester Cooper was a member of the OSS (Office of Strategic Services), the forerunner of the CIA. He served as a commando in China, operating behind Japanese lines. McNamara's own experience in the war was given prominence in the Academy Award–winning documentary film by Errol Morris, *The Fog of War: Eleven Lessons From the Life of Robert McNamara*. The film won the 2004 Oscar for Best Documentary Feature. McNamara's World War II service is also examined in some detail in Blight and Lang, *Fog of War*, pp. 112–37.

17. See, for example, the long conversation between Johnson and Senator Richard Russell, May 27, 1964, in *Taking Charge: The Johnson White House Tapes, 1963–1964*, ed. Michael R. Beschloss (New York: Simon & Schuster, 1997), pp. 363–70.

18. Colonel Howard Burris to Johnson, November 15, 1961, Lyndon Baines Johnson Library, Vice President Security File, Box No. 4. The Vietnam Documentation Project at the National Security Archive also has a copy. Burris endeavors to explain, in more detail than was perhaps warranted or desired by Johnson, how he (Burris) had tried (unsuccessfully) to inform LBJ of the National Security Council meeting. Ironically, Johnson's absence from the meeting may have caused Burris to take unusually copious notes, which turn out to be posterity's only record of that pivotal meeting.

19. Horace "Buzz" Busby was primarily a speechwriter for Johnson. He was a longtime friend of Johnson's from Texas.

20. Johnson not only was aware of these issues, as Prados points out, according to McGeorge Bundy, LBJ had a firm position on the issue of sending combat troops to South Vietnam. See **Document 3-3**, Bundy's "Memorandum for the President," November 15, 1961, where Bundy writes: "This conclusion [to commit *limited* U.S. combat units, if necessary for *military* purposes (not for morale)] is, I believe, the inner conviction of your Vice President . . ."

21. The further into the Vietnam quagmire LBJ sank, the more retrospectively significant became his opposition to the coup against Diem. For example, in a telephone conversation with Minnesota Senator (and future rival of Johnson's for the presidential nomination in 1968) Eugene McCarthy, LBJ plays the Diem card in an effort to convince McCarthy that JFK and his people are responsible for the mess in Vietnam. McCarthy says little in the conversation, but obviously he remained unimpressed by Johnson's credentials as a peace president in 1966 or a peace candidate in 1968. To listen to the conversation, accompanied by scrolling text, visit the Presidential Recordings Project at the Miller Center, University of Virginia, available online at http://tapes.millercenter.virginia.edu/clips/1966_0201_lbj_mccarthy_vietnam.html.

22. The conversation between Johnson and McNamara excerpted in **Document 5-2** occurred on February 20, 1964. In the film *The Fog of War* this conversation is central to the view, implicit in the film, that LBJ in effect "tames" McNamara in early 1964, as the defense secretary shifts nimbly (but tragically) from being an advocate of withdrawal to an advocate of escalation. In another telephone conversation on March 2, 1964, McNamara gamely attempts to explain to his new boss that the signs coming from Vietnam are all bad and increasingly confusing, and that the president ought therefore to be more cautious in making public threats at the North Vietnamese, whom LBJ has just stated publicly "are playing a deeply dangerous game." McNamara makes no headway with LBJ in this conversation either. Gradually, his resistance to LBJ's views diminishes. In *Taking Charge*, ed. Beschloss, pp. 256–60.

23. ARVN refers to the Army of the Republic of Vietnam—the U.S.-backed, -trained, and -supplied South Vietnamese Army.

24. See, for example, the State Department's estimate, from INR, dealing with the period from January 1961 to February 1962, just as the Kennedy administration was settling into office, found in W. Dean Howells, Dorothy Avery, and Fred Greene, *Vietnam 1961–1968 as Interpreted in INR's Production*, released May 2, 2004, part 1, "The Problem Confronted," available at www.gwu.edu/~nsarchiv/NSAEBB/NSAEBB121/index.htm. See also the essays that accompanied the release of the study—sometimes called the State Department's own "Pentagon Papers"—by two of the Musgrove conference participants, Thomas Hughes and John Prados.

25. The ultimatum to which Naftali refers was to conclude a separate peace with the German Democratic Republic (GDR) turning Berlin over to East Germany within six months unless the three Western powers—the U.S., Britain, and France—agreed to withdraw. A bilateral Soviet-GDR treaty would have threatened the West's access rights to Berlin and could have triggered a crisis and war.

26. Roswell Gilpatric, the deputy secretary of defense (speech to the Business Council, Hot Springs, VA, October 21, 1961). The speech was drafted by a young Pentagon strategist, Daniel Ellsberg, later to become famous for leaking the Pentagon Papers to the press during the Nixon administration. Gilpatric recited, in detail, just how powerful the U.S. nuclear force actually was, relative to the much smaller and much less accurate Soviet arsenal. See Michael Beschloss, *The Crisis Years: Kennedy and Khrushchev, 1960–1963* (New York: HarperCollins, 1991), pp. 329–32.

27. Eugene Staley led a delegation to Saigon as a follow-up to LBJ's May 1961 fact-finding trip. The Staley Committee made many economic recommendations but, as Arthur Schlesinger, Jr., writes, "it seemed impossible to stop the disintegration" in Saigon. See Schlesinger, *A Thousand Days*, p. 503.

28. See Newman, *JFK and Vietnam*, pp. 2–23. See especially Newman's account of the Joint Chiefs of Staff's additions to the April 27, 1961, National Security Council report, "A Laos Annex for the Vietnam Report," pp. 19–20. See also Gravel, *Pentagon Papers*, 2:40–41 for the context and background of Newman's remarks.

29. John Kenneth Galbraith (Kennedy's ambassador to India), cable to John F. Kennedy, November 21, 1961, in *John Kenneth Galbraith's Letters to Kennedy*, ed. James Goodman (Cambridge, MA: Harvard University Press, 1998), p. 93. Galbraith had stopped off in Saigon and Bangkok on his way back to New Delhi from Washington, DC. This cable, marked "Top Secret/President's Eyes Only," was not sent via regular State Department channels (which were not trusted either by Galbraith or by Kennedy), but through a back channel, CIA director John McCone, whose instructions were to deliver it directly to JFK.

30. See Parker, *John Kenneth Galbraith*, pp. 372–77.

31. See Gareth Porter, *Perils of Dominance: Imbalance of Power and the Road to War in Vietnam* (Berkeley: University of California Press, 2005), especially chapter 5, "Kennedy's Struggle With the National Security Bureaucracy," pp. 141–79.

32. Joseph Alsop was a hard-line, anti-communist, Washington columnist. See Richard Reeves, *President Kennedy: Profile of Power* (New York: Simon & Schuster, 1993), pp. 178–79, for examples of Alsop's glorification of what he supposed (wrongly) to be Kennedy's willingness to risk a nuclear exchange with the USSR in the wake of the Vienna summit in June 1961.

33. Khrushchev's speech was given two weeks before Kennedy's January 20, 1961, inaugural. The speech was only one of many public statements of Khrushchev's nascent enthusiasm for "wars of national liberation," which he began embracing publicly in late 1960. In the speech referred to by Hughes, Khrushchev said:

> Liberation wars will continue to exist as long as imperialism exists, as long as colonialism exists. These are revolutionary wars. Such wars are not only admissible but inevitable, since the colonialists do not grant independence voluntarily . . .
>
> What is the attitude of Marxists toward such uprisings? A most positive one.

Cited in James A. Nathan and James K. Oliver, *United States Foreign Policy and World Order*, 2nd ed. (Boston: Little-Brown, 1981), p. 254.

34. Barbara Tuchman, *The Guns of August* (New York: Bantam, 1980). When it was first published in 1962, JFK gave copies of it to all the members of his senior national security team. For reactions of those who received copies from JFK see, for example, Robert F. Kennedy, *Thirteen Days*. According to RFK, the president told him during the missile crisis that he was committed to preventing a scenario he called "the missiles of October," a reference to the central theme of *The Guns of August*: that war often starts due to miscalculation and the inflexibility of leaders who must respond in the midst of crises. See also Robert McNamara's recollection of Kennedy's enthusiasm for the book in his memoir *In Retrospect*, p. 96.

35. These phrases ("Let us never negotiate out of fear. But let us never fear to negotiate") are from Kennedy's inaugural address, January 20, 1961. Published in *Public Papers of the President, 1961* (Washington, DC: U.S. Government Printing Office, 1962), p. 2.

36. Roger Hilsman, then assistant secretary of state for INR, recalled in his memoir the surreal and frightening discussions about Laos in February 1961, less than a month after Kennedy became president. Over and over again, he recalled, the officials could come to no plausible scenario other than a "dead end of hideous war or ignominious and far-reaching defeat." Hilsman, *To Move a Nation: The Politics of Foreign Policy in the Administration of John F. Kennedy* (New York: Doubleday, 1967), p. 130.

37. Presidential Special Counsel and speechwriter Theodore C. Sorensen has written that in September 1961, JFK told him, "Thank God the Bay of Pigs happened when it did. Otherwise we'd be in Laos by now—and that would be a hundred times worse." Sorensen, *Kennedy*, p. 644.

38. CORONA was a project designed to provide a more accurate assessment of Soviet nuclear capabilities via spy satellites. The CIA commissioned a history of the project, which was written in 1973 but not published until 1995, in Kevin C. Ruffner, ed., *CORONA: America's First Satellite Program* (Washington, DC: Center for the Study of Intelligence, 1995).

39. McNamara, memorandum to JFK, November 8, 1961, point 2 [**Document 3-1**].

40. Transcript by the Presidential Recordings Program at the Miller Center, University of Virginia, of a White House conversation on Wednesday, October 2, 1963, 6:05–6:30 p.m. It seems clear that Bundy's understanding of JFK's position is that the president wants to "win the war." Yet it is clear from the subsequent conversation over the wording of a statement to be released to the press that McNamara has no such "understanding." There are a number of these apparent anomalies in the Vietnam-related Kennedy transcripts.

41. Galbraith to Kennedy, November 21, 1961, in *John Kenneth Galbraith's Letters to JFK*, ed. Goodman, p. 91.

42. It is worth noting an underlying assumption in James Hershberg's position, which is that JFK would have faced the same situation LBJ faced in February 1965, when crucial decisions were made that led rapidly to the Americanization of the war in Vietnam. Hershberg argues that because LBJ faced pressure to escalate the war—pressure of a certain kind and magnitude, and in response to given events—Kennedy would also have faced the same situation. But it is not clear to us that Kennedy would have made the same decisions made by Johnson between November 22, 1963, and February 1965, and thus it is also far from clear that Kennedy would have faced the situation confronting Johnson by early 1965. A key question is the extent to which the situation faced by LBJ was derived from his own decisions versus those made by Kennedy. See chapter 6 for more on this.

43. See Robert Buzzanco, *Masters of War: Military Dissent & Politics in the Vietnam Era* (New York: Cambridge University Press, 1996), especially pp. 125–28 on the U.S. military's surge of optimism and enthusiasm for Americanizing the war in January 1962.

44. Kennedy met Nikita Khrushchev on June 4 at a summit conference in Vienna, Austria.

45. A major new covert action program aimed at overthrowing the Cuban government was developed during a meeting at the White House on November 4, 1961. The new program, codename Operation MONGOOSE, was to be run by counterinsurgency specialist General Edward Lansdale. A high-level interagency

group called the Special Group—Augmented (SGA) was created for the sole purpose of overseeing MONGOOSE. A memorandum formally establishing MONGOOSE was signed by Kennedy on November 30, 1961. See Blight and Kornbluh, eds., *Politics of Illusion*, especially chapter 5, "Operation MONGOOSE and the Fate of the Resistance," pp. 107–32. The Kennedy brothers seemed to have assumed that an operation like MONGOOSE, which did very little damage to Cuba and its revolutionary government, could hardly have created much of a stir on the island. But if this is what they believed, they were wrong. The Bay of Pigs invasion—along with Operation MONGOOSE, another manifest failure involving Cuban exiles in paramilitary roles—in fact spurred the Cubans to seek assistance from Moscow. Thus what we know as the Cuban missile crisis began to unfold, already, in 1961, as Khrushchev and his Kremlin colleagues debated how to come to the aid of Fidel Castro and his Cuban Revolution. For the Cuban perspective on these events, see the fascinating account of former Cuban chief of counterintelligence, General Fabian Escalante, *Executive Action: 634 Ways to Kill Fidel Castro* (Melbourne, Australia: Ocean Press, 2006). The title of Escalante's epilogue, "Chronology of Crimes," reveals in one telling phrase the official Cuban view of MONGOOSE and similar programs.

46. On June 11, 1963, a Buddhist monk, Quang Duc, burned himself to death in the middle of an intersection in downtown Saigon to protest the policies of the U.S.-backed government of President Ngo Dinh Diem. Other self-immolations followed. The response of Diem's regime was to resort to ever more desperate and brutal efforts to suppress the Buddhist activists. For Kennedy, the sense of political crisis derived in large part from the embarrassment of having such a ruthless and brutal regime as a dependent of the U.S. These events are discussed at length in chapter 4.

47. This is a paraphrase from Daniel Ellsberg, *Secrets: A Memoir of Vietnam and the Pentagon Papers* (New York: Viking Penguin, 2002), p. 196. See pp. 193–97 for Ellsberg's perspective on the November 1961 decisions.

48. See, for example, David G. Marr, "The Rise and Fall of 'Counterinsurgency': 1961–1964," in *Vietnam and America: The Most Comprehensive, Documented History of the Vietnam War*, revised and enlarged 2nd ed., ed. Marvin E. Gettleman, Jane Franklin, Marilyn B. Young, and H. Bruce Franklin (New York: Grove Press, 1995), pp. 205–15. Marr, a U.S. Marine intelligence officer during the war in Vietnam, later became an eminent historian of Vietnamese nationalism.

49. Frances FitzGerald refers to Neil Sheehan, *A Bright Shining Lie: John Paul Vann and America in Vietnam* (New York: Random House, 1988) and David Halberstam, *The Best and the Brightest* (New York: Random House, 1972).

50. Marr, "Rise and Fall of Counterinsurgency."

51. For a more detailed account of the interplay between Kennedy and his

advisers during October and November 1961 on the question of introducing U.S. combat troops in Vietnam, see Dallek, *An Unfinished Life*, pp. 443–56. Dallek repeatedly highlights Kennedy's skepticism, citing, for example, General Maxwell Taylor's notes that Kennedy "is instinctively against introduction of U.S. forces" (p. 450) and Assistant Secretary of Sate for East Asia William Bundy's belief that "the thrust of the President's thinking was clear—sending organized forces was a step so grave that it should be avoided if this was humanly possible" (p. 452).

52. Buzzanco, *Masters of War*, p. 111.

53. Freedman, *Kennedy's Wars*, pp. 477–78

54. See Goodman, *Letters of John Kenneth Galbraith to Kennedy*, especially Galbraith to Kennedy on November 21 and 28, 1961, and April 4 and 5, 1962.

55. This is a paraphrase of a portion of Kennedy's speech: "We cannot, as a free nation, compete with our adversaries in tactics of terror, assassinations, false promises, counterfeit mobs and crises" (address at the University of Washington's 100th Anniversary Program, Seattle, WA, November 16, 1961).

56. One of the most enigmatical figures who reported on the war in Vietnam was the French journalist and scholar Bernard B. Fall. He was French and, following World War II, Fall had covered the so-called First Indochina War between the French and Ho Chi Minh's Vietminh forces. Fall married an American woman and settled into Washington in the late 1950s while continuing to report on the conflict in Vietnam, this time involving the Americans and the communist forces. In 1961, Fall published a classic of comparative journalism, *Street Without Joy* (New York: Stackpole, 1961). The "street" of the title is the infamous Highway 1, north of Hue in the northern extremity of South Vietnam. Fall was killed on the "street without joy" by a mine in 1967 while reporting on the war. McGeorge Bundy began reading Fall's *Street Without Joy* when it was first published in 1961, with the objective of avoiding a repeat of the mistakes made by the French in Vietnam. Fall's book was explicit: neither the French nor the Americans understood revolutionary war—a war of total commitment—fought by the Vietnamese communists, both North and South. Because of this, Fall believed the outcome of the "Second Indochina War" (the American war) would be no different than the first, even though the U.S. was vastly more powerful militarily than the French. Bundy rejected Fall's analysis. Even in 1966, at the time of his resignation from the Johnson administration, he still felt the comparison with the French was inappropriate. Bundy's response was roughly that whereas the French were incompetent, Americans were not. According to Bundy, "There has been no serious proof of French political effectiveness since 1919," quoted in Kai Bird, *The Color of Truth: McGeorge Bundy and William Bundy: Brothers in Arms* (New York: Simon & Schuster, 1998), p. 18. See also pp. 203–4.

57. See Chester L. Cooper, *The Lost Crusade: America in Vietnam* (New York: Dodd, Mead, 1970), chapter 9, "Death of a Mandarin," for an account of Cooper's meetings with Diem and Nhu. Cooper, with a fine sense of the absurd, pro-

vides a rare personal view, in detail, of the utter strangeness of dealing with the Ngo brothers. See also Cooper, *In the Shadows of History: 50 Years Behind the Scenes of Cold War Diplomacy* (Amherst, NY: Prometheus Books, 2005), pp. 210–12.

Chapter 4

1. See Hope Harrison, *Driving the Soviets Up the Wall: Soviet–East German Relations, 1953–1961* (Princeton, NJ: Princeton, 2003) and the older but engagingly written book by journalist Norman Gelb, *The Berlin Wall: Kennedy, Khrushchev, and a Showdown in the Heart of Europe* (New York: Crown, 1987).

2. See Francis X. Winters, *The Year of the Hare: America in Vietnam, January 25, 1963–February 15, 1964* (Athens: University of Georgia Press, 1997) and Ellen J. Hammer, *A Death in November: America in Vietnam, 1963* (New York: Dutton, 1987).

3. General Maxwell D. Taylor, chairman of the Joint Chiefs of Staff.

4. JFK's press secretary was Pierre Salinger.

5. The Military Assistance Command, Vietnam, or MACV, divided South Vietnam into four "corps," or areas of responsibility. At this time, the insurgents of the NLF, also know as "Vietcong," were especially strong in IV Corps, the extreme south, including the rice-growing regions in the Mekong Delta.

6. This issue, whether to state publicly a probable date for the completion of the projected U.S. withdrawal from South Vietnam, was highly controversial within the Kennedy administration. It appears that committing to such a date publicly was opposed not only by McGeorge Bundy, but by almost all of JFK's senior national security advisers, other than McNamara, possibly Taylor, and JFK himself. See McNamara, *In Retrospect*, pp. 78–81. In the DVD extras to the Errol Morris film *The Fog of War*, McNamara says that he was determined to obtain a public announcement of the withdrawal in order to lock it in, so as to make it relatively invulnerable to the maneuvering of the many who did not want to set a date. Most of these advisers, according to McNamara, objected to the very idea of planning to withdraw from South Vietnam.

7. The Cessna L-19 Bird Dog was a light, two-seat aircraft used by the U.S. Army and Marines for scouting and low-level reconnaissance.

8. Major General Tran Van Don was chief of staff of the South Vietnamese Army.

9. Although the editors of the transcript list the speaker as unidentified, we believe this is McNamara speaking. He reliably says *Arabic* and *Roman* aloud when reviewing a draft memorandum that uses both forms of organization.

10. See Parker, *John Kenneth Galbraith*, especially pp. 372–77 on Galbraith's contribution to Kennedy's evolving views on Vietnam, and 416–23 on Galbraith's

eventual estrangement from Johnson on the issue as Galbraith evolved into a highly visible and trenchant critic of Johnson's handling of the war.

11. *SecDef* refers to the Secretary of Defense, Robert McNamara. SecDef meetings were regular gatherings of civilian Defense Department officials and uniformed service officers held in Honolulu, at the headquarters of the Commander of the Pacific Fleet (CINCPAC).

12. General Paul D. Harkins was commander of the U.S. Military Assistance Advisory Group (MAAG) in South Vietnam from 1962–1964.

13. ARVN: the South Vietnamese army. ARVN was the acronym for the Army of the Republic of Vietnam.

14. MAAG, the Military Assistance and Advisory Group, was the forerunner in Saigon of MACV, the Military Assistance Group, Vietnam.

15. See Robert K. Brigham, *ARVN: Life and Death in the South Vietnamese Army* (Lawrence: University of Kansas Press, 2006).

16. See James Galbraith's citation of the Taylor memorandum, which he read into the transcript of the conference in his opening provocation in the previous section of this chapter.

17. "The President's News Conference of April 21, 1961," in *Public Papers of the Presidents, 1961*, pp. 307–15, pp. 312–13. On the Bay of Pigs fiasco as viewed from a number of diverse perspectives within the U.S. government and Cuban exile community, see Blight and Kornbluh, eds., *Politics of Illusion*.

18. See Fredrik Logevall, *Choosing War: The Lost Chance for Peace and the Escalation of War in Vietnam* (Berkeley: University of California Press, 1999), especially pp. 1–16 on de Gaulle's August 29, 1963, statement. Coming from an ostensible ally, it was a hard pill for U.S. hard-liners to swallow. De Gaulle made it clear he opposed the U.S.-led attempt to carve two countries from Vietnam, that he thought Vietnam should be united, and that France would be pleased to facilitate this process. Stanley Hoffmann of Harvard, who grew up in France and admires de Gaulle immensely, was also a young colleague of McGeorge Bundy's in the 1950s. Hoffmann recently recalled some correspondence he had with Bundy during the escalation of the war in Vietnam. Hoffmann told Bundy he doubted the Americans could succeed where the French had failed. Bundy replied: "We are not the French—we are coming as liberators, not colonialists." Hoffmann says he was never able to convince Bundy that "acting with all one's might to do good can be seen as a form of imperialism." Stanley Hoffmann is quoted in Craig Lambert, "Le Professeur," *Harvard Magazine*, July/August 2007, pp. 34–35.

19. The interview with Walter Cronkite of CBS News took place on September 25, 1963. Kennedy famously told Cronkite, "In the final analysis it is the people and government [of South Vietnam] itself who will win or lose this struggle. All we can do is help." Yet Kennedy concluded by saying: "But I don't agree with those who say we should withdraw. That would be a great mistake." Quoted in Gravel, *Pentagon Papers*, 2:827.

20. Thomas L. Hughes, "Experiencing McNamara," *Foreign Policy*, Fall 1995, pp. 155–71. He was reviewing McNamara, *In Retrospect*.

21. See John Prados, *The Blood Road: The Ho Chi Minh Trail and the Vietnam War* (New York: Wiley, 1999), especially pp. 56–68 for a discussion of the escalation in Laos as an attempt to interdict supplies along the Ho Chi Minh Trail. Prados is especially good on the role of the relentless Walt Rostow in pushing his policy of "preventing further infiltration." After Kennedy's death, according to Prados, "if there was a Vietnam option that suffered from lack of defenders it was not Rostow's offensive action, it was withdrawal, which, when mentioned at all, was held up as the horrible alternative that must compel action" (pp. 68–69).

22. During the Johnson administration, one of the ways McNamara tried to rein in the open-ended escalation of the war sought by the Joint Chiefs and civilians such as Walt Rostow was in his advocacy of explorations of Hanoi's willingness to move to a cease-fire as a first step toward beginning negotiations to end the war. All the initiatives failed. On these failed initiatives, see especially McNamara et al., *Argument Without End*, especially chapter 6, "Negotiating Initiatives," pp. 218–313.

23. See Hughes, "Experiencing McNamara"; see also McNamara's exchange with Hughes's deputy at INR, Louis Sarris, in the *New York Times* in September 1995. The exchange is reprinted as an appendix to the paperback edition of McNamara's memoir *In Retrospect*, pp. 391–99.

24. Consult William Conrad Gibbons, "Lyndon Johnson and the Legacy of Vietnam," in *Vietnam: The Early Decisions*, ed. Gardner and Gittinger, pp. 119–57; Chomsky, *Rethinking Camelot*; Stanley Karnow, *Vietnam, A History*, revised edition (New York: Penguin, 1991); Gary R. Hess, *Vietnam and the United States: Origins and Legacy of War* (New York: Twayne, 1990); and Bird, *The Color of Truth*.

25. See Marilyn B. Young, *The Vietnam Wars, 1945–1990* (New York: Harper, 1991).

26. Schlesinger, *A Thousand Days*; Peter Dale Scott, *Deep Politics and the Death of JFK* (Berkeley: University of California Press, 1993); Newman, *JFK and Vietnam*; and Howard Jones, *Death of a Generation: How the Assassinations of Diem and JFK Prolonged the Vietnam War* (New York: Oxford, 2003). The problem many historians have had with these scholars is that those who conclude that JFK would have withdrawn from Vietnam are, as many historians see it, either (a) members of a "Camelot" fraternity of Kennedy worshipers or (b) have become obsessed with, and sentimental about, Kennedy's assassination. Jones's *Death of a Generation* was in some respects a real breakthrough—a book of dispassionate and thorough scholarship, devoid of histrionics, that comes to a tragic conclusion: that Kennedy had decided to withdraw but, according to Jones, the withdrawal he intended was itself made impossible for his successor to carry out due to the two November 1963 assassinations, of Diem and Kennedy.

27. On MONGOOSE, see Blight, Allyn, and Welch, *Cuba on the Brink*; and Blight and Kornbluh, eds., *Politics of Illusion*. Just how "restrained" Operation MONGOOSE was depended on whether you were carrying it out or were the recipient of its acts of sabotage and assassination attempts.

28. Sir Robert G. K. Thompson, a British specialist in counterinsurgency warfare, is credited with masterminding British success in putting down an insurgency in Malaya in the early 1950s. Thompson was in Saigon, at the invitation of Diem, at the same time Taylor and Rostow were there, in October 1961. Thompson's key strategy was the creation of "strategic hamlets" to insulate the population from the insurgents. Roger Hilsman, an academic with experience as a guerrilla fighter in Burma during World War II, went to Saigon at Kennedy's request in December 1961 and returned with great enthusiasm for Thompson's approach. Hilsman later wrote that Kennedy was opposed to committing combat troops to Vietnam, but was very interested in what could be accomplished via counterinsurgency warfare. Kennedy soon made Hilsman his assistant secretary of state for Far Eastern affairs. See Hilsman, *To Move a Nation*, especially chapter 34, pp. 524–37, "If Kennedy Had Lived." See also Freedman, *Kennedy's Wars*, pp. 331–37.

29. See McNamara, *In Retrospect*, pp. 77–83.

30. See Prados, *The Blood Road*, pp. 33–38. Throughout the spring and summer of 1961, the administration debated what to do about infiltration into South Vietnam of men and materiel from North Vietnam via what would soon become known as the Ho Chi Minh Trail. SEATO, a mutual security group modeled to a degree on the European NATO alliance, came up with Plan 5/61 (or Plan 5) and Plan 5 Plus. Intuitively, Kennedy doubted the possibility of "sealing" off Laos, through which the Trail passed from North to South Vietnam. The military analyses of its likely effectiveness were not much more optimistic. Plan 5 and Plan 5 Plus would have required U.S. forces in numbers ultimately compatible with the 205,000 estimate in the McNamara memorandum under discussion.

31. In February 2003, on the eve of the U.S. invasion of Iraq, General Eric C. Shinseki, the U.S. Army chief of staff, appeared before the Senate Armed Services Committee. He was asked how many troops would be required to complete the mission in Iraq if the invasion went forward. His reply was "something on the order of several hundred thousand soldiers." His civilian superiors at the Pentagon, especially Defense Secretary Donald Rumsfeld and his deputy defense secretary, Paul Wolfowitz, were irate. The Army had nowhere near this many troops to devote to the Iraq campaign. A few days later, Wolfowitz told a congressional committee, "It's hard to conceive that it would take more forces to provide stability in post-Saddam Iraq than it would take to conduct the war itself, and to secure the surrender of Saddam's security forces and his army. Hard to imagine." Quoted in George Packer, *The Assassins' Gate: America in Iraq* (New York: Farrar, Straus & Giroux, 2005), pp. 114–16. Shinseki was reprimanded and ultimately

fired as Army chief of staff. But he turned out to be right. Wolfowitz's and others' inability to imagine the need for so many troops was due to their failure of imagination, not an overly conservative estimate by Shinseki.

32. Lisa Howard was an ABC TV reporter who landed a famous interview with Fidel Castro in Havana, which was broadcast in May 1963. She also offered herself as an intermediary between Castro and Kennedy, whom she briefed at the White House about her discussions with Castro. She was herself committed to helping find a way to a rapprochement between Washington and Havana. Kennedy encouraged her in her efforts, and her "citizen diplomacy" was used as a model later in 1963 for an attempt to begin U.S.-Cuban discussions at the UN. These talks involved U.S. diplomat William Attwood and the Cuban ambassador to the UN, Carlos Lechuga. High-strung and with a fiery temper, Lisa Howard committed suicide in July 1965 after suffering a miscarriage. See Talbot, *Brothers*, pp. 222–32.

33. John Kenneth Galbraith to John F. Kennedy, November 21, 1961, in Goodman, ed., *The Letters of John Kenneth Galbraith to Kennedy*, pp. 89–94.

34. Following a brief visit to Washington (which included a dinner at Kennedy's Virginia retreat, Glen Ora) and before heading back to New Delhi to resume his duties as U.S. ambassador to India, Galbraith wrote to Kennedy on April 5, 1962, a memorandum that is vintage Galbraith. He told JFK, "I have put a lot of time in the last three or four days on the scene of my well-known guerrilla activities, namely, South Vietnam. This included a long and most reassuring discussion with Bob McNamara. We are in basic agreement on most matters and for the rest I think Bob appreciated having some arguments from my side of the fence." Galbraith concludes with the kind of edgy wit that Kennedy relished. "Last, but not least, I must tell you how much I enjoyed the other evening at Glen Ora, our survey of the problems of the nation and the world, and the chance to reflect on the unique capacity of your advisers to solve them" (ibid., pp. 100–101). If Galbraith's reading of the coincidence of his views with McNamara's is correct, then already in early 1962, a year and a half before the audiotaped discussions of the Vietnam conflict under discussion by our conference participants, McNamara had reached this conclusion: whatever the solution to the Vietnam dilemma, if it had one, Americanizing the war was not going to help. The April 5, 1962, memorandum from Galbraith to Kennedy finds Galbraith concluding, in part, as follows: "We should resist all steps which commit American troops to combat action and impress upon all concerned the importance of keeping American forces out of actual combat commitment" (ibid., p. 103). This is roughly a year and a half before the audiotaped discussions about the withdrawal being debated by the participants in the Musgrove conference.

35. See McNamara, *In Retrospect*, pp. 62–82. The withdrawal idea emerges within the larger context of trying to decide what to do about Ngo Dinh Diem's government—to encourage a group of military men who are eager to stage a coup,

or to give Diem one last chance to reform and to rid his regime of its brutality, corruption, and plain incompetence (as viewed by the Kennedy administration). Marc Selverstone's reading of the record jibes with our own. McNamara had concluded that Kennedy was not going to Americanize the war in Vietnam. Precisely *why* he had reached this conclusion is unclear, though, as James Galbraith says, the most likely explanation is that Kennedy and McNamara had discussed it between themselves, probably on several occasions. Just how to manage the withdrawal, however, was left to the resourceful, quantitatively oriented McNamara. Is JFK hearing for the first time in the conversation recorded on October 2 about the specifics of the 1,000-man withdrawal, with the rest to pull out by the end of 1965? It is impossible to say for certain. We believe McNamara understood JFK's intentions in this way by the end of 1961, which accounts for his alteration of the November 8, 1961, memorandum to Kennedy that is much discussed in the previous chapter.

36. Like Marc Selverstone, we have seen no "smoking gun" document from Kennedy to McNamara ordering him to begin withdrawing U.S. forces from Vietnam. In his 2003 exhaustive account of the withdrawal plan, however, Howard Jones cites an oral history by Roswell Gilpatric, McNamara's deputy secretary of defense. Where McNamara has been circumspect on Kennedy's motives and intentions, Gilpatric was direct and unequivocal. According to Gilpatric, Kennedy was "particularly restive" throughout 1963 about what he called the "exit point." Gilpatric recalls receiving assurances from McNamara throughout this period that the withdrawal plan "was part of a plan the president asked him to develop to unwind this whole thing." In all likelihood, this was done orally between the president and McNamara, for Kennedy would have known that many of his other aides, notably McGeorge Bundy, Dean Rusk, and the Joint Chiefs, would have opposed such a plan. Thus, when McNamara and Taylor returned from Saigon in early October, they obviously believed the plan they presented to the president was one that fulfilled his own wish to begin disengaging from Vietnam because (as Kennedy saw it) the conflict could not be won via the introduction of U.S. combat troops. See Jones, *Death of a Generation*, pp. 381–82.

37. See, for example, Goodman, ed., *John Kenneth Galbraith's Letters to Kennedy*, pp. 83–97 (letters of September 19, 1961, October 9, 1961, and November 21, 1961).

38. See Ted Sorensen, *Counselor: A Life at the Edge of History* (New York: HarperCollins, 2008), p. 233, for another example of McNamara understanding Kennedy's position, accommodating himself to it, and helping his president get what he wants.

> ". . . [D]uring the 1961 Berlin crisis, the president convened a smaller private meeting to hear the pros and cons of declaring a national emergency. Walter Heller, Douglas Dillon, and I attended, along with the secretaries of state and defense and the national

security advisor. After hearing warnings about the harsh signal his decision would send to both anxious allies and the Soviets, and the implications of emergency powers in a free market, JFK called upon McNamara, who extemporaneously presented a brilliant, logical, clear-cut argument in favor of an emergency declaration, speaking in well-structured paragraphs supported by the facts. After the president decided against the declaration, we all filed into the Cabinet Room for the formal meeting of the NSC, and the president called upon the secretary of defense to open the discussion. McNamara then proceeded to deliver, again without notes, a brilliant, logical, clear-cut argument *against* the issuance of an emergency order. I was impressed" (italics in the original).

39. Two weeks after the assassination of Diem and Nhu, at a press conference, Kennedy reiterated U.S. policy: "Now, that is our object, to bring Americans home, permit the South Vietnamese to maintain themselves as a free and independent country, and permit democratic forces within the country to operate . . ." (The President's News Conference of November 14, 1963, in *Public Papers of the Presidents, 1963* [Washington, DC: U.S. Government Printing Office, 1964], p. 495).

40. Jones, *Death of a Generation*, p. 456.

41. Dallek (*An Unfinished Life*) presents a detailed account of the run-up to the coup against Diem and the assassination of Diem and Nhu, along with Kennedy's reactions. See pp. 669–86. Dallek then infers, as we do, that the aftereffects of the coup would not have tempted Kennedy to introduce U.S. combat troops into Vietnam. In fact, to the contrary, Dallek believes that "The failed coup had—just as the Bay of Pigs had in Cuba—pushed Kennedy further away from direct engagement" (p. 684).

42. James C. Thomson, Jr., was an East Asian specialist who worked for William Bundy in the Far East division of the State Department, as well as for McGeorge Bundy at the National Security Council. Thomson's remarks were given at a Harvard seminar attended by Marilyn Young. Thomson seems to have been a skeptic about the war from a very early point. In a controversial 1968 article, written after he left the government, Thomson quotes anonymously "one of the very highest figures in the administration," as saying, early in 1965, "I'm convinced that we don't have to worry about this [Americanizing the war in Vietnam] because, before the bombing can be undertaken, there will be a neutralist government in Saigon and we will be invited out" (Thomson, "How Could Vietnam Happen?" *Atlantic Monthly*, April 1968, p. 51. In 1986, George Kahin revealed the identity of the official in his book *Intervention: How America Became Involved in Vietnam* (New York: Anchor, 1986), p. 272. The official was Vice President Hubert Humphrey. See also Porter, *Perils of Dominance*, p. 208.

43. janet Lang is referring to Kennedy's extreme caution during the missile crisis, and his resistance to the majority of his advisers, who were strenuously pushing for an air strike on Soviet missile sites in Cuba and an invasion of the

island by U.S. forces. She is also referring to Kennedy the politician, who must see security issues politically as well as strategically. When his advisers, on the critical Saturday, October 27, 1962, pressed Kennedy for military action against Cuba, Kennedy worried about a Soviet response, perhaps on NATO missiles in Turkey, which might have spiraled into an uncontrollable nuclear war, all because the U.S. wouldn't "trade" missiles with the Soviets, in effect removing both sets of missiles as part of a deal to avert war. Believing that the possibility of the missile trade would ultimately be discovered, Kennedy told his advisers, "If that's part of the record, I don't see how we'll have a very good war." May and Zelikow, eds., *The Kennedy Tapes*, p. 602. Kennedy made many such appeals to his subordinates throughout the crisis to imagine the kind of war that might be about to begin and to join him in trying to find a face-saving way to avoid it. See Blight and Welch, "The Eleventh Hour of the Cuban Missile Crisis"; and Bundy and Blight, "October 27, 1962: Transcripts of the Meetings of the ExComm."

44. On the conflict in Vietnam as a "crisis in slow motion," see McNamara et al., *Argument Without End*, pp. 396–97.

45. Listen to this recording, accompanied by a scrolling transcript, at the Miller Center collection, http://tapes.millercenter.virginia.edu/clips/1963_1104 _jfk_vietnam_memoir.html.

46. See Winters, *The Year of the Hare*, pp. 20–23, on Mansfield's views on Vietnam and their possible influence on Kennedy. The letter from Mansfield to Winters was dated October 24, 1989.

47. Bartlett was a Washington journalist who was a favorite of Kennedy's.

48. Winters is paraphrasing Nolting's comments as reported in the minutes of a White House meeting on August 28, 1963, in *Foreign Relations of the United States, 1961–1963 (Vietnam)* (Washington, DC: United States Printing Office, 1964), 4:3. See also Winters, *The Year of the Hare*, pp. 67–68.

49. See Halberstam, *The Best and the Brightest*, pp. 161–65 for a scathing indictment of Nolting, whom he characterizes as "a man of the surface . . . who commits himself only to the upper level of the host government and the society, not to the country itself. If you get along with the government and pass on its version of reality, then you are doing your job. It was not his job to ask questions . . ." (p. 164).

50. Gordon Goldstein is referring not only to the specific letter from Mansfield to Winters, but to Mansfield's view, which he shared with many people over many years, that Kennedy had told him that he was pulling out of Vietnam after he was reelected.

51. Herring, *America's Longest War*, pp. 105–7.

52. Operational Plan 34-A was a CIA program involving covert acts of violence carried out in North Vietnam by South Vietnamese commandos conveyed into North Vietnam with significant CIA assistance, including CIA planes and pilots. James Galbraith is pointing out that under Kennedy, this program was to be

carried out contingent on the development of the South Vietnamese government's ability to do so on its own, but that between the moment of JFK's death on November 22, 1963, and November 26, when LBJ signed NSAM 273, the phrase "government of Vietnam resources" has been deleted, thus rendering 34-A a primarily U.S. program rather than a South Vietnamese endeavor. See also Galbraith, "Exit Strategy."

53. It is possible that the "two principals" alluded to, but not identified, by Bill Moyers are the U.S. ambassador in Saigon, Henry Cabot Lodge, and CIA Director John McCone. In 1975, Moyers recalled a conversation he had with LBJ on Sunday, November 24, 1963, less than forty-eight hours after JFK's assassination and just after LBJ's first meeting on Vietnam as president. Others attending that meeting, which Moyers did not attend, were Dean Rusk, Robert McNamara, and George Ball. Moyers stopped by just after the meeting broke up. He recalled that Johnson was particularly struck by the pessimistic assessments of Lodge and McCone, whose views Johnson summarized by saying of South Vietnam, "it is going to hell in a handbasket." Moyers asked LBJ what he was going to do. Johnson responded by saying that he would give "this crowd" (i.e., his advisers) what they want, to prevent "Vietnam from going the way of China." See A. J. Langguth, *Our Vietnam: The War, 1954–1975* (New York: Simon & Schuster, 2000), pp. 267–70. See also Jones, *Death of a Generation*, pp. 444–47.

54. McNamara's memoir does not clear up this puzzling issue. He says that already on November 24, two days after he assumed office, Johnson met with his advisers, including Lodge, who was in Washington for a long-planned consultation. McNamara writes that "President Johnson . . . felt that the United States had spent too much time and energy trying to shape other countries in its own image. Win the war! That was his message" (McNamara, *In Retrospect*, p. 102). McNamara goes on to say, "Two days later National Security Action Memorandum (NSAM) 273 incorporated the president's directives into policy" (ibid., p. 102). Thus McNamara suggests that Johnson was, from the outset, driving Vietnam policy, and driving it in a different direction from where Kennedy intended to go.

55. McNamara has written that in a March 16, 1964, meeting with the president and his senior advisers, "withdrawal seemed unacceptable because of the domino effect. It was the same conclusion that had been put forward earlier on several occasions, and it remained poorly supported then as it had before" (McNamara, *In Retrospect*, p. 113). In strict numerical terms, this may be true. But the decisive difference between the meetings on October 2 and October 5, 1963, on the one hand, and, on the other, the March 16, 1964, meeting, was the respective presidents' support. Kennedy supported withdrawal. Johnson did not. It is difficult to say which direction the causal arrow pointed; was Johnson or McNamara primarily responsible for the loss of interest in the withdrawal?

56. James Fallows, "Getting Out Right," *The Atlantic*, April 2005, available online at www.theatlantic.com/doc/prem/200504/fallows.

Chapter 5

1. See Michael H. Hunt, *Lyndon Johnson's War: America's Cold War Crusade in Vietnam, 1945–1968* (New York: Hill and Wang, 1996), especially chapter 4, "That Bitch of a War," pp. 72–107. The comment was made to historian Doris Kearns when she was assisting Johnson with his memoirs. See Doris Kearns, *Lyndon Johnson and the American Dream* (New York: Signet, 1976), p. 263. In this remarkable book, the close-up view of Johnson may be, for some, a little too close, so outlandish is LBJ's personality, so insecure, so egotistical, and so vengeful. Ultimately, with regard to the war in Vietnam, he is incapable of extracting himself and preventing his country from escalating the conflict to the catastrophe it ultimately became. See Kearns's chapter 9, "Vietnam," especially.

2. ExComm refers to Kennedy's Executive Committee of handpicked advisers, whom Kennedy assembled on October 16, 1962, when he was first informed that the presence of Soviet missiles in Cuba had been confirmed. For a concise listing of the members of Kennedy's ExComm, see Bundy and Blight, "October 27, 1962," p. 34.

3. There were several such "pauses" in the bombing of North Vietnam. The first, code-named MAYFLOWER, occurred between May 13 and May 18, 1965, without eliciting a response from Hanoi. See McNamara, *In Retrospect*, pp. 184–86. For the Vietnamese discussion of MAYFLOWER, see McNamara et al., *Argument Without End*, pp. 262–69.

4. See, for example, Chester Cooper's minutes of a National Security Council meeting on July 21, 1965, ostensibly called to debate whether to send the requested 175,000 U.S. troops to Vietnam. During a morning session, Ball interjects cautionary remarks, only to be ignored by the others, including Johnson. Then LBJ says that following the lunch break, Ball is to make a presentation on a policy alternative, which will then be debated. Ball does this, arguing that LBJ and the others are underestimating the seriousness of what they are about to do in Americanizing the war. McNamara and Rusk brush Ball aside while the president, according to Cooper's notes, "agreed that the situation is serious. He regretted that we are embroiled in Vietnam. But we are there." That was it for Ball's informed, prophetic presentation on the disaster that was about to happen. A frustrated Ball finally ends with, "We won't get out; we'll double our bet and get lost in the rice paddies." Chester L. Cooper, "Memorandum for the Record: Meetings on Vietnam, July 21, 1965," dated July 22, 1965, and stamped "TOP SECRET—EYES ONLY," original in the Lyndon Baines Johnson Library, Austin, TX. A copy is available from the Vietnam Documentation Project, National Security Archive, Washington, DC.

5. On July 1, 1965, McGeorge Bundy forwarded to LBJ four memoranda on possible courses of action in Vietnam, by William Bundy, McNamara, and Ball, with a cover note by himself. McGeorge Bundy wrote, "My hunch is that you will want to listen hard to George Ball and then reject his proposal. Discussion could

then move to the narrower choice between my brother's course and McNamara's." Quoted in McNamara, *In Retrospect*, p. 195. McNamara notes that at the last minute, a memorandum from Dean Rusk was added, in which Rusk predicted that if the U.S. withdrew from South Vietnam, the result would be a catastrophic war, that is, a nuclear war with the Soviet Union and/or China.

6. Telephone conversation between LBJ and Georgia Senator Richard Russell, Monday, July 26, 1965, in Michael Beschloss, ed., *Reaching for Glory: Lyndon Johnson's Secret White House Tapes, 1964–1965* (New York: Simon & Schuster 2001), pp. 407–11. Johnson and Russell are discussing how to call up reservists with minimal political damage to LBJ and the Democratic Party generally.

7. George W. Ball, *The Past Has Another Pattern: Memoirs* (New York: Norton, 1982), p. 316.

8. For example, in mid-1964, LBJ called his old Senate pal Richard Russell to ask for his help in looking for someone to replace the outgoing U.S. ambassador in Saigon, Henry Cabot Lodge: "Now Dick . . . [m]y great weakness in this job is I just don't know these other people. The Kennedys—they know every damn fellow in the country or have got somebody that knows 'em. They're out at these universities and everyplace in the country—New York and Chicago" (telephone conversation between LBJ and Richard Russell, June 11, 1964, in Beschloss, ed., *Taking Charge*, p. 402). Johnson's multitudinous and bottomless insecurities constitute the principal focus of Doris Kearns's uniquely "behind the scenes" book on Johnson, *Lyndon Johnson and the American Dream*.

9. This is a reference to the two positions argued, respectively, by McNamara and William Bundy in memoranda forwarded to LBJ by McGeorge Bundy on July 1, 1965. McNamara urged a radical escalation of the war effort while William Bundy argued that they try to do the best they can without escalating the force levels beyond the roughly 85,000 who were already deployed. See McNamara, *In Retrospect*, pp. 192–95.

10. The principal reason LBJ committed himself publicly to "continuing" JFK's policies seems to have been fear. He told Doris Kearns, ". . . this time there would be Robert Kennedy out in front leading the fight against me, telling everyone that I had betrayed John Kennedy's commitment to South Vietnam. That I had let a democracy fall into the hands of the Communists. That I was a coward. An unmanly man. A man without a spine. Oh, I could see it coming all right" (Kearns, *Lyndon Johnson and the American Dream*, p. 264).

11. For the text of LBJ's November 27 speech to a joint session of Congress, see the *New York Times*, November 28, 1963, p. 20. The passage cited by Bill Moyers appears approximately halfway into the speech. Johnson quotes Kennedy's inaugural statement that the work ahead is enormous, and therefore, "let us begin." Johnson follows with, "Today in this moment of new resolve, I would say to all my fellow Americans, let us continue."

12. Walt Rostow gave the speech at Fort Bragg, "Guerrilla Warfare in the Underdeveloped Areas," on June 28, 1961. See W. W. Rostow, *The Diffusion of Power, 1957–1972: Men, Events, and Decisions that Shaped America's Role in the World—From Sputnik to Peking* (New York: McMillan, 1972), pp. 284–86.

13. Jack Valenti was a jack-of-all-trades aide to Johnson and was often the notetaker in high-level discussions of the war in Vietnam; Joseph Califano was LBJ's chief adviser on domestic affairs.

14. McGeorge Bundy died of a heart attack in September 1996. Bill Moyers and Gordon Goldstein met six weeks later at a memorial service for Bundy at St. James Episcopal Church in New York City.

15. Moyers refers to the February 7, 1965, attack by Vietnamese insurgents on a base near Pleiku, in the Central Highlands of South Vietnam. Bundy had just arrived on a visit to Saigon when word came of the attack. He and his entourage, which included Musgrove conference participant Chester Cooper, flew immediately up to Pleiku and witnessed the carnage resulting from the attack. (Bundy did not literally "hear the firing of the shells," but he was, according to many reports, affected by the experience in the way Moyers describes.) The attack had occurred on the second day of Bundy's very first trip to Vietnam.

16. General Earle C. "Bus" Wheeler was chairman of the Joint Chiefs of Staff, 1964–1970. Bill Moyers appears to conflate two events separated by several years, each of which involved roughly the troop level mentioned by Moyers: the 205,000 U.S. troops McNamara had suggested to Kennedy in November 1961 that might be necessary to defeat the communist insurgency in South Vietnam [**Document 3-1**] and the additional 206,000 troops that Wheeler and the Joint Chiefs told Johnson in February 1968 would be necessary to defeat the insurgents during the Tet Offensive. See McNamara et al., *Argument Without End*, pp. 362–68; and Buzzanco, *Masters of War*, pp. 311–40.

17. Moyers refers to McNamara's tenure as an executive at the Ford Motor Company and a car, the Pinto, which was infamous for its exploding gas tank and other serious flaws. The Pinto did not appear, however, until 1971, eleven years after McNamara left Ford to join the Kennedy administration. McNamara had nothing to do with the creation, design, or distribution of Pintos.

18. Moyers resigned as LBJ's press secretary in January 1967.

19. Ron Suskind, "Without a Doubt," *New York Times Magazine*, October 17, 2004, available online at www.ronsuskind.com/articles/000106.html.

20. Halberstam, *The Best and the Brightest*.

21. Suskind, "Without a Doubt," www.ronsuskind.com/articles/000106.html.

22. All quotations in this paragraph are from the transcript of a telephone conversation between LBJ and Richard Russell on May 27, 1964, in Beschloss, ed., *Taking Charge*, pp. 363–70.

23. A. W. Moursund was, like Johnson, born and raised in the Texas Hill Country. He sold insurance, cattle, and real estate, and was a favorite playing partner of LBJ's in games of dominoes.

24. Transcript of a telephone conversation between LBJ and Richard Russell, Thursday, June 11, 1964, in Beschloss, ed., *Taking Charge*, pp. 400–403.

25. McGeorge Bundy, "Memorandum for the President, Re: Basic Policy in Vietnam," January 27, 1965. Although Bundy drafted the document, McNamara also approved it. Rusk, as Bundy tells Johnson, "does not agree with us," preferring to try to make do with the present policy rather than run the risks either of escalation or withdrawal. This document is known to scholars of the war in Vietnam as the "fork in the road" memorandum. See also McNamara, *In Retrospect*, pp. 166–70.

26. Transcript of a telephone conversation between LBJ and Robert McNamara, July 2, 1965, in Beschloss, ed., *Reaching for Glory*, pp. 381–83.

27. For a general introduction to the events involved in the Tonkin Gulf affair, see Blight and Lang, *Fog of War*, pp. 86–111; For a polemical but insightful analysis of the Tonkin Gulf events, see also Eric Alterman, *When Presidents Lie: A History of Official Deception and Its Consequences* (New York: Viking, 2004), pp. 160–237.

28. The text of the Tonkin Gulf Resolution is reprinted in Blight and Lang, *Fog of War*, p. 102. The document is available online and can be downloaded at www.choices.edu/resources/supplemental_fogofwar.php.

29. Fulbright is quoted in Alterman, *When Presidents Lie*, p. 160. See also Randall Bennett Woods, *Fulbright: A Biography* (New York: Cambridge University Press, 1995), pp. 349–55.

30. LBJ, cited in Logevall, *Choosing War*, p. 205.

31. See especially McNamara et al., *Argument Without End*, pp. 202–5. A portion of this discussion, which took place in 1997, is reprinted in Blight and Lang, *Fog of War*, pp. 106–9.

32. Ted Gittinger, ed., *The Johnson Years: A Vietnam Roundtable* (Austin, TX: LBJ School of Public Affairs, 1993), pp. 33–34. This is a transcript of a March 1991 conference at the LBJ School, University of Texas, of twenty-two former members of the Johnson administration. The principal living "no-show" was the former Defense Secretary Robert McNamara. He declined to participate, he said afterward, because the conversation was not sufficiently prepared and structured by its agenda, nor focused and constrained by declassified documentation regarding the war.

33. Thomas Hughes was born, raised, and educated in Minnesota (he is an alumnus of Carleton College). He was legislative counsel to Hubert Humphrey when Humphrey represented Minnesota in the Senate, and the close personal and professional relationship between Humphrey and Hughes continued after Humphrey became vice president.

34. 34-A operations, which Johnson had approved just after assuming the presidency, were covert attacks carried out inside North Vietnam with CIA-trained and CIA-backed South Vietnamese commandos. Like many such opera-

tions during the Cold War, it was notably unsuccessful, although, again like other such programs, it provoked the North Vietnamese adversaries and helped to convince them that the U.S. was determined to destroy them. See McNamara et al., *Argument Without End*, pp. 184–86.

35. See sections 7 and 8 in **Document 4-7**, especially the directive to move U.S.-backed military operations "up to 50 kilometers inside Laos"—in effect invading Laos in pursuit of insurgent forces.

36. Specially equipped destroyers, operating under the aegis of the DeSoto Program, routinely monitored radars in North Vietnam after they were triggered by 34-A incidents involving South Vietnamese commandos.

37. CINPAC is the commander in chief of the Pacific fleet, Admiral Ulysses S. Grant "Ollie" Sharp.

38. Cyrus R. Vance was deputy secretary of defense, 1964–1967.

39. Poor General Earle G. "Bus" Wheeler must have wondered what in the world he had been thinking of when he sought the post of Lyndon Johnson's chairman. Wheeler had just succeeded General Maxwell Taylor as chairman of the Joint Chiefs the previous month, July 1964.

40. Commander John Herrick was the commanding officer of the destroyer *Maddox*, which was attacked on August 2.

41. See Blight and Lang, *Fog of War*, pp. 94–98 for excerpts from the Department of Defense telephone logs from August 4, 1965, involving conversations between Admiral Sharp in Honolulu and McNamara at the Pentagon. They reveal confusion on all sides. What seems clear is that Sharp's efforts to discover whether an attack had actually occurred were gradually eclipsed by the need LBJ felt to order some kind of retaliation and to do it quickly. The telephone logs also reveal that neither Sharp nor McNamara were sure an attack had occurred, but worried about the risks of not retaliating if in fact an attack had occurred.

42. See the following section for a discussion of the incident at Pleiku.

43. Bill Moyers refers to the dates of the Tonkin Gulf events, which occurred in early August 1964, as roughly halfway through the period of preparation to escalate the war to an American war, which Fredrik Logevall has called "the long 1964."

44. Cater, a journalist, then an aide to LBJ (1964–1966), made his report not long after he had begun his job—he began working at the White House on May 18, 1964. So he was relatively new to his job, having been in the White House for two and a half months prior to the Tonkin Gulf episode. See Gittinger, ed., *The Johnson Years: A Vietnam Roundtable*, p. 21.

45. The document cited by Thomas Blanton is in the State Department's *Foreign Relations of the United States, 1961–1963 (Vietnam)*, 1:290. This conversation was first reported in 1972 by Halberstam, *The Best and the Brightest*, pp. 503–4. But David Kaiser, writing in 2000, believes that "relying on anecdotal evidence, Halberstam severely distorted the tone of this exchange," implying that

Halberstam had exaggerated Bundy's lack of seriousness in his response to Douglass Cater (Kaiser, *American Tragedy*, p. 543). See also Alterman, *When Presidents Lie*, pp. 195–97 and Bird, *The Color of Truth*, pp. 284–87.

46. Logevall, *Choosing War*.

47. See McNamara et al., *Argument Without End*, pp. 211–12.

48. See Logevall, *Choosing War*, pp. 252–99; see also Kaiser, *American Tragedy*, pp. 341–81.

49. McNamara and Harriman became allies in the secret search for a way to move to negotiations—McNamara was from the Defense Department and Harriman was technically from the State Department but operated, as always, more or less independently of the secretary, Dean Rusk. Cooper was the action officer, for several years, regarding the initiatives with which McNamara and/or Harriman were involved. See McNamara, *In Retrospect*, pp. 300–305 and McNamara et al., *Argument Without End*, pp. 219–312. See also Cooper, *In the Shadows of History*, pp. 233–59; and Cooper's earlier memoir, *The Lost Crusade*, pp. 325–68. Finally, see Rudy Abramson, *Spanning the Century: The Life of Averell Harriman, 1891–1986* (New York: Morrow, 1992), especially chapter 24, "Ambassador for Peace," pp. 627–50.

50. Harriman wrote a glowing foreword to Cooper's *Lost Crusade*, and it is obvious in that book that Cooper considered Harriman to be as much a victim of Rostow and the White House as he was.

51. This infamous statement was, according to David Halberstam, given by Bundy to a reporter while both were in the White House barbershop. "Mac," the reporter said, "what was the difference between Pleiku and the other incidents?" Bundy paused and then answered, "Pleikus are like streetcars," to which Halberstam added this clarification: "(i.e., there's one along every ten minutes)" (Halberstam, *The Best and the Brightest*, p. 646). Kai Bird gives this paraphrase of what Bundy had in mind: "In the larger scheme of things, Pleiku was merely a streetcar. If you didn't mount this streetcar, it could head straight to Munich, appeasement and world war" (Bird, *The Color of Truth*, p. 309).

52. See for example Robert Kennedy's 1967 recollection that, in President Kennedy's view, the solution to the Vietnam problem was always "some form of coalition government with people who would ask us to leave." Robert Kennedy quoted in Arthur Schlesinger, Jr., *Robert Kennedy and His Times* (New York: Ballantine, 1978), p. 767. For a detailed analysis, by both Americans and Vietnamese, of the feasibility of such a solution prior to the escalation of the mid-1960s, see McNamara et al., *Argument Without End*, pp. 99–150.

53. Dean Rusk had been the assistant secretary of state for Far Eastern affairs in June 1950, when the Chinese unexpectedly attacked U.S. forces at the Yalu River in Korea. Some, including Hughes, felt that Rusk's fears of a Chinese counterattack in Vietnam were greatly exaggerated. According to Richard Neustadt and Ernest May, Dean Rusk, in 1950, "had underestimated the Chinese. That

mistake he did not make again. Throughout the 1960s, he overestimated them" (*Thinking in Time: The Uses of History for Decision-Makers* [New York: Free Press, 1986], p. 162). Rusk did not deny his fear of the Chinese. He was forthright in his 1990 memoir about the resonance he believed existed between Korea in 1950 and Vietnam in the mid-1960s. See Richard Rusk, *As I Saw It*, ed. Daniel S. Papp (New York: Norton, 1990), pp. 448–49.

54. For an elaboration of the Four Points and a discussion of them by Vietnamese and American scholars and former officials, see McNamara et al., *Argument Without End*, pp. 223–32.

55. Lyndon B. Johnson, "Peace Without Conquest" (address at Johns Hopkins University, April 7, 1965), in *Public Papers of the Presidents, 1965* (Washington, DC: U.S. Government Printing Office, 1966), 1:394–99. For the view taken in Hanoi of LBJ's Johns Hopkins speech, see the remarks of the Vietnamese historian and former diplomat Luu Doan Huynh in McNamara et al., *Argument Without End*, pp. 226–28.

56. W. Dean Howells, Dorothy Avery, and Fred Greene, *Vietnam 1961–1968 as Interpreted in INR's Production*, section V, "Trial by Force: March 1965–February 1966," pp. 5–6. This INR Vietnam study is a 596-page document completed in 1969, sometimes known as "The State Department's Pentagon Papers." This fascinating study is available online at www.gwu.edu/~nsarchiv/NSAEBB/NSAEBB121/index.htm. See also the very helpful introductions to the document by Thomas Hughes and John Prados. It was declassified in May 2004 and was included in the briefing notebook for the Musgrove conference.

57. Logevall's dissertation at Yale was later transformed into his 1999 book, *Choosing War*.

58. Lyndon Johnson, "Peace Without Conquest."

59. In fact, Harriman shamelessly pursued Johnson in hopes of getting a position in the administration. Chester Cooper later said of Harriman, "I wouldn't want to use the word 'grovel,' but I guess I just did," quoted in Abramson, *Spanning the Century*, p. 631. Harriman himself said that he was "shut out by day, squeezed and squeezed and never allowed to see the president" (ibid., p. 635).

60. This bombing pause lasted thirty-seven days, from December 1965 through January 1966, and was initiated and championed by McNamara. During the pause, Harriman and Cooper hit the road to advertise in foreign capitals how interested Johnson was in moving to negotiations. The initiative failed to elicit a response from Hanoi. See also McNamara, *In Retrospect*, pp. 207–31.

61. This was a secret December 1966 initiative, code-named MARIGOLD. It involved a possible meeting in Warsaw of a North Vietnamese diplomat, Nguyen Dinh Phuong, and the U.S. ambassador to Poland, John Gronouski. The meeting never occurred. As Nguyen Dinh Phuong arrived in Warsaw, the U.S. bombing began anew, as Cooper says in his comment. See George C. Herring, ed., *The Secret Diplomacy of the Vietnam War: The Negotiating Volumes of the Pentagon*

Papers (Austin: University of Texas Press, 1983), pp. 209–370. MARIGOLD is also the subject of a forthcoming book by George Washington University historian (and Musgrove conference participant) James G. Hershberg. Until the Hershberg book becomes available, however, an older source by two journalists can be consulted with profit: David Kraslow and Stuart Loory, *The Secret Search for Peace in Vietnam* (New York: Random House, 1968), pp. 55–74.

62. On March 31, 1968, President Johnson, at the very end of a television address devoted to the war in Vietnam, unexpectedly announced, "I shall not seek, and I will not accept, the nomination of my party for another term as your president." Lyndon B. Johnson, "The President's Address to the Nation Announcing Steps to Limit the War in Vietnam and Reporting His Decision Not to Seek Reelection, March 31, 1968," in *Public Papers of the Presidents, 1968–69* (Washington, DC: U.S. Government Printing Office), 1:469–76.

63. Harry MacPherson, *A Political Education* (Boston: Little, Brown, 1972), p. 258, cited in Barbara Tuchman, *The March of Folly: From Troy to Vietnam* (New York: Ballantine, 1984), p. 295. David Halberstam's 1972 characterization of Rostow still rings true. "He was," wrote Halberstam, "the true believer, so sure of himself, so sure of the rectitude of his ideas that he could afford to be generous to his enemies" (*The Best and the Brightest*, p. 194). See also David Milne, *America's Rasputin: Walt Rostow and the Vietnam War* (New York: Hill and Wang, 2008).

64. The reference is to Nicholas Katzenbach, deputy attorney general in the Kennedy administration, later deputy secretary of state in the Johnson administration.

65. Chester Bowles was President Kennedy's first deputy secretary of state. Bowles incurred the wrath of the Kennedy White House following the April 1961 Bay of Pigs fiasco by suggesting publicly that he had opposed the invasion, but his superiors simply would not listen to him.

66. U. Alexis Johnson became undersecretary for political affairs—the number three position in the State Department.

67. In the shake-up, Bowles was moved out of the State Department, George Ball became Rusk's number two, and Rostow was exiled to the Policy Planning Staff at State.

68. Memorandum from Bundy to LBJ, February 2, 1965. See Bird, *The Color of Truth*, pp. 300–301. He notes that all three of the people nominated by Bundy—in addition to Moyers and Hughes, Abram Chayes from the State Department—were liberals, and each had serious doubts about the wisdom of escalating the conflict in Vietnam to an American war.

69. Robert W. Komer was the deputy national security adviser until 1966, when he was sent to South Vietnam to become deputy commander of U.S. operations. A longtime analyst for the CIA, Komer was known for his advocacy of the Phoenix Program, which resulted in the assassination of more than 20,000

suspected Vietcong operatives. He was also known for his hard-driving style, for which he was widely known as "Blowtorch."

70. Cooper recalls a comment from Robert McNamara during the June 1997 conference in Hanoi on the escalation of the war in Vietnam. See McNamara et al., *Argument Without End*, pp. 284–91; see also McNamara, *In Retrospect*, pp. 250–52.

71. See W. W. Rostow, "The Case for the War," *London Times Literary Supplement*, June 9, 1995. The piece is reprinted in an appendix to the paperback edition of McNamara's *In Retrospect*, pp. 425–42.

72. See Harold P. Ford, *CIA and Vietnam Policymakers: Three Episodes, 1962–1968* (Alexandria, VA: CIA Center for the Study of Intelligence, 1998), pp. 106–8. Ford quotes "Memorandum for the Record," William E. Colby, January 1968, on the eve of the Tet Offensive, as follows: "Mr. Rostow criticized the CIA for being 'fixed on certain positions' and urged it to develop new analyses based on certain totally different hypothetical key facts" (p. 108). The (then) CIA director, Richard Helms, also notes the tendency of the Johnson White House, particularly Johnson and Rostow, to avoid coming to grips with pessimistic estimates on the progress of the war in Vietnam. See his *A Look Over My Shoulder: A Life in the Central Intelligence Agency*, ed. William Hood (New York: Random House, 2003), pp. 328–29.

73. Transcript quoted in Beschloss, ed., *Reaching for Glory*, pp. 383–84.

74. Ibid., p. 384.

75. Senator George Aiken, Republican of Vermont, who became a nemesis of LBJ's after 1966 by taking the public position that the U.S. should declare victory, withdraw its troops, and bring them home.

76. General Andrew Goodpaster, former special assistant to Eisenhower for national security affairs.

77. Senator Everett McKinley Dirksen, Republican of Illinois, the Senate minority leader.

78. The memorandum is dated February 15, 1965, but was not delivered to Johnson until February 17. See the epilogue to this book for more on this memorandum.

79. Telephone conversation between LBJ and McGeorge Bundy, February 18, 1965, transcript quoted in Beschloss, ed., *Reaching for Glory*, p. 184.

80. See also Logevall's *Choosing War*, in which he writes that the memorandum from Humphrey to Johnson was "the most significant effort aimed at stopping and reversing the move to war." See especially pp. 346–47 for a concise summary of some of Humphrey's main points.

81. In one of the most stunning speeches ever given at a party convention, Humphrey stepped forward and declared, "The time has arrived in America for the Democratic Party to get out of the shadows of States Rights and walk forthrightly into the sunshine of human rights." Even though, as Moyers says, Truman

was outraged, Humphrey and the speech advocating racial equality may have been instrumental in getting Truman elected—in spite of the fact that the so-called Dixiecrats bolted the party and put up Strom Thurmond for president.

82. The memo itself [**Document 5-6**] is an eloquent summary of the argument against choosing war, but Humphrey probably did not make his case directly to the president. Musgrove conference participant Thomas Hughes worked closely with Humphrey to draft the memo. According to Hughes (personal communication, March 18 and 19, 2008), Humphrey personally delivered the memo to the office of the president, but not to the president himself. He was probably not in the room when Johnson first read it. McGeorge Bundy was either with Johnson when he read it or was summoned immediately after Johnson read Humphrey's memo. Bundy, according to Hughes, was told to "nursemaid the Vice-President from now on . . ." Humphrey did see Johnson shortly after that and describes this meeting in his memoirs: "About that same time, I was to make the main speech at the UN *Pacem in Terris* conference. The State Department suggested that I cancel my participation (. . . in retaliation for the memo?) I refused and . . . went to Johnson, told him I wanted to go ahead with my speech, and he agreed. I showed him the text. He suggested that Mac Bundy review it in detail. There were three sections [about] ideas that were new and constructive. Bundy cut out all the innovative, peace-seeking material." Hubert H. Humphrey, *The Education of a Public Man: My Life and Politics* (New York: Doubleday and Company, 1976), p. 324.

83. See Logevall, *Choosing War*, pp. 392–95.

84. General Wallace Greene was commandant of the Marine Corps, 1963–1967; General Harold K. Johnson was chief of staff of the Army, 1964–1968. In July 1965, Greene told LBJ he thought it might take 500,000 American troops five years to guarantee the survival of an anti-communist South Vietnam. Johnson told the president something even scarier: he believed the Vietnamese communists, North and South, were probably willing to fight for twenty more years, if needed, to achieve their objective—a unified Vietnam under the leadership and control of the Hanoi government. See Buzzanco, *Masters of War*, pp. 218–24, especially p. 223.

85. Logevall, *Choosing War*.

Chapter 6

1. A series of recent books edited by Robert Cowley with the title *What If?* have become best sellers. See, for example, *What If?: The World's Foremost Military Historians Imagine What Might Have Been* (New York: Berkeley Books, 1999); and *What Ifs? of American History: Eminent Historians Imagine What Might Have Been* (New York: Putnam, 2003). That these books have been widely available in airport bookstalls testifies to the popularity of playing the what if

game among general readers. Their availability in airports is doubtless interpreted by many professional historians as proof of the frivolousness of this kind of exercise.

2. Officially, anyway. It is not difficult to find causal claims in historical arguments ("A caused B") that turn on an unstated counterfactual ("if A had not happened, B would not have happened"). Note that this particular inference is not necessarily correct: there might have been several possible pathways to B, some of which did not require A—a condition known as "equifinality." The standard interpretation of McGeorge Bundy's remark, "Pleikus are like streetcars," is an equifinality claim: the attack on Pleiku, according to this view, was not a necessary condition for the Americanization of the war.

3. It's not for nothing that a nickname for the History Channel is "the Hitler Channel," due to their voluminous programming on World War II in Europe. Fascination with the world without a Hitler and Nazi Germany, or the world if the Nazis had won World War II, has been widespread, and a survey and analysis of this mountainous literature is the subject of a new book, Gavriel Rosenfeld, *The World Hitler Never Made* (New York: Cambridge University Press, 2007). The appearance of this book coincides with the rising popularity of a term that emphasizes the hybrid nature of this kind of exploration of alternate histories, "allohistorical fiction." See, for example, Ezra Klein, "What We All Escaped," *The American Prospect*, June 2007, pp. 59–61.

4. Blaise Pascal started the craze to understand history, and much else, via reference to Cleopatra and her nose. According to Pascal, "Cleopatra's nose, had it been shorter, the whole face of the world would have changed." Cited in Daniel Boorstin, *Cleopatra's Nose: Essays on the Unexpected* (New York: Random House, 1994), p. ix. Cleopatra's nose appears to be enjoying a renaissance in the age of the Internet. On July 14, 2007, a Google search for "Cleopatra's nose" yielded more than 391,000 links, ranging from the philosophical (what French philosopher Blaise Pascal really meant when he originated the discussion of the Egyptian queen and her nose) to the metaphorical (whether the ascendancy of George W. Bush to the U.S. presidency represents a "Cleopatra's nose moment") to the illustrative (the evolution of images of feminine beauty since antiquity) to the marvelously absurd—for example, a "Cleopatra's Nose Lifter," a (possibly mythical) device selling for $79.95 designed to enlarge the nostrils until one's face resembles that of a pig. See for yourself at www.davebarry.com/gg/giftguide/2000/docs/gift1.htm.

5. For a comprehensive and penetrating introduction to the history of historians' musings on counterfactuals, see Ferguson, *Virtual History*. See especially pp. 4–8 for his account of anticounterfactual absolutists Oakeshott, Carr, and Thompson. The book is well worth buying for Ferguson's ninety-page introductory essay alone. Alas, most of the so-called case studies in the book, by various historians (including Ferguson) are just exactly the sort of flights of fancy lamented and derided by people such as Oakeshott, Carr, and Thompson.

6. One of the best short pieces on the use of what ifs is Gaddis's "Nuclear Weapons and International Systemic Stability," Occasional Paper No. 2 (Cambridge, MA: International Studies Program, American Academy of Arts and Sciences, 1990). Despite its forbidding title and the focus on the history of the U.S.-Soviet arms race, one will find on pp. 11–25 a great deal of useful common sense about how to use what ifs in ways that help historians assess causality, identify missed opportunities, and draw lessons from whatever may be the substantive subject of the history. See also Gaddis's *The Long Peace: Inquiries into the History of the Cold War* (New York: Oxford, 1987), for Gaddis's subtle use of what ifs to determine whether nuclear weapons and the possibility of mutual assured destruction kept the peace between the U.S. and the Soviet Union after World War II.

7. H. R. Trevor-Roper, quoted in Ferguson, *Virtual History*, p. 85.

8. H. R. Trevor-Roper, "The Lost Moments of History," *New York Review of Books*, October 27, 1988, pp. 61–67.

9. Ferguson, *Virtual History*, p. 85.

10. Ibid., p. 89.

11. The centrality of model-building in virtual history—constructing a model of the behavior the historian wishes to understand—bears considerable similarity, and is heavily indebted to, two relatively recent developments: first, the rise of cognitive psychology and cognitive science—putting the mind rather than "objective" behavior at the core of the explanation and prediction of human behavior; and, second, the phenomenon of computer graphics, for example, constructing *avatars*, or models directly from human subjects. On the first, see the most influential book in the history of cognitive science: George A. Miller, Eugene Galanter, and Karl Pribram, *Plans and the Structure of Behavior* (New York: Wiley, 1960). This marvelous and superbly written book is still unparalleled for the clarity with which it puts forth the case for model building as the fundamental requirement for understanding human behavior. On computer graphics, see, for example, an entertaining but highly illuminating piece by Sharon Waxman, "Cyberface," *New York Times*, October 15, 2006. One graphic artist cited in this piece, for example, says this is the objective of what he does when he builds computer models of human facial movements: "I like to call it 'soul transference.' The model has the actress's soul. It shows through." This is not a bad definition of what virtual history is about: getting to the essence, the invariants, the proclivities—the "soul," if you will—of the key individuals at the center of the propositions of what if.

12. See chapter 3 for discussion of the significance of the attack on Pleiku.

13. Don Coscarelli, *Bubba Ho-Tep* (Phantasm Pictures, 2003).

14. Logevall, *Choosing War*, p. 390.

15. The questionnaire is reprinted in appendix B, "JFK What If Questionnaire for Musgrove Participants," just as it was presented to those participating in the conference.

16. The participants read two selections from Logevall in preparation for this session. See Logevall, *Choosing War*, pp. 375–414 and Logevall, "Vietnam and the Question of What Might Have Been," in *Kennedy: The New Frontier Revisited*, ed. Mark J. White (New York: New York University Press, 1998), pp. 19–62.

17. Transcript of a telephone conversation between Lyndon B. Johnson and John S. Knight, February 3, 1964, in Beschloss, *Reaching for Glory*, pp. 213–14.

18. Kearns, *Lyndon Johnson and the American Dream*, p. 264. In 1970, the ratio of the population of China (roughly 820,000,000) to the population of South Vietnam (roughly 19,000,000) was approximately 43 to 1. Yet Johnson's paranoia apparently led him to judge the possible loss of Vietnam to Communism as orders of magnitude worse than the actual loss of China to Communism.

19. In the first eleven chapters of *Choosing War*, Logevall walks the reader through the fine-grained detail of what he calls the long 1964, from August 1963 through July 1965, from JFK's last days in office through LBJ's first year and a half of his struggle with what to do in Vietnam.

20. The attraction of oddballs to anything associated with the Kennedy assassination was present from November 22, 1963, onward. But the alleged connection between Kennedy's views on the conflict in Vietnam and his assassination got a second wind with the release of Oliver Stone's 1991 film *JFK*. In this brilliant but historically misleading movie, viewers are led to believe that Kennedy's assassination is due to some unholy marriage of the Mafia, disgruntled CIA operatives, and equally disgruntled Cuban exiles—and some involvement of LBJ himself is even suggested.

Ever since the appearance of the film *JFK*, the Kennedy assassination industry has been working overtime, turning out books that "prove" all manner of incompatible hypotheses about who killed Kennedy and why. For two interesting recent efforts, see Talbot, *Brothers*; and Vincent Bugliosi, *Reclaiming History: The Assassination of President John F. Kennedy* (New York: Norton, 2007). Talbot, who believes there was a conspiracy to kill Kennedy and that the murder was related to JFK's propensity to withdraw from Vietnam, weighs in at just under 500 pages of finely crafted, compelling prose. Bugliosi, who believes Kennedy's death was the result of a lone gunman, Lee Harvey Oswald, does not believe in any conspiracy, and his book is a true heavyweight, at 1,612 pages of full-blast agitprop, in which no detail is too small or insignificant. (The endnotes to the book fill two CDs tucked inside the back cover.) Talbot and Bugliosi also debate the issue in the July 2, 2007, issue of *Time*, "The Assassination: Was It a Conspiracy?" pp. 66–67.

21. To get a sense of the extent to which Logevall's book challenged the paradigmatic assumptions of historians of the war in Vietnam, particularly with reference to Vietnam if Kennedy had lived, see the lengthy exchange between Logevall and four critics on H-Diplo, a useful website on which historians of U.S. foreign policy exchange ideas. Reviews of his *Choosing War* by Lloyd C. Gardner, Robert

Jervis, Jeffrey Kimball, and Marilyn Young were posted on February 1, 2000, shortly after the book appeared, along with Logevall's response to each review, at www.h-net.org/~diplo/roundtables/logevall3.html. This debate went on for many months, with Logevall patiently but firmly responding to dozens of critics, some of whom were, to put it mildly, intemperate in their postings. Logevall proved not only to be an indefatigable debater, but a virtuoso capable of reiterating via a rich profusion of examples and arguments his two rock-bottom findings in *Choosing War*: first, methodologically, a good deal can be learned if one articulates empirically based what ifs in a manner we are in this book calling virtual history; and second, substantively, the data strongly suggest that unlike Johnson, Kennedy would not have Americanized the war in Vietnam.

22. Logevall, *Choosing War*, pp. 375–413; and Logevall, "Vietnam and the Question of What Might Have Been."

23. Read and listen to Kennedy's reflections on the coup at http://tapes.miller center.virginia.edu/clips/1963_1104_jfk_vietnam_memoir.html.

24. Three months later, in this phone conversation of February 20, 1964, LBJ removes any lingering doubts McNamara may have had about LBJ's stance on the conflict in Vietnam. "I always thought it was foolish for you to make any statements about withdrawing," Johnson told McNamara. "I thought it was bad psychologically. But you and the president thought otherwise, and I just sat silent" [**Document 5-2**].

25. http://tapes.millercenter.virginia.edu/clips/1966_0201_lbj_mccarthy _vietnam.html. Johnson tells a skeptical McCarthy, "I just can't be the architect of surrender."

26. George Ball, a critic of the war in Vietnam, was the undersecretary of state from November 1961 until he resigned in September 1966. John McNaughton was McNamara's assistant secretary of defense for international security affairs and, by all accounts, McNamara's right-hand man in the Pentagon on matters related to the war in Vietnam. On McNaughton, see Lawrence Freedman, "Vietnam and the Disillusioned Strategist," *International Affairs* 72, no. 1 (1996), pp. 133–51; see also the highly illuminating 2006 Brown University history honors thesis by Christopher M. Elias, "The Company Man: John Theodore McNaughton and the Vietnam War." McNaughton died in a plane crash in July 1967, along with his wife and son.

27. Logevall refers to remarks by General Wallace Greene of the Marine Corps and General Harold K. Johnson of the Army in July 1965. See Buzzanco, *Masters of War*, pp. 221–24.

28. William Bundy, the assistant secretary of state for Far Eastern affairs, argued in his July 1965 paper for a "middle way," essentially capping the number of U.S. combat troops at around 85,000, who ought to seize and hold certain "enclaves." For an insider's account of the role of Bundy's views on enclaves, see McNamara, *In Retrospect*, pp. 192–204.

29. Transcript of a November 29, 1963, taped telephone conversation between LBJ and Senator Richard Russell, Democrat of Georgia and close personal friend of Johnson's. In an effort to persuade Russell to serve on the Warren Commission, the president tells Russell, "We got to take this out of the arena where they're testifyin' that [Nikita] Khrushchev and [Fidel] Castro did this and did that, and that [could end up] kickin' us into a war that can kill 40 million Americans in an hour . . ." in *The Kennedy Assassination Tapes: The White House Conversations of Lyndon B. Johnson Regarding the Assassination, the Warren Commission, and the Aftermath*, ed. Max Holland (New York: Knopf, 2004), p. 197.

30. In 2002, James Galbraith published some formerly classified documents, with commentary, regarding the nuclear balance in mid-1961, which greatly favored the U.S. over the Soviet Union and which led many of Kennedy's advisers, whom Johnson would inherit on November 22, 1963, to seriously discuss the possibility of a preemptive nuclear strike against the USSR. The U.S. advantage was, in the point of view of the more hawkish advisers, a so-called "wasting asset," because sooner or later the Russians would catch up to the U.S., making it too dangerous to contemplate such a "bolt from the blue" because the Russians would at that point be able to retaliate in kind. The documents presented by Galbraith are, even from this historical distance, bloodcurdling, as U.S. officials at a high level debate whether, when, and under what conditions it would make sense to totally destroy the Soviet Union, communist China, and in fact the entire East Bloc, in a rain of nuclear bombs and missiles. The article, including the documents, is available at *The American Prospect* online edition, www.prospect .org/cs/articles?article = did_the_us_military_plan_a_nuculear_first_strike_for_ 1963.

31. John F. Kennedy, "Commencement Address at American University in Washington," June 10, 1963, in *Public Papers of the Presidents, 1963* (Washington, DC: U.S. Government Printing Office, 1964), pp. 459–64. This is often referred to as the "strategy of peace" speech, after its closing sentence: "Confident and unafraid, we labor on—not toward a strategy of annihilation but toward a strategy of peace." The Limited Test Ban Treaty was signed in Moscow on July 25, 1963, prohibiting the testing of nuclear weapons in the atmosphere. The text is in ibid., pp. 599–600.

32. Kennedy was born in 1917, Johnson in 1908.

33. As a congressman and senator from California, Richard Nixon's political career was built in large part on his intimidation of political opponents with half-truths and outright lies alleging their communist connections. In the early 1950s, Wisconsin Senator Joseph McCarthy made communist-baiting, as these intimidation tactics were called by their opponents, into a perverse art form, spilling over into hallucinatory accusations that became so outlandish that McCarthy was censured by the Senate and ultimately was disgraced. The McCarthy era is

the subject of a superb 2005 film by George Clooney and Grant Heslov, *Good Night and Good Luck*, the story of newsman Edward R. Murrow's courageous and successful challenge to McCarthy's intimidation. Murrow would later serve as Kennedy's director of the U.S. Information Agency.

34. Bill Moyers's comment is a tongue-in-cheek reference to Kennedy's aggressive pursuit of the White House upon being elected to the Senate in 1952. Kennedy finished second to Estes Kefauver of Tennessee in the race to be Adlai Stevenson's vice-presidential running mate in 1956 at the tender age of thirty-nine.

35. See Lyndon B. Johnson, "Annual Message to the Congress on the State of the Union," delivered on January 6, 1965, in *Public Papers of the Presidents, 1965* (Washington, DC: U.S. Government Printing Office, 1966), 1:1–9. LBJ used this occasion, his first major address since being elected president in his own right, to stress his own vision for America's future rather than to reiterate (as he had done often during the previous year) that he was "continuing" JFK's policies, retaining JFK's advisers, and so on. He even closed with a homily about growing up poor in the Texas Hill Country in the Pedernales River Valley.

The "we shall overcome" speech referred to by Bill Moyers has been called by Johnson biographer Robert Dallek "Johnson's greatest speech and one of the most moving and memorable presidential addresses in the country's history." Robert Dallek, *Flawed Giant: Lyndon Johnson and His Times* (New York: Oxford University Press, 1998), p. 218. For the speech itself, see Lyndon B. Johnson, "Special Message to Congress: The American Promise," delivered March 15, 1965, in *Public Papers of the Presidents, 1965*, 1:281–87. It was given in the midst of the Selma, Alabama, "freedom marches" organized by Martin Luther King, Jr., and other African-American leaders. The week before the speech, on "Bloody Sunday," March 7, 1965, demonstrators had been beaten with clubs and whips and tear-gassed by deputies of Selma Sheriff Jim Clark. The speech is essentially about democracy and about voting rights as the cornerstone of democracy. But what gave this speech its surreal memorable aura was Lyndon Johnson, a white southerner, pausing in mid-speech, raising his arms for emphasis, and declaring, "We shall overcome," thus embracing the anthem of black protest in the U.S. According to Dallek, "when Johnson said 'We shall overcome,' a moment of stunned silence followed . . . And then almost the entire chamber rose in unison, 'applauding, shouting, some stamping their feet.' Tears rolled down the cheeks of senators, congressmen, and observers in the gallery, moved by joy, elation, a sense that the victor, for a change, was human decency, the highest standards by which the nation was supposed to live" (p. 219).

36. A native of Boston and a product of Harvard Law School, Richard Goodwin was a White House staffer under Kennedy who became Johnson's chief speechwriter soon after Johnson's accession to the presidency. For the background on the Great Society speech, see Goodwin, *Remembering America: A*

Voice From the Sixties (Boston: Little, Brown, 1988), pp. 267–92. The speech itself was delivered as the commencement address at the University of Michigan in Ann Arbor on May 22, 1964. See Lyndon B. Johnson, "Remarks at the University of Michigan." *Public Papers of the Presidents, 1963–1964,* 1:704–7.

37. Thomas S. Kuhn, *The Structure of Scientific Revolutions,* 2nd ed. (Chicago: University of Chicago Press, 1970). The first edition of Kuhn's book, published in 1962, became an unexpected best seller, and Kuhn immediately found himself at the center of a far-flung debate about the nature of scientific inquiry and humanistic endeavor, the extent to which scientific change and political change are similar or different, and the ways in which these issues among intellectuals mirrored the radical social upheaval in Western societies during the 1960s. See also Kuhn, *The Essential Tension: Selected Studies in Scientific Tradition and Change* (Chicago: University of Chicago Press, 1977), especially the essay that gives the collection its title, pp. 225–39.

38. Kuhn's first book was *The Copernican Revolution: Planetary Astronomy in the Development of Western Thought* (New York: Knopf, 1957). In this book, he had only just begun to think about what he meant by *revolution.* Remarkably, for example, the term *revolution* does not appear in the index to the book on Copernicus.

39. See chapter 4 for a discussion of the drafting of NSAM 273.

40. Beginning in March 1965, U.S. combat personnel, mainly Marines, were sent to Vietnam as part of an enclave strategy. They were to take up fixed positions, and their mission was defensive—to defend U.S. and South Vietnamese assets from insurgent attacks. But on July 28, 1965, LBJ decided to give General William Westmoreland, the U.S. field commander in Saigon, the 175,000 troops he requested, but he also signed off on "offensive" operations for the troops, who henceforward were authorized to engage in "search and destroy" missions. See Herbert Y. Schandler, "U.S. Military Victory in Vietnam: A Dangerous Illusion?" in McNamara et al., *Argument Without End,* pp. 353–62.

41. On March 8, 1965, the first two battalions of U.S. Marines arrived at the U.S. and South Vietnam military base in Da Nang.

42. All through 1967, a battle was waged between McNamara and the Joint Chiefs over how to prosecute the war. McNamara saw no virtue in continuing to pursue a military solution. He had concluded that nothing short of literally "bombing North Vietnam back to the Stone Age" was likely to defeat the Hanoi government, and the more than 400,000 U.S. combat troops in South Vietnam had shown no ability to win the war in the South in any definitive way. The Chiefs were irate about McNamara's proposal to reverse the escalation of the air war and other measures, and LBJ was torn over how to proceed. Ultimately, the Chiefs' view prevailed, and McNamara was relieved of his duties as secretary of defense as of March 1, 1968, when he became president of the World Bank. See McNamara, *In Retrospect,* pp. 283–95. See also Karnow, *Vietnam: A History,* pp. 511–27.

43. On November 1961, see chapter 3; the October 1963 decisions are taken up in chapter 4.

44. On the significance of incommensurability, see Kuhn, *The Structure of Scientific Revolutions*, pp. 198–204. In the case of a paradigm shift, the competing theories or viewpoints do not oppose each other or argue directly against one another. Instead, according to Kuhn, they are incommensurable: "When paradigms enter, as they must, into a debate about paradigm choice, their role is necessarily circular. Each group uses its own paradigm to argue in that paradigm's defense . . . Yet whatever its force, the status of the circular argument is only that of persuasion. It cannot be made logically or even probabilistically compelling for those who refuse to step into the circle" (ibid., p. 94).

45. For more analysis along these lines, see Blight and Kornbluh, eds., *Politics of Illusion*; and Peter Wyden, *Bay of Pigs: The Untold Story* (New York: Simon & Schuster, 1979).

46. The entire text of JFK's press conference is worth reading for the light it sheds on how Kennedy responded to this very deep and embarrassing crisis. See John F. Kennedy, "The President's News Conference of April 21, 1961," in *Public Papers of the Presidents, 1961*, pp. 307–15. The comment by Kennedy on being responsible is on pp. 312–13, in response to a question from NBC newsman Sander Vanocur, and in spite of having at the outset of the news conference announced that he did not wish to speak about the ongoing Cuban disaster. See also, for a comparison of JFK with George W. Bush, David Greenberg, "The Goal: Admitting Failure, Without Being a Failure," Week in Review, *New York Times*, January 14, 2007.

47. Taylor was appointed on April 22, 1961, the day following Kennedy's press conference, discussed above. On June 13, Taylor submitted his report, known ever since as the Taylor Report, which informed Kennedy that for an operation as large at the Bay of Pigs invasion, the hand of the CIA was impossible to disguise, and that the planning within the CIA was "anarchic and disorganized." Cited in Blight and Kornbluh, eds., *Politics of Illusion*, p. 169. Corroborating this, a classified CIA report stated that by the time of the invasion, "success had become dubious," and that "plausible deniability had become a pathetic illusion" (ibid., p. 169). The classified Kirkpatrick Report is found in Peter Kornbluh, ed., *Bay of Pigs Declassified: The Secret CIA Report on the Invasion of Cuba* (New York: New Press, 1998).

48. At the first meeting with his advisers following the discovery of the missiles in Cuba, on October 16, 1962, JFK seemed to have assumed that a quick air strike on the missile sites was more or less inevitable. Near the end of the meeting, just before lunch, Kennedy tells his advisers: ". . . that's what we're going to do *anyway* . . . We're going to take out these missiles." Transcript of a tape-recorded meeting, October 16, 1962, 11:50 a.m., in May and Zelikow, eds., *The Kennedy Tapes*, p. 71. Ultimately, we now know, Kennedy became committed to

avoiding any attack on Cuba, which he concluded raised the risk of nuclear war unacceptably high and which would be a disaster for his efforts to improve relations between the U.S. and Latin America via his Alliance for Progress.

49. Kennedy certainly did not assume he would be reelected without a fight in 1964. Chief among his problems was that his belated but strong support of the civil rights movement was already, by 1963, alienating large numbers of white voters in the South, which had traditionally voted solidly Democratic. According to Kennedy biographer Richard Reeves, "Kennedy . . . was going to have to campaign for reelection as the new champion of Negro rights . . . And polls were still showing him losing six or seven white votes for every Negro one he gained . . . If he picked up enough Negro votes to carry California, which he had lost by 35,000 votes in 1960, he could afford to lose a half dozen of the Southern states he had won big that year. But electoral politics was a tricky business." Reeves, *President Kennedy*, p. 626.

50. Ferguson, *Virtual History*, pp. 438–39.

51. John Lewis Gaddis, *The Cold War: A New History* (New York: Penguin, 2005), pp. 48–49.

52. Harry G. Frankfurt, *On Bullshit* (Princeton, NJ: Princeton University Press, 2005), pp. 55, 56, and 61.

53. Kurt Vonnegut, Jr., *Slaughterhouse Five* (New York: Dell, 1968).

54. Harry G. Frankfurt, *On Truth* (New York: Knopf, 2006), pp. 25–27.

Epilogue

1. Arthur Schlesinger, Jr., "Forgetting Reinhold Niebuhr," *New York Times Book Review*, September 18, 2005.

2. This is argued by Richard A. Clarke, the former National Security Council head of counterterrorism, in his *Against All Enemies: Inside America's War on Terror* (New York: Free Press, 2004). According to Clarke, on the evening of September 12, 2001, President Bush said to him, "See if Saddam did this. See if he is linked in any way" (p. 32).

3. Dick Cheney, quoted in Frank Rich, *The Greatest Story Ever Sold: The Decline and Fall of Truth, From 9/11 to Katrina* (New York: Penguin, 2006), p. 236. See pp. 227–307 for Rich's masterful re-creation of a "double timeline" from September 15, 2001 (four days after the 9/11 attacks), to May 22, 2006 (when Rich's book went to press). On the left-hand side of each page, Rich records what seem to have been the facts regarding the war and occupation of Iraq, as they were known at successive moments, while on the right side he records the public comments, made at roughly the same time, by U.S. and British officials regarding the situation in Iraq. The effect is astonishing: the public pronouncements seem completely unhinged from the judgments that emerge from a wide variety of intelligence sources. When Cheney made his remark on CNN, for ex-

ample, it was already known at the highest levels in Washington that defectors whose reports were consistent with Cheney's allegations were either misinformed or lying. CIA specialists and other analysts believed, in fact, that the Iraqis had probably given up their nuclear ambitions some years before. Nevertheless, the mantra was repeated incessantly by U.S. and British officials throughout the next year as the armed forces from both countries prepared to attack Iraq: Iraq under Saddam Hussein is actively seeking a nuclear bomb, and thus the regime must be removed by force.

4. Nearly three years later, after leaving office, Powell told the *Los Angeles Times* that ". . . he was never warned, during three days of intense briefings at the CIA headquarters before his UN speech that he was using material that both the DIA [Defense Intelligence Agency] and CIA had determined was false." Colin Powell, quoted in ibid., p. 263.

5. George W. Bush, quoted in Mark Danner, "'The Moment Has Come to Get Rid of Saddam.'" *New York Review of Books*, November 8, 2007, p. 59. The quotation is from a transcript of the Bush-Aznar conversation published in the Spanish daily *El País* on September 26, 2007.

6. See Charles Ferguson's Academy Award–nominated 2007 film, *No End in Sight: The American Occupation of Iraq* (Magnolia Pictures) and his follow-up book, *No End in Sight: Iraq's Descent into Chaos* (New York: PublicAffairs, 2008).

For estimates of excess Iraqi civilian deaths, see Les Roberts, Riyadh Lafta, Richard Garfield, Jamal Khudhairi, and Gilbert Burnham, "Mortality before and after the 2003 Invasion of Iraq: Cluster Sample Survey," *The Lancet* 364: 1857–64; and Gilbert Burnham, Shannon Doocy, Elizabeth Dzeng, Riyadh Lafta, and Les Roberts, "Mortality after the 2003 Invasion of Iraq: a Cross-sectional Cluster Sample Survey," *The Lancet* 368: 1421–28. The estimate from the first study, covering the period of March 2003–August 2004, was 98,000 excess Iraqi deaths. The second study looked at the period from March 2003–July 2006 and estimated more than 650,000 excess Iraqi deaths. On the *Lancet* study, see the article by David Brown in the October 11, 2006, *Washington Post*, "Study Claims Iraq's Excess Death Toll Reaches 655,000," www.washingtonpost.com/wp-dyn/content/article/2006/10/10/AR2006101001442.html.

For a broad discussion of the human cost of the war for Iraqis, see *www.mit.edu/humancostiraq*.

As of April 1, 2008, the U.S. death toll is 4,012, with all but thirty-nine having died since May 1, 2003, when President Bush announced, "mission accomplished." For details, see http://icasualties.org/oif/. The site also reports 309 deaths among other Coalition forces.

7. Stephen Herbits to Donald Rumsfeld, April 10, 2003, quoted in Bob Woodward, *State of Denial: Bush at War, Part III* (New York: Simon & Schuster, 2006), p. 167.

8. *New York Times* reporting on Iraq, cited in Todd S. Purdom and the staff

of the *New York Times, A Time of Our Choosing: America's War in Iraq* (New York: Times Books, 2003), pp. 212–14.

9. Kennedy made the charge on April 6, 2004, in a speech at the Brookings Institution in Washington, DC. For the text and commentary see CNN's website at www.cnn.com/2004/ALLPOLITICS/04/05/kennedy.speech/index.html. See also chapter 1 for more on the analogy between the wars in Vietnam and Iraq.

10. Google search results as of April 13, 2008.

11. www.foreignaffairs.org/20051101faessay84604/melvin-r-laird/iraq-learn ing-the-lessons-of-vietnam.html.

12. See generally David A. Welch, "The Impact of the 'Vietnam Syndrome' on U.S. Foreign Policy in a Post-Cold War World," in Robert G. Patman, ed., *Globalization and Conflict: National Security in a 'New' Strategic Era* (London: Routledge, 2006), pp. 95–113.

13. Marilyn B. Young, "The Vietnam Laugh Track," p. 39.

14. This is the judgment reported to Johnson on September 12, 1967, in a top-secret memorandum from CIA Director Richard Helms. LBJ did not share the single copy Helms hand-delivered to the president with either his secretaries of state or defense. In fact, it lay buried in the Lyndon Baines Johnson Library until the early 1990s, when Robert McNamara discovered it while researching his Vietnam memoir. See McNamara's *In Retrospect*, pp. 292–94.

15. This is the thesis of Frank Rich's persuasive *The Greatest Story Ever Sold*.

16. Logevall, *Choosing War*, pp. 403–4.

17. Ibid., p. 403.

18. Graham Allison of Harvard's Kennedy School of Government used to recommend that we "wear our social science the way a burlesque queen wears her clothing —casually and briefly."

19. Daniel Kahneman and Jonathan Renshon, "Why Hawks Win," *Foreign Policy* January/February 2007, available online at www.foreignpolicy.com/story/cms.php_id=3660&print=1. For a review of the first two decades of behavioral decision research, see Daniel Kahneman, Paul Slovic, and Amos Tversky, eds., *Judgment under Uncertainty: Heuristics and Biases* (New York: Cambridge University Press, 1986). For an introduction to the basic point of view taken by Kahneman, Tversky, et al. see David A. Welch, *Decisions, Decisions: The Art of Effective Decision Making* (Amherst, NY: Prometheus, 2002), pp. 135–95. For an application of this framework to foreign policy, see David A. Welch, *Painful Choices: A Theory of Foreign Policy Change* (Princeton, NJ: Princeton University Press, 2005), especially pp. 45–51.

20. Kahneman and Renshon, "Why Hawks Win."

21. Ibid.

22. Ibid.

23. Quoted in Amy Dean, *Night Light: A Book of Nighttime Meditations* (Center City, MN: Hazelden, 1996), p. 31.

Appendix A

1. In William Conrad Gibbons, *The U.S. Government and the Vietnam War: Executive and Legislative Roles and Relationships* (Princeton, NJ: Princeton University Press, 1986), 2:86–87.

2. The original is in the Kennedy Library, Boston, MA. A copy is available in John Prados, *U.S. Policy in the Vietnam War, Part I: 1954–1968* (Washington, DC, and Ann Arbor, MI: The National Security Archive and ProQuest Information and Learning, 2004), item number VI00862.

3. The original is in the Kennedy Library, Boston, MA. A copy is available in Prados, ed., *U.S. Policy in the Vietnam War, Part I: 1954–1968*, item number VI00875.

4. In Gibbons, *The U.S. Government and the Vietnam War*, 2:96–98.

5. In *Foreign Relations of the United States, 1961–1963 (Vietnam)*, 3:656–57.

6. In *Public Papers of the Presidents, 1961*, pp. 724–26.

7. In *Foreign Relations of the United States, 1961–1963 (Vietnam)*, 3:265–70.

8. In *Foreign Relations of the United States, 1961–1963 (Vietnam)*, 3:628–29.

9. Ball, *The Past Has Another Pattern*, p. 371.

10. In McNamara, *In Retrospect*, pp. 77–79. McNamara has excerpted the most important parts of the report and presented them in his memoir. The complete text is in Gravel, *Pentagon Papers*, 2:751–66.

11. The Presidential Recordings Program at the Miller Center of Public Affairs, University of Virginia, available at www.whitehousetapes.org.

12. Transcript by the Presidential Recordings Program at the Miller Center of Public Affairs, University of Virginia. Available at www.whitehousetapes.org.

13. The original is in the Kennedy Library, Boston, MA. A copy is available in Prados, ed., *U.S. Policy in the Vietnam War, Part I: 1954–1968*, item number VI01021.

14. "White House Statement Following the Return of a Special Mission to South Vietnam," October 2, 1963, in *Public Papers of the Presidents, 1963*, pp. 759–60.

15. John F. Kennedy, "The President's News Conference of October 9, 1963," in ibid., p. 774.

16. Robert S. McNamara, *In Retrospect*, pp. 79–80.

17. In *Foreign Relations of the United States, 1961–1963 (Vietnam)*, 4:637–40.

18. McGeorge Bundy, initial draft of National Security Action Memorandum No. 273, November 21, 1963, quoted in James K. Galbraith, "Exit Strategy."

19. Galbraith, "Exit Strategy."

20. CAS refers to "close air support" provided to South Vietnamese fighters mainly by CIA pilots flying U.S. aircraft.

21. In Max Holland, ed., *The Kennedy Assassination Tapes*, pp. 281–83.

22. In Michael Beschloss, ed., *Taking Charge*, pp. 248–50 and 256–60.

23. See Blight, Nye, and Welch, "The Cuban Missile Crisis Revisited," pp. 170–88; see also Blight and Welch, *On the Brink*, pp. 82–84 and 113–15.

24. McNamara, *In Retrospect*, pp. 96, 206.

25. In Beschloss, ed., *Taking Charge*, pp. 494–95, 498, and 509–10.

26. The original is in the Johnson Library, Austin, TX. A copy is available in Prados, ed., *U.S. Policy in the Vietnam War, Part I: 1954–1968*, item number VI01386.

27. See McNamara et al., *Argument Without End*, pp. 170–72.

28. McNamara, *In Retrospect*, p. 168.

29. The original is in the Johnson Library, Austin, TX. A copy is available in Prados, ed., *U.S. Policy in the Vietnam War, Part I: 1954–1968*, item number VI01409.

30. See McNamara et al., *Argument Without End*, pp. 170–74, 186–90, and 205–12.

31. Cooper, *The Lost Crusade*, p. 260.

32. In Hubert H. Humphrey, *The Education of a Public Man*. Reprinted in Ted Gittinger, ed., *The Johnson Years*, pp. 155–58.

33. Details of this story may be found in Thomas L. Hughes's 1999 State Department oral history, available from the National Security Archive, Washington, DC.

34. Tom Lehrer, "Whatever Became of Hubert?" from the album *That Was the Week That Was* (1965), track 9. See the following website for lyrics and a performance by Tom Lehrer: www.metrolyrics.com/whatever-became-of-hubert-lyrics-tom-lehrer.html

35. In Beschloss, ed., *Reaching for Glory*, pp. 345–47.

36. The original is in the Johnson Library, Austin, TX. A copy is available in Prados, ed., *U.S. Policy in the Vietnam War, Part I: 1954–1968*, item number VI01617.

37. Logevall, *Choosing War*, xiii–xxv.

38. See especially Fredrik Logevall, "'Ain't No Daylight': Lyndon Johnson and the Politics of Escalation," in *Making Sense of the Vietnam Wars: Local, National, and Transnational Perspectives*, ed. Mark Bradley and Marilyn B. Young (New York: Oxford University Press, in press).

39. The classic statement of this view is due to Leslie Gelb and Richard K. Betts, *The Irony of Vietnam: The System Worked* (Washington, DC: Brookings, 1978).

40. Theodore Draper, *Castro's Revolution: Myths and Realities* (New York: Praeger, 1962), p. 59.

41. John F. Kennedy quoted in Sorensen, *Kennedy*, p. 309.

42. Bowles labeled his memorandum "Personal" and wrote up his notes approximately two weeks after the meeting described in the document. A copy is available in *The Cuban Missile Crisis Revisited: An International Collection of Documents from the Bay of Pigs to the Brink of Nuclear War*, ed. Peter Kornbluh (Washington, DC, and Ann Arbor, MI: The National Security Archive and ProQuest Information and Learning, 2006), item number CU00161.

43. The selection presented here is Bundy's concluding section. A copy is available in Kornbluh, ed., *The Cuban Missile Crisis Revisited*, item number CU00156.

44. The memorandum was classified as confidential and was specifically requested of Schlesinger by Kennedy. Schlesinger drafted it immediately after he returned from a whirlwind tour of European cities. A copy is available in Kornbluh, ed., *The Cuban Missile Crisis Revisited*, item number CU00164.

45. In Mark Danner, *The Secret Way to War: The Downing Street Memo and the Iraq War's Buried History* (New York: New York Review of Books Press, 2006), pp. 87–91.

46. On November 5, 1998, the UN Security Council condemned Iraq's decision to cease cooperation with UN weapons inspectors and demanded that Iraq provide "immediate, complete and unconditional cooperation" with UN weapons inspectors.

Appendix B

1. The "paper" referred to has been superseded by the present book.
2. Logevall, "Vietnam and the Question of What Might Have Been."

AID	Agency for International Development
ARVN	Army of the Republic of Vietnam
CAS	close air support
CI	counterinsurgency
CIA	Central Intelligence Agency
CINCPAC	Commander in Chief, Pacific Command
CNN	Cable News Network
DIA	Defense Intelligence Agency
DOD	Department of Defense
EXCOMM	Executive Committee of the National Security Council
FAO	Food and Agriculture Organization
FOIA	Freedom of Information Act
GDR	German Democratic Republic
GVN	Government of Vietnam
ICC	International Control Commission
JCS	Joint Chiefs of Staff
JFK	John Fitzgerald Kennedy
LBJ	Lyndon Baines Johnson
MAAG	Military Assistance Advisory Group
MACV	Military Assistance Command, Vietnam
NATO	North Atlantic Treaty Organization
NLF	National Liberation Front
NSAM	National Security Action Memorandum
NSC	National Security Council
OPLAN	Operation Plan
OSS	Office of Strategic Services
RVN	Republic of Vietnam
RVNAF	Republic of Vietnam Air Force
SAC	Strategic Air Command
SAM	surface-to-air missile
SEA	Southeast Asia
SEATO	Southeast Asia Treaty Organization
SECDEF	Secretary of Defense

SGA	Special Group—Augmented
UN	United Nations
UNSC	United Nations Security Council
UNSCR	United Nations Security Council Resolution
USIA	United States Information Agency
VC	Vietcong
WMD	weapons of mass destruction

ACKNOWLEDGMENTS

We owe a tremendous debt of gratitude to the participants in the April 2005 Musgrove conference. The edited and annotated transcript that constitutes the empirical core of this book is derived from the conference. The participants were Thomas Blanton, Chester L. Cooper, Frances FitzGerald, James K. Galbraith, Gordon Goldstein, James G. Hershberg, Thomas L. Hughes, Fredrik Logevall, Bill Moyers, Timothy Naftali, John Prados, Marc Selverstone, Francis X. Winters, and Marilyn B. Young. Brief biographies of each are available in chapter 2. These scholars and former officials from the Kennedy and Johnson administrations prepared for the conference by doing a lot of homework. We sent them a nearly 1000-page briefing notebook a month before the conference. It was brimming with declassified materials on issues related to Vietnam policy in the Kennedy and Johnson years. At Musgrove, they engaged one another in an intense debate and discussion over what JFK might have done, or might not have done, with regard to Vietnam, had he lived and been reelected in November 1964. All of them came to the table ready to defend their positions. But they also came prepared to listen to the views of those with whom they disagreed. We are grateful to all.

We also benefited from contributions made behind the scenes by two former officials who did not attend the Musgrove conference due to ill health. Chief among these was Robert S. McNamara, secretary of defense to Presidents Kennedy and Johnson, with whom we discussed the conference at length while we were still in the planning phase. Likewise, we learned a good deal from Harold P. Ford, a former CIA analyst and author of several works on U.S. policy toward Vietnam in the 1960s.

A special word of thanks is due to Fred Logevall. His 1999 book, *Choosing War: The Escalation of War and the Lost Chance for Peace in Vietnam*, was a breakthrough book. Fred Logevall demonstrated in *Choosing War* that it is possible to consider the question of what JFK might have done in Vietnam in a way that is both intellectually responsible and potentially enlightening—about both this particular historical case and the relevance of the JFK/Vietnam case to the present and future direction of U.S. foreign policy. We are grateful to Fred for his advice to us in the planning stage of the Musgrove conference, for his participation in the conference, and for agreeing to write the foreword to this book.

We also thank the filmmaker Koji Masutani, whom we did not meet until after the Musgrove conference. Koji graduated from Brown University in the spring of 2005 with a concentration in International Relations, but also with strong credentials in filmmaking, having already screened two of his student films at the Cannes Film Festival. We met him shortly before he graduated from Brown, in May of 2005. Throughout the summer of 2005, we explored with Koji the possibility of producing a film that would be the complement to this book, and vice versa. That film, called *Virtual JFK: Vietnam If Kennedy Had Lived*, is now finished. Its world premiere was in April 2008 at the Canadian Hot Docs International Film Festival in Toronto, where it was a finalist for both the Jury Prize and the prize for Best International Feature-Length Documentary. The film is historically accurate, highly innovative, and full of implications for U.S. foreign policy in the early twenty-first century. In addition to having produced a first-rate film on JFK and Vietnam, Koji has been a valuable interlocutor for us over the past three years as our ideas for the book have developed and taken shape.

In the summer of 2005, we spent a month together at the Rockefeller Foundation's Study and Conference Center in Bellagio, Italy. We are grateful to the foundation for the opportunity to spend concentrated, undistracted time together in the immediate aftermath of the Musgrove conference, during which this book took shape. We are grateful to Susan Garfield, director of the Bellagio program at the Rockefeller Foundation's New York office, and especially to Pilar Palacia, managing director of the Study Center in Bellagio, and to Pilar's marvelous staff, led by Elena Ongonia and Nadia Gilardoni.

For the opportunity to present our thoughts at various stages of development, we thank the following: the American University's Honors Program; the Department of History, Cornell University; Harvard University's Weatherhead Center for International Affairs; The Rockefeller Foundation Bellagio Center; the National Security Archive's Carnegie Summer School on International Affairs, Gelendzhik, Russia; and the Woodrow Wilson Center's Program on Democratic Institutions in Washington, D.C. We have also benefited from the insights of our students in the International Relations Program at Brown University, who have read various prior incarnations of this book and who have often challenged us to defend our views. We are grateful to one and all.

The original funding for the project of which this book is the result was generously provided by the Social Sciences and Humanities Research Council of Canada, without whose support none of this would have been possible. We also extend our gratitude to the Arca Foundation, Washington, D.C., for a conference grant and an invitation to use their marvelous facility, the Musgrove Conference Center, St. Simons Island, Georgia, for the critical oral history conference that generated the exchanges recorded in this book. We are especially grateful to Arca President Smith Bagley, Arca Executive Director Donna Edwards, and Arca Board Member Nancy Bagley. All three Arca officials attended the Musgrove conference as observers.

The project from which this book derives is centered at Brown University's Thomas J. Watson Jr. Institute for International Studies. The project evolved during a time of transition at the Watson Institute. We owe a profound debt of gratitude to all three directors who have guided the institute over the past several years: Thomas J. Biersteker, Barbara Stallings, and David Kennedy. We thank each of them for their specific interest in and support of the project on Kennedy, Johnson, and Vietnam, and more generally for supporting all our work using the method of critical oral history. In addition, we received enthusiastic support and assistance during the entire duration of the project from James Der Derian, director of the Watson Institute's Global Security Program. We are also indebted to Ellen Darling and Christine Kilgus, executive assistants for the Global Security Program, for their many contributions to this project. We also thank the Watson Institute's Andrew Blackadar, Emily Jodka, Julia Lic, and Jillian McGuire for their valuable assistance in the composition of the photo essay in this book. At the John F. Kennedy Library, Colleen Cooney and Jennifer Quan were especially helpful, assisting us in locating many of the pictures that we use in this book.

The Musgrove conference could never have happened were it not for the stellar contributions of the core organizing staff. Barbara Elias, of George Washington University's National Security Archive, provided assistance with the documentary database that was crucial in the construction of the briefing notebook for the conference. Barbara also expertly transcribed the tape recordings of the conversations at Musgrove. Ellen White, of Brown University's Watson Institute for International Studies, assisted us at Brown during the run-up to the conference and on-site during the conference at the Musgrove Conference Center. She was instrumental in working with the Musgrove staff to make the entire operation run like a well-oiled machine. We also thank Mircea Munteanu of the Woodrow Wilson Center's Cold War International History Project, who took charge of producing the briefing notebooks and distributing them to the Musgrove conferees.

We thank our friends at the Rowman & Littlefield Publishing Group: CEO Jonathan Sisk; Vice President for History, Geography and International Relations Susan McEachern; and our editor during the early phases of the project, Laura Roberts Gottlieb. We are grateful that both Susan and Laura were able to attend the Musgrove conference as observers, during which our initial discussions with them about this book first occurred. We have published several previous books with Rowman & Littlefield and we are pleased to be back in the fold.

Finally, we have dedicated this book to the memory of two dear friends. Chester L. Cooper was a mentor and friendly critic of all our work on the war in Vietnam. He died in October 2005, just a few months after the Musgrove conference, to which he (as usual) made many important contributions. We miss Chet: his thick Boston accent, his wit, and his courage. We also miss C's thick Boston accent, and everything else about this singular woman.

Note: Page numbers in *italic type* indicate photographs.

At the heart of this provocative book lies the fundamental question: Does it matter who is president on issues of war and peace? The Vietnam War was one of the most catastrophic and bloody in living memory, and its lessons take on even more resonance in light of America's current devastating involvement in Iraq. Tackling head-on the most controversial and debated subject in U.S. foreign policy, this unique work explores what President John F. Kennedy would have done in Vietnam if he had not been assassinated in 1963. Drawing on a wealth of recently declassified documents, frank oral testimony of White House officials from both the Kennedy and Johnson administrations, and the analysis of top historians, this book presents compelling evidence that JFK was ready to end U.S. involvement well before the conflict escalated. With vivid immediacy, readers will feel they are in the president's war room as the debates raged that forever changed the course of American history—and that continue to affect us profoundly today as the echoes of Vietnam stretch into Iraq and Afghanistan.

James G. Blight is CIGI Chair of Foreign Policy Development, Balsillie School of International Affairs at the University of Waterloo. He was professor of international relations at the Watson Institute for International Relations at Brown University, where he pioneered the application of the method of critical oral history to the study of major U.S. foreign policy decisions. He is the author of more than a dozen books on the recent history of U.S. foreign policy, including *Wilson's Ghost: Reducing the Risk of Conflict, Killing, and Catastrophe in the 21st Century* (with Robert S. McNamara).

Janet M. Lang is research professor, Balsillie School of International Affairs at the University of Waterloo. She was associate adjunct professor at the Watson Institute for International Relations at Brown University. She, along with James Blight, served as an adviser for the Academy Award-winning film by Errol Morris, *The Fog of War*. She is the author, with James Blight, of the companion book, *The Fog of War: Lessons from the Life of Robert S. McNamara*.

David A. Welch is CIGI Chair of Global Security, Balsillie School of International Affairs, and professor of political science at the University of Waterloo. He was professor of political science at the University of Toronto and has held visiting fellowships at Brown University, Harvard University, and Princeton University. He has written widely on national and international security decision making, including *Painful Choices: A Theory of Foreign Policy Change* and *Justice and the Genesis of War*.